Discovering Bengaluru

HISTORY · NEIGHBOURHOODS · WALKS

Discovering Bengaluru

Author/Editor: Meera Iyer

Photo Management: Aravind C, Meera Iyer, PeeVee
Illustrated Maps: Sneha Prasad,
Samanvita SreeHarsha, Varsha Kodgi
Cover Design: Pooja Saxena

ISBN: 979-87-6374388-3

First Print: October 2019
First Reprint: January 2020
Second Reprint: March 2021

Copyright © 2019 selection and individual matter, Meera Iyer; individual chapters, the contributors

Published by
INTACH BENGALURU CHAPTER
245, 9th A Main,
3rd Block, Jayanagar,
Bengaluru - 560011
intach@intachblr.org

Designed by
Zinc & Broccoli
2/1, 2nd Floor, OJUS House,
Yelachenahalli, Kanakapura Road,
Bengaluru-560062 | enquiry@zandb.in

Printed at
SCPL, Bengaluru
No 10A,11,11A, JC Industrial Estate,
Bikasipura Main Road, Kanakapura Road,
Bengaluru-560062 | enquiry@scpl.net

All rights are reserved. No part of this publication may be reproduced, stored in a retrieval system or transmitted, in any form or by any means, mechanical, photocopying, recording or otherwise, without prior written permission of the publisher.

Discovering Bengaluru

HISTORY · NEIGHBOURHOODS · WALKS

Written and edited by
Meera Iyer

With contributions by:
Krupa Rajangam
Hita Unnikrishnan, B Manjunath
and Harini Nagendra
S Karthikeyan

CONTENTS

1 | Foreword by *Chiranjiv Singh*

2 | Introduction: A Potted History of Bengaluru

12 | Chapter 1 The Beginnings of the City: The Pete and the Kote

76 | Chapter 2 The Origins of the Parallel City: The Cantonment and Cubbon Park

110 | Chapter 3 More than Just a Temple: Halasuru or Ulsoor

130 | Chapter 4 The Expanding City: Basavanagudi and Its Vicinity

168 | Chapter 5 Temples, Tanks and Trees: Malleswaram

196 | Chapter 6 Towns of the City: Fraser Town, Richards Town, Cooke Town

234 | Chapter 7 The Eurasian and Anglo-Indian Pensioners' Paradise: Whitefield

248 | Chapter 8 The Watery Past of a Modern Stadium: Sampangi Kere

268 | Chapter 9 From Royal Gardens to Urban Green Lung: Lalbagh

313 | Epilogue The Future of Bangalore by *CJ Padmanabha*

318 | Glossary & Bibliography

330 | List of Contributors

332 | Acknowledgements

334 | Index

Foreword

INTACH has been conducting heritage walks in Bengaluru for quite some time. For the general reader who is interested in knowing about the heritage and history of Bengaluru, but who might not be able to participate in the walks, INTACH has put together this book aptly titled *Discovering Bengaluru: History / Neighbourhoods / Walks*. Dr Meera Iyer and the other authors are knowledgeable and entertaining guides. During these walks they answer the questions which may arise in people's minds but are seldom answered. After all, how many can answer questions such as why a particular street is called Market Road Street or who was Sajjan Rao of the Sajjan Rao Circle?

The area that comprises the Bengaluru urban agglomeration had ancient settlements. Begur inscription, which is from around 890 CE, mentions '*Bengaluru kaalaga*', the battle of Bengaluru, which took place between the Ganga and Nolamba dynasties. This inscription is located in the Parvathi Nageshwara temple not far from the Indian Institute of Management on Bannerghatta Road. Roman coins have been found at Yeshwantpur, a suburb of Bengaluru. Evidently inhabitants of this area had trade links with the wider world. Globalisation is not new to the city. There have been waves of globalisation; the IT one is only the latest. The many plant species which were brought to Lalbagh, acclimatised there and then disseminated widely is another dimension of the earlier globalisations. That is how *Araucaria columnaris* became a signature tree of Lalbagh and the roads of Bengaluru have a rangoli of exotic flowering trees such as jacaranda, *Tabebuia*, *Spathodea*, *Peltophorum* and others—reminders of the 'Garden City' that it once was.

Bengaluru got the moniker 'Garden City' not because of Lalbagh but because of the gardens in the compounds of numerous bungalows and houses. When urban land ceiling was imposed in 1976, those gardens became victims of the legislation; many owners subdivided their land to save it from acquisition by the government. Then came builders and developers, and Bengaluru was never the same. Old bungalows were demolished and replaced by nondescript new buildings. Gone were the gardens. Some of the old houses that remain are described in the book.

Public buildings hardly fared better. Heritage buildings were demolished thoughtlessly by the government. Orders to display Sir M Visvesvaraya's portraits in offices were issued by the government, which also issued orders to demolish his house. When I suggested that the house be preserved as a memorial to Sir MV, the suggestion was not accepted, but the name of the building was changed from LIC Building to Visvesvaraya Towers. In place of that gracious house stand the towers designed by Charles Correa. The structure came up in violation of by-laws. The government has been the first to violate the by-laws, whether it was for this building or the Public Utility Building on MG Road or the Telecom Building near Vidhana Soudha. When I asked Charles Correa whether his design violated the environment of Vidhana Soudha, he just said, 'Sometimes beauty lies in contrast.'

While talking of Bengaluru's history, or heritage, one often tends to be nostalgic. The merit of this book is that while it celebrates the old, it does not lapse into nostalgia; it rejoices in what is there. For you can walk only in the present. And here, the history of Bengaluru is built around walks. In spite of all the changes that have occurred and the inevitable destruction owing to a galloping increase in population, there is still left enough of the historical Bengaluru, and the book is at its best in its descriptions of these historical sites. The walk through Gavipura (in chapter 4) is one of those informative and interesting walks. The uncle–nephew duo Thomas and William Daniell had visited these sites in 1792 and sketched them. Aquatints of Gangadhareshwara temple and Hariharagudda tower are included in their monumental work, *Oriental Scenery*. Antonio Martinelli followed the trail of Thomas and William Daniell between 1995 and 1997, and photographed the same spots the Daniells had sketched using their camera obscura. In a conversation Mr Martinelli told me that the remarkable thing was not that so much had changed but that there was still so much left since the time of the

Daniells for him to photograph. This can be said about the INTACH walks as well: there is still so much left to observe and learn about.

The city planners of Bengaluru have no attachment to the past. As one of them said, 'Our job is to give sites and we do it wherever we can.' This one can see all around. Bengaluru celebrates newness. Every phase of the city's development shows the new of that era, from turn-of-the-century colonial architecture to the latest aluminium-clad office blocks. For students of architecture there is enough to see and for students of urban planning there is enough to learn what not to do. Either way, the city is interesting to walk through.

Then there is the intangible heritage of the city: the Bengaluru of poets, writers, singers, dancers, musicians, scientists, artists, sportsmen, engineers, leaders. We do not have a system of markers like the Blue Plaques of London to commemorate such people. They *made* Bengaluru. It would be interesting to have a walk designed around the houses of the greats of the city: this is where Venkatappa lived, this is where CV Raman lived, this is where Doreswamy Iyengar lived, this is where Shanta Rao lived, this is where RK Srikantan lived ... all this in one part of Bengaluru alone. The history of the city is the history of its culture as well.

I have not taken part in any of the INTACH walks, but I have learnt a lot from this book. This is a welcome addition to the books on Bengaluru.

Chiranjiv Singh
Former Ambassador of India
to UNESCO; IAS (retd)

Introduction: A Potted History of Bengaluru

The Legends

A young chieftain went out hunting one day. After long hours in the jungle, he grew weary and decided to take a short break. As he rested under a tree, he was startled awake by a commotion nearby. Imagine his surprise when he saw his hunting dogs come dashing out of the jungle, with a hare hot on their heels! The king was struck by the hare's courage. 'If a hare could be so brave as to chase my dogs,' he thought, 'surely there is something about this land. This must be a land of the brave.' And so he decided to build a new city there. The young ruler's name was Kempegowda and the new city he built was Bengaluru.

This is what legend tells us about the foundations of our city. Given that similar stories involving dogs and either rabbits or hares are told of other forts in India, including Bidar, Hampi and Ahmedabad, we can safely assume this particular legend does not, in fact, have a basis in fact!

There is another famous story concerning the city that anyone who has been here even a few weeks has probably heard. This one tells of another ruler, a king of the Hoysala dynasty, who went out hunting. After some time, he grew hungry. As he wandered in the forest, wondering how he was going to get food, he came upon a clearing where stood a hut. The king knocked on the door and asked the old woman who lived there for some food. She rummaged around in the kitchen and then served him a dish of boiled beans, *bendha kalu*. And so the city that came up there was named after boiled beans, goes the story.

Cute but quite untrue because the name Bengaluru has been around long before the name Hoysala was a gleam in anyone's eye. And we know this because there is an inscription dating back to around 890 CE that mentions a 'Battle of

Bengaluru'.[1] This historical object lies in the premises of the Panchalingeshwara temple in Begur. In the Someshwara temple in Madiwala, near Silk Board, we come across a Tamil inscription dating to about 1247 CE which refers to 'the big tank of Vengalur'.[2] We do not know exactly where this settlement called Bengaluru was. One suggestion is that it was where Kodigehalli is today, about 5 km southwest of Yelahanka.[3] On the other hand, it is also likely that it was where the old city is, centred round the Avenue Road area.[4] As for the inscriptions that speak of the settlement of Bengaluru, they still exist where they were recorded all those years ago. You can see these proofs of the antiquity of the name Bengaluru for yourself.

Place names change through history, as the inscriptions reveal. We have used the current spelling Bengaluru throughout this book, even where it might appear anachronistic, except when quoting from sources which use the older spelling, Bangalore, and when referring to names of institutions. Similarly, we have used the modern names Chennai, Kolkata, Mumbai and Mysuru, although the former kingdom is referred to as Mysore. In the case of localities in Bengaluru where the spelling in English is not standardised, we have used the spelling most commonly used in official correspondence. Where that was not possible, we have used the spelling that most closely matches the name as it is pronounced in Kannada; hence Chickpete, Tharagupete and so on. For people, as far as possible, we have used the spellings used by the people themselves; hence Annasawmy and Seshadri rather than Annaswamy and Sheshadri, for example. The transliteration from Kannada of the name of the Mysore royal family would best be written as Odeyer or Odeyar. However, it is usually written as Wodeyar or, nowadays, as Wadiyar. We have used Wodeyar throughout, the spelling most often used by the people referred to in this book.

Early History

Of course, there have been settlements in and around Bengaluru long before the Begur inscription was chiselled. The area around Bengaluru is rich in evidence of settlements from the Early Iron Age (approximately 1000 BCE–200 CE in this region). Archaeologists have found megaliths and other remains in Kannur, Chikkajala, Managondanahalli, Jadigenahalli, Bannerghatta, Begur and even in Lalbagh.[5] When the foundations for the new gopuras in Begur's Panchalingeshwara temple were being dug around eight years ago, it brought to light several Black and Red Ware potsherds, probably dating from the Early Iron Age.[6] Lalbagh's relics are untraceable but you can see the finds from some of the other sites in Bengaluru's Government Museum. As for the sites themselves, many are now either completely lost or in the process of being destroyed. The former archaeological site of Chikkajala was converted into a residential layout.

Begur, the Bengaluru Inscription and INTACH

The Begur temple and its famous inscription mentioning the battle of Bengaluru have a special place in the city's history. The temple also has a special place in INTACH's history: this was where the first of our popular Parichay heritage walks was held in March 2008.

Inscriptions in Begur, safely mounted and highlighted after an intervention by INTACH Bengaluru Chapter, with financial support from Advaith Hyundai. The Bengaluru inscription is third from the left. © Aravind C

INTACH's earliest trysts with the temple were in the early 2000s when, thanks to a small grant from the Department of Archaeology (as it was called then), the state chapter of INTACH worked on the surroundings of the Panchalingeshwara temple. In those days, the temple was on the banks of the Begur lake, or *kere*. We cleaned up the surroundings, created seating areas and so on. (These improvements have since been almost obliterated by the construction activity in the temple.)

In those early days, very few people knew about the inscription which mentioned the name Bengaluru. On one of our earlier visits, we finally found the inscription hidden under a dirty rag. Later visits were more alarming: the inscription was often under firewood, tin sheets or cement blocks! This despite conversations with people associated with the temple and others. In the meantime, three new gopuras were built around the temple; two more are in the works.

Simultaneously, volunteers also trekked to the Department of Endowments and Department of Archaeology, pressing for the Bengaluru inscription to be protected, to no avail. Eventually, we said, 'Give us permission and we will do what's required.' Permissions in place, we consulted with temple priests and elders, archaeologists HM Siddhanagoudar and Arun Raj and epigraphist HS Gopala Rao, secretary of the Karnataka Itihasa Academy. Based on their inputs, we chose a spot within the temple complex where the inscriptions could be displayed. Another interminable wait followed: devotees were building a new compound wall that had to be completed before we could begin our work. Finally, in April 2018, six years after we first started the work to safeguard it, the Bengaluru inscription was safely mounted on a pedestal in its new location. Go check out this important historical artefact!

Most of the others are being lost to quarrying and to treasure seekers who often use excavators to dig up these millennia-old relics in the hope of finding buried gold and other treasure.

Further evidence of Bengaluru's ancient past are the inscriptions that were and are still found in and around the city. These inscriptions not only provide rich data on dynasties and language, but are also useful in tracing the early history of areas in and around Bengaluru. Ecologist Harini Nagendra has analysed these inscriptions to draw some fascinating inferences on the early ecological history of the city, tracing how settlements were determined by the undulating terrain of the area. Agricultural settlements came up in the valleys towards the north and east, irrigated by lakes and wells, while pastoral communities dominated the scrub jungle and dense forest that abounded towards the south and west of the city.[7]

For the next few centuries, we have a wealth of inscriptional evidence to show the hand of various dynasties in shaping Bengaluru's history, including the Gangas, the Cholas and the Hoysalas.

1500s to the Present

But we will skip ahead to the 1500s, or 1532 to be precise, when the ruler of the powerful Vijayanagar kingdom Achyutaraya, conferred the title Nayakatana on the feudatory lord Hiriya Kempegowda or Kempegowda the Elder, who is popularly regarded as the founder of the city. Kempegowda was the son of the chieftain Kempa Nanje Gowda, or Kempanachayagowda as he is referred to in inscriptions. The family ruled the region near Yelahanka because of which they are referred to as the Yelahanka Nadaprabhus, or rulers of the Yelahanka area. It was in 1537 that Kempegowda requested Achyutaraya's permission to construct a fort, and was granted the request.[8]

After Kempegowda, his son—Immadi Kempegowda or Kempegowda II, builder of the four (or more!) famous Kempegowda towers—reigned from 1569.[9] An important episode in Bengaluru's history was when some chieftains of the region invited Bijapur's Mohammad Adil Shah to send his army to conquer Bengaluru. In 1638, the Adil Shahi ruler sent his redoubtable commander Ranadulla Khan and his deputy Shahaji Bhonsle (Chatrapati Shivaji's father), who defeated Kempegowda II's army and captured Bengaluru. According to *Shivabharat*, a poem about Shivaji, 'The Rajah of Bingarool was expert in the art of fighting and after a bold stand lasting for many days, he surrendered the fort of Bingarool.'[10] Kempegowda II was forced to retreat and move to Magadi, and the family's role in the story of Bengaluru came to an end.

After this victory over the Kempegowda family, Mohammad Adil Shah appointed Shahaji as the governor of Bengaluru; he ruled over this area as a feudatory of the Adil Shahis, but more or less independently. 'Being pleased with the sight of Bangalore, the security of its fortress and the salubrity of its climate,' Shahaji decided to make Bengaluru his headquarters. Shahaji further beautified the city by adding more gardens and also built himself a palace called Gowri Mahal (popularly identified as being in Chickpete).[11]

Bengaluru remained with Shahaji until his death in 1664 after which its governorship passed to his son Ekoji (also called Venkoji). While Shahaji had based himself out of Bengaluru, Ekoji transferred his capital to Thanjavur in 1675. Two years after this came the battle of the brothers as Ekoji's famous sibling Shivaji (who had spent some of his childhood in Bengaluru) laid claim to and conquered the territory. He then bestowed Bengaluru on Ekoji's wife Dipabai, with the express condition that Ekoji could govern this territory but not lay claim to it. To this potent, turbulent mix of wars and rivalries was added the growing prowess of Chikkadevaraja Wodeyar of Mysore. Several skirmishes took place between the Marathas and the Wodeyars in which the Marathas often came out the poorer.

Events came to a head in 1687 when Bengaluru became the stage where a number of actors converged for a denouement. Ekoji, who by all accounts was neither as accomplished nor as shrewd as his illustrious brother, realised he could not hold on to Bengaluru much longer and offered to sell it to Chikkadevaraja Wodeyar for Rs 3 lakhs. In the middle of these real estate negotiations, fresh from his victory over Bijapur a year earlier, the Mughal Emperor Aurangzeb sent his general Kasim Khan to Bengaluru to seize the city. Almost simultaneously, Chikkadevaraja also landed up at Bengaluru. Meanwhile, Shivaji's son Sambhaji also sent a force hurrying towards Bengaluru to pre-empt the Mughals. But they were too late. Kasim Khan captured the fort with a little help from Chikkadevaraja who allied with the Mughals. A little later, the Mughals sold Bengaluru to Chikkadevaraja Wodeyar. And with that opened a new chapter in the city's colourful history.[12]

Chikkadevaraja is said to have built a new fort to the south of the mud fort that Kemepgowda had built about 150 years earlier. This is the origin of the *kote*, a portion of which still exists. Bengaluru remained with the Wodeyars (with brief Maratha-ruled interludes towards the mid-1700s) until the father–son duo of Hyder Ali and Tipu Sultan took over in the 1770s.

By then, Bengaluru had become one of the most important cities in Mysore State, second only to its capital, Srirangapatna. Bengaluru was a commercial hub for silks and textiles, an important centre for the manufacture of arms and ammunition, and was well protected and fortified. Its mud fort, a deep ditch and a bound hedge of bamboo, aloe and other thorny bushes protected the *pete*, or town. Immediately to its south, a strong stone fort with a deep, wide moat protected the royal establishments along with foundries, magazines and barracks.

A street scene in Bengaluru, early 1900s. *Courtesy of Jane Smith, from the collections of Fred Goodwill.*

The vast and prosperous kingdom of Mysore became the cynosure of the East India Company's eyes from the 1780s. The implacable Tipu, however, put up stiff resistance so that it took several protracted battles, including one fierce encounter in Bengaluru, before the British finally defeated him. After Tipu's death, the British placed the kingdom of Mysore back in the hands of the Wodeyars. In 1807, Bangalore Cantonment was created, as a separate entity from the *pete*, and administered by the British. But in 1831, alleging misrule, the British took back the reins and all of Mysore came under their rule. This state of affairs continued till 1881, when the Rendition took place: the administration of the Mysore kingdom reverted to the Mysore royal dynasty. The city was once more organised into two different administrative zones: the Civil and Military Station (C&M Station, formerly the Cantonment) under British administration, and the city under the Maharaja's administration. These two cities continued independently until 1949 when the twain finally met and were merged into one.

Thanks to its location in the peninsula, the terrain around it, and its altitude, Bengaluru has had a particularly diverse history, coming under the influence of several cultures and dynasties. And just as geography has determined history, history has in turn shaped the current city. Bengaluru is not a city focused on a few monuments; rather, it is a city with multiple centres and historic areas, a palimpsest that bears the stamp of its varied past. This book explores this past that is still present around us.

The book has been brewing in our hearts and minds for over a decade, right from when we began the INTACH Parichay heritage walks in 2008. The walks were meant to introduce people, both residents and visitors, to the city's rich and diverse history. The impetus for Parichay was really frustration—at having to constantly hear that Bengaluru was a city with no past, that it was a young city with no great history, that it was a city of the future. Sure, it had been a pensioner's paradise once upon a time, but it was now a pub city and an IT city. It was disheartening to hear this despite the many excellent books about the history of the city that have already been written.[13]

This book is a history of the city told through what you can see, feel and experience in some of the neighbourhoods of Bengaluru. It explores the stories of people, events and places in the streets of the city. This is by no means an exhaustive history of the city. We have restricted ourselves to some of the older areas, especially those neighbourhoods where we have had particularly popular Parichays. One cannot think of Bengaluru without thinking also of lakes and trees. For this reason, we have also included a chapter each on the lost Sampangi *kere* and its evolution into a stadium, and on the oldest of the city's green spaces, Lalbagh.[14]

Through this book, we hope you will gain an appreciation and understanding of Bengaluru's history and its place in the grand narrative of Indian and world history. It is our sincere and humble attempt to share with you our love for this, our city, *namma* Bengaluru.

Notes

1. Report on the working of archaeological researches in Mysore during 1914–15, 16.
2. EC IX Bn 68; see also Krishnamurthy 2011, 40–49; Karthik 2016.
3. Hasan 1970, 1; Rao 1930b, 42–43.
4. Karthik 2015.
5. Srivatsa 2014; Iyer 2010.
6. Conversations with archaeologists Dr SK Aruni and Dr Smriti Haricharan, 2010–2018.
7. Nagendra 2016.
8. Kamath 2008; Rice 1897b; Rao 1930b.
9. Some sources contend that Kempegowda II was Hiriya Kempegowda's grandson, from his son Gidde Gowda or Giddappa Gowda. For more on the Kempegowda family, see Puttaya 1923.
10. Muddachari 1965.
11. Muddachari 1966.
12. Muddachari 1965.
13. These include Harini Nagendra's *Nature in the City*, Fazlul Hasan's incomparable *Bangalore Through the Centuries*, Janaki Nair's *The Promise of the Metropolis*, *Deccan Traverses* by Dilip da Cunha and Anuradha Mathur, and Suryanath Kamath's books, to name a few. This book draws on several of them.
14. A caveat: Several of the places highlighted in the book are in private hands, including some schools, churches and clubs. These are generally not open to walk-in visitors.

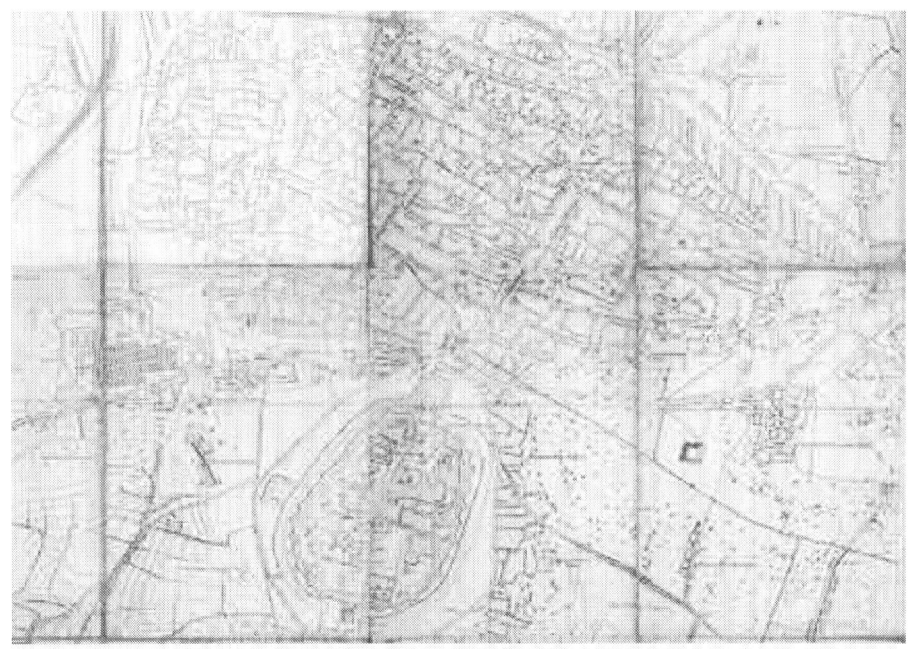

The *pete* and *kote* in 1884-85. From, Survey of India. *Cantonment and City of Bangalore and Environs, Season 1884-85.* Courtesy of Mythic Society, Bengaluru.

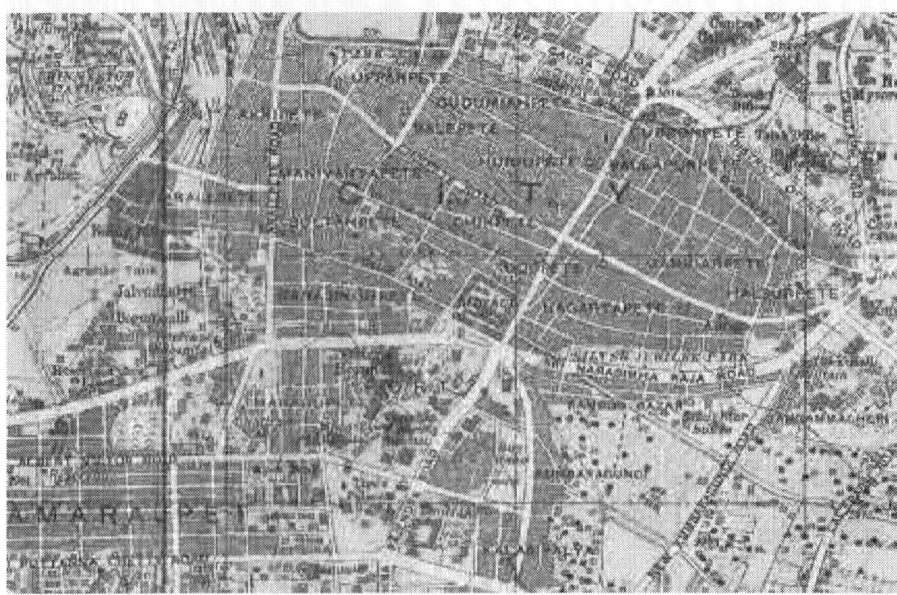

The *pete* and *kote* in 1935-36. From, Survey of India. *Bangalore Guide Map. Surveyed 1935-36.* Courtesy of Naresh Narasimhan.

CHAPTER 1

The Beginnings of the City: The *Pete* and the *Kote*

We begin our story of Bengaluru with Kempegowda, who is ubiquitous in Bengaluru, starting from the airport, to institutions and roads, as well as the many statues of him that dot the city. And unsurprisingly so, since Hiriya Kempegowda, or Kempegowda the Elder, is considered by many to be the founder of the city.

When Hiriya Kempegowda made Bengaluru his capital, he constructed a mud fort to protect it (this fort no longer exists—more on this later). He is also popularly credited with building many tanks, including Kempambudhi *kere* (tank or lake) and Ulsoor *kere*. Besides, he is popularly said to have built or renovated several temples including the Bull Temple in Basavanagudi and Gavigangadhareshwara temple in Gavipuram.

Like other medieval cities—in India and elsewhere—the populous commercial and residential part of Bengaluru, or *pete* (pronounced 'paytay', meaning town or area), was organised according to professions. Workers organised themselves into guilds and usually lived and worked in clusters. In modern London, for example, Bread Street, Threadneedle Street and Milkman Street are vestiges of that period of organisation. Similarly, medieval Bengaluru was organised into several *petes*, each devoted to one profession. Kumbarpete was where the potters lived and worked (located close to the edge of the new city so that the kiln smoke did not engulf the city), Ganigarapete was the domain of the oil millers, Balepete was where bangles were made and sold, and so on.

One of the earliest descriptions of Bengaluru comes from 1670 and is written by the Marathi poet Kavindra Paramanand, who describes the city of 'Bingarool' in his *Shivabharath*, an epic poem on Shivaji.[2]

That matchless city with smart fortifications and towers,
Had tall whitewashed mansions topped by banners
That tickled the skyline.
Houses stood testimony to craftsmen's keen artistry,
And the city resounded with the content coos
of countless pigeons, safe in their nests.
Animated by the calls of peafowl dashing in and out of skylights,
The city boasted a great market,
Selling everything under the sun.
The city teemed with deep lakes, each house was graced by a well,
Fountains gurgled at every square,
Spouting a fine mist.
Trees thick with flowers and shade lined each home garden,
And the walls had lovely murals
That transfixed passersby.
Striking barracks, built with rocks of assorted hues,
And a strong city gate topped with turrets,
Elegant, with fine inlay and plaster.
A fort well guarded by a regiment of veteran soldiers,
And cannons in unreachable watch towers
atop tall ramparts.
Girdled by a bottomless moat glimmering with water,
And dotted with countless lakes,
Each as big as a sea.
Picturesque parks festooned with creepers swinging daily in the breeze,
And temple towers gleaming like the golden peaks of Mount Meru,
All adorned this city.

The fountains and the turrets described by Paramanand are long gone, but incredibly, the footprint of the old fort still lives on, as does its character. Avenue Road is and was the main thoroughfare through the old *pete* area. Veer off into one of the small lanes to the left or right of this main road and it is almost like walking back 500 years. The dwellings have changed, but the temples built by the various communities of the area—the oil pressers, the gold merchants, the weavers—still stand. The shops of the jewellers and cloth merchants are still where they were, and as you wander around, you will still see entire streets where all the shops sell only provisions, or only dry fruits, or only spices. One of the most striking constants are the *kattes* (pronounced 'cut-tay'): open spaces that reveal themselves suddenly as you walk through the narrow lanes. Usually, these *kattes* have a peepal tree in them. Often there is a temple or a dargah next to it. In the times when Kempegowda rode through these areas on horseback, were there many more such open areas? Did some of them have the fountains that Paramanand speaks of?

Where once horses and bullock carts clattered through, today, two-wheelers zip past you, loaded with merchandise. Elsewhere, men carrying heavy loads call out impatiently, 'Side, side.' The nature of the commodities traded has sometimes changed. Shops that once sold leaf plates now sell disposable plates of thermocol (or styrofoam); 'golden' plastic baubles, polyester sarees and colourful plastic trinkets now fill the shelves in many other shops. But everywhere, the air is thick with commerce. And this, in fact, is how it has always been. Thanks to its position at the centre of the southern peninsula, Bengaluru has essentially been a traders' town—and not, say, a temple town like Madurai or Thanjavur. This strategic position also gave it a military advantage, which impacted its history, as we have seen.

Between Kempegowda building his mud fort and a second, stone fort coming up to its south, between the coming of the British and the return of the Wodeyars, and between the many battles that were fought here both for control of territory and against disease, the surroundings here have changed with time. For example, many of the neighbourhoods were refashioned in the wake of the 1898 plague *(see chapters 4 and 6)*. Many of the old areas—such as old Tharagupete—were demolished and either rebuilt or relocated in the early 1900s. New roads were laid out to 'open up congested areas' (a phrase much used in the late 1800s–early 1900s in India by colonial town planners appalled by crowded Indian cities and trying to impose new town planning ideas). A second round of minor changes took place in the 1930s or so, when drainage was provided and more streets widened. The many large public wells that existed even in the 1930s are no longer traceable. And yet, despite all these changes, the heart of Bengaluru, its oldest core, remarkably retains its original footprint.

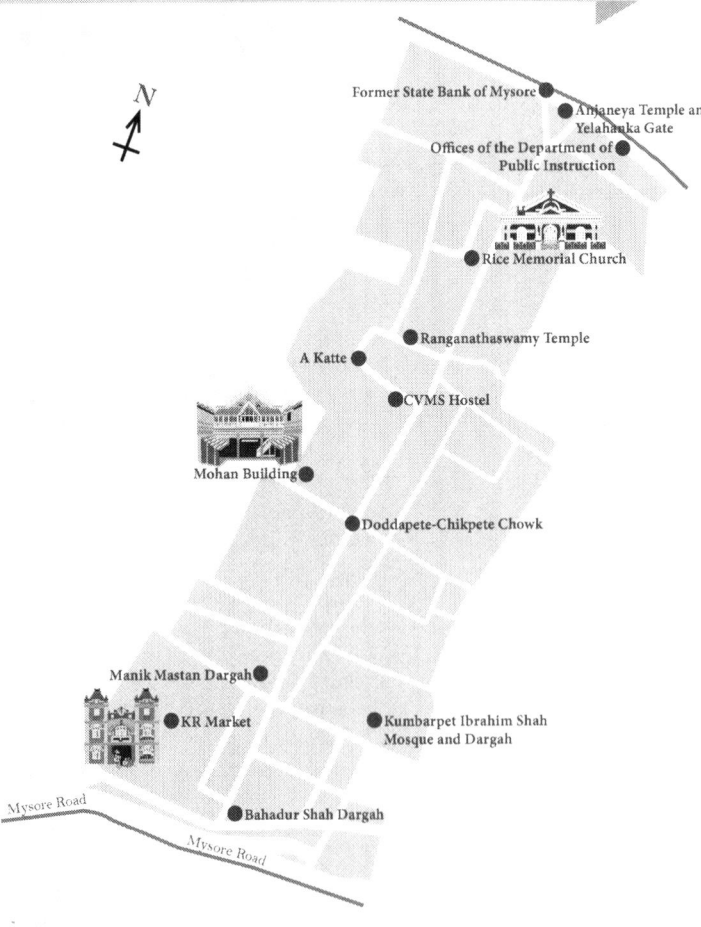

Walk 1: Through the Pete. © *INTACH Bengaluru Chapter*

1. Anjaneya Temple of Yelahanka Gate

Begin your walk at the Anjaneya (Hanuman) temple, at the so-called Mysore Bank Circle at the junction of Avenue Road and Palace Road. The temple is much transformed, especially the exteriors. But in the slightly darkened interiors, the constant flow of the quietly faithful subdues the constant roar of the traffic outside. There is still a semblance of the old here, especially because of the stone pillars and of course, the deity—a relief carving of Hanuman, done in a style that became popular in the Vijayanagar period. Two adjacent shrines are dedicated to Vishnu and Lakshmi.

This temple dates back to when Kempegowda built the mud fort. It was common during the Vijayanagar period for Hanuman to grace and protect major entryways. As a vassal of that empire, it was but natural for Kempegowda to adopt that custom. The temple watched over one of the major entrances into Kempegowda's city, the Yelahanka Gate, on the road leading to Yelahanka. The gate no longer exists; the same goes for the other gates of the time such as the Ulsoor Gate, Anekal Gate, Mysore Gate and so on.

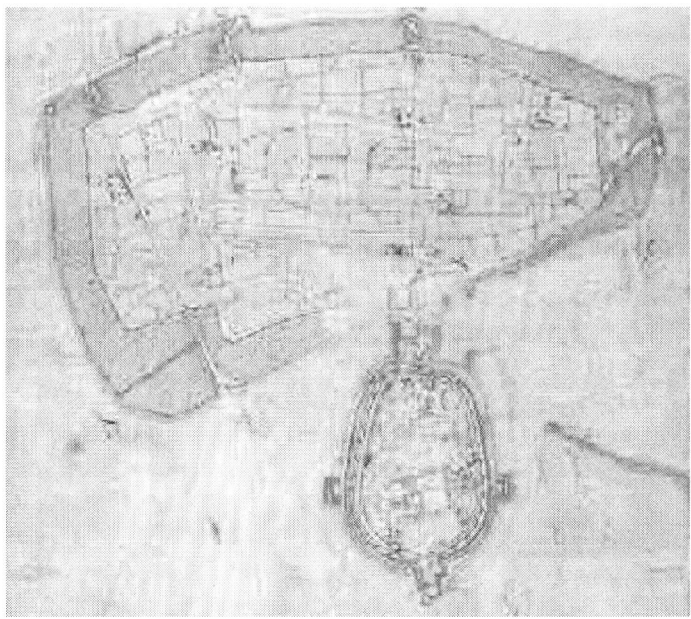

Plan of Bangalore (with the attacks) taken by the English army under the command of the Rt Hon'ble Earl Cornwallis, by Robert Home. *Courtesy of British Library, Shelfmark WD3775(26)*

The Battle for the 'Pettah'

At 4 am on 7 March 1791, a column of men, beasts and weapons moved silently towards Yelahanka Gate. The group comprised His Majesty's 36th and 24th Bengal Native Infantry. Along with them were four 18-pounder guns and two 12-pounders.[5] The infantry was led by Lt Cockerell, and the artillery was led by Lt Col Joseph Moorhouse. About 45 minutes later, the inhabitants of the *pete* woke up to the clamour of battle as the British trained their guns on the gates from about 100 metres away. The Mysore Army returned fire with rocketry and musketry. Soon, the outer gate of the entrance fell. Past this, a narrow passageway lined with prickly pear and 'jungle' on either side impeded the passage of the invading soldiers. With some difficulty, they reached the inner gateway. This, the British found, was stronger than the outer gate; the 12- and 18-pounders were useless against these gates. Bigger guns were summoned. Meanwhile, the Mysore troops kept up their defence, during which several men, including Lt Moorhouse, were killed.[6]

View of the Pettah Gateway where Colonel Moorhouse fell, by Robert Home. Courtesy of British Library, Shelfmark W2567 (3)

Soon enough, the big guns arrived and a breach was made in the gate. A small-built officer named Lt Ayre was hoisted up into the gate, while Gen Medows, the then Governor of Madras who was also present at this attack, is said to have jauntily rallied the troops, saying, 'Well done. Now, whiskers! Try if you can follow and support the little gentleman.'[7] Another version of this incident, narrated by a young British officer, describes Gen Medows as saying: 'Now is the time for you, my brave lad with the whiskers, there are plenty of fine girls within, and here is a little fellow [who] will presently show you the way at them.'[8]

More men crawled through, opened a sally port, and as the rest of the British army rushed in, a bloody battle ensued. Bayonets struck, swords flashed. The sound of constant gunfire mingled with screams and shouts rent the air. Within two hours, and despite fierce resistance by the Mysore Army, the old mud fort was captured. In fact, the very next day, there was a renewed attack by the Mysore troops, when once again, they 'yielded with much unwillingness'. More men were killed. During the fall of the *pete*, 2000 Mysoreans were killed, while 131 British soldiers lost their lives.

The result was a windfall for the British in terms of supplies of grain, fodder and other resources. Though Tipu had ordered that the stocks of grain be destroyed, the commander of the fort, Bahadur Khan, did not follow instructions, perhaps believing that the *pete* would not fall. This proved critical for the British. In many ways, the fall of the *pete* sealed the fate of the bigger stone fort, thanks to the strategic attacking points it afforded the British, the resources they acquired, including food and fodder for men and animals, and of course, its effects on morale.

It may not be an exaggeration to say that a battle at this location changed the course of the city's history. It all goes back to the late 1700s, when the Mysore kingdom was the greatest enemy the British had in India. The British had already fought and lost two wars against Hyder Ali and his son Tipu Sultan, when in 1789, they declared war on Tipu, launching the Third Anglo-Mysore War. The war reached Bengaluru in 1791, when Charles Cornwallis led his 'Grand Army'—a combination of armies of the East India Company, the British government and 'native' states that supported the British—here. By early March 1791, the British forces were just a few kilometres outside Bengaluru. On 6 March, there was a major skirmish in the hills near Gavipura: several hundred men and horses were lost; the leader of the British cavalry, Col John Floyd, was severely injured; and the morale of the British took a severe hit.[4] This disastrous encounter and, of course, the lure of much-needed supplies, prompted Cornwallis to launch his attack on the 'pettah', as the British called the *pete*. The attack began at this very Yelahanka Gate.

II. Former Bank of Mysore

Just opposite the temple you will see a branch of the behemoth State Bank of India (SBI). But until 2016, this was the Bengaluru branch of the State Bank of Mysore, a historic bank that began life in October 1913 as The Bank of Mysore Limited (popularly known as Mysore Bank). It was established thanks to the patronage of the then Maharaja of Mysore, Krishnaraja Wodeyar IV, and was the brainchild of his remarkable Dewan, or Prime Minister, Sir M Visvesvaraya.[9] As with many other things, Visvesvaraya was forward-thinking when he pushed for the establishment of the bank. Mysore State was on the cusp of industrialisation, and there were very few modern financial institutions to provide credit to businesses. In June 1912, Visvesvaraya called for a state-aided bank to fill this gap. The Maharaja agreed and Mysore Bank was born.

Edinburgh, where the Bank of Mysore was first housed.
Courtesy of Nenapu Museum, State Bank of India.

Last day at the old Mental Hospital, 1935. The hospital and Mysore Bank were housed in the same compound until the new NIMHANS building was constructed. *Courtesy of NIMHANS*.

The bank was initially headquartered in a house (named Edinburgh, incidentally) in Chamarajpete. Shortly afterwards, it moved to this location, to the same compound as the Lunatic Asylum, as it was then called.[10] (The asylum was later moved to Jayanagar and reborn as NIMHANS—the National Institute of Mental Health and Neurosciences.) In 1953, the bank was appointed as an agent of the Reserve Bank of India to undertake government business and treasury operations. One year later, it was made an associate of the State Bank of India and rechristened the State Bank of Mysore. Even as it grew in strength, the bank was seen as *namma* bank (our bank). In 2016, the State Bank of Mysore merged with SBI.

This handsome stone building was constructed in 1923. From the outside, the windows on the front facade are the most eye-catching feature, with their pillars, projecting sills, lintels and brackets. Towards the rear, the windows are slightly simpler, with semi-circular hooded arches. Note also the oval ventilators.

As you step up towards the interior, your attention is first held by the entrance door itself, which has an unusual curved shape and wood-framed glass panes. Inside, the building opens out onto an impressive, capacious double-height hall. The eye is immediately drawn to the slim cast-iron columns standing on huge rectangular bases that mark out a central space. On either side, prominent arches separate the space into bays. Note the clerestory windows through which natural light streams in. Originally, the building was symmetric about its central axis. Later, several additions were made to it, especially at the rear of the building.

Check out the small museum, named Nenapu (memory), which houses letters, photographs, equipment, old safes and other paraphernalia from the bank's earliest days to more recent times.

The bank was and is an important enough landmark for it to bestow its name on the intersection where it stands, which was known formerly as Mysore Bank Square and is today called Mysore Bank Circle, or simply, Mysore Bank. During the tumultuous days of the freedom struggle, this was the locus of many a protest. Diagonally opposite, in the backyard of the small Shanishwara temple, is a martyrs' memorial, erected in memory of those who lost their lives in the freedom struggle. The memorial was erected in 1972, as part of the celebrations of the 25th year of Independence. Over the years, buildings grew around it, and today it lies rather dwarfed and almost overlooked in the compound of the Shanishwara temple.

The Bank of Mysore, c.1930s. *Courtesy of Nenapu Museum, State Bank of India.*

Quit India in Bengaluru

In 1942, soon after Gandhiji called for the British to quit India, protests began in Bengaluru too. In August that year, there were repeated gatherings in and around the Mysore Bank area. Protests gathered pace and came to a head in the third week. On 17 August, a large gathering nearby turned restive. Police, the District Magistrate, editors of some local papers and some eminent lawyers are reported to have appealed for peace, but passions ran high. Arrack shops were looted, as was a government rice centre; roads were blocked with carts. Protestors hurled soda bottles and stones at the police from the houses and rooftops. One mob set fire to the Aralepete post office and tried to do the same to the one in Chickpete. They also attempted to enter a police station. The police resorted to firing during which six people were killed and 32 were injured. The then Dewan, N Madhava Rao, held a meeting with senior officials to see how to deal with the situation.

The Martyrs' Memorial. © Aravind C

Unrest continued the next day, 18 August. Two people mentioned in the memorial plaque——Shamanna Bete Rangappa and GV Thirumalaiah——were killed when police fired again that day. Some reports suggest that these were students. Of the other two mentioned, Gundappa is said to have died during a protest in 1937 in Banappa Park, a short distance away, when the Congress leader KF Nariman made a speech. Nothing is known of the other person named——Prahlad Shetty. It is also not known why only these four names are mentioned in the plaque.

III. Offices of the Department of Public Instruction

On the eastern side of the Anjaneya temple, at the junction of Avenue Road and District Office Road, stands a red building partly obscured by a canteen, banners and a high compound wall. This spot has undergone some radical changes: from being part of a deep ditch, it housed a school building, and now accommodates government offices.

The London Mission High School in 1904, now the offices of the Department of Public Instruction. From, *The story of the London Mission Society upto 1904.*

Maps of the late 18th century show that the area where this building stands formed a part of the dry ditch that surrounded the mud fort built by Kempegowda. In those times, this would have been filled with thorny bushes like cacti to deter enemy horses and men. Cut to the 1800s by which time European missionaries had established themselves in the city. In 1847, an Anglo-vernacular school (so designated because both English and Kannada were taught here) was established, which initially functioned from an old chapel on Avenue Road, and then from a rented house opposite the chapel. In 1861, shortly after the administration removed the thorny plants and filled up the ditch, Rev Benjamin Rice *(see below)* bought this parcel of land and the school finally moved to its own building.[12] This was the germ of the London Mission High School that has educated generations of old Bengalureans. In 1932, this school merged with the Wesleyan Mission High School to form the United Mission High School, which was located on Mission Road. That same year, this red building became Central High School.[13] Several decades later, the school closed and the building was taken over to house offices of the Department of Public Instruction.

The two-storeyed brick masonry building has three wings. Externally, it is largely symmetrical though the symmetry does not hold in its internal layout, which has been changed considerably over the years. The building largely conforms to a colonial style, combining European elements like pillars, large volumes and symmetrical planning, with vernacular elements like Madras terrace roofing (on the ground floor), Mangalore tile sloping roofs (on the first floor), the use of lime mortar, and so on.

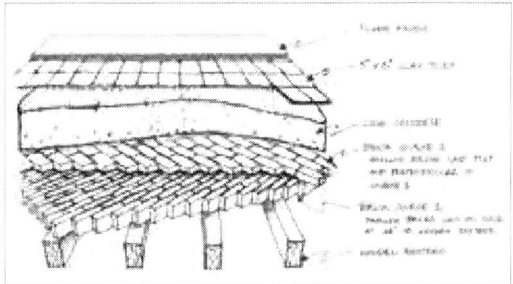

The construction of a Madras terrace roof, a style that was used throughout southern India in the 19th century. *Illustration by Prajwal KA.*

IV. Rice Memorial Church

A short walk of about 300 metres down Avenue Road brings you to this charming building, bright red in colour and distinctly colonial in architecture. This church, in its present form, dates to 1917. But it has been a Christian place of worship since 1834.

The London Missionary Society (LMS) first came to Bengaluru in 1820. (The LMS was constituted in London in 1795 with the express purpose of spreading the word of God to places where Christianity had not yet reached.[14]) In 1834, the preacher William Campbell bought this piece of land and used it as a makeshift school and a place to preach from. The Pettah Chapel, as Europeans referred to it, was constructed here in 1837[15]; it was expanded two years later, and then again six years later.[16] As the congregation kept growing, the old chapel was felt to be too small and not ecclesiastical enough. It was razed and a new one built at a cost of Rs 3500; it opened for worship in October 1852, with

The so-called Canarese Chapel which stood at the site of today's Rice Memorial Church. From, *The Missionary magazine and Chronicle*, No 188, January 1852.

the Rev Benjamin Rice preaching the first sermon in Kannada. Incidentally, one of Bengaluru's early Indian pastors, Rev Job Paul, served in the London Mission Kanarese Church (as it was then called) from 1871 to 1898.

In 1907, there was a major rupture in this church's history: a Municipality engineer noticed cracks in the building and issued a notice asking for it to be vacated as the structure was unsafe. For the next few years, services were held either in Central College or in Mitralaya Girls School nearby. In 1912, the old building was finally demolished, and a year later, plans were drawn up for a new building. But all-too familiar hurdles arose: the Municipality widened the road, and with that, the old plans became useless. After two years of negotiations with the Municipality, the adjacent site was bought which made a new building possible. The new church cost Rs 16,000 to build; the funds came from donations, loans and by selling some furniture from the old building. Finally, on 27 January 1917, the new church, named after Rev Benjamin Rice, was opened for services.[17]

The church's simple but striking exterior features a small porch with a classic pediment. Double Tuscan columns flank the entrance door, which is topped with a Roman semi-circular arch. Two simple windows on either side of the entrance also have semi-circular arches. Ornamentation is minimal, with a simple entablature above the columns.

Of Rice and Men

Courtesy of Douglas Rice

It is strange that there should have been not one but two men named Benjamin Rice who made immense contributions to the city and the state. This father—son pair accomplished an astounding amount of work through passion and sheer force of will.

Benjamin Rice the elder, after whom the Rice Memorial Church is named, was born in 1814 in London. From a very early age, Benjamin was both studious and spiritual, and in 1833, he joined the London Missionary Society as a student. Ordained in 1836, Rev Rice and his wife Jane set sail later that year for Madras (now Chennai) and finally arrived in Bengaluru in January 1838.[18]

Since both his job and his conviction required him to preach to Indians, Rev Rice immediately took up the task of learning Kannada. In five months, he could speak the language, albeit haltingly. Within a year, he was confidently preaching in Kannada in the 'Pettah'. When the LMS required him to take care of the Tamil-speaking congregation, with characteristic assiduity, he learnt that language too within a few months.

The LMS was a pioneer in education in Bengaluru. They ran Kannada-medium and Tamil-medium schools for boys, and later, Kannada-medium schools for girls as well. Rev and Mrs Rice were involved in many of these schools, and not merely in their organisation. As he wrote, 'The education of the young is a very interesting part of our work here.'[19] Since the schools sorely felt the need for appropriate textbooks, Rev Rice went ahead and wrote them. Beginning in 1839 and over the next 30 years, he wrote several textbooks for subjects such as English, arithmetic, geography, history and the Bible. Rev Rice was also Secretary in the Tract and Book Society. He helped revise the Kannada edition of the Bible, and wrote a hymn book that contained 250 hymns in Kannada.

Rev Rice also took on other issues. For instance, in 1886, when a Christian family in Sidlaghatta was prevented from using a public well, it fell to him (and his son EP Rice, also a missionary) to meet the then Dewan, Seshadri Iyer, and plead on behalf of the wronged family.[20]

Benjamin Rice died on 9 February 1887 just a month after a celebration was held to celebrate 50 years of his service. He lies buried in the cemetery on Hosur Road.

The second Benjamin Rice was the first son of the first Benjamin Rice: Benjamin Lewis Rice was born in 1837 and grew up in Bengaluru. He went to England to obtain a BA degree and returned at the age of 23 when he was offered a job as the Principal of Bangalore High School, the precursor to Central College. Rice distinguished himself in successive posts: as Inspector of Schools for Mysore and Coorg (1866); Director of Public Instruction for Mysore and Coorg (1868); Chief Census Officer (1881); Secretary, Education Department (1883).

Courtesy of Douglas Rice

As a child, it is said that young Benjamin could speak Kannada equally or more fluently than English; he picked up Hindi and Sanskrit as well, and also learnt Tamil and the ancient Grantha script later. But he had a special love for the language of the land where he lived. After Rice had retired and moved to England, when he met a Kannadiga in London in 1924, he burst out: '*Ayya, Kannadadalli matanadonave? Muddada Kannada kiviya mele biddu thumba dinagaladuvu*' (Shall we speak in Kannada? It is many days since I heard that sweet language).[21]

While on tours inspecting schools, Rice came across many inscriptions written on stone. Around the same time, the then Chief Commissioner, LB Bowring, commissioned the photography of about 150 inscriptions, mostly from northern Karnataka. Rice's tryst with epigraphy began in 1872 when these photographs were given to him to translate at his leisure. Most of the inscriptions were in Hale Kannada (Old Kannada) and so had archaic letter forms which neither Rice nor most scholars or priests knew. But with perseverance and the aid of a Sanskrit and Kannada scholar, Rice finally managed to decipher the inscriptions.

In 1879, he brought out the volume *Mysore Inscriptions*, which contained translations of these inscriptions. Several more volumes on inscriptions followed, including his magnum opus, *Epigraphia Carnatica*—12 hefty tomes on inscriptions in various parts of Karnataka. Overall, Rice translated almost 9000 inscriptions from all over Karnataka. This was the first systematic survey of inscriptions in India, containing translations, complete transliterations and transcriptions of inscriptions. Rice is thus well deservedly eulogised as 'Shasanapitamaha'—the grandsire of inscriptions.

Impressed with his methodical manner of gathering information, the government gave him the task of preparing Gazetteers for Mysore State as well as for every district. Hence came about Rice's other magnum opus, the *Mysore Gazetteer*, the first of which was published in 1876; the second came out in 1897. The comprehensive information in Rice's books was based partly on his archaeological research tours around the state. These tours on his faithful white pony, often to remote areas, seem to have been adventures in themselves: in one of his reports, for example, Rice notes blandly, 'Some danger was encountered from a large cobra.'[22]

Rice lived in a large, beautiful bungalow he built on Sankey Road, which today houses an upmarket boutique. In 1906, he retired and moved to England. In April 1927, he wrote to his friend and protégé, the distinguished archaeologist R Narasimhachar, 'Remember me to those who still enquire about me. My love for Mysore is unending.'[23]

V. Ranganathaswamy Temple

As you walk down Avenue Road, take a right at BT Street (Basavanna Temple Street) and then a left at 5th Cross. A short walk of a few hundred metres will take you to the market behind and adjacent to the Ranganatha temple. As you walk along, notice how most of the enterprises in this area are gold testers, refiners or otherwise working with gold or gemstones. This gives you a flavour of how the old *pete* was organised by professions.

As is often the case in the old *pete* area, stepping off the road and past the temple gateway means leaving behind the noisy chaos of one world and stepping into another that is far more peaceful. As you cross the threshold of the gopura, typical temple smells waft towards you, including the fragrances of incense, fire and faith. As you walk in, take a closer look at the granite pillars of the *mantapa* (pillared hall): showing riders atop rearing horses, they are derived from the Vijayanagar style but bear the stamp of the Wodeyar period. Notice that the horses are shown stamping another animal underfoot, which in turn is shown attacking people. No two pillars are exactly alike.

The pillars inside the *mantapa* are of different styles, also carved of course, some with the avatars of Vishnu, others with other episodes from the epics, or with dancers, wrestlers, lions and other motifs typically seen in south Indian

Yalis and riders on the pillars of the Ranganathaswamy Temple. © *Aravind C*

temples. The temple is dedicated to Ranganatha, or Vishnu in his reclining form, shown here with his two wives: Bhoodevi and Niladevi. There is a *pradakshinapatha* (circumambulation path) around the *garbagriha*, the sanctum sanctorum, but this is open to visitors only on the occasion of Vaikunta Ekadasi (which falls in late December/early January).

As in many of Bengaluru's old temples, the original granite floor has long been replaced by black and white kitchen/bathroom tiles, which are easier to clean but do perhaps mask the temple's antiquity.

For history buffs, an inscription inside the temple is sure to be of interest. Embedded in a wall on the left is a Telugu inscription which begins: 'In 1628, when the *rajadhiraja rajaparameshwara vira pratapa vira* Rama Deva Maharaya was ruling the empire of the world, seated on his jewel throne, when the Yelahanka Nadaprabhu Kempegowda's grandson, Kempegowda's son, Immadi Kempegowda, was ruling a peaceful kingdom in righteousness, the people of Bengaluru *pete* entered into the following agreement…' The inscription goes on to mention that merchants from a number of villages had decided to pay some money to the Ranganatha temple of Mutyalapete.[24]

VI. A *Katte*

Just a little past the temple on RT Street, on the other side, is a small lane that looks barely wide enough for two people to squeeze past each other. Fear not, and boldly step into this lane. It broadens a little a few steps inside and then zigzags a short way towards the right before suddenly, unexpectedly, leading right into a largish open square, dominated by a peepal tree.

Several of these *kattes* dot the *pete* area. They come as welcome surprises amidst the dense matrix of shops and dwellings. Many of them have a darker history. During the 1791 battle for Bengaluru *(see box)*, these open squares—graced with trees and often a temple—were the places where British troops set up their batteries of guns from which to fire on the fort. In fact, it was right at this spot, and also in the then open area opposite the Ranganatha temple (where the small Tuppada Anjaneya temple now stands), that on 12 March 1791, the attacking troops opened 12-pounder enfilading batteries: these were batteries used in the initial stages of a siege and usually at vantage points from which they could direct sweeping fire upon a target, whether it was a line of troops or a fort, as in this case.[25]

VII. CVMS Hostel

Head east from the *katte* along MT Street and back towards Avenue Road. Once on the main road, turn right. Shortly, you will come upon a gate within which is the Karur Vysya Bank. Step in and take a look at the building in front of you. If you exclaim 'Wow!', you would not be the first to do so in front of the beautiful Chinthalapalli Venkatamuniah Setty's (CVMS) Free Boarding Hostel and Choultry, established in 1911.

Students with CVM Setty and others in front of the CVMS Hostel, 1911-12.
Courtesy of SVS Gupta, nephew of CVM Setty.

The building is named after its founder who hailed from Chinthalapalli in Kolar district, moved to Bengaluru as a small yarn merchant, and prospered. And like many in those perhaps gentler and more genteel days, he gave generously to society. In 1909, a meeting of the Arya Vysya Mahasabha, an institution of the Arya Vysya community that CVM Setty belonged to, discussed the need for children of their community to have facilities and support for their education. Two years later, Setty established the CVMS Hostel for boys from the Arya Vysya community to stay free of cost during their education in Bengaluru.[26]

When CVM Setty passed away, his wife Lakshmidevamma and her brother SV Srinivasa Setty ably managed the hostel. In 1930, she had the old building demolished and the present building constructed in its place. Speaking at the opening ceremony of the new building on 21 May 1930, Dewan Sir Mirza Ismail remarked how CVM Setty 'had a real affection for children'. He was 'himself not highly educated', but was able to achieve immense success in business, because 'though he started life with a very small capital, he possessed a large stock of pluck and enterprise'.[27]

The main hall of the CVMS Hostel. © *PeeVee*

Incidentally, apart from the hostel, Lakshmidevamma also donated Rs 63,000 for the construction of a children's hospital (called the Lakshmidevamma Block) in the Vani Vilas Hospital. Her daughter Rukkamma and brother SVS Setty continued the work after her death. A yarn merchant and astute businessman, SVS Setty was also for long President of the Vysya Bank. He was awarded the title 'Dharmaprakasha' for his social service and, later, was declared a Justice of Peace.

The ground floor of the building was earlier a *choultry* or wedding hall, where some of the family members were also married. Today, it houses a branch of a bank. Incidentally, it was here, when the *choultry* was to be given to the bank on rent a few years ago, that a trunk full of memorabilia was found, including old photographs, letters, citations and other treasures. These were carefully cleaned, and are now preserved in the hostel and the residence of SVS Gupta, son of SVS Setty.[28] Within the hostel (the first and second floors) though, there is no whiff of commerce. In fact, it feels like a warm and rambling old home, both in architecture and atmosphere.

The building is a repertoire of artisanship. For a start, take in the winged figures flanking the plaque at the entrance, the decorative balcony grills on every floor and the slender cast-iron columns above them, the tasteful stucco and wooden fascia on every level, and at the very top, a decorative parapet including a figure of Krishna playing the flute. Beautiful wooden brackets support the large girders which support the roof. Notice how the horizontality of the floors is defined by the ornamental cornice bands.

A narrow staircase with wooden banisters takes you to the first floor which has a large central hall with a polished red-oxide floor and a Madras terrace ceiling. The hall functions as a gathering space into which all the rooms open. The walls here are decorated with photographs and several citations of the founder and his family, many of which make for very interesting reading. Note also the decorative Corinthian pilasters with their little winged deities carved in wood. If you look carefully, you may be able to spot the name Dorman Long and Co on some of the iron beams which were shipped in from England. Everywhere, the attention to detail is evident.

This three-storeyed building is set back from the road. When it was first built, a large foreground would have added to the visual interest that it offers to the street, though that is now hidden by the shops in the front. Around the hall are rooms in which the students lived. When the building was constructed, and even in the 1940s and 1950s, this was the tallest structure along Avenue Road. Though it is now hemmed in by other buildings, you can still get a good view from the upper floor.

This building received an INTACH Award in 2017.

Motifs in the hostel reveal great attention to detail.
© *Aravind C*

VIII. Mohan Buildings

For your next destination, take the right onto AM Lane, and in about 100 metres, take the second left towards Chickpete Road (also called Old Taluk Cutcherry Road). You will be walking adjacent to the Mohan Buildings. On Chickpete Road, turn left and enter.

What is the connection between this building, an administrative office, a cinema, the police and a hotel? Read on to find out.

The Mohan Buildings. © *Aravind C*

This derelict but still handsome building once housed the old taluk *cutcherry*, or office, which is why the road is so named.[29]

According to popular lore, when Shivaji's father Shahaji ruled over Bengaluru, he lived in a palace named Gauri Mahal, that was located here. When we first encounter this structure in written records, it is as a government-owned building housing the taluk *cutcherry* or office, hence the name Old Taluk Cutcherry Road for the street it stands on. Besides the cutcherry, at various times, it also housed the municipal dispensary, an eye infirmary, the City Central Police Station, the District Police Office and the Sub-Registrar's office, among other things. In the early 1900s, the police complained that the building was too old, too cramped and in too crowded a locality, and suggested that it be auctioned off so that they could raise money for a new building elsewhere. Accordingly, in 1905, the building was sold to the businessman Haji Ismail Sait *(see chapter 6)* for Rs 30,000 on condition that he would demolish the old building and erect a new one.[30] Accordingly, Sait constructed a new building in 1909, which he named Ahmed Buildings, the name by which some old-timers still call this structure.

Ironically, after having complained about the location, in the 1930s and 1940s, the police department took two rooms on the first floor here on rent to house a police station![31]

In the mid-1940s, the building was taken over by the Income Tax Department and auctioned. This is when an enterprising young man from Mumbai named Nand Lal Kapur sensed a good business opportunity and bought it for Rs 5 lakhs, a princely—nay, kingly—sum in those days. He renamed the building after his youngest son, Mohanlal.[32] The structure remained a commercial centre: the ground floor was occupied by various shops while the upper floor was used as a lodge by the Bombay Anand Bhavan. A few years later, Kapur moved to Bengaluru with his family. And the cinema connection? Kapur also bought over a cinema hall in the cantonment area, called Paul's Rex (also on auction, incidentally). Bengalureans, of course, know it by the slightly edited name that Kapur gave it: Rex. (This iconic cinema had its last show on 31 December 2018; it is to be demolished and replaced by a multiplex.) The Bombay Anand Bhavan closed down about a decade ago. At the time of writing, the current owner of Mohan Buildings is said to have decided to demolish the structure.

The long facade with its exposed brickwork and the rich ornamental features in iron, wood and lime plaster make this two-storeyed building visually arresting and rather unique; there are also the semi-circular arches on its upper floor, the wooden carvings and the brick walls. Inside, the building has Madras terrace flat roofs and sloping tiled roofs. A colonnade around the central courtyard connects the retail shops on the ground floor. The verandah on the first floor overlooks the street.*

Motifs at Mohan Buildings. Notice the gandabherunda in one of them. © *Aravind C*

---

* Architectural description by Pankaj Modi, Coordinator, INTACH Bengaluru Chapter

IX. Doddapete–Chickpete Chowk

Exit the Mohan Buildings and turn left till you reach the intersection. Tarry a while here, traveller, for this chowk or intersection, according to legend, is the very heart of the city that Kempegowda built. After Kempegowda had decided where he was going to build his new capital, the story goes that on an auspicious day in 1537, his priest brought along four pairs of white oxen, each attached to ploughs. At the appointed hour, these pairs of oxen were set loose and they went forth, ploughing the land in four different directions. The distance they traversed marked the limits of the fort, while the paths they took became the new city's main roads: Doddapete and Chickpete.

The pillars and shop fronts that define this intersection date from the 1930s, when the City Municipality went on a beautification drive and also widened some roads in the *pete*. Sadly, not much effort has gone into the maintenance of the pillars and some of the shop fronts have been replaced by modern structures that do no service to the past.

X. Manik Mastan Dargah

Walk about 400 metres down Avenue Road, keeping a sharp lookout for a small gap between shops with a small sign for MP Traders and another for the Dargah Hazrat Manik Mastan. The inconspicuous entrance is almost opposite Kusum General Stores on the left of the road. (Incidentally, Kusum stopped giving plastic bags to customers 19 years ago, making it one of the first shops in Bengaluru to do so!) Step into the little opening and be dumbstruck by the remarkable contrast between the spacious and quiet surroundings of the dargah and the clamour and hubbub of the main road outside.

We begin here with a story from the time of Hyder Ali, when he was getting the mud fort that had been built by Chikkadevaraja redone in stone. Several labourers worked on this project, including three men—Tipu Mastan, Manik Mastan and Tawakkal Mastan—who, Hyder noticed, were never around when salaries were paid. Intrigued, he asked one of his men to follow the three labourers to see what they were up to. Hyder's man was told that the three prayed and slept in a mosque every night. But when he followed them, he found that though prayers continued, the three men's bodies had separated into different pieces. And yet, there they were back at work the next day, ready to lift the huge stones as usual! When he reported back this story, Hyder immediately realised that the three were no ordinary men, that they were saints.

Of the three, Manik Mastan lies buried here, Tawakkal Mastan's dargah is at Cottonpete, and Tipu Mastan's is near Arcot in Tamil Nadu. Manik Mastan belongs to the Suharwady Sufi *silsila* (order).

XI. Kumbarpet Ibrahim Shah Mosque and Dargah

Across the road from the Manik Mastan dargah, turn left onto Sadar Patrappa Road. A short walk of a few metres leads you to the mosque named after Ibrahim Khan, who was *killedar* or commandant of the fort of Bengaluru for ten years under Haider Ali. While one authority dates this masjid to 1761, other sources state that the mosque was built at the site of Ibrahim Khan's grave by the British after the Third Anglo-Mysore War, in gratitude for Khan's kindness towards his (British) prisoners.[33]

Ibrahim Khan is believed to have been in charge of rebuilding Chikkadevaraja's mud fort in stone; he also set up cannon and gun foundries in Bengaluru.[34] We do not know exactly where these foundries were, but isn't it exciting to think that high-quality armaments, including cannons, muskets and rockets, were being manufactured in the old city of Bengaluru more than 250 years ago?

Incidentally, this complex of dargah and mosque is another one of the open spaces in the area that served as convenient points from which to fire during the siege, storming and capture of the fort in the 'Battle for Bengaluru' in March 1791.

XII. KR Market

At the end of Avenue Road is an iconic market whose origins go back 200 years. There was probably already a market in this area from the early 1800s. In about 1907, officials of the City Municipality, along with the then Dewan, PN Krishnamurti, visited the market. Finding it unsanitary, they suggested that a new one be built near Kalasipalyam. However, this plan was later modified as the area selected was found unsuitable, and it was decided to redevelop the old market instead. But, for want of a good map of the city and of town planners, nothing much happened for a few years.

In 1913, the reconstituted Bangalore City Improvement Committee *(see chapter 4)* proposed that a new and bigger market be built here.[35] Accordingly, streets and shops in this area, then called Siddikatte, were acquired. (Incidentally, the name Siddikatte derived from a tank purported to have been built during Kempegowda's times by a wealthy woman named Siddi. This tank existed in the late 1700s, according to 18th century maps, but by the early 1900s, it had dried up and become the residence of well-to-do Brahmins.[36]) However, for several reasons including funding, work on the market began only in 1918.[38]

The new market was designed by the State of Mysore's Chief Architect, SH Lakshminarasappa, with Calcutta's Stuart Hogg Market (better known

Krishnarajendra Market. © *Aravind C*

as New Market) as the model. The market, now called Krishnarajendra or KR Market, was opened on 11 October 1921. In its early days, the revamped market was called, appropriately, the New Market or the New General Market, City New Market and City Market, the last being the same as the moniker that had graced the old market which had been razed.

In the early days, a Market Inspector was appointed to ensure that the premises remained clean and sanitary.[39] Improvements and additions to the market continued well into the 1930s. Special efforts (and a few lakhs) were lavished on the market frontage and the Market Circus, as the then large open area in front was called. In January 1930, the City Municipality held its first 'Market Show' since the buildings were completed.

Though the market's layout is said to be modelled on Calcutta's New Market, in architectural terms, especially with its twin tower-like structures topped with mansard roofs and ornate railings, it takes its cue more from Victoria Hospital across the street. Both are colonial, Victorian-inspired styles of architecture.

Only the frontage remains of this once-elegant and clean market. The building that you see inside was constructed in 1997 when the market was expanded and modernised, with facilities like lifts and cold storage. However, most of the stalls in the upper floors remain unoccupied while the cold storage facility remains unavailable and unused. There have been repeated announcements and attempts at improving the market, which at the time of writing, have not materialised.

XIII. Bahadur Shah Dargah

Across from the market, at the intersection of Silver Jubilee Park Road and Avenue Road, stands the Dargah Hazrath Mir Bahadur Shah Al-Maroof Syed Pacha Shaheed. Like many of the other dargahs in the area, this one too is linked to the tumultuous wars of the late 1700s.

On 21 March 1791, when the British Grand Army (led by Gen Charles Cornwallis) attacked the fort of Bengaluru, the Mysore Army in the fort put up a stiff fight. One man in particular stood out—the *killedar* or commandant of the fort, Bahadur Khan. Tipu had only recently had him transferred from Krishnagiri to Bengaluru. Tall, fair and striking, with a white beard that reached almost to his waist, the 70-something veteran fought with all the vigour of a youth.

Contemporary British accounts recount how he led the fight from the front, urging his men to make a last stand against the enemy. The gallant soldier battled on till his last breath, dying of a shot in the head and multiple stab wounds. You can gauge the admiration the British felt for the old soldier from the encomiums they heaped on him. Roderick Mackenzie, a lieutenant in the British infantry who participated in that battle, wrote, 'Wherever gallantry is recorded, Bahadur Khan, *killedar* of Bangalore, will hold a conspicuous place among the heroes of our times. True to his trust, he resigned it with life, after receiving almost as many wounds as were inflicted on Caesar in the Capitol.'[40]

After the battle, Cornwallis sent word to Tipu informing him that he could take the mortal remains of Bahadur Khan. Tipu is said to have wept with despair when he learnt of the loss of his trusted *killedar*. But to Cornwallis he responded that the spot where a soldier fell was the most honourable place

Bahadur Shah's dargah attracts both Muslim and Hindu faithful.
© *Aravind C*

where he could be interred. Accordingly, the British buried Bahadur Khan with full military honours near where he died.

The one-roomed dargah has granite cladding, a dome and four small turrets. In the centre is a grave draped with a red embroidered shawl, festooned with several garlands. Every day about a hundred men and women stream in, touch the grave and pray silently, believing that a wish made at this dargah will come true. The famous Karaga procession, too, makes a stop here. (One of Bengaluru's oldest festivals, Karaga comprises rituals mainly centred round the city's water bodies; the festival culminates in a procession that halts at religious centres in the *pete*.)

Bahadur Shah died years ago, but here, close to where he perished, he is still very much a part of people's lives.

Incidentally, the road on which the dargah stands, Silver Jubilee Park Road, was named after the Silver Jubilee celebration of Krishnaraja Wodeyar IV. On 8 August 1927 Krishnaraja Wodeyar IV, affectionately known by the people of Mysore State as Nalvadi, completed 25 years of rule. Today, the road is best known for shops selling electronic components and hardware.

A plaque commemorates the British assault and victory over the Bengaluru fort in 1791. © *Pankaj Modi*

Walk 2: *Through the* kote *area*

In which you experience military, royal and hospital zones, and also encounter some rocket stories

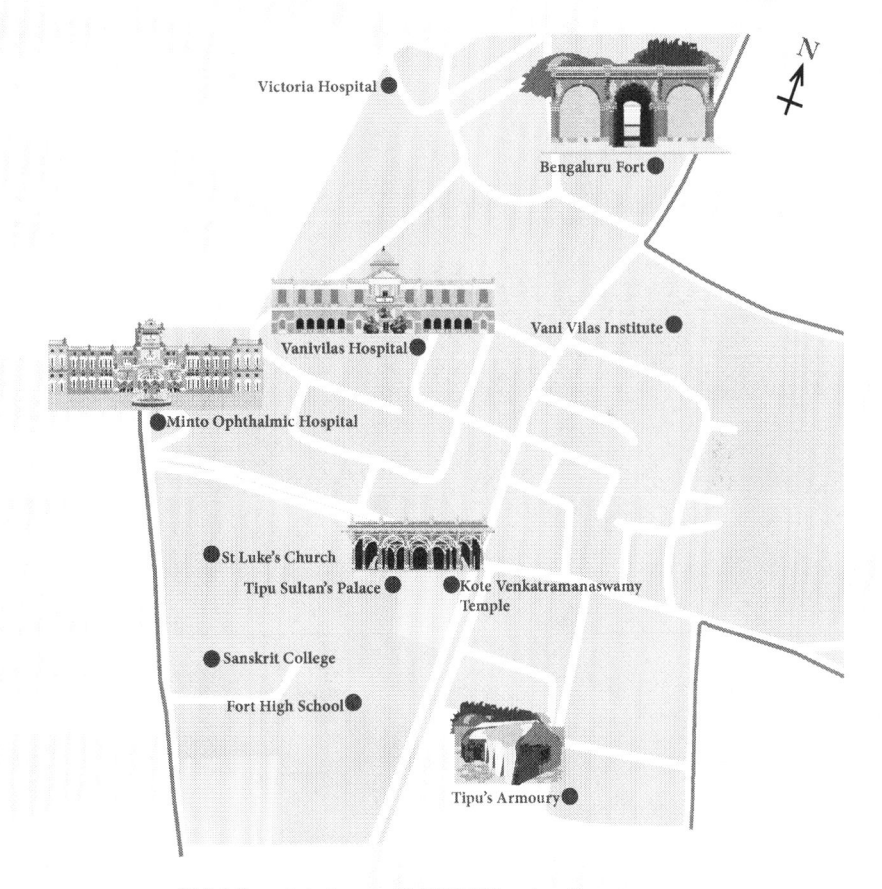

Walk 2: Through the kote area. © *INTACH Bengaluru Chapter*

I. Bengaluru Fort

Our walk begins at the ever-busy junction of KR Road and the road leading into Victoria Hospital. Every single day, hundreds, nay thousands, of people pass by the *kote*, or fort, which stands at this intersection, thanks to the bus stand and hospital that are just outside this historic structure. And yet, like the Muggles in the Harry Potter series who never notice the magic all around them, most people do not really register the big stone structure. This may be because they are too focused on the hawkers who sell their wares on the footpath outside the fort, or because crossing the roads here generally engages all senses if you want to stay alive. Of course, most people also do not know that the fort was the site of a pitched battle in 1791 (see box), nor that it came close to being completely demolished not very long ago, not once, not twice, but several times.

A fort with many lives

After his defeat in the Battle for Bengaluru in 1791, it is said that an upset Tipu Sultan had the Bengaluru fort dismantled. It is also said that Dewan Purnaiah, Prime Minister of the Mysore kingdom under Hyder, Tipu and, later, Krishnaraja Wodeyar III, had the fort rebuilt in 1799.[43]

After the death of Tipu Sultan in Srirangapatna in 1799, a few British troops were garrisoned in the fort in Bengaluru. Their numbers increased steadily. In 1807, the new British cantonment of Bangalore was established a few kilometres northeast of the old city. But the fort was included as a disjunct part of the Cantonment. This was because, when the British troops moved from Srirangapatna, they also moved their large stores of arms here. This immense arsenal that was stored in the fort weighed heavily on British minds and was a crucial point in subsequent deliberations over the fate of the fort—discussions that went on for more than 50 years.

The Bengaluru Fort in the late 1800s. *Courtesy of British Library, Shelfmark 394 (86)*

The Battle for Bengaluru

View of the Delhi Gateway after it was repaired, by Robert Home.
Courtesy of British Library, Shelfmark WD3775 (7)

After the capture of the mud fort by the British following the battle with the Mysore Army on 7 March 1791, the attacking army set up batteries at various points in the *pete*, from which they fired at the stone fort. With each new battery, they moved closer to the fort. First came ten 18-pounders and two enfilading batteries, erected about a kilometre from the fort, then came two 24-pounders, a 24-pounder breaching battery, seven 18-pounders and so on.[41] Even as this was going on, Tipu's army made repeated attacks on the British, and on several occasions, men, horses and supplies were lost. But the British movement was inexorable.

On 18 March, Capt Alexander Beatson, a valued engineer and surveyor in Cornwallis' army and the one who had guided him to Bengaluru, suggested a different point of attack. Accordingly, all guns were now trained at a point a little east of the Delhi Gate, almost exactly where KR Road runs near the fort today. The action culminated in a pitched battle that took place right here on 21 March 1791. At 11 pm that moonlit night, the Grand Army snaked its way over a two-foot passage that had been left in the causeway across the moat. Lt Roderick Mackenzie recounts that, as they neared the bastion and wall that had been breached, they faced stiff opposition from Mysore Army soldiers inside the fort. 'Multitudes crowded tumultuously to the point of attack,' he says and describes how blue lights and fireballs thrown at the British turned the night as bright as day. 'A blaze of musquetry and a general discharge of rockets contributed to the awful grandeur of an exhibition in itself truly tremendous. And one universal roar of cannon at once struck the spectator with consternation and terror.' The invading army made its way through the breach and streamed left and right down the ramparts. Stiff fighting followed, but in less than two hours, the battle was over. About 2000–3000 people died in what Mackenzie describes as a 'momentous event which put Britain in possession of probably the strongest and most important fortress in Mysore'.[42]

In the 1820s, the fort was said to be in such a 'ruinous' state that it could be captured 'with no special bravery'![44] But the Company (for this was still the East India Company) baulked at the expense of repairing it, and sanctioned only the bare minimum work required to ensure that it would be 'tenable against a Native Force' and that the all-important arsenal was safe. Cut to the 1830s and it was a similar story all over again. The picture painted is of a rather dilapidated *kote*, with shrubs and grasses growing over it; parts of its ramparts were filled with ditches gathering rainwater. But the fort needed to be in good repair because, so the reasoning went, the city had fertile soil and a temperate climate; it also had good and safe communications with the Malabar coast, the Nizam's dominions, and the rest of south India. The recommendation was to repair it by putting a few companies of Pioneers and Sappers on the job. But no sooner had they started work than the five companies were withdrawn, just a few months later. Interestingly, while Roderick Mackenzie and others who took part in the 1791 battle had called it one of the strongest fortresses in Mysore State, once it was securely in their possession, it was derided just 40 years later as being 'the worst fort I ever saw'.[45]

Some 20 years later, along came yet another proposal to 'let the fort fall to ruin'—of course, after ensuring that the arsenal was properly secured. New barracks were being constructed in Bangalore Cantonment and there seemed little need to keep the fort in good repair. But ultimately, it was allowed to survive for two rather opposing reasons. One official—British Commissioner of Mysore Sir Mark Cubbon, no less—states that the fort 'suggests no other idea to the native mind than the hopelessness of trying to defend the strongest fortresses against British skill and valour'. It would remind the 'natives', he says, 'of the fearful carnage' when the fort was taken by storm. At the same time, it has 'moral influence', says a Gen Beresford, Commanding Officer of the Mysore Division. It reminds people of the 'palmy days of Tippoo Sultaun's rule'.[46] Tread cautiously, he advises, for there are many who live within the fort who are against British rule. Ultimately, caution prevailed and the fort survived.

The fort in 1881, or, the curious case of the missing mention

In 1881 the Rendition took place: the administration of the Mysore kingdom, which the British had appropriated from the Wodeyars in 1831 on the pretext of misrule, reverted to the Mysore royal dynasty. This seminal event brought with it several bureaucratic tangles in which the fort, too, was ensnared for a while.

After the Rendition, the Cantonment of Bangalore, as it had been known till then, became the Civil and Military Station (henceforth referred to as the C&M Station), and was also known as the Assigned Tract. This latter term comes from the Gazette Notification issued on 28 April 1881:

> Whereas His Highness the Maha Raja of Mysore, by an instrument dated the 25th day of March, 1881, assigned, free of charges, to the exclusive management of the British Government, for the purposes of a Cantonment, certain lands within the limits specified and described in a schedule and map and annexed to the said instrument, and forming the Civil and Military Station of Bangalore; and whereas by the said instrument His Highness the Maha Raja of Mysore renounced all jurisdiction in the lands so assigned...

The problem was that though it was shown on the official map accompanying the documents as a big, detached, non-contiguous block of the C&M Station, the fort—the fort! With its huge arsenal!—was entirely missing from the Schedule, which only described the contiguous portions of the C&M Station.[47] In terms of possession on the ground, this omission did not matter much since the British authorities assumed jurisdiction in the fort. But when this omission was pointed out some months later by a British General, there was minor panic until the then Resident, Sir James Gordon, stepped in to assert that the omission was deliberate because 'the Bangalore Fort was British territory by conquest' and so did not have to be 'assigned' by the Maharaja. Even other British officials were uncomfortable with this statement—as was obvious in subsequent correspondence.

Eventually, in 1888, when the arsenal was moved to the Cantonment, the British government gave the fort over to the Maharaja's administration in exchange for the Residency grounds (today's Raj Bhavan), which had been under the Mysore Maharaja's administration.[48]

Death of a fort

A new chapter began in the history of the *kote* when it was taken over by the Mysore administration. In 1881, when British military authorities dismantled part of a wall to repair some entrenchments, the then Dewan, CV Rangacharlu, had complained against the demolition of a building that held 'sentimental interest' for Mysore State.[49]

But beginning in 1889, the growing city began to eat away at the historic monument. In 1889, as part of a slew of roads, Lt Col AH Macintire, Deputy Commissioner of Bangalore, suggested the opening of the road that ran east–west through the stone fort, dismantling these parts of the fort wall and filling in the 'ditch' where necessary; breaking down one of the old fort gateways to allow for a road to pass through; and the setting up of a grain bazaar in the fort glacis (a sloping bank in front of a fort).[50] This seems to have been the beginning of the gradual cannibalisation of the fort, a process that continued over the next 50 years or so, leaving only a portion of the Delhi Gate complex intact for us today. In 1894, the President of the City Improvement Committee, listing all the city 'improvements' that had taken place, describes how the north gate of the fort was dismantled and widened 'to admit of a 30' road'. In 1899, the southern gate, called the Mysore Gate, was dismantled.[51] And so it went, with the fort being gradually broken apart to extend a playground here, widen a road there. Some of the fort's stone was broken down to build the road, and sometimes the stone was sold to institutions that came up nearby, such as the Theosophical Society on KR Road.[52]

A portion of the Delhi Gate. ©*Aravind C*

The Delhi Gateway's imposing entrances were made large enough to allow elephants to enter. © *Meera Iyer*

Iron spikes precluded the use of elephants to break open the doors. © *Meera Iyer*

Today, of course, what we call the Bengaluru Fort is really only a portion of its northern gateway, the Delhi Gate complex. The Delhi Gate itself was once a massive complex of three courtyards and gateways. As for the fort, before it was dismantled, it extended from here till just beyond Fort High School in the south, where the Mysore Gate stood.

Military architecture in 18th century Mysore State

Though only a fraction of the old fort still stands, what is left is still impressive. One is reminded of the fabled comment by Vitruvius on the symbolism of architecture and war, about how a feeling of strength could be imparted (to a building) to deter attackers.[53] It is also a good example of Mysore State's military architecture in the 1700s.

Most scholars think that the fort was initially built in the 1600s by Chikkadevaraja Wodeyar, in mud, and then rebuilt in stone by Hyder Ali and still more extensively strengthened by Tipu Sultan.[54] However, not all scholars agree. Some believe that both the fort surrounding the *pete* and this fort were built at the same time, by Kempegowda.

By the 1700s, gunpowder was playing a stronger role in warfare; military architecture had to respond to this change. This is one of the reasons why mud forts were replaced by stone. But appearances can be deceptive. Though we call it a stone fort, in reality, it is a mud and stone fort, or a rubble and stone fort. The inner core is made of rubble and the outer two surfaces are wedge-shaped granite stones with the wedges facing inward. You can see an example of a wedge-shaped stone near the path to the dungeons. The combination of outer stone and the core of rubble gave such forts both strength and the ability to withstand the shock of cannon fire. A similar style of construction is visible in the fort at Hampi/Vijayanagar and other places built in the 1400–1500s, though bastions in the forts of earlier, pre-Islamic influence were often square, not circular.[55]

As you walk in, note the many defensive features, in common with well-built fortifications the world over. The first things to notice are the menacing iron spikes on the back of the door. These were to prevent elephants from being used as battering rams to break open the door.

Also notice how each huge doorway is placed at a right angle to the previous one: this was deliberately done to slow down invading armies. If you were part of an army trying to capture the fort, you would have made an easy target for the snipers standing behind the gun slits in the parapet above you. Look back up at the parapet from here and from the courtyard past the second doorway, and you can see the gaps in the parapet from where cannons once fired (the technical term for them is embrasure), and the slits through which muskets once blazed (called loopholes in military fortification parlance). Beyond the gate out of the courtyard there were originally two other courtyards like this one, with more gates.

Maps from the 1790s and photos from the 1800s show how this oval fort was once surrounded by a wide and deep moat.[56] There was no drawbridge to cross the moat; a causeway was the only means of entering.

Other things to linger over in the fort are the carvings at various places, both on the stone walls and in the stucco work along and above the doorways. They reflect an eclectic mix of Hindu and Islamic influences. The scrolls

A motif in stucco in the Bengaluru Fort. © *Meera Iyer*

of creepers along the doorway are similar in style to those you might see in Hindu temples. Yet the stucco carvings are typically Islamic. There are parrots, flowing floral designs, foliage. Don't miss the abundance of peacocks: in procession, singly, doubly; there are even double-headed peacocks. Peacock motifs were ubiquitous in Islamic art. The beautiful bird was associated with paradise and also symbolised royalty.

Speaking of carvings, did you notice the *gandabherunda*, the symbol of the Mysore Wodeyars, on the Ganesha temple just inside the fort? This suggests that the temple was added after the 1800s. The fact that the temple obscures decorative motifs on the walls behind also suggests that it was added sometime after the fort walls were rebuilt in stone. However, the 1791 maps of the fort do show a structure here. Further, the plinth of the temple, especially on the eastern side, has a series of small carvings of peacocks, women dancing, people playing instruments, and so on. Stylistically, these belong to the 16th–17th centuries or so. Yet, these carvings are not placed in any order and appear to have been brought here from elsewhere. This would suggest that there was an earlier structure here, perhaps a temple, which was renovated or rebuilt, and the *gandabherunda* added after Tipu's death.

One of the most exciting parts of the fort remains mostly hidden from view today. The steps along the fort's outer wall on the south lead to the wall walk (literally, the part of the fort walls behind the parapet and along which soldiers could walk). If you get permission to go up, you can see other fortification features. Along the base of the merlons are the banquettes—ledges or platforms on which defenders would stand to fire over the top of the parapet, and then duck back down while reloading their muskets. You can also see that the embrasure openings are splayed on the firing side, to enable a wider angle of fire. Both these features are a sign of the influence of French engineers on the designs of Tipu's forts.[57]

From there, steps lead down towards the infamous dungeons, securely sited and almost invisible until you are actually inside them. Two sets of dungeons exist, one of which is more intimidating. It is not difficult to imagine the chamber of horrors this must once have been. On the door over this dungeon is a board proclaiming that it was where Sir David Baird (who led the attack against Tipu Sultan in 1799) and several others were imprisoned for many years in the 1780s. This, in fact, is the reason the Delhi Gate escaped being reduced to stone, so that the monument where this celebrated officer of the British Grand Army was imprisoned could be showcased! Though one suspects it was also so that the British could boast of their triumph over Tipu in general: witness the victory plaque on the fort wall along KR Road.

II. Victoria Hospital

Ready for some medical tourism—of a fashion? Just outside the gate to the fort is the road that leads into the Victoria Hospital campus, the first hospital we encounter in a zone filled with some very handsome hospital buildings.

Modern medicine entered the old city in 1833, when a small dispensary was established in the fort area. Six years later, a second dispensary with a clinic accommodating 50 patients was opened. Over the years, several additions were made to this, the last being in 1866. Meanwhile, in the then Cantonment side, the Bowring Civil Hospital was opened in 1868. In 1872, the flourishing hospital in the *pete* was demoted to a dispensary and patients were transferred to the new hospital in the Cantonment. Then came the Rendition, and the Wodeyar-administered city portion of Bengaluru found itself without any hospital at all. In 1886, the then Maharaja of Mysore, Chamaraja Wodeyar X, donated 20 acres to the Good Shepherd Sisters to set up St Martha's Hospital, which was opened on 28 July 1886—the eve of the feast of St Martha, a friend of Jesus.[60] For some years, the *pete* dispensary was merged with St Martha's.

But it was obvious that another hospital was urgently needed, especially near the more densely populated areas of the city. Accordingly, in 1897, Kempananjammanniavaru, popularly known as Vani Vilasa Sannidhana, the queen regent of Mysore State from 1895 to 1902 and widow of Chamaraja Wodeyar, laid the foundation stone for a new hospital. Also responsible for

The Victoria Hospital, a Wiele's postcard. *Courtesy of Harish Padmanabha.*

the setting up of this hospital was the then Senior Surgeon and Sanitary Commissioner, Lt Col Terence Joseph McGann. It was he who chose the site and also pushed for its construction.[61] The foundation stone-laying ceremony was organised and attended by the then Dewan, the ever-capable Seshadri Iyer, and took place on 22 June 1897, the day Queen Victoria's diamond jubilee was celebrated. The Maharani had particularly wanted the hospital to provide free medical care and to be open to all.

The hospital was built with approximately Rs 4 lakhs and was opened three years later on 8 December 1900, by the then Viceroy and Governor General of India, Lord Curzon. In his speech on the occasion, he said:

"Its architectural features, and the excellence and completeness of its contemplated arrangements, show that Her Highness the Maharani Regent has resolved that no expense should be spared to give to the chief city of the State a hospital accommodation and equipment which should make it the envy of its neighbours. This is in entire keeping with the enlightened policy, as regards public institutions and buildings, which has been consistently followed by the Mysore Durbar."

With its steeply sloping, four-sided, mansard roofs, ornate parapets and segmental arches, the building is another example of the colonial and Victorian neo-Gothic styles of architecture. Note that the stone used in the building here was likely once a part of the Bengaluru Fort.

Electricity Comes to Bengaluru

> **Bangalore.**—Messrs. Binny and Co. have recently introduced the electric light into their oil mill in the Pettah. The cost of the whole of the machinery amounted to a little over 2,000 reals, and Messrs. Binny and Co. hope, says the *Indian Engineer*, to make a saving by the introduction of the light before long, as the same engine that is used on the works will also work the dynamo. The cost of candles and oil amounted to about 3,000 reals a year, and the whole system of lighting was unsatisfactory.

Binny and Co were using electricity in their oil mills as early as 1891.
From, *The Electrical Engineer, December 4th, 1891.*

The beginnings of electricity distribution in Bengaluru lie not far from here.

When did electricity come to the city? The usual answer is 1905. In fact, it would not be wrong to say that it happened 16 years before this. Way back in 1891, the *Electrical Engineer* reported that Binny and Co had introduced electric lighting in their oil mill in the *pete*.[63] They managed this by attaching a dynamo to the oil-fuelled engines that ran their oil-pressing machinery. Prior to this, the premises had been lit by candles and oil lamps. Keep in mind that the very first commercial electric incandescent light installation anywhere on land was in New York in 1881. Then, as now, Bengaluru was ahead of the curve in adopting new technology!

In 1896, India's first hydroelectric power station was set up near Darjeeling to supply electricity to that town. Over the next few years, various electricity generation projects were proposed all over India. But it was the ambitious Cauvery Falls Power Scheme that first transitioned from plan to reality, thanks to the government of Mysore State.

In the late 1890s, Messrs Taylor and Sons requested electric power to run their mining operations in Kolar Gold Fields (KGF). Dewan Seshadri Iyer recognised the merit of the scheme and the Mysore government moved rapidly on the proposal. Very quickly, supply channels were built at the Cauvery Falls at Sivasamudram; the power station, transformer and transmission houses were readied; staff quarters were built; the machinery and paraphernalia required to generate electricity were put in place; and perhaps most important, key personnel were identified, recruited and sent for training abroad to learn this still relatively new technology.

On 30 June 1902, within three years of approving the scheme, KGF began to receive electricity generated at Sivasamudram. This was then Asia's second hydroelectric power station (after the one at Darjeeling), the continent's largest. It also had the longest power transmission anywhere in the world at that time——almost 150 km from Sivasamudram to KGF.[64]

In 1904, the Maharaja's government sanctioned a scheme to provide electricity to Bengaluru, which was only 100 km from Sivasamudram. The scheme sanctioned 18 circuits covering both the city and the Cantonment. By early 1905, transmission lines and other infrastructure for this were in place, and Bengalureans were at the cusp of the electric age. But then the infamous British bureaucracy made its presence felt. Special sanction was required under the Indian Electricity Act before the Cantonment could get electricity. Military authorities objected to the alignment of the transmission lines and to trees being lopped or cut for these lines. The Telegraph Department was unhappy with transmission lines that passed too close to telephone lines, fearing they would affect the latter's working.[65]

All this necessitated a last-minute redrawing of plans. Since the substations in the Cantonment could not be used, the city substation was redesigned to take on an additional load. It was July 1905 before everything was finally ready for at least the city to be lit up.

The actual inauguration happened on 3 August 1905, near the fort. At 6.30 pm that evening, the streets leading to the fort were filled with expectant, chattering crowds. Just outside the Delhi Gate stood two large tents where the who's who of Bengaluru had assembled, including Dewan PN Krishnamurthi, Secretary to the Government of Mysore, HV Nanjundayya, and many other worthies.[66] The person chosen to take the city from darkness to light was Sir John Hewett, head of the Government of India's Department of Commerce and Industry. In his brief speech, Sir Hewett highlighted the role of Major ACJ de Lotbiniere, the Deputy Chief Engineer of Mysore, who conceptualised the scheme, and Harry Parker Gibbs, Chief Electrical Engineer of Mysore, who oversaw its installation and execution; he also lauded the Maharaja's government for its 'far-seeing wisdom'.

Finally, the British Resident, A Williams, escorted Hewitt to the substation where he threw the switch, and lo and behold, 104 lamps, came on as if by magic! The crowd cheered, and the applause grew even louder when additional circuits were switched on. In just a few minutes, 800 street lamps around the city blazed brightly.[67]

The Cantonment had to wait a few more years to see the light. Some establishments in the military station such as the Bowring Hospital were electrified in 1907, but it wasn't until 1908 that 250 street lights in that part of the town were finally lit with electricity.

There is no trace now of the substation where this exciting event took place. However, it was most likely located where the Karnataka Power Transmission Company's transformers now stand, near Victoria Hospital, just a few hundred metres from Delhi Gate.

III. Vani Vilas Hospital

Our next stop, Vani Vilas Hospital, is just behind the KR Market Metro Station on KR Road.

Around 1808, a little church called the Drummer's Chapel was built here to cater to the small (European) Christian community that had settled here after the death of Tipu Sultan in 1799.[68] With the building of other churches elsewhere, this chapel fell into disuse, even being used for a while as military stores.[69] In the late 1920s, when the Mysore Maharaja's government decided to set up a maternity hospital, they naturally wished to build it in what was already a hospital zone, thanks to the Victoria and Minto hospitals. Accordingly, Krishnaraja Wodeyar requested the Church of England for the land where Drummer's Chapel stood, granting it another site to build a new church (which became St Luke's Church – *see below*).

The Vani Vilas Hospital was commissioned by Krishnaraja Wodeyar. Its foundation stone was laid in 1930 by Kantirava Narasimharaja Wodeyar, the then crown prince. And it was named after their mother, former Queen Regent Kempananjammanni Vani Vilas Sannidhana.

The imposing two-storeyed granite structure has a large, open, central quadrangle. If the hospital building reminds you of the Corporation Buildings

Vani Vilas Hospital, 1980s. © *INTACH*

Chief Architect

Srinivasarao Harti Lakshminarasappa was born around 1885. He obtained a Bachelors degree in engineering and worked in the Department of Public Works in the Mysore government as an architectural engineer, during which time he designed a public library in Mysuru.[71] Soon after, the Mysore government sent him to study abroad and he graduated with a degree in architecture from the Liverpool School of Architecture. On his return, he continued as an architect with the government and later also served as Principal of the College of Engineering, Bengaluru. During 1935–1940, he was Chief Architect in the government of the Maharaja of Mysore. SH Lakshminarasappa lived on HB Samaja Road, Basavanagudi.[72]

Bengaluru has Lakshminarasappa to thank for many of its majestic buildings. Apart from Vani Vilas Hospital, he designed the offices of the Municipality, Bruhat Bengaluru Mahanagara Palike (BBMP) on JC Road, the Krishnarajendra Silver Jubilee Technological Institute and NIMHANS, among others.[73]

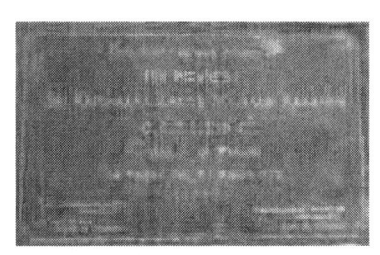

Plaque at Vani Vilas Hospital.
SH Lakshminarasappa designed the building.
© Aravind C

on JC Road, that might be because they were both designed by the same architect, SH Lakshminarasappa. 'The building is fitted with the latest type of electric lights and fans, electric lifts and telephone communications, while the sanitary fittings are of the most modern and up-to-date description,' engineering contractor B Munivenkatappa wrote in 1936.[70]

The two side wings of the hospitals were built thanks to donations from two prominent philanthropic merchants of Bengaluru: Sajjan Rao and SVS Setty (of CVMS Hostel fame) donated generously to build the Sajjan Rao Block and the Lakshmidevamma Block respectively.

IV. Vani Vilas Institute

Across the road from the Vani Vilas Hospital is the Vani Vilas Institute. This institution has a hoary past and is living proof of the attention given to girls' education by the Mysore government. This school for girls was established in 1918, and in 1926, was made an Intermediate college specialising in mathematics and science.[74] This was also a prelude to the establishment of a residential college for women. In the 1930s, the Women's Intermediate College was moved from here to its own building in Seshadri Road, an institution we now know as Maharani's College.

The Vani Vilas Institute, 1980s. © *INTACH*

Sri Lakshmi Nivas, former residence of Sajjan Rao and family, stood opposite the Bangalore Medical College. Until the 1970s, the area had several large bungalows. Very few of these still stand. *Courtesy of Malini White.*

The building was built at a cost of about Rs 69,000.[75] Like most buildings of that period, this one too is a blend of colonial and vernacular styles. The two-storeyed structure is built with brick and lime mortar. The front portico is emphasised with a pediment set in the parapet wall. The ground floor pillars are in the Doric style, while on the first floor, there are rectangular pilasters with Corinthian capitals. The building has arched openings with mouldings. The cornices define the horizontality at various levels. The inner side facing the courtyard has a colonnade.

V. Tipu's Armoury

To get to the armoury from Vani Vilas Institute, walk up KR Road. At the intersection, turn left, then take the next right at the petrol pump. Follow the road as it curves. You will see the armoury on your left.

This brick-and-mortar structure was built in the late 1700s when Hyder Ali and Tipu Sultan ruled over Mysore State. It was used to store arms, ammunition and rockets. British army maps drawn in the 1790s call this building the Grand Magazine. There were at least five armouries in Bengaluru Fort.

All of Tipu Sultan's armouries are partly underground and within a sunken court, which helped shield them from enemy eyes. More importantly, accidental fires were contained and would not have spread outside the court. Again, in case of accidents, the vaulted roof would collapse inward, thus restricting damage to the court and the building alone. The vaulted roof also kept inside temperatures much lower than in buildings with flat roofs, obviously an important consideration for a structure used for storing arms and ammunition.

Apart from rockets, Hyder and Tipu's armies were known for their guns and artillery. After the British captured Bengaluru Fort from Tipu Sultan in 1791, they seized about 120 cannons. Most of these were manufactured in the Mysore kingdom, but there were also many that were of French and English make. The Mysore Army's muskets were usually made locally, though they also used guns made by the English. The armoury would have once stored these and other weapons.

Tipu's Armoury. © *Aravind C*

The Rocketman and the Star-Spangled Banner

Tipu was famous for both firearms and rockets, and was also known to be quite an innovator, both in design and purpose. It wouldn't be too far from the truth to say that he was one of Bengaluru's first nerds! At a time when most armies in Indian states were using matchlocks, even in the 1800s, Tipu had already discarded them as antiquated; his soldiers used the more efficient, more modern flintlocks. These firearms, rockets, cannon and ammunition were manufactured in foundries in Srirangapatna, Chintamanai, Devanahalli and even Bengaluru.[76]

Tipu Sultan and Hyder Ali pioneered the use of iron rockets in warfare. Their designs were studied by the British Army who later introduced modified versions in their wars in Europe. Dr Roddam Narasimha, formerly of the National Aeronautical Laboratory, has researched these rockets extensively. In a speech delivered in 1985, he outlines how a simple modification—replacing the paste or cardboard cylinder containing gunpowder with an iron cylinder—led to the rockets having far greater range and accuracy. In fact, these rockets had ranges of about 2.4 km![77]

After the fall of Tipu, samples of these rockets were carried to England, to the Royal Woolwich Arsenal, where Sir William Congreve studied and improved on them. These improved rockets were soon being used by the British in the Napoleonic Wars and in their confrontation with the United States during the wars of 1812–14, when they were called Congreve Rockets.

We shall turn our attention to a particular battle that took place on the night of 13–14 September 1812, when Fort McHenry was bombarded from Baltimore harbour. The attack was witnessed from on board a truce ship by Francis Scott Key, a young American lawyer who was there to negotiate the release of an American civilian prisoner of war. As he watched, a huge American flag fluttered, defiant, in the red glare of the rockets that were fired at the fort. Key was overcome by the sight and by the victory it represented, and he quickly jotted down a poem which began with the following lines:

O, say can you see, by the dawn's early light,
> What so proudly we hail'd at the twilight's last gleaming,
> Whose broad stripes and bright stars through the perilous fight

O'er the ramparts we watch'd were so gallantly streaming?
> And the rocket's red glare, the bombs bursting in air,
> Gave proof through the night that our flag was still there,

O, say does that star-spangled banner yet wave
O'er the land of the free and the home of the brave?

The poem became the national anthem of the United States of America. Think of that song when you step into the armoury in Bengaluru where early versions of those very rockets were stored!

VI. Fort High School

Head back to the traffic signal at KR Road. Fort High School is about 100 metres south along this road, opposite Bangalore Medical College.

This school building was constructed in 1907. The origins of the school, however, date back to the 1800s when the City Municipal English School was established in the fort area, though we do not know exactly where. In 1890, this school was shifted to a former barracks.[78] When plague struck in 1898, the school was shifted to Tipu's Palace, along with the Municipal Kannada School, and functioned from there for a few years.[79] In 1899, the government set aside the current site to build and house the Municipal Kannada School. However, when the building was completed in 1907, it was occupied by the Municipal English School, which was later renamed the Government Anglo-Vernacular School.[80] Over the years, other changes took place. The lower (elementary) classes were moved out and it was renamed Fort High School in 1928, but was also known as Government High School, Fort.[81] Today, Fort High School functions as a Kannada-medium high school for boys.

Several eminent personalities have passed through the portals of this school, including cricketer GR Vishwanath, freedom fighter HS Doreswamy, Kannada poet TP Kailasam, and former Chief Minister Kengal Hanumanthaiah. The school is also famous as the venue of Bengaluru's biggest classical music extravaganza. Every April since 1939, musicians from around the country participate in a month-long festival of Carnatic and Hindustani classical music organised by the Sree Ramaseva Mandali Trust of Chamarajpete.

Fort High School, 1980s. © *INTACH*

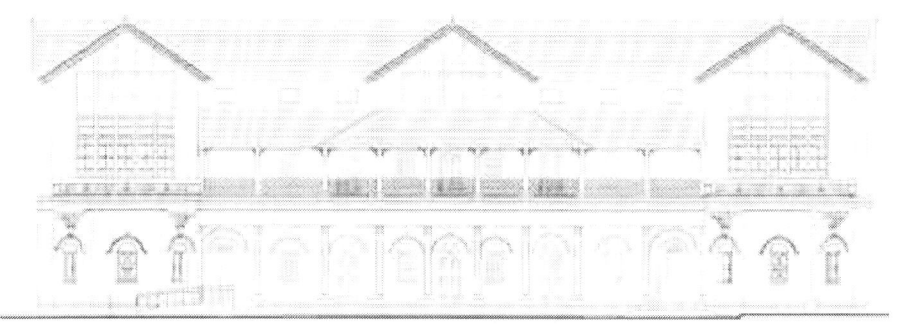

Fort High School. © *INTACH Bengaluru Chapter*

This imposing building has evolved over several different phases. It showcases how colonial and vernacular elements of architecture can be synthesised to produce a handsome whole. Colonial features, such as the emphasis on a central point, projecting ends, colonnades, gabled roofs, semi-circular lintels and monkey tops—steeply pointed hoods over windows and doors, with decorative vertical wooden slats—are combined with vernacular features such as the sloping tiled roof, Madras terrace flat roofs and a central courtyard.[*]

Originally, the central entrance of the building led into a large central hall that was partitioned with foldable doors. In 1927, the building was expanded considerably. A U-shaped block was added to the original structure, thus forming the courtyard. These details were revealed thanks to the conservation and restoration work on the school undertaken by INTACH in April 2018. This restoration was made possible thanks to Basant Poddar, whose Mineral Enterprises Ltd is the major donor for the project. KC Venugopal of Prakash Café, Chamarajpete, has also chipped in with a small contribution.

---

[*] Architectural description by Pankaj Modi, Coordinator, INTACH Bengaluru Chapter

VII. Kote Venkataramanaswamy Temple

This Vishnu temple is at the traffic signal on KR Road. The temple was built by the Mysore king Chikkadevaraja Wodeyar in about 1700.[82] Its architecture strongly resembles that of the temples in Hampi, though certain details—including its particular layout and some of its pillar carvings—are more characteristic of a Wodeyar style of architecture. The idol is similar to the one at the famous temple of Balaji in Tirupati. The Lord is flanked by his consorts Sridevi and Bhudevi.

A narrative frieze depicting the marriage of Shiva and Parvati runs around the outer wall of the temple. © *Aravind C*

The charming frieze on the temple's outer walls is typical of the Bengaluru region: it depicts the marriage of Shiva and Parvati and the various guests at the marriage procession, including the *ashtadikpalas* or guardians of the eight directions, the *saptarishis* or the seven great sages, and others.

A special feature of this temple is the four central pillars that frame the *mukhamantapa* or the central hall of the temple. At first glance they may look like the typical Vijayanagar-style pillars with riders on mythical horse–beast amalgamations (called *yalis*) that you see in most temples built in this period. What makes these four pillars special is that they have four *yali*-rider pairs, rather than two or three such riders per pillar, as is usual.[83]

In 1791, during the battle between the British and Tipu Sultan, a cannon ball hit the pillar just outside this temple. It is said that this saved Tipu's life, because of which he had a great fondness for this temple. The original pillar, which was slightly chipped by the cannonball, was replaced by a new one a few years ago.

VIII. Tipu Sultan's Palace

Tipu's Palace. © *Ajay Ghatage*

Adjacent to the temple, to its west is the Abode of Happiness, the Envy of Heaven. This is how a plaque inside describes this palace which was begun by Hyder Ali in 1781 and completed by Tipu Sultan ten years later. Interesting factoid: as per one particular plan for the palace, this was to have been the residence of the Maharaja of Mysore.

Here is a translation of the inscription in Tipu's Palace. The language of the inscription is Persian, the style is poetic:

> *As soon as the foundation of this palace was laid, its head was raised to heaven with joy. Oh, what a lofty mansion, a home of happiness, its summit being above the skies. It is a house of glass in purity, all who see it are struck with wonder. In magnificence it rivals the sky, which hangs down its head with shame. The description alone of this palace, when heard by Faridun [a mythological Persian king known for his justice, generosity and his victories] caused him to go to his long sleep. I sought by computation according to Zar [a system of calculating dates, devised by Tipu himself] for the date, and an unseen angel said: 'A house of happiness,' 1196 [1781 CE] When the painting of this new palace was finished, it cast the beauty of China into oblivion. I sought for this date from Khizir, the Wise [an angel, or a servant of God], who said: 'Doubtless, it is envied by heaven,' 1206 [1791 CE].*[84]

Plaque in Tipu Sultan's Palace. The gist of this inscription is that the palace is an Abode of Happiness, the Envy of Heaven. © *PeeVee*

When it was built, this palace was well within the fort of Bengaluru. After 1799, the fort and this palace were occupied by British army officers and officials. The large palace complex then comprised a parade ground, fountains, music room, gardens and many more quarters. In December 1831, a few months after the British took over the administration of the kingdom of Mysore from the Wodeyars, they decided to refurbish some parts of the palace to accommodate the Mysore Commissioners.[85] After 31 October 1831, the Mysore kingdom's administration was made the responsibility of a Board of (British) Commissioners. They were assisted by a British Resident who handled political relations with the Maharaja. The palace was whitewashed, plastered, old walls removed, new walls built and so on, for Rs 1131. Incidentally, this also served as the offices of the famous, long-serving and popular administrator, Sir Mark Cubbon, after whom we have a road and a park named in Bengaluru.

At that time, the palace comprised two distinct wings, which the British referred to as the No 1 and No 2 palaces. Of these, the larger No 1 Palace, a part of the palace complex that no longer exists, was later converted into offices for the Commissioner and senior military officials.[86] The smaller No 2 Palace, the existing part of the complex, housed the various offices of the British administration, including departments such as treasury, military administration, posts, forests, police, press, revenue and so on.

By the 1850s, the palace was getting to be rather crowded and the administration decided they needed a new building. Plans were made and things might have materialised pretty soon but for the First War of Independence, or the Sepoy Mutiny as the British called it. It was only in 1868 that the new Mysore Public Offices building—today's High Court—was built in the Cantonment.

Over the following two or three decades, ideas mooted for the now-vacated palace swung between restoration to outright demolition. In the early 1870s, it seems to have been nobody's baby. Reports speak of it being used occasionally as a venue for dances, even![87] Later, a plan was mooted to have it repaired and fitted up 'for the ultimate reception of the Maharaja of Mysore', then Chamaraja Wodeyar X, who was a few months short of six years.[88] The No 1 Palace was said to be too dilapidated and would have to be razed. The central building, today's existing palace (the No. 2 Palace as it was called then), was in fairly good repair, though lots of additions had been made over time with mud which had been ravaged by white ants. Walls and screens had been added between the pillars to create office spaces, and the walls had been whitewashed. Shortly after, the Government of India sanctioned Rs 50,000 towards restoring the No 2 Palace. Eventually, the plan to house the Maharaja here was dropped, but other ideas for the palace cropped up: demolish it and rebuild an entirely new one instead; restore it and use it as a Town Hall[89]; build a fountain in its garden.

In the 1890s, the fort shortly was transferred to the City Municipality, a few offices of the Mysore government began functioning from the palace, including the Inspector General of Police, the Excise Commissioner and the Conservator of Forests.[90] Later, the palace was also used as a school.[91]

Eventually, after so many twists in its life history, the palace was finally recognised as a monument of historical importance.[92] The glazed partitions and screens that had been erected during the British administration's stint here were finally removed. In 1950, the monument came under the aegis of the Archaeological Survey of India (ASI).

Living life king size: Architecture and layout

If you think the extant palace is rather small for a king, you'd be right. Like the fort, the original palace—which was a complex comprising buildings, grounds, gardens and fountains—has been whittled down considerably. As we have seen, the entire so-called No 1 Palace was demolished. What remains is only a portion of the original.

Originally, the only entrance into the palace complex was from the eastern side. In front of the palace on that side was a large parade ground enclosed with a high wall. Gates led from there towards the armoury and the fort.

Thanks to Britons' fascination with all things Oriental, several of those who visited or worked in Bengaluru in the 18th and 19th centuries wrote about what they saw. These descriptions help us construct, in the mind's eye, an image of the opulence and magnificence that once was. Many visitors spoke of this as the most beautiful building in Bengaluru. One British army officer declared that the palace was 'the most airy and elegant of any in the East', that it had 'an air of grandeur that is seldom to be met with in any country', and 'rich carpets covered the floors, superb hangings decorated the walls'.[93] The artist and army officer, Robert Home, praised how it 'displayed to the four winds of heaven as many ample fronts', with fountains in front of each face. Yet another described how the palace was decorated with 'rich carpets, gold and silver cloth' and had 'rooms filled with china and glass'.[94]

The northern and southern sides of the palace had gardens where the 'pink of Europe vied with the variegated flowers of the East',[95] and 'water and shade most happily blended to form delightful retreats from the sun'.[96] The allusion here is to the fountains that once graced these areas. You can see the fountain in the 1792 painting by Robert Home (displayed in the museum inside the palace). More excitingly, you can even see remnants of the fountain on the southern side of the palace, a feature that was uncovered by the ASI just a few years ago.

On the northern side, from where we enter today, was a *naubat khana* where musicians used to play.[97] On the upper storey is a large central hall, flanked by rooms on the west and east. There are three balconies. The balconies on the

The cusped arches in Tipu's Palace are one its most attractive features. © *PeeVee*

northern and southern sides would have served as places for Tipu to hold court. Lt Roderick Mackenzie describes how one of these balconies had a canopy over it. The throne was lacquered all around and ornamented with gilding of various colours, so that it appeared quite 'magnificent', especially with the fountain in front.[38] This, then, was the Darbar Hall; people would come here to meet the king and air grievances. The balcony facing the southern side is said to have been where Tipu met with officers from his administration and military. A similar balcony on the western side was where Tipu's wife held court.

The palace is a tasteful blend of various elements and influences. The wooden brackets and the fluted and carved pillars are reminiscent of those found in south Indian temples. Flowers, trees and bands of foliage are carved on the brackets holding up the roof. Some people reckon they can spot human masks or faces on these brackets, especially when they are viewed from directly below. Take a good look to see if you can see these too! The scalloped arches are similar to those in Mughal architecture. In its overall layout, this palace, or at least the portion that remains, strongly resembles the Shivappa Nayak Palace in Shimoga. Perhaps Tipu liked what he saw there and decided to make something similar here? Incidentally, the teak for the pillars is believed to have been brought from the forests near Shimoga.

The palace is also very similar to Hyder and Tipu's three palaces in Srirangapatna; only one of these still stands, the remaining two having been demolished by the British in the 1800s.

A painted palace

Like the palaces in Srirangapatna, this palace was also once famed for its richly painted walls, only mere traces of which now remain. The two best places to get an idea of past splendour are the small room in the northwest and the room on the first floor, in the northeast. Notice the floral motif on the ceiling that resembles a star pattern, enclosed within a framework of entwining leaves. The wall–ceiling junction has a wide border of stylised carnations and chrysanthemums, again encased by free-flowing vines. Such floral motifs within geometric frameworks are typical of Islamic art. The artists who worked on these paintings blended diverse elements to convey a sense of unity and order in line with Islamic principles.*

Notice how each room has different motifs in its ceilings and walls. In the room on the northwest, bunches of grapes are repeated just above

---

* Portions of this section were written by Swathi Reddy, former Co-convenor, INTACH Bengaluru Chapter.

the oval frames. Ribbons in oval frames with bows on top recur throughout, the endlessly repeating and interlacing patterns symbolising the infiniteness of God.

This particular motif of the ribbons and bows is rather uncommon in India. In fact, it has distinct French influences. Most likely, this is a direct influence of the gifts that Tipu received from Louis XVI via his ambassadors, when he sent them to France in 1788. Among these gifts received were Savonnerie carpets in which these kinds of ribbons with bows are commonly used.[99] Interestingly, there was already a healthy exchange of materials and designs between France

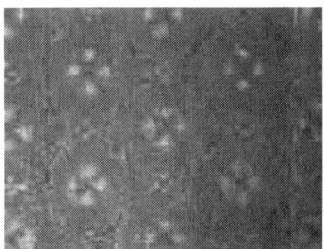

A motif on a ceiling in Tipu's palace. © *Meera Iyer*

Paintings on the walls of one of the rooms in Tipu's palace. Note the ribbons and bows, an uncommon motif in India. © *Meera Iyer*

and India at that time, including textiles. Most of the exchange was one way, from India to France.[100]

Just as in the architecture of this palace, Mughal influence stands out in this mural: the natural-looking plant form was a Mughal design innovation that spread through trade routes in the 17th century.

The upper-storey room in the northeast is a good spot from where to appreciate the different techniques used to decorate the ceilings and the walls. The paintings on the ceiling were done on strips of canvas which were then pasted onto the wood. If you look carefully, you can see evidence of the strips here. The wall paintings, on the other hand, were directly painted onto the fine-grained lime plaster. The pigments were made from ingredients like linseed oil, lead, aloe vera and sap from Ficus trees.

Of Gums and Pigments

In 1799, after Tipu Sultan was killed, the Mysore government asked Francis Buchanan, a Scottish physician, naturalist and geographer, to survey their newly acquired territories. The resulting tome—*A Journey from Madras through the Countries of Mysore, Canara and Malabar*—was published in 1807. Here is an extract from the book, detailing the processes used to repair the painting in Tipu's Dariya Daulat palace in Srirangapatna. Buchanan based this account on information he gathered from local craftsmen. The techniques and materials used in this palace in Bengaluru are likely to have been very similar.

At first sight, one would imagine that much gilding is used in the ornaments; but in truth, not a grain of gold is employed. The workmen use a paper covered with false gilding. This they cut into the shape of flowers and paste these on the walls or columns. The manner of making this false gilded paper is as follows: Take any quantity of lead and beat it with a hammer into leaves as thin as possible. To twenty-four parts of these leaves, add three parts of English glue dissolved in water and beat them together with a hammer till they be thoroughly united, which requires the labour of two persons for a whole day. The mass is then cut into small cakes and dried in the shade. These cakes can at any time be dissolved in water and spread thin with a hair brush on common writing paper. The paper must then be put on a smooth plank and rubbed with a polished stone till it acquires a complete metallic lustre. The edges of the paper are then pasted on the board and the metallic surface is rubbed with the palm of the hand which is smeared with an oil called 'gurna' and exposed to the sun. On the two following days the same is repeated when the paper acquires a metallic yellow colour, which however, more resembles the hue of brass than that of gold.

The 'gurna' oil is prepared as follows: Take three quarters of a maund of *agashay yennay* (linseed oil) half a *maund* of the size called 'chunderasu' and a quarter of a *maund* of *musambra* or aloes prepared in the country. Boil the oil for two hours in a brass pot. Bruise the *musambra* and put it into the oil. Boil them for four hours more. Another pot having been made red hot, the 'chunderasu' is to be put into it, and will immediately melt. Take a third pot, and having tied a cloth over its mouth, strain into it the oil and *Musambra*. These must be kept in a gentle heat and the 'chunderasu' added to gradually. The oil must be strained again and it is then fit for use.

The 'chunderasu' is prepared from the milky juice of any of following trees: *Ficus glomerate*, Goni, (possibly *Ficus drupacea*), bayla, bayvina (*Azadirachta indica*), gabali etc. It is therefore an elastic gum.

The oil used for painting consists of two parts of linseed and one part of 'chunderasu.' [01]

IX. Minto Ophthalmic Hospital

About 300 metres west of the palace along AV Road is Minto Ophthalmic Hospital, named in honour of Lord Minto, Viceroy and Governor General of India from 1905 to 1910. The genesis of ophthalmic care in Bengaluru goes back to 1896 when an eye infirmary was established in a small building somewhere in Chickpete.[102] Later, this was moved to the Lalbagh Lodge, which was on Lalbagh Road. This saw a steadily increasing number of patients every year, going up from 199 in 1901 to 648 five years later.[103] By 1907, the Mysore government had decided to establish a separate hospital for eye care.

This came closer to fruition on 17 December 1910, when Nalvadi Krishnaraja Wodeyar laid the foundation stone for the hospital. During the ceremony, the Maharaja alluded to this need articulated by Lt Col John Smyth, who had been the Senior Surgeon and Sanitary Commissioner for Mysore State when the building was commissioned. To quote the Maharaja: 'I am glad that it has been possible for my Government to take one more step forward in a policy which aims at giving Mysore a leading place among the provinces and

Minto Ophthalmic Hospital © *Meera Iyer*

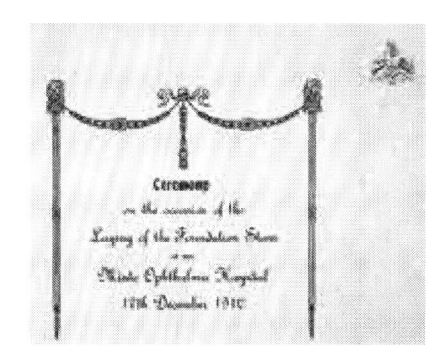

A page from the programme held on the occasion of the foundation-laying ceremony of Minto Ophthalmic Hospital. From file Med 135, Sl 5,6,8. KSA.

States of India in regard to its Medical Institutions.' Though not the oldest, it was indeed one of the earliest specialised ophthalmic hospitals in India. At the Maharaja's request, the hospital was named after Lord Minto, who he said was, 'a true friend to India and her people'.[104]

The hospital was built at a cost of about Rs 3 lakhs and took two years to construct.[105] It was inaugurated on 31 January 1913 by the Maharaja, accompanied by Dewan Sir M Visvesvaraya, the Yuvaraja and Sir Hugh Daly, among others.[106] Dr Ramaswami Iyengar was its first Superintendent. At that time, the hospital had two operating theatres and wards accommodating 34 men, 34 women and 12 children.[107] Today, it has 300 beds and is one of India's largest eye hospitals.

The granite building has an imposing, almost brooding facade. With pointed arches in its parapet decorations and ornate details like its balustrades, this grand building's architectural style combines the colonial with shades of Victorian neo-Gothic. Inside, there is a central courtyard with a fountain. Mansard roofs, like the ones at the Victoria Hospital, define each corner. The result is a pleasing, pleasant composition, quite un-hospital like. Some of these design elements are due to the influence of Lt Col Smyth.[108]

Don't miss the *gandabherunda* in the pediment on the two wings on either side of the entrance porch.

X. St Luke's Church

The church lies about 150 metres south of Minto Hospital, on Pampa Mahakavi Road.

The antecedents of St Luke's Church go back to the Drummer's Chapel (*see above*), also called Fort Church, that was built near here. Later, when the Mysore government decided to build the Vani Vilas Hospital, it acquired the land that the old church stood on and granted the present plot for a new church to be built. The then Dewan Mirza Ismail laid the foundation stone of the new St Luke's church in 1932 and it was opened for worship in 1935. According to church sources, the church bell, the baptismal font, some pews and part of the pulpit came from the old church building.[109] The Cross was donated by KN Guruswamy, founder of the *Deccan Herald* newspaper, while the Lord's Table made of mahogany was a donation from Mirza Ismail.[110]

St Luke's Church. © *Aravind C*

XI. Sanskrit College

Next to the church is the Sri Chamarajendra Samskrita Graduation and Post-Graduation Centre, one of the oldest Sanskrit colleges in the state. A constituent college of the Karnatak Sanskrit University, it was established as Vaani Vidya Patashalaa in 1885. In 1889, the two departments, Kavya and Shastra, were amalgamated into one institution, which was then named the Sanskrit College.[111] In 1896, its name was changed to Sri Chamarajendra Sanskrit College.

Shri Chamarajendra Sanskrit College. © *Aravind C*

Interestingly, in its early days, the college functioned out of various diverse and rather unusual locations. For a few years, the college was even housed in what was called the Lower Arsenal which stood near today's Vani Vilas Hospital.[112] Lest we imagine an entire college crammed into a small arsenal like Tipu's armoury, we must hasten to add that the arsenal that the college functioned from was considerably larger. The college continued here until November 1931, when the arsenal was demolished (during the construction of the Vani Vilas Hospital) and the college then moved to Tipu's Palace. It was only in the mid-1930s that the stately building you see today was built at a cost of about Rs 40,000.[113]

This linear building has elements of Islamic and Hindu architecture. The central bay is emphasised by projecting it out and having a masonry dome on top of it, which is surrounded by miniature domes. A projecting balcony on the first floor, supported on stone brackets, defines the entrance. The end of the building has also been defined with smaller domes. The linear colonnade, with stone columns and stone parapets at both the floors, leads into the rooms. The domes have brass finials.

Among the college's illustrious alumni is Sri Bala Gangadharanatha Swami of the Adichunchanagiri *math*.

●●●●●

There are several other buildings, nooks and streets that you will probably like to explore in this area—streets full of stories, named after people who lived there or philanthropists who helped build the area. There are garadi manes—traditional gyms—that still function, houses whose beauty lies dimmed and begrimed by the passing of the years, but which still speak of the care and attention invested in their design and creation. We suggest you walk the winding lanes here at your leisure. The fort area, the petes and the markets here are likely to draw you back again and again. Enjoy the journey!

The Bengaluru Fort and Tipu's Palace. © *PecVee*

Notes

1. Many believe it was Kempegowda who built a second fort just south of his mud fort. Parts of this second fort still stand. This is what is today called the Bengaluru Fort (described in this chapter). See Aruni 2007, 11.
2. This translation, by Naresh Keerthi, is from Nagendra 2016.
3. See also Sharma 2016.
4. Vibart 1883, 222; Hasan 1971, 198.
5. Wilks 1817; Mackenzie 1793, 29.
6. Stubbs 1877.
7. Wilks 1817, 124.
8. Matthew 1793, 23.
9. *Karnataka State Gazetteer* 1989, 98; Urs 2016.
10. See 1885 map. Note that there is still a road named Hospital Road, parallel to the District Office Road.
11. 'Fresh trouble in Bangalore: Six killed and 32 injured', *The Times of India*, 19 August 1942; '2 killed, 42 hurt in new India riots', *The New York Times*, 18 August 1942.
12. Bowring 1893, 152; Rice nd, 152.
13. *Karnataka State Gazetteer* 1990, 691.
14. Fisher 1890, 586.
15. Anon 1852.
16. Sewell 1858.
17. Anon 1917; *Rice Memorial Church Centenary Celebration*, 1917–2017 (booklet).
18. Rice nd.
19. Rice nd, 122.
20. Hudson 1893, 48.
21. Sundara 1989, vi.
22. Rice 1889.
23. Sundara 1989, vii.
24. EC IX Bn 1.
25. Stubbs 1877, 119.
26. Moona 2011.
27. Mirza 1930.
28. Personal communication with SVS Gupta, son of SVS Setty, February 2018.
29. Subba Rao 1926.
30. File POL 129 of 1904-05; Sl 1-8; KSA.
31. Proc Gov Mys (Prisons) March 1940, 39, KSA.
32. Personal interview with Kamal Kapur, son of Mohanlal Kapur, April 2018.
33. Kamath 1996, 245; Manjunatha 2010.
34. Manjunatha 2010.
35. File ML 1 of 19, Sl 2, KSA.
36. Rao 1930b, 95.
37. File ML 1 of 19, Sl 2, KSA.
38. Harini Nagendra, quoted in Ram 2017.
39. Anon 1945, 26.
40. Mackenzie 1793.
41. Stubbs 1877, 118.
42. Mackenzie 1793.
43. Rice 1897b, 47
44. IOR/F/4/1029/28194, British Library.

45. IOR/F/4/1442/56940, British Library.
46. IOR/Z/E/4/33/B44, British Library.
47. IOR/R/2/Box1/20:1880-1924, British Library.
48. Defence B 1934/MAR /2171/2183/KW, NAI.
49. IOR/R/2/Box1/20: 1880–1924, British Library.
50. File ML 76 of 1894, Sl 1–2, KSA.
51. File Sani 48 of 1899, Sl 1–4, KSA.
52. File GM 228 of 18, Sl 1, 3, 7, KSA.
53. Vitrivius, quoted in Hourihane 2012, 300.
54. Rice 1897b, 46.
55. Lewis 2012.
56. Rajani 2007.
57. Personal communication, Barry Lewis, historian and anthropologist, Emeritus, University of Illinois, Urbana Champaign, USA, June 2008.
58. See, for example, comments on this matter in Anon 1913c.
59. Anon 1909, 258.
60. http://stmarthas.in/history.html, accessed 10 August 2018.
61. Ismail 1930, 495.
62. Curzon 1902, 149.
63. Anon 1891, 530.
64. Hobble 1906.
65. 'Electric lighting of Bangalore', *The Daily Post*, 7 June 1905.
66. Iyer 2017.
67. 'Electric lighting for the city', *The Daily Post*, 4 August 1905.
68. Anon 1963, 578.
69. Penny 1922.
70. Munivenkatappa 1936, 782.
71. Urs 1953, 195.
72. Personal communication, K Jairaj, great grand-nephew of Lakshminarasappa, August 2018; interview with Krishna Rao Jaisim, grandson of Lakshminarasappa, 2 September 2018.
73. File No Defence/B/1950 Feb/ 5514-5520, NAI.
74. Anon 1931, 20.
75. Rao 1929, 362.
76. For more on the firearms of Tipu, see Wigington 1992.
77. Narasimha 1985.
78. File ML 12 of 90, Sl 1–2, KSA.
79. File ML 318 of 04, Sl 1–3, KSA.
80. File ML 241 of 15, Sl 1–2, KSA; File Edu 105 of 11, Sl 1–2, KSA.
81. Review of the Progress of Education in the Mysore State for the decennium 1922–23 to 1931–32, 1935, 57.
82. EC IX Bn 118; this inscription, recorded by Benjamin Rice, was considered lost till recently. It was rediscovered in August 2018 by heritage enthusiasts in JP Nagar.
83. Aruni 2007, 114.
84. EC IX Bn 7.
85. IOR/F/4/1464/57516, British Library.
86. IOR/R/2/ Box 44/410 File 78 of 1885, British Library.
87. Sankey 1873.
88. IOR/R/2/Box44/410: File 78 of 1885, British Library.

89. File ML 5 of 1888, Sl 1–5, KSA.
90. File GM 26 of 1895, Sl 1–21, KSA.
91. Rao 1930a, 373.
92. File GM 228 of 1918, Sl 3, 10, 14, 17, KSA.
93. Mackenzie 1793, 46.
94. Skelly 1791, quoted in Stronge 2009, 9.
95. Home 1808, 3.
96. Anon 1791, 234.
97. Buchanan 1807, 31.
98. Mackenzie 1793, 47.
99. Bremer-David 1997.
100. Martin 2014.
101. Buchanan 1807, 74–75.
102. Rao 1929, 439.
103. See Reports on the Administration of Mysore for the years 1902 and 1907.
104. Wadiyar 1921, 122.
105. Anon 1913, 169.
106. 'New Mysore hospital', *The Times of India*, 3 February 1913.
107. Anon 1913a.
108. Anon 1913a.
109. Dhanraj, Isaac and Mercy 2010, 14.
110. Henry 1962, quoted in Nair 2005, 358.
111. Review of the Progress of Education in the Mysore State for the decennium 1922–23 to 1931–32, 1935.
112. File Muz 32, 1895-96, KSA.
113. Review of the Progress of Education in the Mysore State for the decennium 1922–23 to 1931–32, 1935, 116–117.

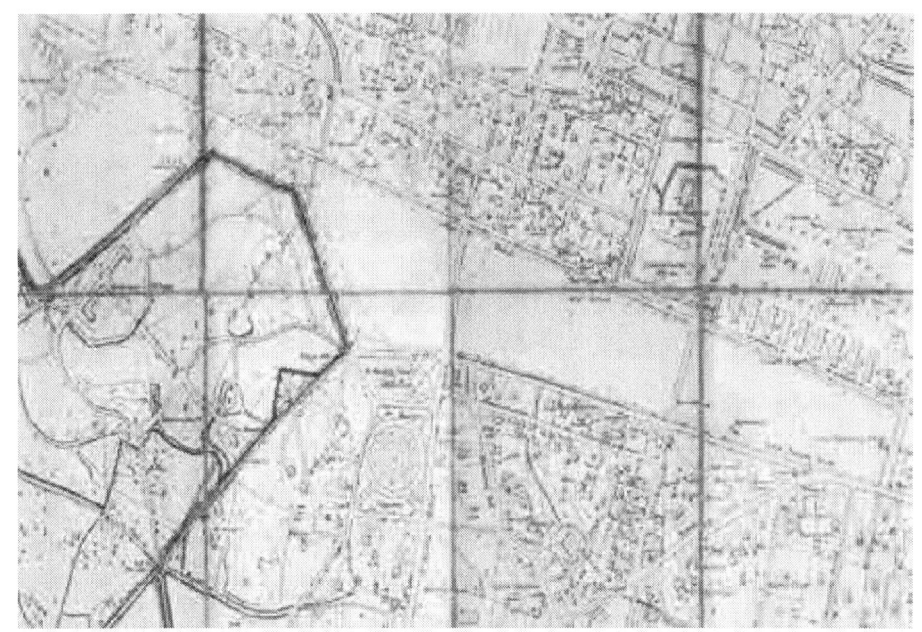

Cubbon Park and its vicinity in 1884-85. From, Survey of India. *Cantonment and City of Bangalore and Environs, Season 1884-85.* Courtesy of Mythic Society, Bengaluru.

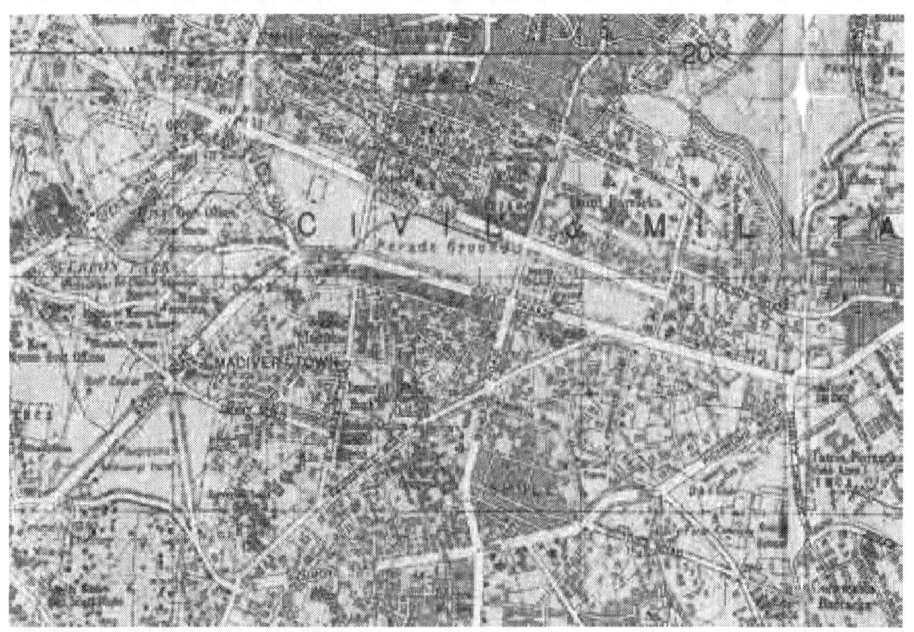

Cubbon Park and its vicinity in 1935-36. From, Survey of India. *Bangalore Guide Map. Surveyed 1935-36.* Courtesy of Naresh Narasimhan.

CHAPTER 2

The Origins of the Parallel City: The Cantonment and Cubbon Park

A stroll through the Cubbon Park area two centuries ago would have taken you through a landscape very different from the tree-filled park of today. Two centuries ago, a portion of this expanse was chequered with fields. Farmers drew their ploughs across their lands, and sowed and harvested ragi and other crops. Drainage channels wound their way across other parts of the undulating terrain, leading towards Sampangi *kere (see chapter 8)* nearby. This idyll might well have continued till today if it hadn't been for some particularly fierce opposition to the incipient British Raj by a certain Tipu Sultan, who ruled over Mysore kingdom from his capital Srirangapatna. In the year 1799, after many years of battles against the British, Tipu Sultan was finally killed by the British East India Company.

With the enemy destroyed, the British handed back the kingdom to the Wodeyar dynasty, the erstwhile rulers of Mysore before Tipu's father Hyder Ali seized power from them. The handover provided for the maintenance of a British force for the defence and security of His Highness' dominions, to be stationed within the territory restored to the Wodeyars. Under this treaty, a British garrison settled into the fort and palaces of 'Seringapatam', as the British referred to Srirangapatna, no doubt looking forward to some rest and rehabilitation. But it was not to be. After the euphoria over their victory subsided, things did not quite work out for the British at Tipu's capital.

It was the mosquitoes that did them in. Droves of British soldiers were felled by malaria. This was a time before the link had been made between mosquitoes and malaria (a link that, incidentally, was first made by Sir Ronald Ross while at Bengaluru, only a couple of kilometres from here). Instead, malaria was attributed to *mal aria*, or bad air. British medical journals of the time are full of scholarly articles on the hazards of tropical climates. 'Seringapatam' began to feature in them regularly for the 'fevers' which prevailed there and it soon became notorious as 'the most unhealthy spot in Mysore'.[1]

The search was on for a suitable place for the British garrison to move to. Kolar, Sira, Bengaluru and Chitradurga were among the contenders.[2] Two things clinched the deal in favour of Bengaluru. The first was its importance as a trading centre and its proximity to other such centres of trade and population including Hosur, Chennai and Srirangapatna itself. The second unassailable fact was that no other location compared to Bengaluru in terms of its salubrious climate. At about 915 metres above sea level, it was considered 'one of the most temperate and healthy places in the Indian peninsula'.[3]

Setting up a Cantonment

Accordingly, in 1806–07, after parleys between the Maharaja of Mysore and the East India Company, the Company was given land some 6 km east of Bengaluru *pete*, near Agram, adjacent to Ulsoor Tank. A new cantonment came up here to house the Mysore Division of the Madras Army. Bengaluru was initially made a station for two European and five 'native' regiments, and a sum of a little over 54,000 *pagodas* was set aside for constructing barracks and other buildings.[4] (The *pagoda* was one of several currencies circulating in the early 1800s, and was equivalent to about Rs 4 in those days.[5])

The business of building the cantonment fell to a Lt John Blakiston of the Corps of Engineers in the Madras Army.[6] Blakiston had thus far experienced temporary military camps more intimately than settled cantonments, moving quickly from one battlefront to the next. However, impressed with his part in crushing the 1806 Vellore Mutiny ('no quarter was given', Blakiston says of his role there), the British military authorities gave the 21-year-old the task of building the new cantonment. The lack of experience in building barracks and parades didn't seem to deter him. In less than a year, the brand-new Bangalore (as the British called the place) Cantonment was up and running.[7]

The site picked for the Cantonment encompassed two small valleys and two ridges, all running roughly northwest to southeast; a third ridge, bordering its southern valley, was outside the Cantonment area. On the higher slopes of the northern valley, nearly on the crest of the northern ridge, Blakiston chose to lay the centrepiece of the Cantonment: the vast, central Parade Ground, 2 miles (approximately 3.2 km) long, running nearly east–west.[8] (The present parade ground, named after the Field Marshal Sam Manekshaw, is only a part of the original.) Along the perimeter of the Parade Ground ran a broad, tree-lined track, probably fashioned after the famous Rotten Row of Hyde Park, which

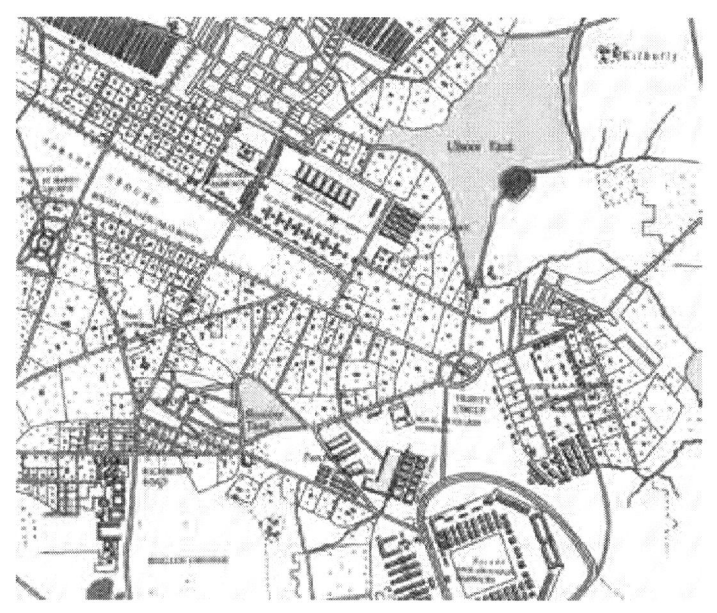

The layout of the Cantonment of Bangalore in the 1860s. Redrawn by Apoorva Gundmi from a map in *Report on the Station, Barracks and Hospitals of Bangalore 1865*. Gantz Brothers: Madras.

was what it came to be called in later years. Around the nucleus of the Parade Ground were barracks for European and 'native' regiments, bungalows for the European officers, and all the other paraphernalia of a military establishment, including hospitals.

To the north of the Parade Ground were the European infantry barracks (hence the name Infantry Road), the European cavalry barracks (and hence Cavalry Road, the old name for Kamaraj Road), and the guardhouses of four of the 'native' regiments. In the northeast, behind the cavalry, were the lines of the 'native' cavalry, and behind the European infantry barracks, a 'great bazaar'—today's Shivajinagar.[9] (Incidentally, a story is sometimes told that Blackpully, as Shivajinagar was once called, was named after Blakiston. Other oft-repeated stories are that it was so named because it was first settled by people who grew *bili akki*—white rice—or because it was the 'black', aka 'native', town. However, a newspaper report from 1924 states that Blackpully was so named after a Colonel Blake of the British Army who once lived there.[10]) South of the Parade Ground, at No 1, South Parade (as MG Road was called then), was St Mark's Church (designated a cathedral much later). To its east were several commercial establishments that catered to the officers, public rooms, the Gymnasium and a few bungalows. At the extreme eastern end of the Cantonment were the horse and foot artillery lines.

European officers of the 'native' regiments had their bungalows on the northern side of Parade Ground, beyond the barracks. Company officers and staff had theirs to the south, extending from the horse and foot artillery lines, parallel to Parade Ground. Shivajinagar, Ulsoor and other such areas were primarily populated by Indians who worked with and for the military. They lay interspersed with the areas where the Europeans lived.

The European bungalows were the subject of much admiration. Writes George Bell, a soldier who served in Bengaluru in 1827:

> *The bungalows where the officers live are all detached from each other, like so many villas in the neighbourhood of a large city in Europe, each having a large compound from one to twelve acres of ground, laid out partly in garden, grass, and walks planted with very beautiful trees of various kinds, shrubs and flowers. There are also strawberries in many gardens, and all kinds of European vegetables. All houses have stabling, coach-houses, and a set of servants' apartments, with many other conveniences, detached a little way from the dwelling.*[11]

Through the years, visitors to the Cantonment were struck by the very English air these bungalows lent to the area, noting with surprise how it looked just like a 'European village or small town, the buildings were almost the same and the bungalows had great sweeping lawns and front gates like anywhere in

Cubbon Park. © *Aravind C*

England'. 'The smallest bungalow has something of a compound. In the larger premises, it is literally a good walk for an invalide *(sic)* from the house to the back hedge,' wrote a reporter in the early 1900s.[12]

In the layout of this new cantonment, Blakiston and subsequent planners appear to have been influenced by ideas on town planning that were current in Britain at the time, which laid a great deal of emphasis on aesthetics. Whether by principles of town planning or because the military needed open spaces, the new cantonment had an abundance of open areas that were used for the military and also for recreational purposes, so that all visitors were of one accord in considering the cantonment of 'Bangalore to be one of the best stations in the whole country'.[13] Very quickly, the cantonment grew into a large military establishment. Blakiston was not far off the mark when he looked back on his creation nearly 20 years later as 'one of the largest and finest cantonments in India'.[14]

Growth of the Cantonment

In 1831, there was an upheaval in Mysore State that gave a further fillip to the Cantonment's growth. In October of that year, the Governor-General of India William Bentinck assumed administration of the State for the East India Company, alleging misrule by Krishnaraja Wodeyar. The administration of Mysore State passed to a Board of Commissioners, which was assisted by the Dewan in financial matters and by the British Resident in political matters.[15] The offices of the Mysore government were shifted from Mysuru to Bengaluru, leading to a further influx of people into the Cantonment. As the Bengaluru chronicler Fazlul Hasan puts it, 'The Burra sahib, dressed in tweeds, with the inevitable bowler hat and often sporting a moustache, and the Mem Sahib, smartly attired, charming but imperious' moved in, along with the inevitable retinue of 'native' ayahs (domestic helpers), gardeners, cooks and so forth.[16]

From the 1840s onwards, the garrison here generally consisted of four European regiments, including the cavalry, infantry, horse and artillery regiments. In addition, there was a 'native' cavalry regiment, and two to four 'native' infantry, and 'native' horse and artillery regiments.[17] In the 1850s and 1860s, there were a number of changes in the regiments and their lines, and new barracks came up. In 1865, the Sappers and Miners made Bengaluru their headquarters. They occupied the former 'native' cavalry lines near Ulsoor lake and have remained here ever since, renamed and known to us now as the Madras Engineer Group (MEG).

With more barracks, more regiments, more people, there were naturally more churches: Holy Trinity Church was consecrated in 1852. With this, the two ends of South Parade were defined by St Mark's Church and Holy Trinity

Church. Other buildings, both military and civil, sprang up and the town began to spread. Apart from increasing numbers of European (and Indian) soldiers, Bengaluru attracted European and Indian civilians too, including administrative staff, teachers, businessmen and others. European pensioners and Anglo-Indians settled in bungalows on the slopes of St John's Hill (earlier known as Mootoocherry), north of Shivajinagar's bazaar; later, this became a part of Cleveland Town, established in 1883 and named after General John Wheeler Cleveland, who died that year.[18] Today, Cleveland Town is considered a part of Fraser Town *(see chapter 6)*. Towards the south, the expanding population led to the formation of the suburbs of Richmond Town and Langford Town. Bengaluru also became home to 'a plentiful supply of invalids from all quarters of the presidency'.[19] In fact, because its climate was considered particularly suited to the European constitution, Bengaluru was used as a convalescent base during the Crimean, Afghan, and First and Second World Wars.[20]

Life in the Cantonment

Military life revolved around the Parade Ground, both physically and socially. Military review days were occasions of great pomp and splendour on the Parade Ground, and visitors were usually suitably impressed. Writes one:

> *The long and apparently interminable line of soldiery, from the dashing hussar, and the not-less-handsomely-equipped horse-artilleryman, down to the humbly-clad sepoy of a 'native' infantry corps' made for quite a striking spectacle. Adding to the drama were 'the oceans of spectators of every hue and*

Parade marking the coronation of King George V and Queen Mary, held on 12th December 1911, with St Mark's Church (now Cathedral) in the background. This part of the parade ground is now Cariappa Park. *Courtesy of The Madras Sappers Museum and Archives.*

costume, and on every imaginable conveyance' all watching the 'the aides-de-camp rapidly executing orders of their grey old chief; the hoarse shouting and screaming of commanding officers; the boom of the loud cannon; the clattering of musketry, and the rush and scramble of the natives to pick up unexploded cartridges.[21]

That was on military review days. Most other days, such as the military parades and field days that took place once or twice a week, the troops were up and about by daybreak, but were all done by 9 or 10 o'clock in the morning, leaving the rest of the day free for other amusements.[22] If Bengaluru today is known for its pubs and its parties, things were not very different in the 1800s and 1900s, at least in the Cantonment, which soon acquired a well-deserved reputation for its festivities and lifestyle. Even in the 1820s, 'monthly balls, private parties, amateur theatricals, mess dinners, riding, driving, horse-racing, &c., were the order of the day', all seasoned with salacious gossip and scandals.[23] Writing in the early 1830s, Emma Roberts says, 'The fancy balls are upon a grand scale,' adding that 'no expense is spared upon these entertainments; the bands of the several regiments are in attendance', with the result that 'the effect of the whole is magnificent'.[24]

The Royal Engineers' polo team in the early 1900s. Polo was another popular pastime for soldiers posted in the cantonment of Bangalore. *Courtesy of The Madras Sappers Museum and Archives.*

The road running around the Parade Ground came to be known as Rotten Row, as we have noted, after its famous London counterpart. In the evenings, once the heat of the afternoon sun had waned, everyone went out for a ride,

A Wiele's postcard of much-loved boulevard and South Parade
(today's MG Road), late 1800s / early 1900s. *Courtesy of Rohit Hangal.*

either on horseback, or in carriages, which in earlier days were usually bullock-drawn. Until the late 1850s, when new barracks were built on the old racecourse (near today's Austin Town), one favourite round for riding was along the Parade Ground and round the racecourse. Others preferred to ride up Rotten Row all the way up to near St Mark's Church where a bandstand once stood, whiling the evening away in the company of the people who gathered there. Rotten Row witnessed many a romance blossom as the Cantonment's debonair army men flirted with the station's many fetching European women. All too often, these romances ended in scandal, to the vicarious thrill of the residents. Engagements that were entered into one night only to be broken the next morning, when both penitent parties were sober, were not uncommon! Even in the 1800s, they drank 'a great deal of pale ale at Bangalore'.

After riding, the most popular sport amongst the residents was undoubtedly cricket. One sought-after ground was near the main gate of the European infantry barracks (formerly cavalry barracks; the Army Public School now occupies a part of these barracks) where the British soldiers played cricket every day at least eight months of the year.[28] For troops serving in the heat and dust of the rest of the subcontinent, a climate that allowed this very English sport was welcome: 'a splendid sward and a mild temperature made cricket in the mornings and evenings an agreeable and healthy pastime.'[29] In the winters, the chief amusements were the picnic parties at the many interesting sites in and around the city, including Lalbagh and Nandi Hills (or Nundydroog, as it was known to the British).[30] And of course, there was shooting all through the year, in and around Bengaluru, as well as the races.

And so life passed peacefully, at least for the European residents of the Cantonment, as ball succeeded grand ball, party succeeded raucous party, and game succeeded joyous game. Occasionally, to relieve the monotony of the idyllic existence as it were, came along the sporadic court martial, usually to chastise soldiers who had committed minor offences in a fit of drunkenness.

But then, in late 1832, there occurred an event that shattered the idyll—an event grave enough to award capital punishment to six people. This was the 'Mutiny of Bangalore' *(see box)*.

A view of South Parade (today's MG Road), or Rotten Row as it was popularly called, near Mayo Hall. *Courtesy of The Madras Sappers Museum and Archives.*

The Mutiny of Bangalore

Resistance towards the British had always existed in Bengaluru, manifesting itself in pro-Tipu and/or anti-British sentiments in songs sung by itinerant holy men and preachers, and even puppet shows.[31] The simmering sentiments came to a boil in 1832, only a few months after the British takeover of the administration of Mysore kingdom.

The plan in the Bangalore Mutiny, or Bangalore Conspiracy, as it was also euphemistically known in later years, was simple, if audacious: seize the fort, massacre all Europeans, and then incite mutiny among troops in the rest of the country.[32] The principal conspirator was a button maker who was also a havaldar of the 9th Infantry named Syed Tipu, who claimed to be a descendant of his illustrious namesake, and is described as a 'fine, handsome fellow'.[33] On 28 October, the havaldar was to be posted as a guard at one of the gates of the fort. The plan was that he would open the gates and let a party of mutineers inside the fort. With this force at his command, he planned to kill the General in the fort, and then fire a gun as the signal for the mayhem to begin throughout the Cantonment. The 'native' artillery in the Cantonment were to have turned their guns on the two European regiments stationed there at the time. Another 'native' troop would cut the horses loose from the European cavalry, while another small group would deal with the officers in their bungalows. Incidentally, strict instructions had been given to spare all women.

Meticulous as the planning was, the Europeans were saved by a sepoy from the 'native' infantry who informed his Colonel about the mutiny that was to take place that very night. By that afternoon, about 30 mutineers had been arrested. An inquiry was held. Four of the mutineers——Syed Tipu, Badaruddin, Shaikh Ismail and Kallandar Beg——were sentenced to be 'blown away from a gun'.

The executions took place on Christmas Eve that year and were possibly one of the goriest moments of the Cantonment. As the entire garrison assembled on the Parade Ground to watch, and a band played Handel's 'Dead March', four of the mutineers were blown away by guns, their feet lashed firmly to the wheels of 12-pounders, their bodies touching the barrels of the guns. Two others were shot to death at the same time. Walter Campbell, a witness, records the last words of Syed Tipu:

> I took service under the accursed Firangis who slew my ancestor Tipu Sahib and possessed themselves of his dominions. I did so for the purpose of seeking revenge. I have made the attempt and I have failed. They can take my life but they cannot destroy my spirit. This shall revisit the earth and rouse my fellow soldiers to action, and 'ere long, you shall see the accursed *kafirs* driven from the land.

Campbell, who described the execution as 'the most awful and imposing scene I ever witnessed', records that the 'bodies of the victims were blown into fragments, strewing the ground in front of the ground with portions of flesh, which were greedily pounced upon by hosts of kites and vultures'. He also records that Tipu's head, severed from his body, retained a smile.[34]

Syed Tipu's prophecy about fellow soldiers rising to drive out the British came true 25 years later when the First War of Independence, or the Sepoy Mutiny as it was called then, engulfed the country in 1857.

A Park Marks Clear Lines and Divisions

After 1857, the government passed from the East India Company into the hands of the Crown. In 1881, there was yet another change in Bengaluru's status with the Rendition, when Mysore State was handed back to the Wodeyars. On 5 March 1881, Maharaja Chamaraja Wodeyar turned 18. Exactly a month later, on 5 April, the Maharaja signed a Deed of Assignment, making over to the exclusive management of the British government all lands forming the military station of Bengaluru, including some adjacent villages, free of charge. The Maharaja renounced all jurisdiction in the lands so assigned. Until then the Cantonment had been considered 'a station in a foreign territory'. Now, it was renamed the Civil and Military (C&M) Station and came under the direct control of the Government of India.[35] From the date of the Rendition, the Chief Commissioner of Mysore became Resident in Mysore and Chief Commissioner of Coorg. He was invested with the powers of a Local Government and of a High Court in respect of the Bangalore Assigned Tract.

In Bengaluru, as elsewhere in India, the arrangement of the Cantonment displayed influences of European mores as much as the uneasy relationship between the British and the 'natives'. As elsewhere, the military portion consisted of the field or parade ground and the lines. The 'lines' originally referred to the rows of tents for 'native' troops that were sited in front of rows of officers' bungalows. Originally, the military lines were organised in defensive formation,

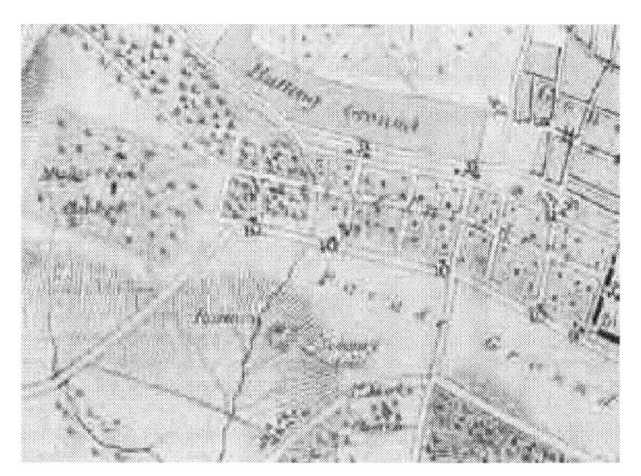

Section of an 1854 map, showing drainage channels and a ravine in the area that later became Cubbon Park. From *An atlas of the southern part of India, including plans of all the principal towns & cantonments*. 1854. Pharoah and Company: Madras.

well away from the enemy. Often in India, the parade ground also served as a buffer between the rulers and the ruled, a separation that persisted even when the need for military preparedness disappeared. Bengaluru's Parade Ground, however, was more the nucleus of social and military life of the Cantonment. The vast land between the 'Pettah' and the Cantonment was what served as a buffer between the two.

Cubbon Park was established on this extensive area in 1870. With this, the separation between the two Bengalurus—the old city or *pete* and the new, very British, Cantonment—was reinforced. Perhaps it is no coincidence that the park was laid out after 1857, when British attitudes towards Indians had hardened even further, and suspicion and fear were uppermost in British minds. Incidentally, the two cities of Bengaluru met and merged into one Municipality only in 1949. Until then, there were also toll gates between the twin cities where people had to pay for goods entering the Cantonment; one such gate was called Ulsoor Gate *ukkad* (toll gate), near Ulsoor Gate (where the Halasuru Gate Police Station now stands).

An 1854 map shows that the area now covered by the park then had numerous water channels running through it, which drained into Sampangi *kere*. Some of these channels had cut such deep troughs into the ground that they were used by the British soldiers for escalading practice![36] There are also reports of fields and a few 'huts' on some parts of the park, which were removed in the 1870s and the owners compensated.[37]

Bengalureans are rightly proud of this approximately 200-acre expanse of green. © *PkeVee*

When it was first established, Cubbon Park had the landscaped look a formal English garden. *Courtesy of British Library, Shelfmark 43041 (3)*

This vast expanse of green covers about 200 acres. Many names have been associated with it. The idea for the park came from Lewin Bentham Bowring, the Chief Commissioner of Mysore State from 1862 to 1870. The park was laid out by Lt Col RH Sankey *(see box)* and was first christened Meade Park, after Sir Richard Meade, who was Chief Commissioner after Bowring. Later, it was renamed in honour of Sir Mark Cubbon, the longest serving and most popular British Chief Commissioner of Mysore. His statue still stands in the park. In 1948 (after a proposal first made in 1927), the park was officially renamed Sri Chamarajendra Park.

Apart from several buildings that reflect the history of the Cantonment and the city, Cubbon Park, as most people still call it (even its Metro station is called the Cubbon Park Metro Station), has more than 6000 plants and trees, of about 90 different species. When it was first established, the park had the landscaped look characteristic of a formal English garden. But this changed over the years, thanks partly to extensive planting. In the early 1900s, many trees and tree avenues were planted in the park, including African tulip trees, mast trees, casuarinas and others. Don't miss the grand old silk cotton trees in the northern parts of the park, the magnificent Java fig avenue leading from the bandstand to the museum, and the old and gnarled mango trees scattered around the park. Do also take a walk through the quiet and picturesque bamboo groves between the Victoria Statue and the bandstand.

A Walk in the Park

In which you encounter a haughty empress, buildings built in a style named for her and one built to upstage them all

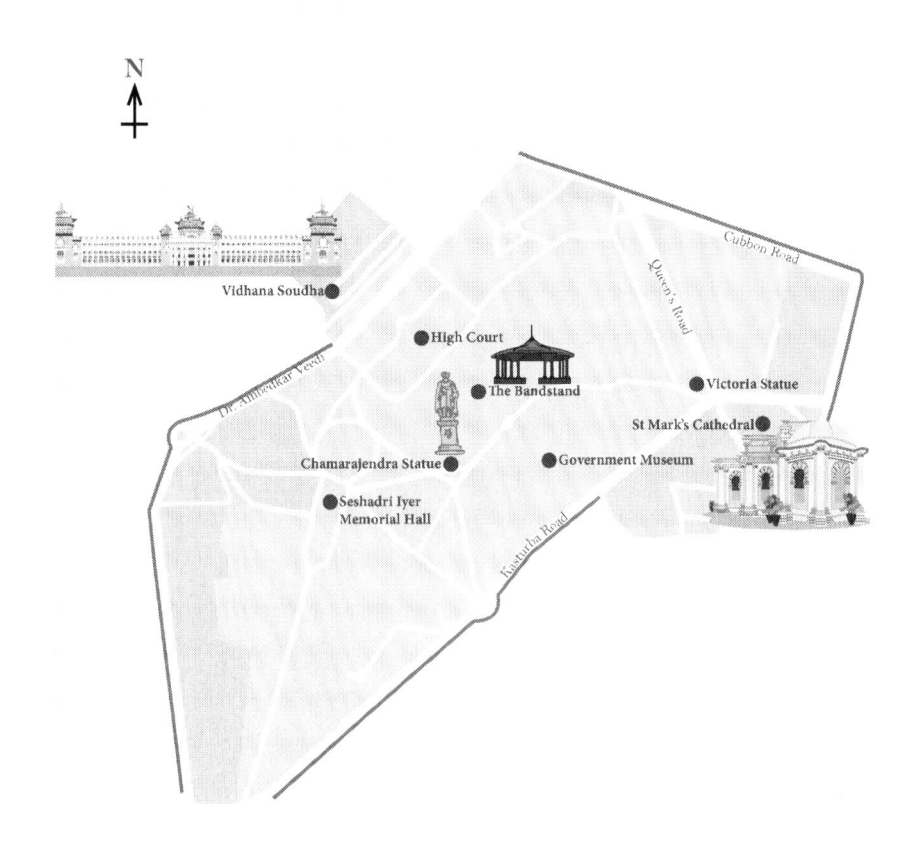

N

Vidhana Soudha

High Court

The Bandstand

Victoria Statue

St Mark's Cathedral

Chamarajendra Statue

Government Museum

Seshadri Iyer Memorial Hall

Cubbon Road

Queen's Road

Dr. Ambedkar Veedi

Kasturba Road

A Walk in the Park. © *INTACH Bengaluru Chapter*

I. St Mark's Cathedral

We begin our walk at 1, MG Road—no, not the mall, but the church that stands at the intersection of MG Road with Queen's Road. There is an entrance to St Mark's Cathedral along MG Road. However, as this is closed on most days, you can enter the church from the road next to that Bengaluru landmark, Koshy's.

St Mark's Church (now Cathedral) sometime between 1902 and 1906, showing the collapsed dome. *Courtesy of The Madras Sappers Museum and Archives.*

This, the oldest Protestant church in the Cantonment, has a fascinating history full of highs and lows. When it was built in 1808, the church was a rather utilitarian structure, with no dome, no bell and little by way of ornamentation. It was universally pilloried for its 'unredeemed ugliness'.[38] In March 1901, a bell tower was added, the aim being to mark King Edward VII's coronation with a peal of bells. A chancel and transepts were also added, and the entire roof was raised. Unfortunately, in December 1902, the tower and the bells collapsed, destroying much of the new additions in the process. It took another four years for the building to be repaired, now with a dome and turret combined. Some 20 years later, disaster struck once again. On the night of 17 February 1923, a fire broke out in the church. It was quickly put out, but not before causing considerable damage. It is said that only two bent steel girders survived to indicate where the great organ had once stood.[39] Repair work began and the church was nearly ready for use a year later when the dome collapsed again.

It was only in 1927 that the church was fully renovated and finally reopened for worship. In place of the much-derided 'matchbox' of yesteryears stood the handsome and stately edifice that you now see. Semi-circular arches, Ionic columns and pilasters, and prominent domes echo the neo-Renaissance or the classical Greco-Roman style of architecture that was then popular in England.

In 1928, the two-manual pipe organ, encased in Burma teakwood, was installed. This was a gift from the mother of the English cricketer Michael Colin Cowdrey. A plaque on the southern outer wall, dedicated to Maj Joseph Dickson, is the oldest tablet in the church. Photographs taken in the 1800s show an obelisk next to the church which was probably built in memory of the Major. This was torn down during the post-fire renovations in the late 1920s and the memorial tablet incorporated into the building itself. Another interesting relic is on the northern side: a tethering place for horses.

The memorial tablets that dot the walls inside the church reflect its beginnings as the garrison church for the Cantonment. Among the many tales of untimely death that these plaques tell, one on the western wall is in memory of Lt Col Sir Walter Scott. He was the eldest son of the famous Scottish poet and novelist of the same name, the author of the Waverly novels, Ivanhoe and many other works.

Take a look also at the list of chaplains who have served St Mark's over its 200 years. Many of them were closely associated with some of Bengaluru's oldest schools. Rev Posnett founded St John's School in 1854 while Rev Pettigrew established Cathedral School and the Bishop Cotton schools. Others like Pakenham-Walsh and GU Pope were wardens at the Bishop Cotton schools where they have School Houses named after them.

St Mark's Church was made the Cathedral of the Mysore Diocese of the Church of South India in 1947.[40]

View of St Mark's Church in the early 1900s, from near the Victoria's Statue. *Courtesy of Rohit Hangal*

Stained glass in the church

— by Swathi Reddy

Stained-glass panels inside the church unfold like a visual sermon, much like in 12th century France, when stained-glass windows were first used as a storyboard of biblical scenes to reach out to a largely illiterate public. The artwork on glass all around the church stands out for its range of detail and technique. The chancel windows at the altar end display the Adoration of the Magi with the three wise men bearing gifts of gold, frankincense and myrrh for the Christ Child. There is another of Christ Blessing the Children. Along the north arm or transept, between the altar and the nave, is the Annunciation when the angel Gabriel tells the Virgin Mary that she will be the Mother of God. Much of the stained glass seen here was shipped from studios in England. Church records state that after the fire of 1923, glass for the upper or clerestory windows came from Chennai. The church takes its name from Saint Mark the Evangelist. His symbol—a winged lion—is on the extreme right of the semi-circular glasswork right above the door opposite the altar. The saint is kneeling, hands folded in prayer, in deference to Christ.

II. Victoria Statue

Diagonally opposite St Mark's Cathedral, at the corner of Queen's Road and Kasturba Road, is a statue of Queen Victoria standing haughty and imperious, hidden behind a screen of trees.

This statue of Queen Victoria once occupied pride of place in the Cantonment. It was unveiled on 5 February 1906 with much fanfare and oratory. The then Prince of Wales, George Frederick Ernest Albert (later King George V), did the honours. By then, the Prince was a veteran in this sort of thing, having already unveiled a Victoria statue in Agra, Victoria memorials in Kolkata and Yangon, and a Victoria Technical Institute in Chennai in just the first three months of his India tour. From Bengaluru, the Prince's tour took him to Karachi, where he was to unveil yet another statue of the late Queen Empress. Nevertheless, in his speech, the Prince alluded to something about the Bengaluru statue that gave him 'especial pleasure': 'It is the association of the Maharaja of Mysore and his people with the inhabitants of the Civil and Military station of Bangalore.' The Prince was referring to the fact that the statue would not have been erected at all but for a generous contribution from the Maharaja.[41]

Soon after Queen Victoria's death in January 1901, committees sprang up all over India and other colonies to deliberate on ways to commemorate her memory. Bengaluru's Queen Victoria Memorial Fund met in Mayo Hall, a little over a year after the Queen died, to mull over the matter. A technical

The statue of Queen Victoria in the early 1900s, with cannons standing guard. *Courtesy of TucksDB.*

institute was mooted, to be called the Bangalore Victoria Technical Institute, which would also have a statue of the late empress in front. But the committee finally decided to commission only a statue. The memorial was to be funded by public subscription. When, after six months of fundraising, the public had only contributed Rs 10,000 (almost all of it by Annasawmy Mudaliar; *see chapter 6*),[42] Krishnaraja Wodeyar IV donated a generous amount that finally saw the project through.

The statue was made by Thomas Brock, a prolific and celebrated sculptor in England whose most famous work is the Victoria Memorial in front of London's Buckingham Palace. Brock made a 11-foot tall marble statue for Bengaluru, which, together with its 13-foot granite pedestal, cost Rs 25,500. It was shipped from England and arrived in July 1905.

Bengaluru's statue is a copy of an earlier one that Brock had made for his hometown of Worcester in England in 1890. It was quite a popular prototype: another replica of it was requested for the city of Cape Town in 1889, Birmingham in 1901, Carlisle in 1902 and Belfast in 1903.[43] In all, Brock made 14 Victoria statues during his career.[44] In all these statues, the Queen wears her flowing Order of the Garter robes decorated with roses and tassels, and carries a sceptre and an orb. Other details—such as the tilt of the monarch's head and the angle at which she looks down her nose—vary.

The years had taken a toll on the Empress's regalia. Her sceptre broke, as did a finger of her right hand. Her orb lost its cross during a political rally in the

1990s when one end of a banner was attached to it. In 2017, the Department of Horticulture restored the statue: Victoria now has a repaired but shortened sceptre and her orb now bears a miniature version of the original cross. Of the more than 50 statues of Victoria that were installed in India, only five still remain at their original locations. Bengaluru's statue is one of them.[45]

The period building housing Cubbon Park Police Station, with its monkey-topped entrance and the year 1910 proudly emblazoned on top, has a link to the Victoria Statue. Originally, the police station was even closer to the statue. John Cameron and subsequently GH Krumbiegel, both Superintendents of the Government Gardens and Parks, asked for its removal so an ornamental railing could be provided that would both beautify and protect the statue. The proposal to move the police station from its original spot near the statue was finally approved in 1909 and the new building was constructed in 1910.[46]

III. The Bandstand

Enter the park through the gates near the statue and walk about 550 metres to reach the bandstand.

Bandstands are a by-product of the Brass Band Movement of the 19th and 20th centuries in the United Kingdom, when bands playing in parks drew large audiences. In Victorian England, tens of thousands of people would gather to listen to these free concerts. And so it was that bandstands began to sprout all over parks in the UK. The first such bandstand was built in 1861 in the Royal

Cubbon Park's first bandstand was built near today's Bowring Institute.
Courtesy of British Library, Shelfmark: Photo 254/4(2)

Horticultural Gardens in Kensington near London. We don't know exactly when Cubbon Park jumped onto the bandstand bandwagon, but photographs show that by the 1870s, it most certainly had.[47]

Cubbon Park's bandstands have been rather peripatetic. The earliest bandstand in this area did not come up here, but stood roughly where a petrol pump stands today, adjacent to Bowring Institute. It was demolished in about 1888, when Bowring Institute was allotted the site where it stood.[48] Around 1909, there was a proposal for a new bandstand. This time, the site chosen for it was close to Seshadri Iyer Memorial Hall, at Ringwood Circle. Work on it began in 1913 and the structure, paid for by the Mysore Maharaja, was completed the next year. The roads around it were laid out at that time.[49] In the late 1920s, that old bandstand was dismantled and a new one built here, where it stands today.

Though built some years after the death of Queen Victoria, this bandstand is still typical of the Victorian period. Like most bandstands built during that time and still seen in parks in England, our bandstand has cast-iron columns with a timber frame, cast-iron railings and decorative roofline details, sloping roofs, an octagonal shape and a raised plinth. Almost certainly, the bandstand would originally have had a false wooden roof that served as sounding boards for the band playing in the bandstand. The current roof is a modern one, fitted during a renovation in September 2013.

Regardless of its location, for many Bengalureans the bandstand used to be one of the main attractions of Cubbon Park. In its early days, bands of both the British and Mysore armies (the latter the army of the Maharaja of Mysore) as well as of the police used to play here at least once a week. One of the grandest concerts is said to have been during the celebrations of the Silver Jubilee of Krishnaraja Wodeyar IV in 1927.

Today, after several years of disuse, every Sunday, when the park is closed to vehicular traffic, musicians and bands are invited to play in the bandstand, which is once again enjoyed by people of all ages.

IV. High Court

A short walk of about 100 metres in a north-westerly direction brings you to a flight of steps flanked by cement lions. Beyond the tall grill gates lies the High Court. This slice of Victoriana was built in 1868 to accommodate government offices which, until then, had been housed in Tipu's palace in the fort. Consequently, it still sometimes goes by its old name of Attara Kacheri, or 18 offices. Proposals for new digs for the British administration had been made in 1857, but then the First War of Independence broke out and things were kept in abeyance for some time. The first plans sent in 1860 to the Government of India for sanction were rejected. Fresh plans were made for the building, this time by Lt Col Richard H Sankey, who also designed Cubbon Park, and work began on it in 1864. It was built at a cost of Rs 3.68 lakhs.[50] The contractor for the project, Wallace and Co, had the work done by Narrainsawmy Mudaliar, whose name is now inextricably linked with the building.

With the Rendition in 1881, these offices came under the control of the Maharaja's government, rendering the British administration of Bengaluru homeless. For almost two decades, the offices of the C&M Station—including

A postcard by S Mahadeo and Sons, of the Attara Kacheri (now the High Court). This is now the rear of the building. *Courtesy of Rohit Hangal.*

those of the District Magistrate, the Civil Court Judge and so on—were housed in various rented accommodations. It was only in 1904 that they got themselves new digs, when another set of Public Offices were erected next to Mayo Hall (*see chapter 6*). The Mysore government offices continued here till 1956 when they moved to the Vidhana Soudha. The High Court, which till then had been housed in one wing, then occupied the entire building.

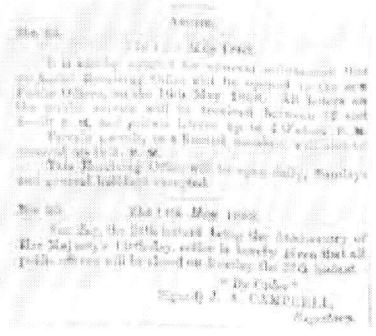

An announcement in the Mysore Gazette of May 1868 intimating that the post office would henceforth be located in the new Public Offices (today's High Court). From, KSA.

The long arcades and the Ionic columns hark back to classical forms of architecture that were popular in Europe during the Renaissance period and enjoyed a revival in the 19th century. But it has some distinctly local features too. For example, the verandahs running around the building, which the designer, Sankey, was particularly proud of: 'Hardly a ray of direct sunlight finds its way into the building while at the same time there is abundant light and ventilation,' he writes. The roofing was originally of the type called the Madras terrace roof. Other local elements that were used were granite for the ground floor walls and flooring, and bamboo matting for the roofs of some of the verandahs.[51]

Don't miss the statue in front of the building, which shows Sir Mark Cubbon astride a horse. Sculpted by the Italian-born Frenchman, Carlo Marochetti, whose works are found in England, Italy, France and elsewhere around the world, it was cast at Marochetti's foundry in London and shipped here. The inauguration took place at the Parade Ground on 16 March 1866, and 'natives congregated in thousands', wrote one observer. The statue was moved to its present location when the Attara Kacheri building was completed.[52] In the 1990s, some activists wished to have this, and the Queen and King's statues, removed. However, Sir Mark stayed put and, in fact, even got a new pedestal for his statue.[53] At the time of writing, there is once again a move to knock him off his pedestal.[54]

This side of the building, overlooking the bandstand and the museum, was once the main entrance into the building. Today, the entrance into the High Court is from opposite the Vidhana Soudha, from what was once the rear of the building.

Like a cat with nine lives, this building is already on its third, having come close to demolition twice. In the 1950s, Chief Minister Kengal Hanumanthaiah was keen to have this symbol of colonial power demolished. However, he was prevailed upon to retain the structure, which he did on the condition that the new legislature then being built—the Vidhana Soudha—should tower over this colonial relic. And so it was that the Vidhana Soudha was built exactly where it is, opposite the old Attara Kacheri, with a flight of steps that makes it soar over the old building![55]

In 1984, once again, the court sanctioned the demolition of this building, and approved of a plan to build a new structure in its place. The move sparked one of the first public movements to save a heritage building in Bengaluru. A Public Interest Litigation (PIL) was filed by a group of concerned citizens, brought together by the late film producer and director, M Bhaktavatsala. Other eminent citizens including the first Convenor of the INTACH Bengaluru Chapter, Naomi Meadows, and several other INTACH members worked to raise public awareness about the building.[56] The PIL was heard in the very building that was supposed to be demolished. M Bhaktavatsala had this to say about this seminal case: 'At that time, it was a sensational case, this PIL! All those lawyers sitting there, they'd be spitting at me, saying, "Why do you want to save this building? The building is crumbling." We were Enemy No. 1.'[57] The court dismissed the petition and the case went to the Supreme Court. But meanwhile, taking heed of popular public opinion, the state government rescinded its decision to demolish the building; it was expanded and, happily, it still stands.

Architect, Engineer, Designer

Richard Hieram Sankey, an Irishman from far-away Tipperary, designed the first of his many buildings, Nagpur's Anglican Cathedral of All Saints, in 1851, at the ripe old age of 22, when he was posted as Superintending Engineer at Nagpur. During his stint at Nagpur, Sankey's wide-ranging interests became obvious: he published a paper on the geology of the Nagpur region, discovered the coalfields of the Kanhan Valley, and also found 250-million-year-old plant fossils. After being posted in Kolkata, Kanpur, Allahabad, Lucknow, the Nilgiris and Myanmar, Sankey came to Mysore State in 1861, where he served for 13 years, as Assistant to the Chief Engineer, then Chief Engineer and, finally, Secretary to the Chief Commissioner of Mysore.

One of Sankey's first projects here was to carry out a systematic survey of the old tanks and to map the catchment area of each. He then organised the repair of several of the old channels, bunds and tanks, including the pristine-looking Sulekere tank near Maddur. The engineer in Sankey recognised and admired the genius of the tank system. In a report written

This urn, near the museum, was a gift from RH Sankey. © Aravind C

in 1866, he says, 'thanks to the patient industry of its inhabitants', 60 per cent of Mysore State was under tank irrigation. In fact, he adds, 'it would now require some ingenuity to discover a site within this great area suitable for a new tank'.

But this is precisely what he did in Bengaluru. Then (as now!) Bengalureans continually bemoaned the state of their water supply. The Cantonment depended largely on the Ulsoor tank (see chapter 3) and wells near it, and people fretted both about the quality and quantity of the water. In 1868, Sankey designed a project to collect and store water to supplement the needs of the Cantonment. The plan was sanctioned in 1874, and then, partly because of a terrible famine that intervened, it was only completed in 1882. For many years, because the tank still did not quench the city's thirst and initially leaked, Sankey Tank went by the name Sankey's Folly!

Apart from the tank and the High Court building, Sankey did a frenetic amount of building and designing here. In 1864, he worked on his second church when he helped build St Andrew's Kirk in Bengaluru. In 1870, he designed and laid out Cubbon Park. Sankey seems to have recreated on the ground the romantic landscapes that he painted on canvas, with winding paths and picturesque waterways. (Incidentally, this was not the only park Sankey worked on: later, he beautified the botanical gardens in Chennai, where he also helped lay out Marina Beach.) He also designed Bengaluru's Mayo Hall (1883) and another imposing structure in Cubbon Park——the Government Museum——completed in 1877.

Vegetable Seller, Contractor, Philanthropist

A vegetable seller who became a prince; a penniless ten-year-old who grew up to become one of the richest men in the city, established several educational institutions, helped build one of Bengaluru's most iconic buildings, and set up orphanages and homes for needy people. This is the story of Dharmarathnakara Rai Bahadur Arcot Narrainsawmy Mudaliar.

Arcot Narrainsawmy Mudaliar was born into an aristocratic family. His great-grandfather was Secretary to the Raja of Gingee. But by the time Narrainsawmy was born on 14 May 1827, the family was in dire straits. His father had moved the family to the recently established Cantonment of Bangalore but died soon after. It fell to the ten-year-old Narrainsawmy Mudaliar to support his widowed mother and his two younger brothers. How he managed it for the first few years, we do not know, but in 1850, when he was 22 years old, he began to trade in vegetables, buying them in Bengaluru and selling them in Chennai.[62]

The venture was successful and he soon expanded into the lucrative salt trade, buying 'Madras salt' as it was known, to sell in Bengaluru. Business prospered and, before long, Narrainsawmy Mudaliar had set aside enough capital to open a shop in the Cantonment. As he established a name for himself, his list of customers quickly grew. His most illustrious client was the then Maharaja of Mysore, Krishnaraja Wodeyar III, who became a patron in 1859. From then on, Narrainsawmy Mudaliar remained forever devoted to the Maharaja. As a token of his gratitude, he changed the name of his shop from Mysore Hall to Mysore Maharaja Hall.

When the plan for the new Public Offices (that is, the High Court building) was approved, the contract for construction was awarded to Wallace and Co. Learning that the firm planned to subcontract the construction work, he sensed an opportunity, partnered with a banker named Bansilal Ramrathan, and bid for and won the project. The Attara Kacheri, which now houses the High Court, was built to exacting standards. Its timely and satisfactory completion earned Narrainsawmy Mudaliar considerable respect and money. He used this windfall to diversify into other businesses, including an auctioneering firm called the Bangalore Agency on South Parade. This venture, too, flourished. In fact, his success in business earned him the sobriquet 'Merchant Prince of Bangalore'.

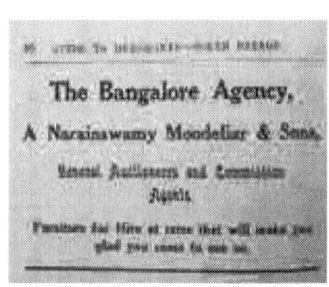

An advertisement for Narrainsawmy Mudaliar's The Bangalore Agency. From *A Soldier's Guide to Bangalore*, 1917. YMCA: Bangalore.

The Prince used his wealth to help those who were less fortunate. He had a particularly keen interest in education. He established a free English primary school for Indians in 1873, the first in the Cantonment. Other branches and schools soon followed, including a technical training institute and some schools exclusively for girls. In 1893, at the foundation-laying ceremony of an orphanage that Narrainsawmy Mudaliar established, the then Viceroy of India, Lord Lansdowne, spoke warmly of the many charitable institutions the generous merchant had founded. He recalled how, during the great famine of 1876–77, Narrainsawmy Mudaliar had built rest houses, and taken up the maintenance and care of many destitute children. To quote Lord Lansdowne, Bengalureans 'owe a deep debt of gratitude to the benevolence of Mr. Narrainsawmy Mudaliar'.[63]

Narrainsawmy Mudaliar's The Bangalore Agency. It was replaced by Plaza Theatre which was later replaced by the MG Road Metro Station.
Courtesy of Sanjeev Narrain.

In recognition of his services, in 1877, he was given the title 'Rai Bahadur' (also sometimes written as 'Rao Bahadur') by the British. Later, in 1894, Maharaja Chamaraja Wodeyar gave him the additional title 'Dharmarathnakara'. Today, the 15 educational institutions that bear his name are run by the RBANM's Educational Charities that is managed by his descendants.

V. Government Museum

Head back in the direction of the bandstand and then walk about 100 metres past it to reach the red building that houses the Government Museum.

This museum opened on 18 August 1865, making it one of India's oldest. The man behind the museum was Edward Green Balfour, a surgeon. Balfour had already established the Madras Museum in 1851, and served as its Superintendent for nine years when he came to Bengaluru in 1861. Within a couple of years, he had convinced the government of the need for a museum here. Accordingly, the government asked its officers everywhere to send in interesting artefacts that might be suitable for display in the museum. These were supplemented with objects donated by the public and some that were also purchased: today, we would say the exhibits were crowd-sourced![64]

The museum initially opened in a room in the Cantonment Jail, which was then situated in a section of the compound that housed the Good Shepherd Convent and the Sacred Heart School. It moved to another rented building on Museum Road before finally settling in this handsome building in 1878.[65]

The museum (painted white) in a Wiele's postcard from the late 1800s/early 1900s. *Courtesy of Harish Padmanabha.*

Designed by Col RH Sankey, the new building came up on an axis with the Attara Kacheri (now the High Court) in Cubbon Park. A fig tree-lined avenue connected the museum with the Attara Kacheri, with an urn decorating the intersection with the perpendicular road. Sankey chose for this building a classical Greco-Roman style that was all the rage in Victorian England and so naturally was also popular with the colonials. The classical detailing above the doors and windows (with the Greek/Roman god in the keystone), the different window styles for the two floors, with taller and pedimented windows on the upper floor and semi-circular arches on the lower, are all characteristic of this style. Don't miss the urn in the garden behind the museum—a gift from Richard Sankey.

The main entrance to the museum was originally on the eastern side of the building—the side that now faces the Visveswaraya Museum. In 1960, construction began on a new wing, built in the same style as the original. The extension—the western wing—was opened in 1962.

The museum is a veritable treasure house of artefacts, even though one does need to exercise considerable imagination and effort to look past the poor lighting, labelling and arrangement of exhibits. Among its priceless collection are sculptures, some of which date from the first century CE, wooden carvings, musical instruments, Mysore style paintings, and of course numerous archaeological relics. For a Bengalurean, some things that might be of special interest are the massive and exquisitely carved hero stone near the museum entrance, brought in the 1860s from the temple in Begur by Commissioner LB Bowring; the Neolithic and Early Iron Age (also sometimes called Megalithic) relics that were found during archaeological excavations in and around Bengaluru, including in Savanadurga and Jadigenahalli; and the many paintings showing Bengaluru in the 1700s. It is also not every day that you get to see objects from Mohenjo-daro! So take a look at the museum's collection of pottery, bricks, dice and toys from there. Another very important artefact here is the Halmidi inscription (from the village of Halmidi in Hasan district), the oldest known inscription in Kannada.

VI. Chamarajendra Statue

Head back towards road leading to the bandstand. At the road, turn left and walk about 200 metres. The statue is on the right fork.

Chamaraja Wodeyar, also called Chamarajendra Wodeyar, ruled over Mysore State from 1881 until his death in 1894. He was just 31 years old when he died. During his brief reign, this young and well-loved king laid the foundations of a modern and progressive Mysore State. It was during his rule that the first moves towards democracy were made, making Mysore the first princely state in India to make this attempt. He also took special care to promote the education of women.

The statue of Chamaraja Wodeyar.
© PeeVee

This marble statue of the king was executed in 1927 by GK Mhatre, a sculptor from Bombay (now Mumbai). Don't miss the *gandabherunda*—the double-headed eagle—above the inscription, the symbol of the Wodeyar dynasty.

VII. Seshadri Iyer Memorial Hall

Walk west along the road for about 450 metres to get to Ringwood Circle. Seshadri Iyer Memorial Hall is across the circle. This handsome structure, which houses the State Central Library, was built in 1905 but fully completed only in about 1910.[66] It commemorates Seshadri Iyer, the longest serving Dewan of Mysore State: he served from 1883 to 1901. Seshadri Iyer is often referred to as the 'Maker of Modern Bengaluru'. It was during his administration that extensions such as Basavanagudi, Malleswaram and Seshadripuram were established; the Chamarajendra Water Works which supplied water to Bengaluru from Hesaraghatta lake was set up; and India's second hydro-electric generating station came up at Sivasamudram near Bengaluru.

The Seshadri Iyer Memorial Hall is one of the many publicly-funded structures in Cubbon Park.
© PeeVee

The building was paid for by money donated by the public, and it was meant to be used for public purposes, specifically 'for a Public Hall with a statue and a Library'.[67] But it has a curious early history. From about 1908 to 1920, parts of the structure were used for a decidedly non-public purpose as they were rented out to a Bangalore Club (not to be confused with today's Bangalore Club): the large hall on the right of the building was used as a billiards room by the club.[68] There were even tennis courts adjacent to the Hall. From 1909, the building was occupied by both an educational museum and the Bangalore Club. In 1914, the Public Library was finally housed here as well.[69] This rather crowded state of affairs continued till 1920 when the structure was made over to the Municipality. The club then vacated the premises and the Public Library occupied the entire building—or almost the entire building, for in the 1920s, there was also a restaurant located here which apparently did thriving business.[70]

The building has an interesting mix of architectural styles and features, including an unusual apsidal plan, wooden roofs that soar to a height of almost 14 metres, very prominent curved Dutch gables, and

The foundation stone of the Seshadri Iyer Memorial Hall was laid on 15th October 1903.
© Aravind C

several Indian motifs and details, including the use of granite pillars. Early photographs show that the large arched windows along its outer facade were originally open arches.

The bronze statue of Dewan Seshadri in front of the building was sculpted by William Colton, a French-born British sculptor and President of the Royal British Society of Sculptors. The statue was paid for by public subscription and unveiled by Lord Hardinge, the then Viceroy of India, in 1913.

When the building was built, this area was not included in Cubbon Park. In fact, Seshadri Road passed right through the area where the garden around Seshadri Iyer's statue is laid out. When the statue was installed, this portion of the road was diverted. Later, in 1910 or so, the lands around this building, including a hamlet named Sillubande, all the way up to Hudson Memorial Church, were acquired and incorporated into the park.[71]

VIII. Vidhana Soudha

To get to the Vidhana Soudha, you could take some of the trails that cut through the park. Else, walk around Ringwood Circle which lies behind the State Central Library, towards the Vidhana Soudha Metro Station. The building lies across the road from the High Court.

Unfortunately, visitors are not allowed inside this grand building which houses Karnataka's legislature and part of its secretariat. It is India's largest such legislature-cum-office complex. Begun in 1952 and completed in 1956, it was the brainchild of the state's second Chief Minister, Kengal Hanumanthaiah. Hanumanthaiah wanted a building that would 'reflect the power and dignity of the people'. He particularly wanted the architecture of the building to reflect Indian traditions, rather than western. To this end, he took great personal

The Vidhana Soudha in the 1980s. © *INTACH*

interest in the building's design, making very specific suggestions for decorative details to be drawn from particular temples, palaces, houses and even a dam. The northern portico, for example, was modelled after the gateway to the Krishnarajasagar dam near Mysuru.

The Vidhana Soudha is built of granite quarried from places around Bengaluru. Porphyry, a pinkish-tinged variety of granite, from near Magadi, was used for the decorative elements. About 1500 artisans, including chisellers, wood carvers and stone masons, worked on this building. Don't miss the parapet designs. They are inspired by the *gavakshas* (literally, cow's eyes), the horseshoe-shaped arches that decorate most south Indian temples.

A newspaper clipping from the 1950s, about the construction of the Vidhana Soudha

Incidentally, when Jawaharlal Nehru laid the foundation stone for this building in 1951, the plan was for a modest, two-storeyed structure. This original plan was shelved in 1952 in favour of the grand building that you now see.[72]

Soldiers from the MEG (earlier called Queen Victoria's Own Madras Sappers and Miners) erecting the Oriental Building (now the LIC Building), 1926. *Courtesy of The Madras Sappers Museum and Archives.*

⁕ ⁕ ⁕ ⁕ ⁕

Our walk exploring Cubbon Park, the beginnings of the Cantonment of Bangalore, and life in the Raj ends here, at this building which symbolises the end of the British era.

The British have long gone but the Cantonment and the armed forces they established here still play a large role in Bengaluru. The city is home to several branches of the defence forces including the MEG, the Army Service Corps, the Corps of Military Police, the Paras (Parachute Regiment Training Centre) and the Air Force. Soldiers, particularly from the MEG, have literally built much of the city: records of Queen Victoria's Own Madras Sappers and Miners as they were earlier called, show that MEG's soldiers built not just army buildings but also the LIC (Life Insurance of India) office (which initially housed the Oriental Insurance Company) and the BRV Theatre (now an army canteen) on MG Road, for example, besides carrying out other miscellaneous building work such as additions to the Indian Institute of Science and Bowring Hospital, a pipeline to a tobacco factory in Fraser Town, and even some roads in Yeshwantpur.[73] We have the defence to thank for much of Bengaluru's natural heritage (most defence lands are large swathes of green that include some very venerable old trees) and colonial-era built heritage, including some lovely offices, messes, barracks, memorials, houses and hospitals which dot various parts of the city.

Notes

1. Hall 1833, 45.
2. Wellesley 1851.
3. Annesley and Pettigrew 1855.
4. A brief note on the origin and development of the Assigned Tract of Bangalore, KSA; IOR/F/4/260/5798, British Library.
5. To give you an idea of how much this would be: a rupee in those days would have bought you about 3 kg of rice. See Rice 1897b, 459.
6. WP1/166/5. Letter from Lieutenant Colonel R. Barclay to Major General Sir Arthur Wellesley, containing news of various outstanding Indian matters and of mutual friends and acquaintances in India, 3 March 1807, http://www.archives.soton.ac.uk/wellington/results.php?count=1, accessed 12 August 2018.
7. Blakiston 1829, 315.
8. Nicholson 1873, 315.
9. Williams 1840, 144.
10. 'Housing the poor', *The Times of India*, 7 November 1924.
11. Bell 1867, 267.
12. Troup 1997, 56; 'Pleasant Bangalore: Phases of Indian life', *The Times of India*, 16 April 1908.

13. Hervey 1850, 45.
14. Blakiston 1829, 316.
15. Shama Rao 1936. The Board was abolished in June 1832 and administration of the state entrusted to one single Commissioner. Sir Mark Cubbon, one of the most popular and well-respected Commissioners to hold the post, also held it the longest, from 1834 to 1861, and was succeeded by Lewis Bentham Bowring.
16. Hasan 1970, 125.
17. Report on the Medical Topography and Statistics of the Mysore Division of the Madras Army 1844, 54.
18. Rajangam 2013.
19. Anon 1854.
20. Jain, Murthy and Shankar 2001.
21. Anon 1854, 182.
22. Compton 1897.
23. Bell 1867, 268.
24. Roberts 1837, 315.
25. Anon 1854; Marryat 1868.
26. Roberts 1837.
27. Anon 1854, 183.
28. Bowring 1871; Troup 1997. The barracks were till recently known as Baird Barracks and are today called Abdul Hamid Barracks, named after a war hero who died during the 1965 war with Pakistan.
29. Clark 1885, 64.
30. Roberts 1837.
31. See, for example, File No. 385, 1782–1888, NAI, which deals with a sect of 'Caliphs and Mureeds' in Bengaluru who were 'employed in exciting the religious feelings of the Mussalmans' against the British; IOR/F/4/219/4808, Nov 1806–Feb 1807, British Library; Bentinck 1809, 133.
32. Doveton 1844; James 1998.
33. O'Callaghan 1832, 84; Doveton 1844, 622.
34. Campbell 1864, 397.
35. Aitchison 1909, 188; A brief note on the origin and development of the Assigned Tract of Bangalore, KSA.
36. Sankey 1873.
37. 'Our own correspondent', *The Times of India*, 19 August 1874.
38. Anon 2008, 13.
39. 'St Mark's Bangalore: Gallant salvage work at the fire', *The Straits Times*, 19 March 1923.
40. Anon 2008, 55.
41. Reed 1906, 501.
42. 'The late Queen-Empress: Technical Institute for Bangalore', *The Times of India*, 18 February 1902.
43. Steggles 2000, 202.
44. Stocker 2014.

45. Steggles 2000, 178–214.
46. Annual Report of Government Gardens and Parks in Mysore for the official year 1908–1909.
47. For more on this, see Herbert 2000.
48. File Resy 699 of 1886, Sl 1–30, 34–45, KSA.
49. Annual Report of Government Gardens and Parks in Mysore for the official year 1913–1914.
50. Sankey 1873.
51. Sankey 1873, 4.
52. Dobbs 1882, 221–222.
53. Steggles 2000, 70.
54. Shyam Prasad 2018.
55. Nair 2005.
56. Interview with PK Venkataramanan, *INTACHer* 1, no. 2, http://www.intachblr.org/files/IntacherVol1Issue2.pdf.
57. Interview with M Bhaktavatsala, *INTACHer* 1, no. 1, http://www.intachblr.org/files/IntacherVol1Issue1.pdf.
58. Lang, Desai and Desai 1997, 77.
59. Sankey 1853.
60. Rao 1930a, 157.
61. Nair 2005, 203–208.
62. Personal communication with TV Annaswamy, great-grand-nephew of Narrainsawmy Mudaliar, a former President of RBANM's Educational Charities and author of *Bengaluru to Bangalore*, a book on Bengaluru's history.
63. Anon 1909, 477–478.
64. Reports for the Administration of Mysore for the years 1863–64 and 1864–65.
65. Iyer 2015.
66. Annual Report of Government Gardens and Parks in Mysore for the official year 1906–1907, 4; File ML 457 of 1908, Sl 1–2, KSA.
67. File GM 209 of 17, Sl 1–7, KSA.
68. File ML 457 of 1908, Sl 1–2, KSA.
69. File EDU 45 of 1909, Sl 6–7, KSA.
70. File ML 213 of 26, Sl 5, 6, KSA.
71. Annual Report of Government Gardens and Parks in Mysore for the official year 1908–1909, 10.
72. For more on this, see Nair 2005, 203–213.
73. Annual Record of Queen Victoria's Own Madras Sappers and Miners for 1923–24.

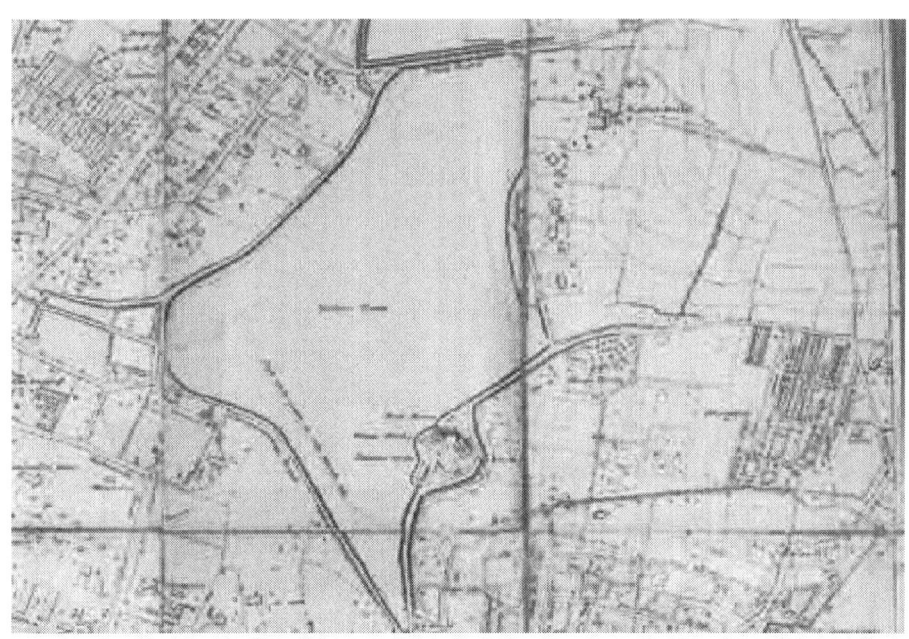

Halasuru and its vicinity in 1884-85. From, Survey of India. *Cantonment and City of Bangalore and Environs, Season 1884-85.* Courtesy of Mythic Society, Bengaluru.

Halasuru and its vicinity in 1935-36. From, Survey of India. *Bangalore Guide Map. Surveyed 1935-36.* Courtesy of Naresh Narasimhan.

CHAPTER 3

More than Just a Temple: Halasuru or Ulsoor

Halasuru, or Ulsoor, is one of Bengaluru's most vibrant settlements and also one of its oldest. Here you can find bustling streets, lively markets, ancient temples, old water bodies, distinctive traditional architecture and a colourful street life.

Halasuru probably began as a small settlement clustered around the 1000-year-old Someshwara temple. After Kempegowda developed the city of Bengaluru in the mid-1500, Achyutaraya, the then ruler of the Vijayanagar empire, is believed to have granted Kempegowda 12 *hoblis* (clusters of villages), as a reward for his loyalty and commitment. One of the *hoblis* was Halasuru. In those days, Halasuru would have been just inside the bound hedge that surrounded Bengaluru *pete* at a radius of about 6 km from the fort.

Halasuru is said to be named after *halasina hannu*, the jackfruit. One story relates that the area had many jackfruit trees. One day, a man watched as a monkey took a jackfruit, and without tasting it, threw it on a small heap of mud nearby. Curious, the man dug up the mud, and lo and behold, there was a linga there! This was eventually installed in the Someshwara temple. This temple would have formed the nucleus of the earliest settlement in Halasuru, with a cluster of houses around the temple, and a sea of fields and farms around it.

Fast-forward to the 1500s and you would have seen a significant addition: the Halasuru *kere* (properly 'tank', but nowadays more commonly translated as 'lake'). For over a thousand years, people in south India have been building small dams to capture and store rainfall (*see chapter 8*). The reservoirs or *keres* so formed served both irrigation and household needs. These *keres* were usually interconnected so that overflow from a tank upstream led to another downstream. Like all of Bengaluru's lakes, Halasuru lake is also a man-made reservoir. It is popularly believed to have been built by the Kempegowda family.

British poet and artist Edward Lear visited the Ulsoor kere in August 1874 and was charmed by it. *Courtesy of Houghton Library, Harvard University. MS Typ 55.26 (2185)*

Halasuru village—then full of coconut gardens and orchards—once depended on Halasuru lake and on numerous wells for its water. In the 1800s, the Cantonment too relied on this lake for its water. In the early days, water used to be supplied by water carriers on bullock carts. Later, the British laid pipes to supply water to the barracks. Today, the area's water supply no longer comes from Halasuru *kere*. But the lake still plays an important ecological role providing a rich habitat for diverse birds, aquatic plants, fish and other fauna.

Another landmark of Ulsoor, as it is now more commonly known, is the so-called Kempegowda Tower, built on a rock near the *kere* by Immadi Kempegowda, the son of the founder of Bengaluru, Hiriya Kempegowda. It is one of four, or possibly more, towers that he built. Popular legend says that the towers were built to mark the extent to which Bengaluru would grow. They were more likely to have been built as watchtowers. The Ulsoor Kempegowda Tower falls under land belonging to the army and is inaccessible to the public. You can, however, get a glimpse of it as you drive down from MG Road to Ulsoor, if you crane your neck a little. You can also see it from across the lake. British maps drawn in the 18th century after the 'Battle for Bengaluru' show that during the 1791 battle, the British used this tower as a vantage point from which to fire on Tipu Sultan's army.

In 1807, the new Bangalore Cantonment was established just west and south of Ulsoor lake. The *pete*, or old city near Bengaluru Fort, was already a commercial centre. The setting up of the Cantonment made Ulsoor another

The Kempegowda tower in Ulsoor. © *Meera Iyer*

trading hub. New avenues for employment opened up. Contractors and labourers were needed to construct buildings. Suppliers were needed for vegetables, oil, salt and other essentials. Tailors, barbers and other servicemen were needed to provide services to the growing population. The economic opportunities attracted many migrants from surrounding areas, including Tamil-, Marathi- and Telugu-speaking people. Ulsoor's distinctive character today is partly due to the synthesis of the various cultures of people who made it their home many generations ago.

Because of its proximity to the Cantonment, Ulsoor's evolution was different from that of the old *pete* area. The old city housed businesses and bazaars filled with both retailers and wholesalers. Like any typical Indian settlement, it also had thriving communities of artisans. But here in Ulsoor, you won't hear the click-clack of looms, nor will you find the streets of wholesale merchants so characteristic of the *pete*. This is because this area's residents were almost all engaged in the service sector, many of them working in the Cantonment, while its bazaars catered mainly to local residents. And yet, despite its proximity to the Cantonment, Ulsoor essentially remained a very typical Indian settlement, as you will see. This is still evident in the settlement pattern of several narrow lanes, many of them centred around the temple. It is also obvious in its architecture.

The new British cantonment (later the C and M Station) was a major source of livelihoods for the people of Ulsoor. © *PeeVee*

Ulsoor's winding roads still have several old buildings, the majority of them traditional houses, very different in character from the bungalows of the rest of the Cantonment.

Houses of Traditional Build

Question: What would you call a microclimate modifier that provides plenty of light and ventilation to a whole house, but requires zero electricity?

Answer: A courtyard.

Many of the traditional houses in Ulsoor have a courtyard like this, sometimes two. © *PeeVee*

An open-to-sky courtyard in the centre of the house, with rooms all around opening onto it, ensures light and air circulation in all the rooms. Several houses in Ulsoor are planned around a courtyard. Some also have a second courtyard towards the back of the house. The courtyard is often a focal point for many activities. In the mornings, it may serve as an extension of the kitchen with some preliminary food prep occurring here. Later in the day, it often functions as a centre for family gatherings and activities. It can also double up as a washing and cleaning area. Hindu households often have a tulsi plant at the centre of the courtyard.

Out of more than 80 old buildings in Ulsoor, at least 25 still have courtyards.[1] Today, architects and homeowners in India and abroad are reintroducing courtyards into modern, contemporary homes. The courtyard is now recognised as a trendy, eco-friendly, cost-effective way of modifying the inner climate of the house, a way of bringing the outside in, without compromising on privacy.

Several old houses in Ulsoor also have some very interesting roofing techniques that are now disappearing from most other parts of Bengaluru. This is one of the very few places in Bengaluru where you can still see bamboo pitched roofs. Such roofs are built with thin bamboo poles that are placed very close together, supported by a framework made of either wood or bamboo. Add a layer of tiles on top of the bamboo and you have a roof that is sturdy, economical, stable and cheap. As long as the bamboo is treated to keep insects away, these roofs will last a long time. In fact, bamboo often outlasts steel. This simple traditional roofing system also allows for movement of air, which helps keep interiors cool.

A few decades ago, the most popular floors in houses were red-oxide floors. However, because of the time and labour involved in getting a well-made red-oxide floor, most new houses have abandoned this style. Several houses in Ulsoor are still proud owners of red-oxide flooring. Lokeshwari, who lives on Masjid Street, recalls how in their house, 'If coins fell to the ground, you couldn't find them—the floor was so polished!'[2]

The Mystery of the Chinese Bell

The Chinese bell in the Kempegowda tower in Ulsoor c. early 1900s.
Courtesy of Jane Smith, from the collections of Fred Goodwill.

In the early 1900s, a large metal bell used to lie in the Kempegowda Tower in Ulsoor. An inscription in Chinese said that the bell was made in China in 1741. How did it come to be in Bengaluru? The answer reveals a tenuous link between the Opium Wars and Ulsoor.

In 1842, towards the end of the First Opium War, British soldiers from the Madras Horse Artillery took a bell from a temple in Nanjing, China, and brought it back to Chennai, as part of war booty. From there, the bell was brought to Bengaluru, where it was kept near their barracks. It was struck once every hour, and could be heard 4 km away, or so they say! One rainy night, rather than go out in the rain to strike the bell, a sentry threw a large piece of ammunition at it instead and permanently damaged it. The bell lay unused for some years until the 1870s, when it was moved to the Kempegowda Tower where it stayed till the early 1900s. Sometime later, the bell was moved to the grounds of the Madras Engineer Group (MEG).[3]

The Chinese bell in the premises of the MEG Officers Mess. © *Meera Iyer*

A Walk through Ulsoor

In which you see a 1000-year-old temple, a 200-year-old settlement, and the timeless impulses of coexistence, philanthropy and commerce

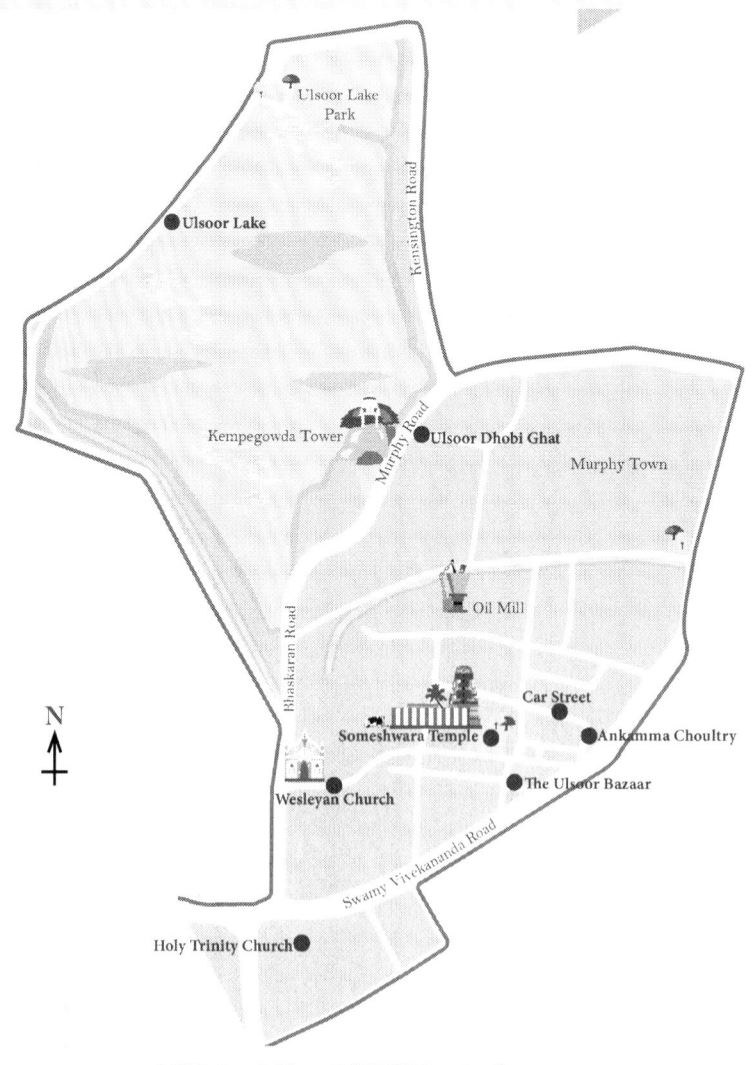

A Walk through Ulsoor. © *INTACH Bengaluru Chapter*

1. Someshwara Temple

We begin our walk at one of the most beautiful temples in Bengaluru, which is also one of the city's oldest. According to legend, Kempegowda was once out hunting in this part of his kingdom, which in those days was a dense jungle, teeming with animals. After a strenuous bout of hunting, he lay down under a tree to rest a while. The god Someshwara appeared to Kempegowda in a dream and told him about a treasure that lay buried nearby in seven brass vessels. 'Retrieve it, and build me a temple,' he commanded. And Kempegowda joyfully did so.

For a temple this large, strangely (and sadly for us), there are no inscriptions to speak of. Based on architectural styles and context, historian Dr SK Aruni of the Indian Council of Historical Research ascribes the temple's *garbagriha* (sanctum sanctorum) and its inner hall to the Cholas who ruled this area about a thousand years ago. The main *mantapa* was built during the Vijayanagar period in the 1500s or 1600s. The Kamakshi Amman shrine within, according to Dr Aruni, was probably built in the 1700s, though according to others it dates from the 1600s.[4]

Take some time to look around the main *mantapa*. Its beautifully carved pillars— showing rearing horses and riders, the square carved panels on each column, the elegant *yali*-shaped balustrades—are typical of the Vijayanagar style of architecture: a slice of Hampi in the heart of Bengaluru. As in many of the pillars of the temples in that famed capital city, here too, you can find carved on the pillars scenes depicting stories of devotees, saints, geometric designs, monkeys, yoga asanas, seated lions, frolicking monkeys, dancers, hunters and many, many more.

The Someshwara temple in the 1890s.
Courtesy of British Library, Shelfmark BL 43041 (25)

Parvati weds Shiva. Brahma officiates as the priest while her father Himavan is on the left (with the crown of rocks). © *PeeVee*

The sculptures alone can keep you engaged for hours. Two particularly interesting motifs to look out for are the *gandabherunda* or double-headed eagle (shown here in an anthropomorphic form), and a shepherd wearing a cloak and resting on a staff. Often, this latter image is erroneously pointed out as being of Kempegowda.

A unique feature of the temple is the rather rare depiction of the Nava Nathas or the nine Shaiva saints, shown seated on nine different wild animals. Historian Anila Verghese first remarked on the unique depiction of all of these nine saints on the southern outer wall of the temple. Nowhere else is this kind of a portrayal—of all nine together—seen.

The 'Girija Kalyana' story—the marriage of Shiva and Parvati—is depicted in a number of temples in the region around Bengaluru. The sequence on the outer walls of the Kamakshi shrine is easily one of the finest in Bengaluru. The story begins from the southern wall, where Vishnu, Brahma and the groom Shiva, seated on Nandi, are shown setting out for the wedding. The subsequent figures show the *saptarishis* (the seven great sages), the *ashtadikpalas* (the guardians of

Who were the Nava Nathas?

The Nathas are a sect thought to date back to the tenth century and to have been founded by Matsyendranath, who is usually shown seated on a fish. In some traditions, the sect is said to have been founded by Adinatha, an incarnation of Shiva himself. One of the defining traits of the Natha *panthis* (or adherents of the Natha tradition) was their stress on yogic practices. In fact, one legend describes how Matsyendranath was once fishing somewhere in the Bay of Bengal when he hooked a large whale that swallowed him whole. The whale came to rest on the ocean floor near the spot Lord Shiva had chosen to convey the secrets of yoga to his wife Parvati, who fell asleep in the course of the lesson. When at one juncture Shiva asked, 'Are you listening?', promptly came an affirmative reply from an unexpected source: from within the belly of the whale. Matsyendranath had listened to all of Shiva's teaching. Lord Shiva then made Matsyendranath his disciple and taught him all the secrets of yoga. In this tradition, Matsyendranath is regarded as the one who then brought the science of yoga to the rest of the world.

The names of all the Nava Nathas are not known. The most popular and well-known ones are Matsyendranath and his disciple Gorakshanath, who is also said to be the founder of hatha yoga. The Nathas are depicted as seated on a fish, bear, tiger, snake, scorpion, tortoise, makara (a sea creature), antelope and boar.[6]

The Nathasampradaya or Natha cult became very popular in some parts of Karnataka and Andhra Pradesh in the medieval period. Depictions of Matsyendranath riding his fish are very popular in temples around Hampi. In Bengaluru, apart from the linear depiction here in Ulsoor, you can also see the Nava Nathas sculpted on the pillars in the Jalakantheswara temple near the fort.

The Nava Nathas on the walls of the Someshwara temple. © *PeeVee*

the eight directions), and other ascetics and divinities, all attending the wedding. On the northern side is the actual ceremony. Brahma officiates as the priest, and Parvati's father Himavan gives the bride away. Note the rocks on his headdress, indicating that he is the Lord of the Mountains! Notice also how, after the marriage, Shiva is once again shown on Nandi, but this time accompanied by his wife, the goddess Parvati.

II. A *Kalyani*

Traditionally, south Indian temples have *kalyanis*, small stepped tanks, to their northeast. And indeed, this is where you will find the Someshwara temple's *kalyani*. But, some years ago, you would not have found it at all. It was only in the year 2010 that a strange thing happened in Bengaluru: instead of the usual erasing of the past, we added some built heritage to the cityscape! The Muzrai Department of the state government excavated the old tank associated with the Someshwara temple. The tank, measuring approximately 12 metres by 10 metres, is at a spot where a cowshed and a little shop stood a few years ago.

The tank would have once been used in the temple's rituals, including the annual Teppotsava, a ritual when idols of the Lord and his consort are taken out on a float for a ride around the tank. The unearthing of the tank involved demolition of portions of some houses along its sides. This generated some controversy: the temple tank is mired in a court case and therefore inaccessible to the public, though you can see it from the outside.

As in the case of the temple itself, we have no exact date for the construction of this rectangular stepped tank; it probably dates from when Kempegowda expanded and renovated the temple in the 1500s. Locals say their grandparents remember the tank in the old days and that it was filled up about 150 years ago. Maps of the 1880s clearly show that the tank existed then, but it disappears from maps made in the early 1900s. This would coincide with the time of the plague and after, when the British were particularly concerned about hygiene and unsanitary conditions. That was probably when the tank was filled up.

The excavation of the tank threw up a lot of debris and some interesting artefacts. These include pieces of blue and white willow-patterned porcelain plates, gilt-edged porcelain teacups manufactured in Belgium, Canada and England, plenty of old-fashioned soda bottles and innumerable liquor bottles in all shapes and sizes—the last, no doubt, thanks to the alcohol-guzzling soldiers of the British military establishment nearby!

III. Ankamma Choultry

Continuing on the road past the *kalyani* and then turning left at the T-junction (don't miss the temple chariot in front of you) brings you to this striking building on Car Street. It is an example of the spirit of giving that moved people in the early 1900s. The *choultry*, or wedding hall, was built in 1929 by a Mr Subbaiah Reddy, expressly for charitable purposes. Named after his wife, Ankamma, it was given out rent-free for weddings; only the utility charges had to be paid. According to his granddaughter Gowri Reddy, 'There was this belief that if a thousand weddings happened in your *choultry*, you would get moksha!'[7] She also recalls that every year, during the temple chariot festival, Subbaiah Reddy would organise an *annadanam*, or food donation, in the *choultry*.

Reddy typifies the successful migrant who came to Bengaluru, made it big and then gave back to society. He came to Ulsoor from the village of Jangampalya, near Bengaluru. Beginning his career as a mason and working his way up to becoming a contractor, Reddy soon began working as a contractor for the British authorities. Some of the buildings he was involved in include the Isolation Hospital on Old Madras Road, the plague hospital in Neelasandra, and the Aurobindo Ashram in Ulsoor. He also built a number of large bungalows near Ulsoor.

The *choultry* is a clever, winning combination of east and west. It was built using beautifully wire-cut bricks, with Burma teak for the doors and windows, which are accentuated with pediments. Above the entrance is a bas-relief of Rama, Sita, Lakshmana and Hanuman. The sloping eaves on the lowest floor emphasise the linearity of the building. Hiding under the eaves at each corner are cherubic gargoyles.

The *choultry* is no longer rented out for weddings. It now hosts occasional exhibitions and sales.

Ankamma Choultry's aesthetic mix of vernacular and western architectural elements includes gods and goddesses in its bas relief and brackets. © *PeeVee*

IV. Car Street

Ulsoor's labyrinthine layout has several little lanes that wend their way into fast-disappearing slices of the past. The street on which Ankamma Choultry stands is one such lane, called Car Street, running about 350 metres and slightly wider than some of the other alleys. No, the name has nothing to do with automobiles. Rather, it derives from the temple chariot that is pulled down this street on its way around the temple during some festivals *(see box)*.

A postcard of the temple chariot in a procession in Ulsoor, 1918. *Courtesy of Rohit Hangal.*

As you head west from Ankamma Choultry, you will see some houses that stand out for their architecture, once again combining traditional or vernacular with a colonial style. Note the *jagalis*—the ledges that either line the front walls or the entrance itself. These are a typically Indian element of architecture, reflecting our cultural ethos as a gregarious, friendly society that thrives on social interactions. *Jagalis* embody a space that is neither fully public nor fully private, but is a transition from the street to the home. The *jagali* is multi-functional. In the mornings, you can perch on it as you haggle with the vegetable vendor. In the evenings, you can sit on it and chat with passers-by or watch the world go by. In the afternoons, you could even nap there.

Such vernacular-style houses with *jagalis* and carved wooden doors are still found in many parts of Ulsoor. © *PeeVee*

Another typical Indian feature is the grand entrance. On this street, you can see elaborate lintels over the doorways, combined with some colourfully painted doors, often flanked by niches to hold oil lamps. Look out, too, for that quintessential colonial Bengaluru feature: the monkey top *(see chapter 6)*. Several other decorative and unusual architectural elements catch the eye here. Flamboyantly decorated parapets, Art Deco sunbursts and other designs, intricately carved, almost lace-like wooden eaves, stucco decorated columns and Romanesque pilasters, all still hold their own against adjacent modern constructions.

When the Gods Walk the Streets

The Someshwara temple's many festivals are inextricably woven into the fabric of the lives of many Ulsoor's residents. Come April—May, it's time for the temple's annual Chariot or Car Festival: on the full moon day of the Hindu month of Chaitra, the beautifully decorated wooden temple chariot carrying the utsava murtis (festival idols) winds its way through some of Ulsoor's streets.

Ulsoor's most famous festival, the Poo Pallaki (or palanquin of flowers), takes place in April. It celebrates the marriage of the god Someshwara to the goddess Kamakshi. Spectacularly decorated palanquins carrying images of the god and goddess are joined by temple chariots from several other temples, followed by more than 80 flower palanquins. This grand procession wends its way through several streets in Ulsoor and Jogupalya before arriving at the Someshwara temple. The chariots were traditionally pulled by devotees but nowadays many are attached to tractors.

Many of the chariots in the *poo pallaki* are decorated by Muslim flower vendors. © PeeVee

The procession begins at around 1 am and ends after noon. Roads are lined with vendors, people dance in the streets, others queue up to be blessed by the gods and to make their offerings of flowers or bananas to them. On that special day, Ulsoor stays up all night, celebrating the divine marriage.

This festival draws people from around Bengaluru and surrounding areas. In typical Indian syncretism, the chariots used in the festival are decorated largely by Muslims.

V. Ulsoor Bazaar

Head south on any of the lanes perpendicular to Car Street to reach Bazaar Street, which is usually choc-a-bloc with traffic. The shops lining the street stock all manner of items, ranging from party costumes, false hair and false jewellery to regular clothes and watches. Some stores, like the stationery supplier Sumangali, have been around since the 1930s or earlier.

Opposite the Hanuman temple on Bazaar Street is a little lane through which you can nip into Ulsoor Bazaar. Though the bazaar today is a shadow of its former vibrant self, it is still worth a dekko. Until a few decades ago, it was the lifeline of the residents of the area and drew visitors from as far away as KR Puram, who flocked to its stores for everyday essentials like vegetables, oil, salt medicinal herbs and other essentials. Some of the shops are now being run by third- or fourth-generation members of the same family. Pop into the market if you'd like to stock up on familiar and unfamiliar spices, herbs and medicinal plants, vegetables, items needed for rituals and worship, and other knick-knacks.

VI. Wesleyan Church

About 100 metres west of the Hanuman temple on Bazaar Street is the Wesleyan Centenary Church, opened in February 1913. The presence of the church here dates to 1865 when Wesleyan missionaries first set up a Tamil-medium school for girls and a boarding house near here.[8] Later, Rev Pakianathan was in charge of the school and boarding for several years. The church was constructed in his memory. Built largely of stone, the church has some delicate details for the interested eye, including the lancet windows and the muntins on the main door.

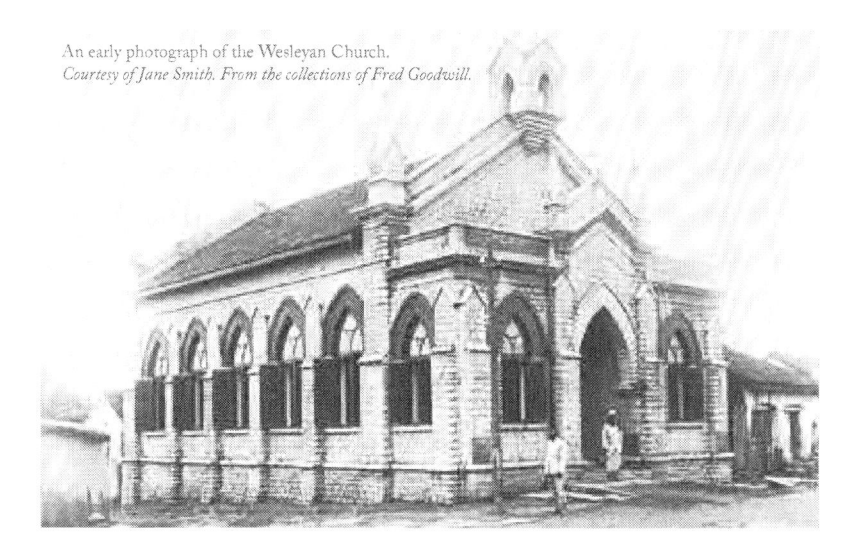

An early photograph of the Wesleyan Church.
Courtesy of Jane Smith. From the collections of Fred Goodwill.

VII. Ulsoor Lake and the Ghats

Continue on Bazaar Street another 250 metres or so and then turn right onto Kensington Road, now officially known as Bhaskaran Road. A walk of 200 metres or so brings you to one end of Ulsoor lake, easily the most loved and best known of all lakes in Bengaluru. The southern corner that you see here is where the overflow weir once stood. About 400 metres down the road and on your right, you can see the Ulsoor dhobi ghats, where there have been dhobis servicing the people of the Cantonment since the 1800s.

In the mid- and late 1800s, European troops were supplied with water from Ulsoor lake. However, the questionable quality of the water in the lake was a continuous cause for concern. Naturally enough, for dirty water from the Shivajinagar area flowed into Ulsoor lake. In the early 1860s, a sewer line was constructed which conducted this sewage under the lake and discharged it about 2 km away. Alongside, several years and a lot of money were spent on erecting pumps, tanks and filtration plants at the base of the rock on which the Kempegowda Tower stands, in order to pump water from the lake and supply it 'in unlimited quantities' and 'within reach of every soldier' (European, of course, not 'native'!) and his family, not to mention the horses.[9] However, because of continued unease over the quality of water in the lake, it was eventually supplied only for non-culinary uses. For drinking, water was pumped from wells in the dhobi ghats and supplied to the troops.

Today, like similar centres elsewhere in the city, the dhobis here primarily cater to hotels though they still do count some families among their clients. The dhobi ghats are also among the few open, tree-filled areas left in Ulsoor.

VIII. Trinity Church

You will need to double back on Kensington Road/Bhaskaran Road for a good kilometre towards MG Road. At the junction with MG Road, turn left onto Swami Vivekananda Road and you will see the entrance to the church a little beyond the petrol pump at the corner.

This is the Cantonment's second oldest Protestant church, after St Mark's Cathedral. By the 1830s, the Cantonment had already grown so much that 2000 people attended services at St Mark's, though the building could only accommodate 450 people. This lack of space finally led to the construction of the Holy Trinity Church. Its foundation stone was laid in 1848 and it was consecrated in 1851 by Rev Dealtry, the then Bishop of Madras. It began to be used for worship in 1852. Incidentally, this made Bengaluru the first military station to flout the 'one station, one church' rule that the East India Company then had.[10]

The church building was designed by Maj JT Pears, then Superintending Engineer in Bengaluru. His initial design was rather utilitarian. In order to 'add to the ecclesiastical appearance', the Bishop of Madras suggested some additions, including that the belfry be an ornamental spire that would be visible from almost everywhere in the Cantonment.[11] Here's a fun factoid: if you grew up listening to the chimes of the Big Ben on the BBC, it may interest you to know that Trinity Church's bell was cast in the same foundry as the Big Ben—the Mears Foundry in London—in 1847.

The church is adorned with an extraordinary number of plaques and memorials, some of them very beautifully executed, which give us a glimpse into Bengaluru's military past. Take a look also at the pews, some of which still carry brass plates with designations and regiments, defining very clearly who was to sit where in the church. The first few rows, naturally, were reserved for bigwigs in the Cantonment including the British Resident, the GOC (General Officer Commanding), military officers, the chaplain and so on.

Trinity Church, a Tucks postcard. *Courtesy of TucksDB.*

After Independence, the church was initially taken over by Indian Christian soldiers and their families, and for a few years it was known as the Holy Trinity Garrison Pastorate. In 1965, it was renamed the Holy Trinity Church. It is now part of the Karnataka Central Diocese of the Church of South India.

The first few pews were reserved for officers in the C and M Station including from Queen Alexandra's Imperial Military Nursing Service for India (QAIMNS, seen here). © *PeeVee*

• • • • •

We conclude our short walk around Ulsoor here. As you would have noticed, the area is undergoing rapid transformation. The street in front of the temple, which was once full of traditional residences housing priests, is now full of modern multistorey buildings. The Metro has riven the neighbourhood into two, with the formerly socially contiguous area of Jogupalya now being separated. But despite the changes in the built environment, and especially away from the main streets, the old settlement lives on. As in the *pete* area, you will see different communities and their respective temples; for example, the small Marathi-speaking community that has built and worships at the Shree Rakhumaee Mandir. Boys still play on the streets, some lanes end at houses, and men and women still stand outside their doors to chat. As in most of India, the old lives comfortably with the new.

Notes

1. Based on an architectural listing of Ulsoor, carried out by INTACH in 2015.
2. Ulsoor resident interviewed by Pallavi Murthy, for INTACH, September 2015.
3. Rice 1905, 26.
4. Aruni 2007; Puttaiya 1923.
5. Verghese 2001; also see Aruni 2007, 31–33.
6. Verghese 2001.
7. Gowri Reddy interviewed by Pallavi Murthy for INTACH, September 2015.
8. Anon 1865.
9. There was also a proposal to build a water tank on top of the Kempegowda Tower that was, however, dropped because 'the natives did regard it [the tower] with veneration'. Romilly 1880.
10. Penny 1922, 154.
11. Penny 1922, 155.

Basavanagudi and its vicinity in 1884-85. From, Survey of India. *Cantonment and City of Bangalore and Environs, Season 1884-85. Courtesy of Mythic Society, Bengaluru.*

Basavanagudi and its vicinity in 1935-36. From, Survey of India. *Bangalore Guide Map. Surveyed 1935-36. Courtesy of Naresh Narasimhan.*

CHAPTER 4

The Expanding City: Basavanagudi and its Vicinity

A Short History of Extensions to Bengaluru

One of the curious things about Bengaluru is how its history and evolution have been shaped so strongly by some rather unwholesome little beasties. The first is the mosquito, the reason the British left Srirangapatna and moved to Bengaluru where the weather and other things beckoned. The second was *Vibrio cholerae*, the bacterium that causes cholera. The third and most potent city shaper was also the most dreaded: *Yersinia pestis*, the bacterium that causes bubonic plague.

Cholera was a frequent unwanted visitor to Bengaluru in the 1800s. Medical journals of the time were full of alarming reports about the insanitary conditions in Indian towns and the resultant cholera epidemics that recurred with dismaying frequency. A *British Medical Journal* volume in 1880, for example, notes how there was 'international interest' in the 'fluctuating prevalence of cholera in its home'.[1] In response, the British government set up Sanitary Commissions in various cities that produced Sanitary Reports detailing the efforts required and the measures taken to clean up.

As we have seen, the Bengaluru of those days was unique in that it was really two cities, administered by two different governments. On one side of the administrative divide, the Cantonment was already being expanded. It was not long before the authorities in charge of Bengaluru city, too, set their minds to planning its growth.

Accordingly, in 1889, at the initiative of the Dewan of Mysore, K Seshadri Iyer, the government of the Maharaja of Mysore constituted a Bangalore City Improvement Committee. The committee comprised several heavyweights including Lt Col AH Macintire, who was then Deputy Commissioner of the district, Col C Bowen, later Mysore State's first Chief Engineer, and others. Two years later, KP Puttana Chetty, who became President of the Bangalore City Municipality, PN Krishnamurti, later Dewan of Mysore State, and others formed part of this high-powered committee.[2] The committee's task was simple: the city's population was growing, and it needed places to expand into. The aim was to ensure that the city's expansion was a planned one. Death and disease weighed heavily on the minds of the committee members, of course, but these were not the only considerations when planning extensions to the city.

KP Puttana Chetty served as President of the Bangalore City Municipality and also as Deputy Commissioner. *Courtesy of Nenapu Museum, former State Bank of Mysore.*

The earliest extension, New Tharagupete, was formed because the old Tharagupete was 'condemned from a sanitary point'.[3] The new extension was formed by buying up lands just west of the fort, including some properties in Pioneercherri; these had been settled by pensioners of the Queens Own Madras Sappers and Miners—the forerunners of the MEG—from when they had been headquartered in Bengaluru, way back in the early 1800s. New Tharagupete was partly a commercial extension, with around a hundred new shop sites, each measuring 30 feet by 100 feet (approximately 9 metres by 30.5 metres).[4]

Meanwhile, residential extensions to the city had already been planned. In a letter to Dewan Seshadri Iyer in 1889, the chair of the City Improvement Committee, Lt Col Macintire, proposed the 'Extension of Guthalli (*sic*) village' including laying connecting roads, all for the princely sum of Rs 6000.[5] Another item proposed was the 'Extension of Town on Gavipur side' for which about 150 acres to the south of the fort could be acquired. These were to become the Western and Northern extensions to the city. From all the (luckily for us) copious letter-writing between the various parties concerned, including officers of the City Municipality, the Dewan, the Chief Secretary and others, we learn that by the early 1890s, these proposals had moved from the realm of thought to that of action.

By 1892, the acquired lands for the Western Extension had already been divvied up in the form of a regular rectangular grid. Some plots had been sold and a few early birds had begun constructing houses there. This, then, was the first residential extension to the old city. Shortly after, the Northern Extension was carved out of a village called Malenahalli. In late 1892, land was acquired from villagers here (who were resettled nearby, close to today's Mantri Mall). Malenahalli and surrounding lands were divided into 109 sites and a few more for large bungalows.[6] The Northern Extension is today known as Seshadripuram. In the mid-1890s, the erstwhile Western Extension was named Chamarajendrapete and is today known as Chamarajpete.

An extension named for a king

Chamarajpete was, of course, named after Chamaraja Wodeyar X, the ruler of the Mysore kingdom between 1881 and 1894.

A total of 1152 sites were marked out over an area of 196 acres, each measuring 30 feet by 108 feet. In addition, four large sites of about 1.5 to 2 acres, and 13 smaller ones of about half an acre each, were also created. These sites were to be sold according to caste and community. For example, there were 270 sites reserved for Brahmins, 42 for Vaishyas, 72 for Nagarthas, 78 for Muslims, and so on. By the mid-1890s, many of these had already been sold, conservancy lanes *(see box)* laid out and avenue trees ('cocoanuts and other trees') planted.[7] Early buyers in Chamarajpete included some eminent personalities such as KP Puttana Chetty among others. The prices of sites in Chamarajpete then are likely to cause bemusement: in the mid-1890s, sites were sold for Rs 20 to Rs 25.

Many of today's Bengalureans will either despair or be tickled to hear that even in those early days, different arms of the government were bickering over their responsibilities, while residents suffered the consequences—a situation that is all too familiar to many of us today. About four years after the extension was formed, residents of Chamarajpete submitted a petition to Dewan Seshadri Iyer (calling him 'the father of the extension'), begging the government to take care of poor lighting, poor roads, poor conservancy and so on. (This petition is also interesting for the diversity of languages the petitioners sign in; Kannada, Telugu, Hindi, English and Urdu are clearly discernible.) The Sanitary Engineer (Standish Lee) and the President of the Municipal Commission (TT Leonard) exchanged some letters about responsibilities in the wake of this petition. The latter describes how, as of 1896, the eastern portion of Chamarajpete was occupied, but the western portion only sparsely so. He also paints a rather sorry picture of things, remarking how, since some of the houses did not have toilets,

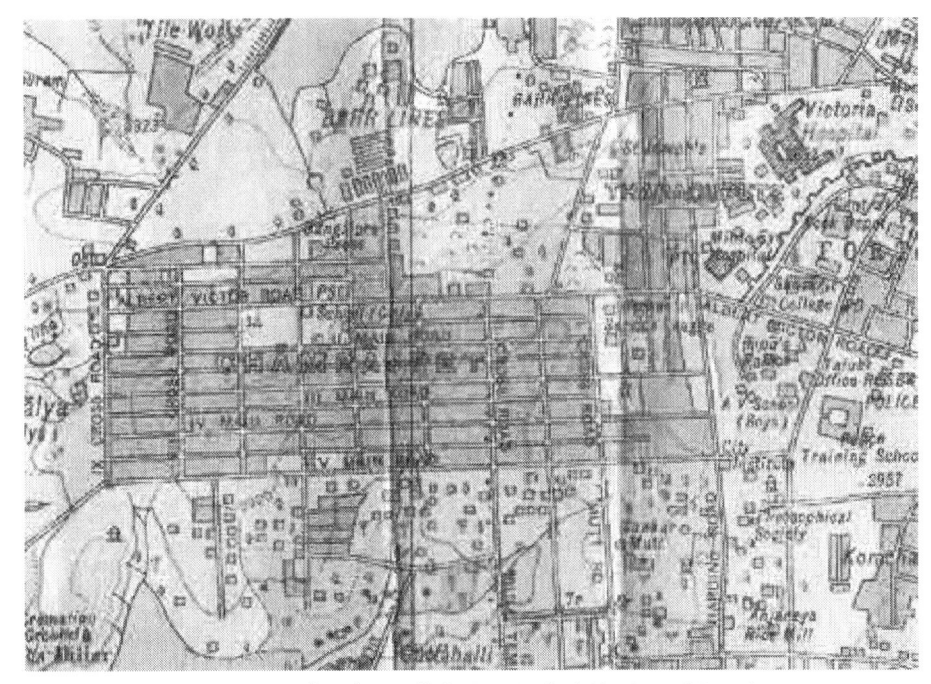

Chamarajpete in 1924-25. From, Survey of India. *Bangalore Guide Map, Surveyed 1924-25.* *Courtesy of Naresh Narasimhan.*

the 'occupiers of such commit nuisance wherever they can, the unbuilt sites being very convenient for this purpose'.[8]

It was only in the second half of the first decade of the 1900s that the government finally got around to providing drains in Chamarajpete. However, perhaps Mr Leonard was being overly critical, or perhaps the extension shaped up soon, or both, because all the plots in Chamarajapete were bought up in just three years. And by 1914, 5000 people called Chamarajpete home.[9]

In the mid-1890s, the President of the City Improvement Committee, Arcot Srinivasacharulu, wrote to the government that the purpose for which the committee had been constituted had been served: 'all the sites in the Northern and Western extensions have been allotted, fair roads made, wells excavated, drains built, and as many of the sites have been built upon and most of the houses occupied.' This being the case, the two new extensions could now be transferred to the Municipality and the committee could hang up its boots, he suggested. The government concurred, saying the 'work of extension has been carried by the Committee with vigor *(sic)* and promptitude, and the best thanks of the Government are due to the gentlemen who served on the Committee'. The committee having served its purpose, it could now be disbanded.[10]

What is a Conservancy Lane?

Conservancy is a euphemism for the disposal of human excreta. In the early days of Indian cities, night soil was disposed of in cesspits. Often, these were cleared only infrequently. In the 1880s, the City Municipality and the C&M Station's Municipal Commission both passed laws that required night soil to be cleared every day. Conservancy lanes were built which allowed access to the backyards of houses: workers would come along these lanes, enter the backyards where the toilets were, and remove night soil every night or very early in the morning every day.

And then came the plague

Bubonic plague. The very name conjures up horrific images of suffering and death. Indeed, just such scenes were visited upon Bengaluru fairly regularly in the past. Frequent visitations of the plague were not uncommon in the 1800s. But the plague epidemic of 1898 was notable for its scale. In October 1898, when the disease became endemic in Bengaluru, more than 2800 people died of plague and approximately 40 per cent of the population left for safer areas.[11]

The first officially recorded case of bubonic plague in India hit Mumbai (then Bombay) in 1896.[12] From there, it spread through the country, hitting some parts—such as Pune, Belgaum, Sholapur and Hubballi (or Hubli)—very hard. The tentacles of plague reached Bengaluru via Hubballi, then under the Bombay Presidency. From 1897 onwards, the Mysore government swung into action, taking several measures to prevent the epidemic from reaching Bengaluru. The railways (which came to Bengaluru in 1864 when the Cantonment station was built) posed one of the biggest dangers. Passengers entering the city were inspected initially at all the entry points to the city: Yeshwantpur and Kengeri railway stations in the north and south respectively, and also at the Cantonment station. Police and railway officials were trained to spot possible cases of infection and ask: 'Did you get ill suddenly? Did you feel fever come on with shivering?' and so on.[13] 'Look at his skin and under his armpits,' they were instructed. If the officers deemed a person infected, a protocol was to be followed: he or she was to be isolated, clothing burned, or if of high value, washed and kept in the sun for several hours; soiled cloth and bandages were to be burnt, and so on. Meanwhile, segregation camps were also made ready.

Ambulances to take plague-infected people to the hospital.
From, *Les Missions Catholiques*, Vol 31, 1899, p606.

But despite their best efforts, the disease did hit Bengaluru. On 12 August 1898, a railway Superintendent and his helper returned to Bengaluru from Hubballi, bringing the plague with them.[14] The helper died, becoming the city's first casualty of the notorious epidemic. The very next day, the plague appeared in the coolies in the goods shed of the Southern Mahratta Railway. From there, it was not long before it spread to the rest of the city. Over the next six months, several thousand people lost their lives to the plague.

One of the consequences of this horrific death toll was the realisation that the old city needed to expand further to relieve congestion and open up some areas. True, plans for new extensions had already been made some years earlier. Given how plots in Chamarajapete had been snapped up and how land prices were increasing, in 1896, TT Leonard, the President of the City Municipal Commission, recommended that 270 acres of land in the vicinity be bought for further extensions, with another 170 acres set aside in reserve. He scoped out the area along with Standish Lee who declared the terrain acceptable from a sanitary perspective.[15] But though the suggestion to buy land was accepted, it was not implemented.

Until the plague. Following a government order dated 16 September 1898, a Special Improvement Division was formed which was tasked with improvements to the city; the immediate aim was to improve sanitation as a measure against the spread of the plague. Four days later, a government order was issued, notifying land that was needed for the Basavanagudi extension.

• • • • • •

The Land of Basava

On 4 October 1898, in the quaint governmentese typical of those times, VP Madhava Rao, the Plague Commissioner for Mysore, wrote to the Secretary of the Government of Mysore for funds: 'I have the honor to request that Government will be pleased to place a sum of Rs 25,000 at the credit of the Deputy Commissioner, Bangalore District, for the acquisition of lands required for the Basavanagudi and Malleswara Extensions and the City Improvement.'[17]

The government immediately sanctioned the money, requesting the Deputy Commissioner (KP Puttanna Chetty) to be 'good enough to expedite the submission of a draft declaration in respect of lands'. The lands identified for acquisition to form the new extension of Basavanagudi were in the villages Karanji Bisara Halli, Upparahalli and Yediyur Nagasandra.[18] The impression conveyed by the subsequent frenetic exchange of letters between the Plague Commissioner, the Deputy Commissioner of Bangalore district, the Sanitary Engineer and the Maharaja's Government, is of men on a mission. Just three months after his first request, Puttanna Chetty (who incidentally was a resident of the newly formed Chamarajpete) reported that Rs 47,000 had already been spent on the new extensions, and would the government be pleased to release a further sum of Rs 50,000?[19]

And so it went: money was sanctioned, lands acquired, extensions were formed. Thus was born Basavanagudi (and Malleswara, also called Malleswaram).

The site chosen for Basavanagudi was a little south of the existing extension of Chamarajpete. It was named after the old temple at one end of the new extension that was dedicated to Basava (or Nandi), the bull regarded as Shiva's mount—hence the name Basavanagudi, or the Bull Temple. Land to the tune of 440 acres was acquired and divided into sites. As in Chamarajpete, here too, different sized sites were marked out, and some were kept aside for larger bungalows or villas. And as in Chamarajpete, sites were marked out for different communities *(see map)*.

Why was this new extension not made contiguous to the slightly older Chamarajpete extension? Was it perhaps because the intervening lands were covered by Karanji *kere*, which was drying up by the late 1890s? Eight years after the establishment of the extension, a group of Basavanagudi's residents wrote a petition to the government in which, among other demands, was this: 'That the tank bed on either side of the main road from the Fort be ordered to be filled up and converted into a public park or play ground. ... In the tank bed are seen pools of water during the greater part of the year, and as such,

An 1890s map showing the lands in villages south of Chamarajapete that were to be acquired for the Basavanagudi extension (in red). *Redrawn by Priyani Pranab from a file in KSA.*

it becomes a fertile breeding ground for mosquitoes and malaria.'[20] In 1913, Karanji *kere* was finally filled up.

Basavanagudi was laid out on a gridiron plan, like Chamarajpete. In other words, the land was divided into rectangular plots, with roads running north–south and east–west. And again like Chamarajpete, Basavanagudi had conservancy lanes 12–15 feet wide, which ran behind the houses. However, Basavanagudi was unique in that of all the new extensions, it alone had a very large public square at its centre, with four diagonal roads extending from each of its corners. The approach roads to the extensions, the boundary and the diagonal roads were all made 100 feet wide. The rest of the roads were between 40 and 60 feet.

The amount to be charged for these newly minted sites was a matter of considerable debate. Standish Lee was of the opinion that the sites should be priced so that their sale would recover the moneys spent on creating the layout. By his recommendation, a site measuring about 30 feet by 108 feet— these were the so-called 'ordinary house sites'—would cost Rs 115.[21] However, given that a similar site in Chamarajpete had sold for Rs 20–Rs 25, the chief administrators were all of the opinion that this was too high a price. As the

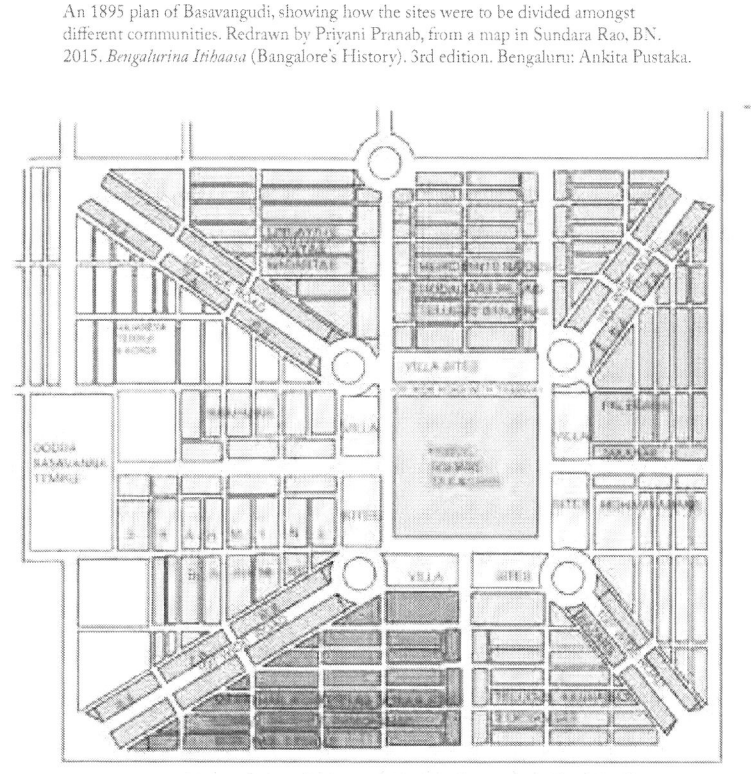

An 1895 plan of Basavangudi, showing how the sites were to be divided amongst different communities. Redrawn by Priyani Pranab, from a map in Sundara Rao, BN. 2015. *Bengalurina Itihaasa* (Bangalore's History). 3rd edition. Bengaluru: Ankita Pustaka.

PLAN OF BASAVANAGUDI EXTENSION 1894 AREA 440 ACRES

Plague Commissioner, VP Madhava Rao, said, 'Extensions were primarily started with a view to relieve the overcrowding in the city and provide accommodation for people whose houses were either dismantled on sanitary grounds or were taken up for opening out conservancy lanes; … the prayer of the people that the hardship suffered by them on account of the plague may be taken into consideration.' And so it was that the prices of sites were fixed at Rs 30 per site, or Re 1 for 100 square feet.

In 1899-1900, a number of people from the Revenue Survey Office bought plots along one particular street, now called Surveyor Street. *From KSA.*

Plague-defined Architecture

The experience of plague affected the architecture of the newer extensions, distinguishing them from the older Chamarajpete. In the late 1800s, the cause of the plague was still not well understood. It was still thought to be induced or exacerbated by such environment-related factors as lack of ventilation and light, dampness and so on. It was in the 1890s that *Yersinia pestis*, the bacterium that causes plague, was discovered in rats, thus suggesting that rodents had something to do with transmission of the disease. But it wasn't until 1908 that the link between rats and the plague was firmly established. It took another decade or so for this link to be popularly accepted.[22] Until then, the emphasis while planning extensions was on ensuring adequate ventilation and open spaces.

This was why houses were built contiguously in Chamarajpete whereas a plague-induced horror of closeness precluded row houses in Basavanagudi (and Malleswaram). Instead, each house was separated from the other by open spaces. According to Krishna Iyengar, Deputy Chief Engineer of the Public Works Department of the Mysore government in the 1910s, the open spaces between houses in the newer extensions 'certainly secures better light and ventilation, although the contiguous houses present a better street picture'.[23]

Plague Camps

About a year after the plague first reached India, by which time an epidemic of the disease was raging across parts of the country, the Mysore government set up plague camps in several parts of the city. These were essentially temporary constructions—huts made of jungle wood, tiles or sometimes thatched roofs—erected for the purpose of isolating people suffering from the disease. Plague Camps, sometimes euphemistically called Health Camps, were set up on Guttahalli Road in Gavipura, Bull Temple Road, Kankanahally Road, Bannerghatta Road, Hosur Road and Magadi Road, among others. The last named was one of the first to be built and was infamous as the place of no return.[24]

Strangest of all was the case of the camp at Basavanagudi, which was right in the heart of the new extension. The next time you stroll down the tree-lined Krishna Rao Road or the genteel HB Samaja Road, imagine a series of sheds along the road, for that is where the plague camp was located. Needless to say, those who had bought sites nearby were not amused. Here they were, thinking they'd move to Basavanagudi to avoid 'congestion' like the ... er ... plague, only to find the plague staring them in the face! Finally, in 1912, one such new resident of Basavanagudi, a Mr Narayanaswamy Iyengar, petitioned the government for the removal of the camp, stating that it was a danger to him and his family. The petition may have been prompted by the resurgence of plague (in a mild form, luckily) in 1910–11, when it originated in these very plague camps.[25]

A segregation camp in north Bengaluru. A similar camp stood near Krishna Rao and HB Samaja Roads till the early 1920s. From, *Les Missions Catholiques*, Vol 31, 1899, p586.

The Municipality, of course, recognised the danger. When they had first established the camp, the area around had been open ground. By the time of Narayanaswamy Iyengar's petition, 'numerous costly dwelling-houses had sprung up to the north, south and west of the camp, and were being constructed east of it too'.[26] However, it was only in the 1920s that this plague camp was removed and the land thus freed up was divided into bungalow sites and sold by public auction. We can imagine what poor Mr Narayanaswamy Iyengar felt, looking out onto the plague camp for so long; he was most likely not amused.

More New Extensions

The success of Basavanagudi (and Malleswaram) and the huge demand for new houses led the City Municipality and the government to come up with new extensions. Shankarpuram was established in 1908,[27] and Visveswarapuram, named after Sir M Visvesvaraya, in 1919.[28]

Today, all these localities have a distinct flavour, different from any other part of the city. It is in their architecture and layout, their communities and faiths, their eateries and culture. Walk through these neighbourhoods to get a glimpse of the quintessence of south Bengaluru.

Walk 1: Through Basavanagudi

In which you experience nature, culture, literature and architecture

- BK Mariappa Charities
- Mahila Seva Samaja
- Sajjan Rao Choultry
- Ramakrishna Math
- National High School
- Vani Vilas Road
- Lalbagh Botanical Garden
- Gandhi Bazaar
- Basavanagudi Union and Service Club
- BP Wadia Road
- Bull Temple
- Bugle Rock Park
- MN Krishna Rao Park and Pavilion
- Anglican Church
- Gokhale Institute of Public Affairs

a. Old East West School Building
b. Indian Institute of World Culture
c. MR Narendra's house
d. Old Home School

Walk 1: Through Basavanagudi. © *INTACH Benglauru Chapter*

I. MN Krishna Rao Park

We begin our walk at Basavanagudi's largest park. This central, large, square open space was inked into the gridiron plan for Basavanagudi from the very beginning. Early photos of the area show that it was just that—an open space. It took the interest of an acting Dewan to change it into the tree-filled park you see today. In the early 1940s, Rajakaryaprasakta Dewan Bahadur (later Sir) Mysore Nanjundiah Krishna Rao, who lived right next to the park, donated Rs 20,000 for its development. Rightly, the park is now named after him. Sir MN Krishna Rao officiated as Dewan in 1931, when Sir Mirza Ismail travelled to England for the Round Table Conference, and later for a brief period after the latter resigned. Rao was conferred a knighthood for his contribution to the Mysore State administration.

Sir MN Krishna Rao.
Courtesy of MR Narendra.

Naturally enough, the park has always served as the locus of activities for Basavanagudi's residents. In its early days, apart from cricket, football and other games, the park also served as a news and entertainment hub. One resident recalled how every evening, a radio would play in the park, beginning with the news at 6 pm, followed by music, and ending with the BBC's news broadcast at 9 pm.[29] At some point, this 25-acre park was set aside expressly for women and children, apparently at the behest of Krishna Rao himself.[30]

The MN Krishna Rao Park. © *Aravind C*

In 1964, the Bangalore Water Supply and Sewerage Board (BWSSB) was constituted and plans were laid to pump water from the Cauvery river all the way to Bengaluru. The reservoir in the northwest corner of the park and the charming, circular BWSSB office near it both date from that time.

The park continues to remain one of Basavanagudi's most popular lung spaces, popular with all sections of society including walkers, joggers, nature lovers, seniors and, of course, children.

The Krishna Rao Pavilion in MN Krishna Rao Park. © *Aravind C*

II. Krishna Rao Pavilion

At the centre of the Krishna Rao Park is the Krishna Rao Pavilion, which was built thanks to a donation of Rs 15,000 from Sir MN Krishna Rao. Completed in 1941, this unusual two-storeyed masonry building has an octagonal plan, a segmented dome and external staircases. It was designed by the German architect Otto Koenigsberger, Chief Architect of Mysore State at the time. It is said that the final design of the building had a lot to do with Sir Mirza, who was partial to domes and axial symmetry; Koenigsberger himself was a little unhappy with the final look of the building![31] Take a look at the foundation stone, which was laid by Sir MN Krishna Rao.

III. Anglican Church

Head out of the park via the southern entrance, turn left and walk about 250 metres, past Arumugam Circle till you see Church Road on your left. A short walk on this road will bring you to the Anglican Church in Basavanagudi. A plaque inside notes that the foundation stone was laid on 8 March 1907, by Mrs Stuart Fraser, wife of the then British Resident, Sir Stuart M Fraser. Incidentally, just five days later, Mrs Fraser laid the foundation stone of a different sort of building in another part of Bengaluru that was also related to the plague *(see chapter 6)*. It appears that the building of the church caused a little unease among some of Basavanagudi's early residents. A year after the foundation stone had been laid, FW Heycock, chaplain at St Mark's, wrote to Stuart Fraser: 'I hope the tension at Basavanagudi will soon be relieved and the church will be enabled to fulfil the purpose for which it was ostensibly built.'[32]

Stained glass window in the Anglican Church, Basavanagudi. © *Aravind C*

The church is said to have been built thanks to the efforts of a YB Ponayya, a teacher at the London Mission School, and one of the earliest settlers in the section allotted to Christians. The stained glass window at the altar end of the church, brought all the way from England, is dedicated to the late Thangamma Ponayya, the wife of Mr Ponayya. CR Ponniah, the founder's grandson (who spells his name differently from his grandfather), and GA Anandhraj now look after this little church. It was CR Ponniah who added the little extensions on either side of the building in order to give it the shape of the cross. The church has services in English and Kannada.

IV. Old Home School

Walk up Church Road, keeping the BS Madhava Rao Circle (named after an eminent mathematician) to your left. Facing the Circle, between Kanakapura Road and Krishna Rao Road, is a two-storeyed bungalow in a large garden. This old bungalow is a little unusual for these parts in having predominantly colonial (rather than vernacular) elements, such as the arched facade and the lack of a courtyard inside the house.

From 1930, this building housed one of Basavanagudi's oldest and most well-known schools, The Home School, started by Ms Robinson, daughter of an American missionary, and Ms Donne, a British lady. In 1999, the school was asked to move out of these premises. After some years, the family that owns the property finally won a legal battle to regain their house. The family still lives here. The Home School continues to function from a new building nearby.

V. MR Narendra's House

Cross Kanakapura Road and head to the corner of North Public Square Road and Kanakapura Road. Dewan Sir MN Krishna Rao's house is said to have been the third house built in the locality. It still stands near the park, in almost pristine, unchanged glory.

According to MR Narendra, MN Krishna Rao's grandson, the *gruhapravesham* (house-warming ceremony) took place on 7 November 1907, at which point only the ground floor had been completed.[33] The first floor was added ten years later, to accommodate the extended and growing family.

In typical vernacular style, the house has a courtyard. Earlier, the large hall adjacent to it served as the dining hall. Rosewood staircases, Ansonia grandfather clocks, gleaming red-oxide flooring, teak doors, an ornate swing, cherished pictures of the Maharaja of Mysore and many other memorabilia are all lovingly looked after by MR Narendra. One of the many interesting artefacts is an antique Scott radio: according to Narendra, the Yuvaraja of Mysore himself had once visited the house just to see this!

In 2017, this house was the well-deserved recipient of an INTACH Heritage Award.

The beautifully maintained interiors of Narendra's house, with traditional red oxide flooring and period furniture. © *PaeYe*

VI. Indian Institute of World Culture

Walk back on Kanakapura Road about 100 metres towards MN Krishna Park and turn right at BP Wadia Road. About 80 metres down this road, you will find the Indian Institute of World Culture, established in 1945. Its founder, the theosophist BP Wadia, had envisioned it as a cultural centre for ordinary people, to 'give them a breadth of outlook resting solidly on the foundation of eternal verities which do not belong exclusively to any age or clime, nation or creed', and to make available 'nuggets of knowledge which make a man more healthy in body, more wealthy in mind, more noble in heart, more self-sacrificing in spirit'.[34]

To promote intercultural exchange and the ideal of universal brotherhood, the institute organises nearly 150 cultural programmes, lectures, seminars and exhibitions every year at its premises, all free and open to the public. Talks in Kannada and English are on such diverse topics as combating loneliness, science in India and aspects of the Ramayana, to name a few; in addition, there are cultural events such as dance and classical music. Luminaries who have given talks at the institute include DV Gundappa, VK Krishna Menon, JBS Haldane, Kengal Hanumanthiah and many others.

The crowning jewel of the institute is its library, which began in a humble way in 1947, with a few hundred books. Today, it has about 45,000 books and a children's section with a further 10,000 books. There is also a reading room, which has subscriptions to about 150 journals and magazines from all around the world.

VII. Old East West School Building

About 200 metres further down BP Wadia Road, at Tagore Circle, a delightful though somewhat derelict building still attracts the attention of passers-by. This building once housed the East West School; classes were held in the rooms of the house and the assembly in the courtyard. The school was established in 1961 by Elizabeth and Sophia TenBroeck, American theosophists. Today, it is housed in a new building near Arumugam Circle, a short distance away. This old house is still standing only because it is locked in a legal battle over ownership.

The house had been bought by Sophia's father and Elizabeth's husband, William Davis TenBroeck. He and Elizabeth were close associates of BP Wadia, the founder of the Indian Institute of World Culture. In fact, early meetings of the institute were held in this very house. Sophia TenBroeck later served as the Vice President of the institute for several years.[35]

Architecturally, it is an extremely interesting building; being located on a corner site also influences its plan. The entrance is provided at the junction and the projecting bays are on both the roads. The entrance is defined by a

The beautiful bungalow where the East West School began. © *Aravind C*
It was demolished in October 2019.

pillared verandah, with an open balcony on the first floor. The building has a combination of a flat roof and a sloping roof.

VIII. Basavanagudi Union and Service Club

Across Tagore Circle on KR Road is Basavanagudi's oldest cultural hub, dating back to 1901. The Union was started thanks to the enthusiasm of Bellave Venkatanaranappa, a professor of physics at Central College, a founder member of the Kannada Sahitya Parishad, and one of Basavanagudi's earliest settlers. He believed people here needed a place where they 'could get together as friends and spend their time in a jolly manner'.[36] In 1907, the members of the Union, with L Sreenivasaiengar as President and Prof Venkatanaranappa as Secretary, petitioned the Maharaja's government for a free site. 'Want of provision for outdoor recreation has often been felt,' they said, adding, 'in consequence of the distance of the Extension from their respective offices, [members] will have no inclination to stop anywhere in the middle for recreatory purposes, however much they may feel the necessity to do so.' However, a new building that would house a reading room and a tennis court, they felt would 'meet the demands of a much larger number of the people of this growing Extension'.[37] The requested site was granted, not free, but at an upset price of Rs 132.

This club was also known as Masti Club, after one of its most illustrious members, the litterateur Masti Venkatesh Iyengar. Other well-known members included DV Gundappa, KS Aiyar (who made a donation for the building of the main hall), LS Venkoji Rao (founder of Vijaya College) and the cricketer G Vishwanath. Prof Venkatanaranappa is said to have built part of the walls himself. The building was renovated in 2007.

Jnanpith award-winner Masti Venkatesh Iyengar was a member of the Basavanagudi Club, which was sometimes referred to as the Masti Club! *Courtesy of K Ranganath, grandson of Masti Venkatesh Iyengar.*

Interestingly, membership to the club was exclusive: only men above the age of 55 were admitted, and membership fees were pegged at Re 1, the same as the price of 100 square feet of land! Not surprisingly, members were largely drawn from the upper class. Many of them were also Brahmins, because of which the club was also called a 'Brahmanara Koota', or Brahmins' Club.[38]

That was then. Today, the club has more than 700 people who enjoy a multitude of services and facilities including badminton, table tennis, billiards, multi gym facilities, a bar, library and party halls. The old structure has been completely rebuilt and little remains of the old building that was the haunt of Basavanagudi's early intellectuals.

IX. Gandhi Bazaar

The market street on which the Basavanagudi Union stands is a visual and olfactory feast. Gandhi Bazaar is lined with flower sellers on one footpath, all of them vying for your eye with their creative display of colourful merchandise.

Gandhi Bazaar is famous for its flowers, fruits, vegetables, spices and items required for worship. © *PeeVee*

Gandhi Bazaar once had several bungalows. Sir SP Rajagopalachari's Lakshmi Bhavan (*left*) built in the 1920s, stood near the intersection of Gandhi Bazaar and Bull Temple Roads. Chief Engineer MG Rangaiah's house (*right*), built in 1926, was on Gandhi Bazaar Main Road. *Courtesy of Krishna & Aruna Chidambi, and the family of MG Rangaiah.*

Along the other footpath are vegetable sellers, equally creative in their display and only slightly less colourful. Also lining the street are several famous eateries and shops selling textiles, shoes and items required for worship. These last are particularly interesting, for here you can find herbs to eat, wash your hair with, keep mosquitoes away, and of course offer during worship.

This street was initially named Northwest Diagonal Road, and later Angadi Beedi, meaning Shop Street. In the late 1920s, on one of his visits to Bengaluru, Mahatma Gandhi is said to have visited this street. According to local lore, he visited one of the buildings near the beginning of the street and gave a short speech there. Apparently, the chair he sat on was preserved for many years. Others say Gandhiji bought and drank some tender-coconut water at a shop here. His visit was immortalised by renaming the road after him.

Old-timers recall how the road was largely residential; shops were limited to near the intersection of the street with DVG Road. Many of the street vendors have been here for several decades; some have stalls that span generations. A few establishments to look out for include the ever-popular Vidyarthi Bhavan, started in 1943 and famous for its crunchy ghee-laden dosas; Srinivasa Condiments, better known as Subbamma Angadi, well known for its spicy-salty 'Congress' peanut snack and other eats like *chaklis*; Udupi Sri Krishna Bhavan, which has its main branch in Balepete and which is famous for its luscious *badam halwa* among other things; and the almost 70-year-old perfumery named Perfumerr. Just off Gandhi Bazaar, near its intersection with Govindappa Road, is Vyasaraja Math, one of the many *maths* (also spelt *matha* and *matt*) or religious institutions that you will find along Basavanagudi's streets.

X. Ramakrishna Math

At the other end of Gandhi Bazaar road, at Ashram Circle, turn right onto Bull Temple Road. A few metres ahead, to your left, is the Ramakrishna Math, built by followers of Ramakrishna Paramahamsa and Swami Vivekananda more than a century ago. Back in 1901, a group of devotees of Ramakrishna formed the Vedanta Society in Bengaluru in 1901. In 1904, the Ramakrishna Math was established in a rented building. The foundation stone for a new building was laid in 1906, and the building inaugurated by Swami Brahmananda on 20 January 1909. Initially called Ramakrishna Mission Institute, its name was changed to Ramakrishna Ashram in 1910, and Ramakrishna Math in 1999.

There are several interesting structures within the campus of the *math*. The Vivekananda *mantapa* and the statue of the seer on it are modern, but the enshrined stone slab is one upon which the great man himself had sat. The story goes that Swami Vivekananda visited Bengaluru in 1892 and stayed for a few days in the Kalappa *choultry*. While there, he often sat and meditated on a stone bench in a house adjacent to the *choultry*. This house belonged to a jeweller named Sri Sugappa. It was several years later that Sri Sugappa realised that the young man he had often seen sitting on his bench was none other than Swami Vivekananda. He and his descendants preserved the bench. In 1997, when the family decided to demolish the house, they donated the bench to the Ramakrishna Math.

Another rock that preserves the memory of another great soul is the Mother's Rock. In 1911, Sarada Devi, also known as the Holy Mother, had come to the ashram. It is said that one day she climbed the 3 metre-high rock to view the sunset. Enchanted by the view, she began meditating here. Out of respect for her, this rock was preserved and the *mantapa* was raised on it in 1967.

XI. Bull Temple

A walk of about 700 metres heading south on Bull Temple Road will take you to the temple after which the road and the locality are both named. The temple, built on a hillock, has several unusual features. For one, it is one of the few dedicated to Nandi, the vehicle of Shiva. For another, it is one of the few temples in south India where you can enter the *garbagriha*. The temple is about 500 years old. Legend connects its origins to a marauding bull that habitually destroyed the groundnut crops in the area. One version of the story says farmers decided to build a temple in the hope of stopping the bull from destroying their crops. A slightly more colourful version has it that one day an irate farmer chased the bull and struck it. Much to his surprise, the bull turned to stone. He realised that the bull was a divine manifestation and decided to build a temple to it. Imagine his surprise when he saw that the bull was growing in size. The farmer prayed to Lord Shiva, who told him he would find a trident in the ground nearby which he must then place on the bull's head. This he did and the bull finally stopped growing.

A tradition arose of offering the bull the first groundnut harvest. Kadalekayi Parishe, the groundnut fair, is still held near the temple during November and December. (Incidentally, groundnut is not a native crop. It was introduced to India via the Portuguese sometime in the 16th century.[39])

The bull, 4.6 metres high and 6.1 metres long, is one of the largest monolithic bulls in India. Basava, the bull, holds his head slightly turned to his left, with his right leg bent and raised. He is beautifully decorated with bells. At its base, notice the stone that bears an inscription in Kannada. In translation, it reads: 'At the feet of this god Basaveshwara, the river called Vrishabhavati rose and flowed with its stream to the west.' It is ascribed to about 1600 CE by BL Rice.[40]

There are several temples within the same complex. One of the most popular is of Dodda Ganapati, the Big Ganapati, at the base of the hill. This temple is especially popular with students, who visit it in droves especially before examinations! The 5.5 metre-tall idol is said to be *swayambhu* (self-manifested).

The Bull Temple, after which the extension of Basavanagudi is named.
Courtesy of Rohit Hangal.

XII. Bugle Rock

The hillock contiguous with the high point on which the Bull Temple is built is Bugle Rock (*kahale bande* in Kannada). It is popularly said that soldiers would blow a bugle here every evening. Another legend is that during the Third Anglo-Mysore War, Tipu's soldiers gathered here to discuss strategy. Today, the rocks are a popular place for children to clamber over and slide down.

In the first decade of this century, the park was given a facelift. That is when the murals of Kempegowda, Sir M Visvesvaraya, Jnanpith award winners and other notable personalities were added to the wall of the water tank here. There is also a statue of DV Gundappa.

Bugle Rock Park is a haunt of the Indian flying fox, one of the most common species of bats. Come evening, the air is filled with hundreds of bats, as they leave their roost to forage for food. It is a sight not to be missed.

XIII. Gokhale Institute of Public Affairs

The Gokhale Institute of Public Affairs was the brainchild of writer and Basavanagudi resident DV Gundappa. DVG, as he was popularly known, decided to name the institute after freedom fighter Gopal Krishna Gokhale. He also decided to imbibe Gokhale's motto: 'Public Life must be spiritualised.' The institute was started on 18 February 1945 with the aim of 'education of the public for democratic citizenship'.[41]

The Gokhale Institute has been housed in its present premises on Bull Temple Road since 1956. With its library of over 60,000 books, a reading room providing newspapers and periodicals, its periodic classes on political science and Sanskrit, and its regular lectures (eminent personalities such as HN Kunzru, Jaya Prakash Narayan and Nani Palkhivala have given talks here), the institute is one of Basavanagudi's important cultural spaces.

Other Notable Institutions in the Area

BK Mariappa Charities Hostel

This charitable institution and hostel is on 3rd Main, Chamarajpete. In March 1914, a young man of 35 wrote a will instructing that his wealth be used for establishing a charity for poor students. Eight days later, he died. The BK Mariappa Charities Hostel was built in 1921 on a large plot, measuring about four cottage sites which the initial trustees bought from the Bangalore Municipality for the purpose.

The BK Mariappa Charities Hostel in Chamarajpete. © *Aravind C*

The hostel is a handsome, symmetrical structure. A very colonial-looking colonnade and verandah runs all along the front. The imposts, semi-circular Roman arches and their keystones are nicely delineated in a contrasting colour. The cornice and some decorative plasterwork above it are also typical of the period. The once open balcony is now covered with a wooden trellis, except at the centre where there is a bust of the benefactor, BK Mariappa, framed by a classic monkey top. Up close, you can see other interesting details emerge, such as the *gandabherunda*, which sits in the middle of every iron baluster in the staircase.

When the hostel opened, it provided free accommodation to 45 students. Today, the main hostel building and the new building adjacent to it house 75 boys who pay a very small fee. A remarkable and important aspect of the hostel is that, as per BK Mariappa's will, one-third of the students admitted into it are from Mariappa's community of Nagartha Lingayats, one-third are Brahmins, and the remaining third are Hindus of any caste. The hostel counts several luminaries among its old students, including physicist Dr H Narasimhaiah, who taught at National College and later became Vice Chancellor of Bangalore University; K Narayanaswamy who was formerly the Chief Secretary of Karnataka; T Siddalingaiah who was a former Congress President and later a minister in the Mysore government; and many others.[42]

National High School

This school, at the corner of KR Road and Vanivilas Road, is yet another of Basavanagudi's institutions and landmarks that owes its origins to the theosophists led by Annie Besant. Founded in 1917, this school was initially located in Chamarajpete near Bengaluru Fort and was named SLN National High School. It was later moved to its present location. Its history is closely entwined with the Indian freedom movement. Prominent freedom fighters who have visited the school include C Rajagopalachari, NS Hardikar and Mahatma Gandhi. The school prides itself on its secularity even today. Famous people pepper its list of alumni, including cricketer Anil Kumble, scientist CNR Rao, hoteliers Sadanand Maiya and Vasudev Adiga, and actor Ramesh Aravind.

Mahila Seva Samaj

This school, located at the intersection of KR Road and Subramanya Temple Road, was started by Parvatiamma Chandrashekhar Iyer, wife of Dewan Bahadur Justice KS Chandrashekhar Iyer. In 1913, she established an organisation called Seva Sadana Society, which later became Mahila Seva Samaja. The express aim was to empower women, especially young widows, through improved literacy. Annie Besant, a supporter of the school, inaugurated the main building in 1920. Incidentally, this building won an INTACH Heritage Award in 2015, under the category of private institutions.

The school was generously supported in the early years by the Mysore Maharaja's government, from granting the site of the school at concessional rates to donating land for the playing field.[43] Step inside the main building to step back in time. The impeccably maintained interiors, the old photographs lining the walls, the memorabilia connected with the school's history (including an old weighing machine used to weigh babies, from the days when the MSS ran an antenatal and baby clinic) all tell of a legacy that is cherished and honoured.

The MSS is still run by a committee comprising only women, and it continues to pursue its commitment to improving literacy and women's empowerment.

Sajjan Rao Choultry and Temples

The Sajjan Rao Circle in VV Puram is replete with memories of this philanthropist of old Bengaluru.

Dharmaprakasa Sajjan Rao Suryavamshe was born in 1868 in a village in Mandya district to a family of limited means. Later, he moved to Bengaluru to help with his uncle's business. Through sustained hard work, he established his own businesses dealing in yarns and textiles, among other things. Within a few years of moving to Bengaluru, he became one of the city's wealthier merchants.

Like many others of the time, Sajjan Rao, too, was seized with the need to give back to society. In 1931, he built the Ganapati temple that overlooks

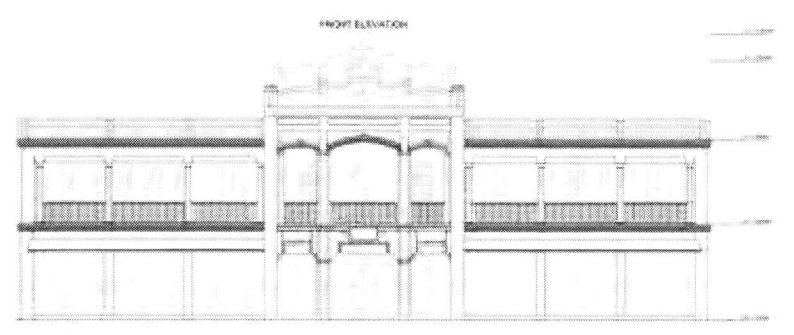

Front elevation of the Sajjan Rao Choultry. © *INTACH Benglauru Chapter*

the Circle. You can still see a statue of the gentleman in a small niche inside the temple. The *choultry* nearby was built in 1934 so that members of his community could have a place for weddings. Adjacent to it is a temple dedicated to Subramanya, also built in the 1930s. A few hundred metres away from the Circle is a school built by Sajjan Rao. All these institutions are still maintained by a trust comprising Sajjan Rao's descendants.

But this was by no means the end of his charity. In the early 1930s, Sajjan Rao donated money towards the construction of a block in the newly built Vani Vilas Hospital (on KR Road). Later, in 1940, he built a dispensary in the name of his mother Laxmibai Jeevan Rao Suryavamshe. He also gave generously to the Mahratta Hostel on Bull Temple Road, which was started by Thakku Bai Venkatarao Bhojagade and is now called the Venkatarao and S Sajjan Rao Mahratta Free Hostel.

The *choultry* itself is an ornament to the Circle. A central entrance with a colonnade provides an attractive frontage to the building. The colonnade leads to shops on either side. The central portion of the symmetrical facade is highlighted by projecting it out of the line of the facade and further emphasising it with ornamental cornice work on the parapet.

Originally, the *choultry* boasted a large, central double-height hall, which had a rather dramatic impact on visitors. In the 1980s, the central space was covered to create a dining hall. The central hall had a ceiling of Madras terrace roof so the spaced-out rafters and beams added to the character of the building. Other interesting features in this brick and stone building are the cast-iron columns and ornamental *chajjas*.*

INTACH Bengaluru is currently working on the restoration of this building.

---

* Architectural description by Pankaj Modi, Coordinator, INTACH Bengaluru Chapter

Walk 2: Through Gavipura

In which you learn more about Kempegowda, hear about two European artists, and learn a bit of astronomy

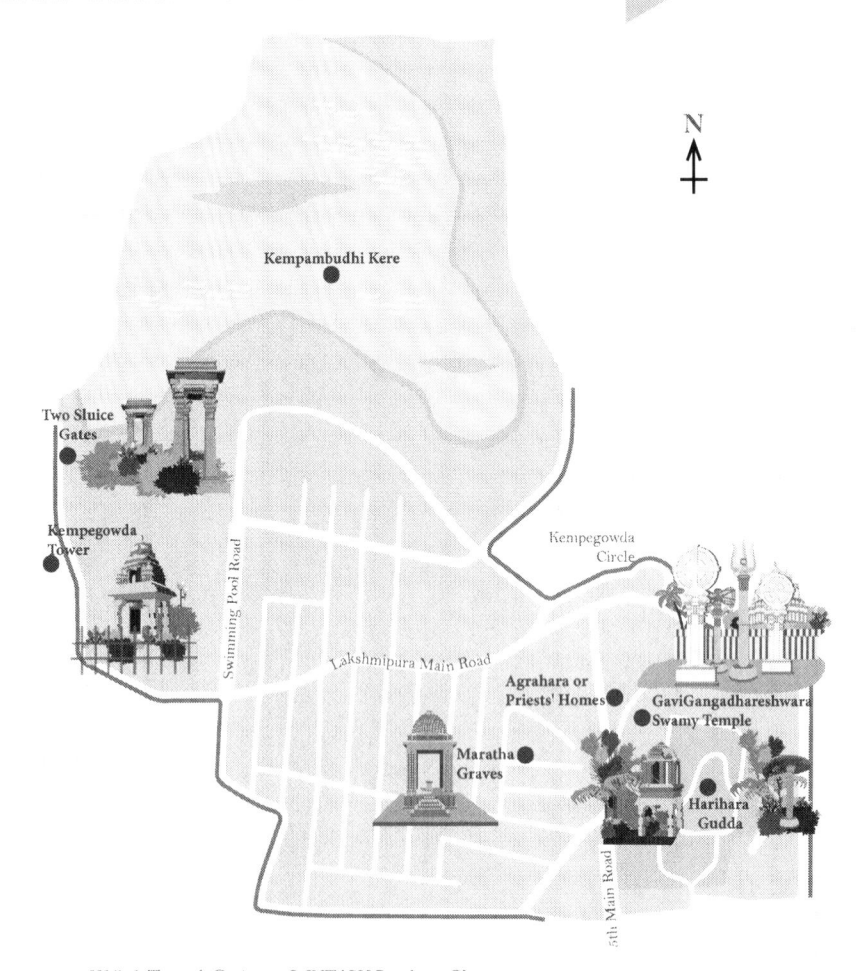

- Kempambudhi Kere
- Two Sluice Gates
- Kempegowda Tower
- Kempegowda Circle
- Swimming Pool Road
- Lakshmipura Main Road
- Agrahara or Priests' Homes
- GaviGangadhareshwara Swamy Temple
- Maratha Graves
- Harihara Gudda
- 5th Main Road

Walk 2: Through Gavipura. © *INTACH Benglauru Chapter*

First, some history… In the year 1792, two Europeans—one a youth of about 22, the other his 42-year-old uncle—wended their way through south India, accompanied by a retinue of men carrying cots and provisions. And their drawing tables. For the two were Thomas and William Daniell, the celebrated English landscape painters. They are best known for their work *Oriental Scenery*, a collection of aquatints of views of India published in six parts between 1795 and 1810.

Passing through the area near Bengaluru, they were entranced by the dramatic scenery of rocky hills and vales, many of them topped with little shrines, temples or *mantapas*. On 1 May 1792, the pair came upon the little village of Gavipura. And as with many people for centuries now, Bengaluru cast its unique charm on them. 'Spent the whole day at the Hills to the southward of Bangalore, where we collected several Scenes,' William wrote in his journal that day, adding, 'the neighbourhood of Bangalore is remarkable for the frequent appearance of the remains of ancient Hindu architecture'.[44]

The Daniells made a number of pencil sketches, some of which were later made into their trademark aquatints. One of the scenes that captivated them was the Harihareshwara temple perched atop a little hillock. They also made a number of sketches of a few *mantapas*. On the same day, they visited the Bull Temple and made a sketch there too. Incidentally, these drawings are among the earliest depictions of parts of south Bengaluru.

Cut to 1914–15. This was when the suburb of Gavipura was officially created. Unlike neighbouring Basavanagudi, Gavipura was established by the City Municipality with no financial assistance from the Mysore government. This small extension comprised 16 cottage sites and 64 house sites.[45] Of course, Gavipura has grown considerably beyond that nucleus today.

I. Kempambudhi *Kere*

A good place to start your Gavipura walk is at this water body which once supplied water for irrigation and hence made the settlement possible. Named after Kempamma, the consort of the Kempegowda family's deity, Kempambudhi *kere* is one of the many tanks said to have been built by the city's founder, Kempegowda. The paved walkway that leads you to the lake is, in fact, the bund. As you start your walk from near the Bandi Mahakalamma temple, keep in mind that you are walking on a 500-year-old dam!

'A 10-year-old Hindoo girl named Byramma swam continuously for 12 hours in a pond at Bangalore yesterday.' Newspapers around the world carried this little item in their pages on 25 April 1934.[46] In reality, Byramma's remarkable feat had taken place on 21 April 1934, and the so-called pond mentioned in many reports was this very Kempambudhi *kere*. Byramma's endurance test had been conducted in front of a committee that consisted of, among others, the

President of the City Municipality and the Second Member of the Maharaja's Council. 'The girl looked quite fresh when she emerged from the water amidst cheers,' we are told![47]

The idea of a ten-year-old creating a record that stunned the world is indeed remarkable, and it points to the existence of an active swimming culture in this area. This was thanks to the swimming club called the Dolphin Club, established here in 1919.

II. Two Sluice Gates

As you walk back from the *kere* towards the road, on your left you will notice two stone structures resembling towers. These are sluice gates that once controlled the flow of water from Kempambudhi *kere* to the surrounding fields. The two sluice gates are now several metres from the *kere*, but when built, they would both have been in the water, close to the bund, each regulating the flow of water in a different channel.

This *mantapa*-like sluice gate is typical of the Vijayanagar period to which Kempegowda belonged. Contrast this with sluice gates from an earlier period which were built in a different style; at Manne near Nelamangala, for example, they are supported on two pillars, rather than four as here. A similar four-pillared sluice gate is also found in Madivala kere. In 2017, de-silting of the *kere* in Hosakerehalli threw up a surprise in the form of a similar sluice gate there as well, which many mistook for a mantapa.[48] This sluice gate has since disappeared under silt once more.[49]

Two sluice gates at the Kempambudhi *kere* likely date to the Kempegowda period. © *Aravind C*

III. Kempegowda Towers

On your way towards the main road, just before the Bandi Mahakalamma temple, a small gate and path lead towards one of the famous Kempegowda towers. This is the symbol adopted by the Bruhat Bengaluru Mahanagara Palike, the Municipal Corporation of the city of Bengaluru.

The story goes that Kempegowda II, son of Kempegowda I, built four of these to mark the points to which the city of Bengaluru would extend. Indeed, a plaque placed at the base of the tower mentions this. (The other three of the so-called Kempegowda towers are in Ulsoor, Lalbagh and Ramana Maharishi Park on Bellary Road.) However, this is not the only Kempegowda tower in Gavipura. There are two similar towers on Harihara Gudda, the hill near the Gavigangadhareshwara temple. There is also a similar tower at the other end of the bund you just came from. The placement of these and the other so-called Kempegowda towers suggests that they were built as lookout points.

The Kempegowda Tower near the Kempambudhi kere. © *Aravind C*

Look at the hillock on which this tower stands. One particular rock has evenly spaced ridges along one of its edges. These ridges are a result of the process of breaking the rocks, probably to build this very *mantapa*. Stoneworkers would make a line of closely and evenly spaced shallow holes along the rock where they wanted to fracture it. Using long rods like crowbars, they would then neatly wedge the rock apart. An alternative method was to insert wooden pegs into these holes and then pour hot water into them. The water would cause the wood to swell, making the rock fracture neatly.

A second feature to note is a series of depressions that have been scooped out of the rock in a line leading up to the tower. These were probably used to hold oil *lamps*.[50]

IV. Maratha Graves

Turning left at Lakshmipura Main Road, walk about half a kilometre. Just before the Kempegowda Circle, turn right and walk up about 110 metres, then take the steps down into the large open ground on your right. At the other end of the ground is a small graveyard where you can find the samadhis or graves of several Marathas, with the oldest dating back to 1897.

The samadhis are square in plan with a simple plinth and a small platform in the centre. This platform usually has a granite stone inscribed with the name of the deceased. Many of the names are no longer legible. Most of the samadhis have four slender columns and are surmounted by a dome. Among them is the samadhi of Muthoji Rao Scindia, a businessman in the 1800s, and of the philanthropist Sajjan Rao. Sajjan Rao's grave was cleared of garbage by his descendants in 2017. Near the graves is a set of footprints carved on stone, which are said to be of a saint who meditated here. There is also a Nandi sculpture of uncertain age.

Several other Maratha graves are found in Gavipura, including along Lakshmipura Road. There are also *maths* and charitable institutions established and run by Marathas in the vicinity.

Maratha presence in Bengaluru dates back to the 1600s. In 1638, Ranadullah Khan, the general of the Adil Shahis of Bijapur—accompanied by his second in command Shahaji Bhosle (father of the celebrated Shivaji)—defeated Kempegowda II. At that time, Shahaji was given Bengaluru and some of its surrounding territories as a *jagir*.[51] According to Maratha lore, Shahaji established a Bhavani Peetha *math* here in Gavipura.[52]

V. Gavigangadhareshwara Temple

The ancient cave temple after which this neighbourhood is named is located on the opposite side of the road from the Maratha graveyard. The temple is said to have been built by Kempegowda. However, it is likely that the cave temple existed earlier, and was renovated and expanded by Kempegowda.

There are several architectural details that are typical of the Vijayanagar period, such as the carved pillars at the entrance *mantapa*. Over the sanctums are two Vijayanagara-style shikharas, or towers, with images in stucco work. The temple has several unique features. The narrow circumambulatory passage has been cut through the rock. Legend has it a tunnel leads from here to Shivaganga, 75 km away.

Dominating the front of the temple are several monolithic structures which are quite unusual. As the two peripatetic Daniells put it, 'The entrance to this temple has a very striking effect, from the size and singularity of the mythological sculpture wrought in stone which appears in the court before the temple.'[53] The monolithic stone *trishul* and *damru*, the trident and the small drum that Shiva holds in two of his hands, are unique to this temple.

Even more interesting are the two monolithic stone discs called the *suryapana* and *chandrapana*. Researchers from the Jawaharlal Nehru Planetarium in Bengaluru have investigated these discs and the phenomenon that occurs on Makara Sankranti each year: on that festival day in mid-January, the rays of the sun fall directly on the linga inside.[54] The study revealed some astonishing details and led the researchers to surmise that the Gavigangadhareshwara temple and its monolithic stone structures are part of an astronomical

The monolithic stone discs were probably used to make astronomical observations.
© *Ajay Ghatage*

observatory, in all likelihood used to monitor phenomena like the solstice and the equinox. Among other exciting discoveries, they observed that if there were no trees blocking the views, the shadow of the western disc would fall exactly on the eastern disc at sunset only on the day of the summer solstice. Similarly, during sunrise on the winter solstice in December, the shadow of the eastern disc would fall exactly on the western disc. As for the phenomenon of the sun's rays falling on the linga in January, given the movement of the sun, the same phenomenon would also happen in late November. The researchers' paper is highly recommended: be warned that it may lead to an itch to do some sleuthing of your own!

VI. Agrahara, or Priests' Houses

A path to the west of the temple leads to the houses where the temple priests reside. Protected by the archaeology department of the state government, the past becomes visible in these humble abodes built of stone and random rubble masonry. Outside some houses are stone grinders to grind ragi and other grains. Today, they often function as places to dry clothes. Through the open doors, you may catch a glimpse of the small courtyards these houses have. These courtyards would ensure enough light and ventilation for the small rooms built around them.

The vernacular character of this place is reflected in the street pattern and the interaction of the houses with the street. A *mantapa*-type gateway defines the passage from each house to the lane which leads to the temple. Paved with stone slabs, it curves in response to the hill profile. The single-storeyed houses line one side of the street. Most of them have low plinths and can be directly entered from the lane; some have a higher plinth with a few steps. There are different typologies of houses here: some have an entrance bay that opens into a courtyard, some open directly into a hall, and one has a verandah in front (which is now closed). Most of the activities from the house spill onto the street which also encourages interaction between the families staying there.

VII. Harihara Gudda

This hillock, which looms behind the Gavigangadhareshwara temple, features in several of the Daniells' paintings and sketches. Apart from the many *mantapas* here that the Daniells drew, an unusual structure here is the stone umbrella, which also fascinated the Daniells, who surmised that it was the 'chakra or discus of Vishnoo, placed horizontally'.[55] The purpose of this structure and its exact age are still unknown.

A small stone umbrella in Harihara Gudda park. © *Pankaj Modi*

Also on the hill is the Harihareshwara temple, which was reported as being empty and abandoned by the Daniells but has since gained an idol. It has also gained some decidedly quirky decorations: the temple was renovated in 1976, which is probably when the aeroplane motifs were added to it!

●●●●●

Our perambulations around these neighbourhoods end on this hillock. However, this is only the merest glimpse of south Bengaluru's heritage and culture. The lanes of Gavipura, VV Puram, Shankarpuram, Chamarajpete and Basavanagudi are full of houses and people, foods and aromas that are best observed, experienced and then loved while on foot. A few hundred metres from the sylvan park on Harihara Gudda are community wedding halls dating to the early 1900s, dhobi ghats, the home of the writer Masti Venkatesh Iyengar (now housing a small museum), dance schools and craft shops housed in old bungalows, the home of the founder of the *Deccan Herald* newspaper, streets that shed their somnolence every night as stalls selling street food open up, and lots more. Be a flaneur.

Notes

1. Anon 1880, 750–751.
2. ML 76 of 94, Sl 1–2, KSA.
3. File Sani 55 of 1899–1900, Sl 1–4, KSA.
4. File ML 76 of 94, Sl 1–2, KSA. In the records all dimensions are usually in feet, as was the norm at the time. Henceforth, we will not provide the conversion to metres for such dimensions, but rely on the conversion supplied here to give an idea.
5. File ML 5 of 1888, Sl 1–5, KSA.
6. File LR 86 of 1891, KSA.
7. File ML 76 of 1894, Sl 1–2, KSA.
8. File ML 229 of 1895, Sl 1–4, KSA.
9. Iyengar 1914.
10. File ML 76 of 94, Sl 1–2, KSA.
11. Report on the Administration of Mysore for the four years 1895–96 to 1898–99, 63.
12. For the social unrest and the political upheavals caused by stringent plague regulations, see Echenberg 2007; Waltraud, Pati and Sekher 2017.
13. File Sani 5 of 1895, Sl 1–5, KSA.
14. Iyer 1914.
15. File ML 231 of 95, Sl 1–12, KSA.
16. File ML 1 of 19, Sl 2, KSA.
17. File Sani 44 of 1898–99, Sl 1–11, KSA.
18. File ML 90 of 1898, 1–87, KSA.
19. File Sani 44 of 1898–99, Sl 1 to 11, KSA.
20. File ML 478 of 06, 1–15, KSA.
21. File GF 68 of 1899, KSA.
22. Butler 1983.
23. Iyengar 1914, 209.
24. File Sani 16 of 97, KSA.
25. File ML 189-12, 1–6, KSA.
26. File ML 189-12, 1–6, KSA.
27. File ML 58 of 08, Sl 1, 4, 5, 7, KSA.
28. File ML 199 of 19, Sl 1, 2, KSA.
29. Interview with Prahlad Rao, 88-year-old resident of Gandhi Bazaar Road, August 2017.
30. File ML 85 of 45, Sl 3–4, KSA.
31. Baweja 2008.
32. Heycock to SF Fraser, 1908, KSA.
33. Interview with MR Narendra, August 2016.
34. Wadia 1947, 231–233.
35. http://www.katinkahesselink.net/his/dtb_3.htm, accessed 31 August 2018.
36. Gundappa 2016.
37. File ML 425 of 1906, Sl 1–6, KSA.
38. 'A club with character', *The Hindu*, 22 May 2004.
39. Smartt 1994.
40. EC 9 Bn 70.
41. http://www.gipa-bng.org/index.php, accessed May 2019.

42. Anon 2014; personal communication, N Puttarudra, Warden at Mariappa Charities Hostel, December 2016.
43. Proceedings of the Government of Mysore, May 1941, 12.
44. William Daniell's journal, quoted in Archer 1980, 159.
45. File ML 1 of 19, Sl 2, KSA.
46. For example, *The Examiner* (Tasmania), 25 April 1934.
47. '12 Hours Swim: Hindu girl's remarkable performance', *The Singapore Free Press and Mercantile Advertiser*, 18 May 1934.
48. Govind 2017.
49. For more on reservoirs, sluice gates and irrigation during the Vijayanagar period, see Morrison 2015.
50. Personal communication, SK Aruni, Director, Indian Council of Historical Research, February 2015.
51. Rice 1897b, 359.
52. Suganya 2011.
53. Quoted in Archer 1980, Plate 102.
54. Vyasanakere, Sudeesh and Shylaja 2008.
55. Quoted in Archer 1980, Plate 101.

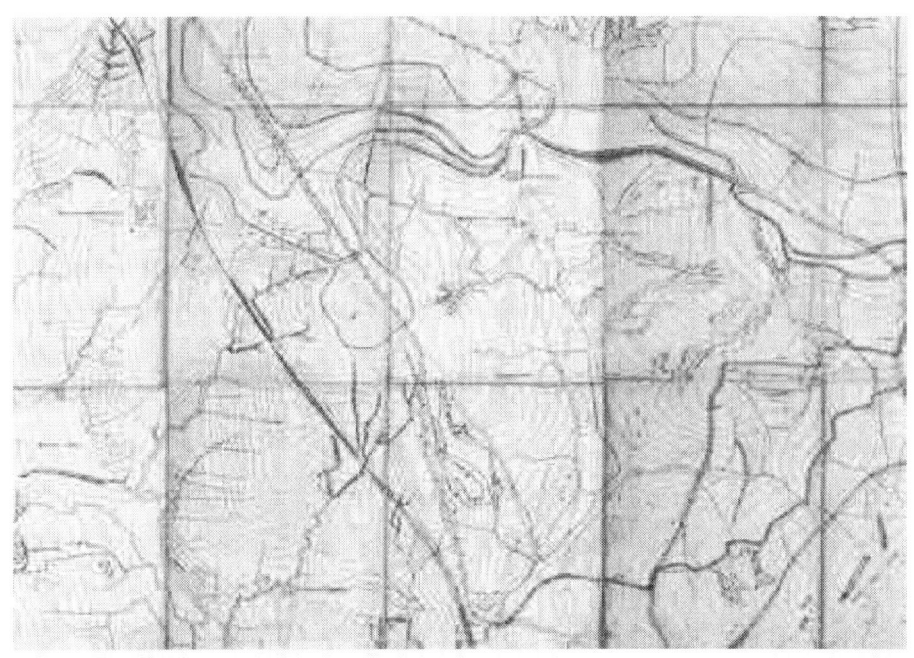

The Malleswaram area in 1884-85. From, Survey of India. *Cantonment and City of Bangalore and Environs, Season 1884-85.* Courtesy of Mythic Society, Bengaluru.

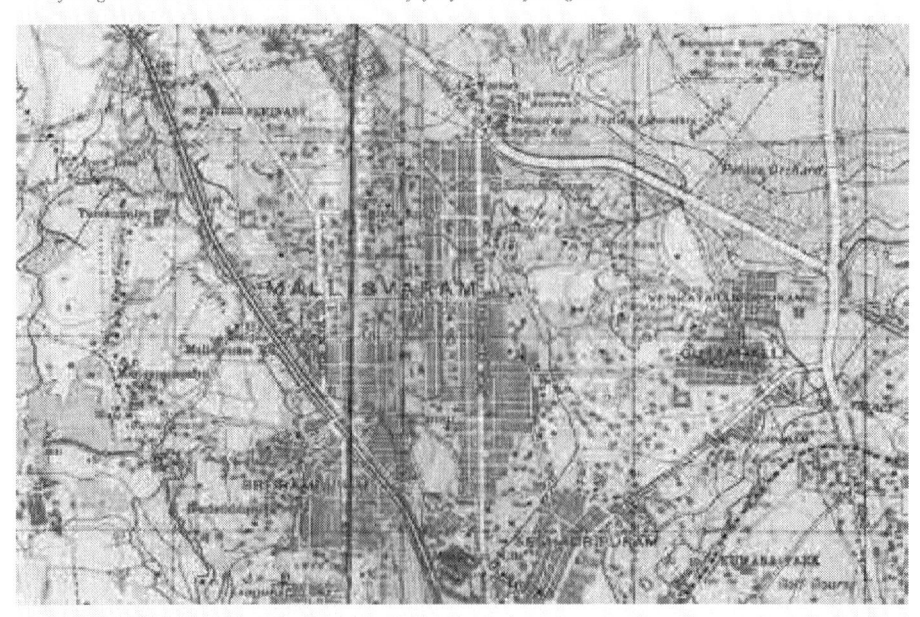

The Malleswaram area in 1935-36. From, Survey of India. *Bangalore Guide Map. Surveyed 1935-36.* Courtesy of Naresh Narasimhan.

CHAPTER 5

Temples, Tanks and Trees: Malleswaram

Two extensions were established by the City Municipality in response to the plague. While Basavanagudi came up to the south of the *kote* or Bengaluru Fort, another was established to the north of the old *pete*. Here, where there were villages called Ranganathanapalya, Jakkasandra and Andandattarapalya, and a large old temple dedicated to the god Kadu Malleshwara, emerged the second, smaller extension.[1] Like Basavanagudi, it took the name of the presiding deity and was called Malleswaram. And like twins separated at birth, Malleswaram was very similar to Basavanagudi, but also quite different.[2]

Malleswaram Takes Shape

As in the case of Basavanagudi, the lands acquired to set up the extension were divided into plots. Here, 291 acres were acquired on either side of the old Tumkur Road and divided into plots of different sizes. Like Basavanagudi, and Chamarajapete before that, Malleswaram, too, was laid out in a grid pattern with no attempt to adhere to the contours of the land (which was considerably undulating and rocky in this case). One reason for this may have been so that the houses could face the auspicious cardinal directions in accordance with 'astrological Hindu usage'.[3] And as with the other two extensions, this one was divided into eight different blocks for as many communities including Brahmins, Lingayats, Muslims and so on. As with Basavanagudi, VP Madhava Rao, then Plague Commissioner of Mysore, and Standish Lee, then Sanitary Engineer of Mysore, played major roles in the establishment and design of Malleswaram.

On the west, the extension was bound by the railway line. To the south were the cloth mills, and beyond that, the vast waters of Jakkarayana *kere*,

170 | Discovering Bengaluru

PLAN OF MALLESWARAM EXTENSION

An 1895 plan of Malleswaram, showing how the sites were to be divided amongst different communities. Redrawn by Priyani Pranab, from a map in Sundara Rao, BN. 2015. *Bengalurina Itihaasa* (Bangalore's History). 3rd edition. Bengaluru: Ankita Pustaka.

which was upstream of Dharmambudhi *kere*—where now stand the Majestic (officially Kempegowda) bus terminus and Metro station. The Jewell Filters *(see below)* initially formed the northern end of the extension. Ten main roads running north–south were laid out. Some of them were named after trees: Sampige Road (originally also called the Champaca Avenue Road or Sampangi Avenue, officially the Venkataranga Iyengar Road; 'sampige' is golden champa/*Magnolia champaca*), and Margosa Road (also earlier called Margosa Avenue Road; 'margosa' is another name for neem). The diagonal 8th Main Road was the old Tumkur Road. There were 18 roads running in an east–west direction, named the crosses.

Today, Sampige Road is an endless stretch of glitzy and not-so-glitzy shops. In the original plan, only a few plots near 8th Cross were set aside as shop sites. Interestingly, at one point, trams were set to trundle along this street; this was to be part of the tramway planned to connect the city to the C&M Station.[4]

However, the idea of a tram network was nixed about ten years after the layout was established.[5]

For the first few months after the extension was set up, sites were sold directly. But from December 1899 onwards, select sites were sold by auction. This ended up being a gauge by which to judge how popular the two sister extensions were: the sites in Basavanagudi fetched good prices but those in Malleswaram sold for far less than expected.[6] One problem may have been that the Malleswaram extension was initially considered a 'malarial site', thanks to several pits in the rocky terrain.[7] It may also have been because unlike Basavanagudi which was well-connected to both the city and the C&M Station, approach roads to Malleswaram, especially from the Cantonment, were lacking in the first few years.[8]

Many of these lacunae were addressed between 1912 and 1917, thanks to the efforts of a few people including S Venkatarangiengar (also spelt Venkataranga Iyengar) and D Venkataramayya, who became Municipal Councillors for the new Malleswaram Division of the Municipal Corporation.[9] The then Dewan Sir M Visvesvaraya asked these two gentlemen what was needed 'to complete the laying out of Malleswaram extension in its entirety'.[10] In response, they provided a detailed list of works required, including completing several roads at the extremities of the extension; establishing underground drainage and conservancy lanes in all parts of the extension; setting up the so-called Ryots' Block west of the railway line (originally meant for ryots who apparently lived in isolated sheds there—afterwards, many of these small plots were sold to Brahmins) later renamed Srirampura; and installing a sewage treatment farm beyond Jakkarayana *kere*.

An India-born Scottish Engineer

Standish Lee was born in October 1838 in India and completed his studies from the Madras Engineering College. No less an engineer than Sir M Visvesvaraya described him as being 'original in many ways', and credited him with being one of the first in India to look at town planning.[18]

Lee had had some experience in municipal affairs before he came to Mysore State, having served as Executive Engineer in Madras in the 1860s, where he worked on the underground sewerage of that city.[19] He also brought water to the city from the Red Hills reservoir, still a functioning and vital source.[20] Much later, in mid-1892, as the Sanitary Engineer for the Mysore government, he worked on the sewerage of the fort and palace in Mysore.[21]

In the 1870s, Lee moved to Bengaluru and established the Steam Woollen Mill in 1877.[22] In the 1880s, this was bought over by the Binnys. Lee was Head Master at the School of Engineering in the C&M Station.[23] He teamed up with Arunachala Mudaliar and C Pappanah to successfully bid for the construction of railway lines. However, in Bengaluru, he is best remembered for helping to design the two extensions of Basavanagudi and Malleswaram.

A Dewan of Three States

Vishwanath Patankar Madhava Rao was one of India's most highly respected statesmen, with the distinction of serving as Dewan in three progressive, so-called native states—Mysore, Travancore and Baroda—and eventually becoming a prominent member of the Congress Party. He was born in 1850 in Kumbakonam, Madras Presidency (now in Tamil Nadu). After joining the Mysore Civil Service in 1870,[6] he served in various posts including as Inspector General of Police, the first Indian to hold that post. When the dreaded plague broke out, it was clear that a strong and efficient administrator was immediately required to tackle the crisis. The British Resident in Mysore, Sir Donald Robertson, had been impressed with Madhava Rao's work as Inspector General and suggested his name; the Maharani Regent immediately concurred and Madhava Rao was appointed Plague Commissioner. To him, then, we owe the speedy and efficient establishments of the Basavanagudi and Malleswaram extensions. Madhava Rao became the Dewan of Mysore State in 1906, retiring from the post in 1909. He died on 1 December 1934.

VP Madhav Rao. From, *Les Missions Catholiques*, Vol 31, 1899, p559.

Like many of his ilk and time, VP Madhava Rao was said to have a strong personality that made an impression on all who met him. He had a strong belief in social welfare and democratic principles.[17] Madhava Rao initially lived in Patan Bhavan, a palatial stone bungalow (that still exists) near Race Course Road, in an area named after him as Madhav Nagar. Later, his family moved to Malleswaram, where many of his descendants still live.

Extending the Extension

Over the years, the original 291 acres that comprised Malleswaram increased incrementally. Within about ten years of the establishment of the extension, more land was added near Sankey Tank. Land was also acquired across the railway line, in Ryots Block. Old-timers and maps both record how, until the mid-1920s, most of Malleswaram lived south of 15th Cross. In fact, many of the roads north of it were still mud roads. By the 1930s, areas north of 15th Cross were also populated. By this time, the extension had increased to about 304 acres.[11] In the 1940s, it expanded further when the Swimming Pool Extension was formed, with 235 sites.[12]

Malleswaram's relatively small size meant everything was easily accessible, whether it was the sports grounds, the cultural venues or the temples. This may explain why the locality became—and still continues to be—such a hub for arts and culture. It was also nurtured in its early days by eminent names in the field of dance, Carnatic music, visual and performing arts and literature, including GP Rajarathnam, Veena Doreswamy Iyengar, K Venkatappa, MS Sathyu and many others. The area's many religious and cultural institutions—Seva Sadan, Ubhaya Vedanta Sabha, Canara Union, Rama temple, Gandhi Sahitya Sangha and several others—serve as venues for regular events.

An Educational Hub

Malleswaram is remarkable for the plethora of educational institutions that dot its streets, including the Government Girls' and Boys' schools. One of the earliest initiatives was the Malleswaram Ladies' Association, which was formed in 1927. Initially set up to organise cultural and social events, it soon began classes for women with a stress on vocational training. Today, it runs several educational institutions, including nursery schools and colleges for women.[13]

The Mysore Education Society (MES) was established in the 1950s with several leaders and academics among its founders, including the Sanskrit scholar MPL Sastry and M Chinnaswamy, advocate and one of the founding members of the Karnataka State Cricket Association.[14] MES today has pre-university and degree colleges, and offers courses in arts, science and commerce streams. Cluny Convent, established by the Congregation of the Sisters of St Joseph of Cluny, opened with two students in 1948 and now educates more than 2000 every year. Bengaluru's premier educational and research institution, the Indian Institute of Science, founded in 1909, lies just outside the northern boundaries of Malleswaram.

The Indian Institute of Science, seen from the Raman Research Institute, c. 1950s.
Courtesy of Raman Research Institute Archives.

The Sporting Spirit

Walk the streets of Malleswaram and you may well hear the resounding cheers of spectators watching some intense matches involving the area's sportspeople. Malleswaram's sports mania probably owes a great deal to the easy accessibility of two large grounds on 5th Cross and 18th Cross. Cricket is popular here, of course: the Friends Union Cricket Club (FUCC) and the Malleswaram Gymkhana still have some of Bengaluru's best cricket teams. Badminton is popular as well, and played in the courts at Canara Union and Malleswaram Association *(see below)*. The legendary Prakash Padukone began his illustrious career in the Canara Union courts.

But the sport that Malleswaram holds dearest, the one that sets most Malleswaram-ites' hearts aflutter, is basketball. Basketball is (and always has been) to Malleswaram what football is to Brazil. Matches are held in the Malleswaram grounds, in people's large compounds, in the grounds of the Government Boys' School on Margosa Road—some portions of which were built by Otto Koenigsberger, Chief Architect of Mysore State from 1939 to 1948 *(see below)*—and elsewhere. The Young Men's Mandyam Association, Bharat Sports Union and Young Pioneers Sports Club were formed in the 1950s. One of the grounds where they played is today the Malleswaram market. Beagles Basketball Club was established a few years later; the members played in a court set up in the grounds of the late BV Patankar, a descendant of Dewan VP Madhava Rao. Later, they moved to East Park Road, where they built their own courts. Basketball is a tradition that still thrives.

All sports including cricket, football and especially basketball, are popular in Malleswaram. © *PeeVee*

A Walk though Malleswaram

In which you meet a genius, some sportspeople, some scholars and several altruists

A Walk though Malleswaram. © *INTACH Benglauru Chapter*

I. Panchavati

We begin our walk through this leafy green suburb in one of its leafiest and greenest corners, the house of India's only Nobel Prize winner in the sciences. This unobtrusive bungalow at the intersection of 8th Main and 15th Cross was for long Sir Chandrashekhar Venkata Raman's home. So low-key is it that many of the youngsters who park their motorbikes outside do not know that the genius and his family lived here for several years.

The house was built in 1905 by B Jagdeo Kumaraswamy Naik, the then Deputy Commissioner of the city.[24] In 1942, Sir Raman bought it for Rs 30,000 from Kumaraswamy Naik's descendant BJ Kumara Krishna Raju, a businessman in the film industry. The story goes that at the time, three of the houses at this intersection were for sale. Raman had his eye on the only one of the three that was a double-storeyed house. However, Lady Lokasundari Raman much preferred one of the single-storeyed houses, which she felt would be quite enough for one's later years. Besides, it had a large space in front in which one could plant a garden. And so it was that the Ramans bought this house, which Lady Raman suggested be named 'Panchavati' after the hermitage where Rama and Sita spent many happy years of their forest exile.[25]

Raman moved here when he retired from the Indian Institute of Science in 1948. When the Ramans bought the house, the garden had only a few coconut trees. They planted most of the trees that you now see. In the days when the Ramans lived here, there was also a rose garden, for Raman loved roses.[26] There was also a cowshed with cows. The rear wing with its kitchen, stores and puja room were modified to make them more convenient. The portico in front and the corridor to the rear wing were added during Raman's time.

Interestingly, the house did not have a courtyard like most Indian bungalows, but resembled colonial bungalows in its plan, with its large central hall and rooms flanking it. The room in the front to the right was Raman's room. On the other side was his library which stocked an extensive selection of books, not just on science but also literature.[27] Later, Raman's son, the eminent scientist Radhakrishnan, and his family, lived in the cottage to the northwest. Lady Raman lived in Panchavati till she passed away in 1980.

The Raman Research Institute Trust maintains the 2.25-acre plot in much the same condition as it was when the Ramans lived here.

Sir CV Raman: The Man, The Genius

Sir Chandrasekhara Venkata Raman, born on 7 November 1888, was India's first Nobel Prize-winning scientist. He was awarded the Nobel Prize in physics in 1930 for his discovery of the 'Raman effect'.

The epitome of genius, young Raman completed his BA at the age of 15, and his MA at the age of 18. When he was 16, he was once measuring the angle of a prism using a spectrometer in his college when he observed some diffraction bands. Further investigations led to his first scientific publication in the respected journal, *The Philosophical Magazine* (London) in 1906, when he was just 18![28]

Sir CV Raman. *Courtesy of Raman Research Institute Archives.*

His deep curiosity about nature was evident early on and endured throughout his life. In one of his lectures, he said, 'The man of science observes what Nature offers with the eye of understanding, but her beauties are not lost on him for that reason. More truly it can be said that understanding refines our vision and heightens our appreciation of what is striking and beautiful.'[29] This lively interest in the world and its phenomena led to his most famous discovery, of course, but also to other avenues of research, and hence to papers and publications on music, the colours of flowers and the acoustic properties of certain buildings. Even his Nobel Lecture, delivered on 11 December 1930, began with the words, 'In the history of science, we often find that the study of some natural phenomenon has been the starting-point in the development of a new branch of knowledge.' He goes on to describe how 'observing the wonderful blue opalescence of the Mediterranean Sea' during a trip to Europe in 1921 led him to surmise that 'the phenomenon owed its origin to the scattering of sunlight by the molecules of the water'. He began experiments 'to ascertain the laws governing the diffusion of light in liquids' but soon realised that the subject 'offered unlimited scope for research. It seemed indeed that the study of light-scattering might carry one into the deepest problems of physics and chemistry...'[30]

Sir CV Raman conducted his Nobel-winning research in Kolkata. He moved to Bengaluru in 1933, when he was offered the post of Director of the Indian Institute of Science (IISc), becoming the first Indian to hold that post. However, political differences, personal jealousies and other factors led to him being stripped of the directorship just four years later. He continued as a professor, retiring from IISc in 1948 and establishing the Raman Research Institute (RRI) a year later.

Quite apart from his scientific genius, anecdotes abound of his quick wit. For example, at the Nobel banquet, when offered a drink, he responded, 'You have seen the Raman effect on alcohol. Please do not try and see the alcohol effect on Raman!'[31] His oratory skills are legendary. He had a gift for explaining the most obtuse scientific concepts in simple terms and with generous doses of humour, as a result of which his public talks were always packed to bursting.

Sir CV Raman died on 21 November 1970. He was cremated at RRI.

A German-born Chief Architect of Mysore State

Otto Koenigsberger was born in 1908 in Berlin, Germany. With the beginning of Nazi rule in 1933, like many other Jews in office, he was dismissed from his government job after which he worked for some years in Egyptian archaeology.[37] In 1939, he was offered the job of an architect from an unlikely source: Sir Mirza Ismail, Dewan of Mysore. The invitation came about thanks to his mother's brother, the physicist Max Born (who received the Nobel Prize in 1954), and indirectly, thanks also to Sir CV Raman. In 1935, Sir Raman invited Max Born to be a visiting professor in theoretical physics at IISc for six months. It was during his stint at IISc that Ismail once asked Born for suggestions for an architect; Born suggested his nephew's name, and Koenigsberger came to Bengaluru a few years later. (Incidentally, Koenigsberger illustrated Born's book, *The Restless Universe*.)

Koenigsberger was the Chief Architect for the Public Works Department in the Mysore government from 1939 to 1948. In Bengaluru, you can see buildings designed by him in IISc, Cubbon Park and Malleswaram.

Koenigsberger also designed parts of the steel city of Jamshedpur and Bhubaneshwar, among others. After Independence, Jawaharlal Nehru appointed him the Director of Housing for the Ministry of Health. In this capacity, he worked on planning and architectural projects for Partition refugees. Koenigsberger later moved to London. He is the author of *Manual of Tropical Housing and Building*, published in 1974, which is still a classic. He died in London in 1999, an Indian citizen.

Sir CV Raman with Max Born (second from right) and Mirza Ismail (fourth from right).
Courtesy of Raman Research Institute Archives.

II. Chitrapur Math

Across the intersection from Panchavati is a spiritual centre of the Chitrapur Saraswat community; their main *math* is in Shirali, in Uttara Kannada district. The crossroads where it stands was named the Chitrapur Circle in 2014.

This old bungalow was bought by the community in 1953, initially to serve as a retreat and accommodation for the spiritual heads of the *math* when they visited Bengaluru. Later, as the *math* became the centre for all of the community's religious and spiritual activities in Bengaluru, the building was renovated and expanded in 1973 and again in 1999–2000, while retaining its original character. An apartment complex and a commercial complex adjacent to the *math* were built in the late 1970s. The porch with its arched facade, the simple parapet and the large halls of the old bungalow have all been retained, as has the extensive garden.

III. Canara Union

A short walk down 8th Main towards the south brings you to Canara Union, one of Malleswaram's most well-known institutions. In fact, 8th Main has been renamed after it. It began very modestly indeed in 1900, when Dr Badakere Venkata Rao founded the centre to promote social and cultural interactions among members of the Saraswat Brahmin community. In the early years, meetings were held in Dr Rao's house.[34] The current building was made possible thanks to a generous donation from Dattatreya N Sirur, a merchant and philanthropist, owner of Minerva Mills and Raja Mills or Mysore Spinning Mills (Mantri Mall now stands where the latter used to be). The building was opened on 21 October 1931. Within a few years, the Canara Union became a very vibrant centre for literary, cultural and social activities for the community, hosting plays, festival events, weddings and games.

It has also been one of the main centres for nurturing talent in indoor games. Legendary shuttler Prakash Padukone first wielded his racquet in the courts here. The Prakash Courts at the institution is named after him. Table tennis tournaments were earlier held in the dining hall and wedding hall of Canara Union; today there are separate areas designated for these. Several national champions have participated in these tournaments, which continue to be held regularly even today.

IV. Malleswaram Girls High School

Continue on 8th Main/Canara Union Road till 13th Cross. Turn left and walk about 400 metres till you reach its intersection with 4th Main. On your right will be the building that was once the home of HV Nanjundayya, the first Vice-Chancellor of Mysore University.

The grand two-storeyed stone building sits at the centre of a large corner plot. According to some of Nanjundayya's grandchildren, their ancestor had a clear view of the buildings of IISc from this palatial house. The porch, the ornamental stone pediments above each window, the distinctive *chajjas* and the stone parapet all add an imposing grandeur to the building. Other interesting features are the unusual star-shaped openings in the gables, the ornate grills and the decorative barge boards.

A large hall on the first floor is lit by coloured glass. The first floor has a combination of flat roof and Madras terrace. At the rear of the building, another structure with some rooms and a central courtyard was added some time later. This is a brick and lime mortar building with a Madras terrace roof.

Nanjundayya's was a very large family and this house was always filled with people. Accounts of it provide a vivid picture of a warm, happy home

A window and ornamentation in the Girls' High School.
© *PeeVee*

The Malleswaram Girls' High School, former residence of HV Nanjundayya. © *PeeVee*

The First Vice-Chancellor of Mysore University

Hebbalalu Velpanur Nanjundayya was born on 13 October 1860 and spent his early years in Mysuru. He received his BA, BL and MA degrees in quick succession; later, he obtained an ML degree while in service. Beginning his career as a sub-registrar in Kollegal, he rose rapidly through the echelons of government service through hard work. By 1907–08, he was Chief Justice of the Chief Court of Mysore.

Nanjundayya is often remembered as the one who *almost* became Dewan after T Ananda Rao retired, instead of his friend——Sir M Visvesvaraya——and indeed, he was a popular contender for the post. However, the two remained friends even after Sir MV took over as Dewan, though they agreed to disagree on some issues. After his retirement from government service in 1916, Nanjundayya's erudition and scholarship made him the ideal candidate to help set up Mysore University, of which he was appointed the first Vice-Chancellor.

HV Nanjundayya, first Vice-Chancellor of Mysore University. From, The University of Mysore, *Silver Jubilee Souvenir*, Bangalore Press, Bangalore, 1941.

In a foreword to a biography of Nanjundayya, the eminent litterateur and freedom fighter DV Gundappa said of him that he was 'distinguished by independence of mind and elevation of character, and his public spirit made use of every available opportunity to promote his people's moral and material improvement'.[37] Nanjundayya had a keen sense of humour, enjoyed horse-riding and also paid attention to detail. According to a family story, he had the carpet in his house made so that it could be easily divided into six pieces, one for each of the children who were to inherit it![38]

His perfectionist streak is certainly evident in his magnum opus, the 24-volume *Ethnographical Survey of Mysore*, a wonderfully detailed exposition on the rituals, social practices and beliefs of some of the state's castes and tribes. He describes each community's origin stories, the ceremonies that are performed at birth, marriage and death, the customs prescribed for divorce, adultery and widow remarriage, their particular cuisines, their superstitions and so on. The amount of information compiled and the attention to detail are astonishing, and yet its presentation is accessible, not pedantic. Nanjundayya authored several other books in English and Kannada, and even translated some of Victor Hugo's poems to English. He was also a founder-member of the Karnataka Sahitya Parishad (later rechristened Kannada Sahitya Parishad), and Vice-President of the Mythic Society.

When the new extension of Malleswaram was established, Nanjundayya was among the first to move here: he bought his site No 12 in early 1899, next to that of his brother, HV Krishnayya. Later, he bought more sites to accommodate his large family. Nanjundayya passed away in 1920. His grandchildren and great-grandchildren still live in the vicinity.

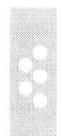

The Former Villa Pottipati

On 4th Main, a little past 9th Cross, stands a lovely bungalow named Vema Lodge. A little further, at the intersection of 4th Main with 8th Cross, stood a similar grand bungalow built in the early 20th century; it was demolished in August 2018, causing much anguish among heritage lovers in Bengaluru.

The elegant Villa Pottipati before it was demolished. © Ajay Ghatage

Both these houses were built by T Baiyanna, a contractor, the first President of the Vokkaligara Sangha, and a respected resident of Malleswaram. Vema Lodge, built in 1910, is named after the 17th century Telugu poet Vemanna. Villa Pottipati, built in 1925, was bought by Baiyanna's son-in-law Dr Pottipati Hanimireddigari Rama Reddy who named it Pottipati House, after the village of Pottipati in Andhra Pradesh where he hailed from.[39] Dr Reddy, a distinguished agricultural scientist, was part of the Indian Agricultural Service, and served in various positions around the country; he was one of the early Principals of the Agricultural College in Hebbal (now the University of Agricultural Sciences), an institute he helped build.

In the 1970s, Pottipati House served as the office of the Karnataka State Forest Industries Corporation. Later, in the 1980s, several of the older residents of Malleswaram used to come here regularly to pay their electricity bills because the bungalow housed a Karnataka Electricity Board (KEB) office.[40]

Some years ago, the Neemrana Group took the building on lease and for the next several years, the bungalow housed one of Bengaluru's finest heritage hotels. The building was maintained with most of its older features intact, including its red-oxide flooring, monkey tops, Mangalore tile roofs and so on.

Vema Lodge and Villa Pottipati were often referred to as twins since they were both built in similar styles, at around the same period and by the same person. Vema Lodge is still beautifully maintained by some descendants of the former Dewans Purnaiah and PN Krishnamurti, who bought it in the 1920s. RIP, Villa Pottipati.[41]

T Baiyanna, who built Villa Pottipati and Vema Lodge. *Courtesy of Vinatha Reddy, great grandniece of T Baiyanna.*

bursting with life, and full of 'old people and children everywhere.'[35] When Nanjundayya passed away, the house was inherited by some of his children and later sold to the government, which repurposed it into a school for girls.[36]

V. Malleswaram Grounds

Further down 4th Main from Vema Lodge, at the next intersection, you will see the Malleswaram Grounds, which is to Malleswaram what Parade Ground was to the Cantonment in its early days. Over the years, it has become a nucleus for the area, catering to all ages, playing host to events of all kinds, from cricket and basketball matches to festivals and major political gatherings.

On the other side of 5th Cross (also known as Mahakavi Kuvempu Road), is the KC General Hospital. In the first few decades of the extension, the land to the south of the Malleswaram Grounds was a large wooded area. By the 1930s, the trees here had been cleared. It was here that, in the mid-1940s, the Sri Kempacheluvajammani Avaru Hospital for Women and Children, named after the then Yuvarani of Mysore, was built.

Today, it is a multi-speciality government hospital, catering to hundreds of people from Malleswaram and elsewhere.

VI. Venugopalaswamy Temple

Walk east on 7th Cross, turn left onto Margosa Road and then walk north (past the old CTR/new Shri Sagar restaurant famous for its dosas) till you reach 9th Cross. Turn right and walk till you hit East Park Road; you will come across a cluster of temples when you turn left here. The Mahaganapati, Rama and Venugopalaswamy temples are all lined up along this road, as are two *maths*. Of these, the Venugopalaswamy temple is the oldest. It was consecrated on 22 August 1902, to commemorate Nalvadi Krishnaraja Wodeyar taking over the administration of Mysore.

Discerning eyes may notice how some of the stones and sculptures in the temple seem considerably older than 130 years; these include the images of the goddess Ganga on either gatepost of the western entrance to the compound. This is because they date to an earlier period than the temple: the edifice has been constructed using materials from older structures, including two Anjaneya temples, one Basavanna temple, and interestingly, one of the sluice gates of Karanji *kere* in Basavanagudi.[42] The *utsava* idol (the metal idol that can be taken out on processions during temple festivals) of Lakshmidevi was originally in the Krishna temple in the Mysore Palace.[43]

Some of the older constructions have been obliterated by recent additions and renovations.

VII. Malleswaram Market

The stretch of 9th Cross Road you'll be walking along before you come upon the temple cluster is called Market Road. This is because this road is where the Malleswaram market was located in the early years of the extension. It has now been reduced to a small lane lined with mostly empty stalls.

A portion of the Malleswaram Market. © *Ajay Ghatage*

In the 1970s, a new, larger market was built on Sampige Road, which was demolished in 2015. A large multistorey is coming up on the site, which you can reach by turning right at the Venugopalaswamy temple and then left onto the ever-bustling Sampige Road. After a walk of about 130 metres, the air will be filled with the heady smell of jasmine, roses and other flowers. A visual extravaganza of colours unfolds on the footpath as sellers vie for your attention with attractive displays of flowers. This is only a very small glimpse of the former Malleswaram market, which was especially famous for its flowers. Behind the footpath and the fence lies the ghost of the market, demolished and now in the throes of rebirth—a mass of cement pillars, concrete slabs and vertical iron rods.

X. Sri Dakshinamukha Nandi Tirtha Kalyani Kshetra, or Nandishwara Temple

From the market, walk a few metres further and then turn right onto 2nd Temple Street. Continue on this road for about 100 metres and then take the right fork to stay on 2nd Temple Street, which is another temple zone in Malleswaram. About 100 metres down this road, the Nandi Tirtha Kalyani temple will be on your right.

In 1997, an almost-everyday event in Malleswaram had a very unexpected outcome indeed. It happened thus: a politician sold a plot of land to a builder who wanted to construct a commercial building on it. Imagine everyone's surprise when the excavators unearthed old temple pillars and roofs. Further careful excavation revealed an intact courtyard with a pillared hall around it, a perfectly preserved *kalyani* and, most interesting of all, a south-facing statue of Nandi from whose mouth there flowed a clear stream of water which fell exactly on a linga placed a little below it. Local people eventually prevailed upon the builder to halt construction. The find caused considerable excitement in Bengaluru. Reports of the newly unearthed temple spoke of it being 400 years old, or even 7000 years old.[44]

The Nandishwara Temple. © *PeeVee*

The *kalyani* is believed to be built by the philanthropist Rao Bahadur Yele Mallappa Setty in the 1880s.[45] Mallappa Setty hailed from a family that had made its fortune by growing and selling betel leaf.[46] He also built the large tank named after him near KR Puram and donated Rs 35,000 towards the construction of a maternity hospital on Nrupathunga Road. This hospital no longer exists, though the tank does. Unfortunately, Setty is one of a large tribe of largely forgotten philanthropists of old Bengaluru.

Water flows continuously from the mouth of Nandi in the Nandishwara Temple. © *Aravind C*

Setty is said to have constructed an underground pipe to bring water from the newly built Sankey Tank to the mouth of the Nandi. The *kalyani* is clearly seen in maps prepared in 1885, three years after Sankey Tank was constructed. It is also possible that the water for this *kalyani* taps one of the drainage channels that arose from Sankey Tank and eventually led to Jakkarayana *kere* to the south and further downstream. A 1935 Bangalore Guide Map of the area (published by the Survey of India) clearly marks the temple. The 1969 Bangalore Guide Map, however, does not show the Nandi temple and *kalyani*, implying this temple disappeared from view and eventually from memory sometime after the mid-1930s.

The *kalyani* is certainly striking in its architecture and design. Apart from the water that flows from Nandi's mouth, other unusual features of the temple are the pillared corridor that runs all around the tank and the fact that it is set below ground level. There are carvings of fish and turtles on the steps of the tank, while within the tank, there are now real turtles.

IX. Kadu Mallikarjuna Swamy Temple and Inscription

A few metres down the road is the temple after which Malleswaram was named. By far the oldest temple in the area, the Kadu Mallikarjuna temple, also known as the Kadu Malleswara temple, is dedicated to Mallikarjuna, a form of Shiva.

We do not know when the temple was first built or consecrated; the linga is said to be *swayambhu*, one that has manifested itself. In addition to the main deity Mallikarjuna, the temple has shrines dedicated to Kashi Vishwanatha, Ganapati, the goddess Brahmaramba and also Vishnu. A little to the north of the main temple is a shrine dedicated to Subramanya.

It is a simple, low-profile structure which when built would have been on a hillock.[47] You will immediately notice the similarity in style between the pillared corridors around the temple here and that in the Nandishwara *kalyani*. This would be explained by the fact that a lot of the temple's present form is owed to Rao Bahadur Yele Malappa Setty who 'improved it at a high cost'.[48] The gopura at the eastern entrance is a recent addition. The tree-filled garden around the temple is one of Malleswaram's biggest and best green spots. Many Malleswaram-ites love to spend a calm evening here after a visit to the temple.

When you exit the temple from the main gateway, turn right and then immediately turn right once again. You will find yourself in a narrow path between the Kadu Mallikarjuna and the Lakshmi Venkateshwara temples. At the end of this path is a boulder enclosed within a cage on which reposes Bengaluru's oldest tangible Maratha connection. The inscription records that Ekoji (Shivaji's half-brother) gave the village of Medaraninganahalli as a *manya* (or a sacred offering) for the god Mallikarjuna of Mallapura.

The record was discovered by archaeologist and Malleswaram resident R Narasimhachar in 1909. The year is recorded as the Hindu year Saumya,

Nagakal or Snake stones in the gardens of the Kadu Malleswara temple. © *Aravind C*

The Kadu Malleswara temple, from where the extension derives its name. © *PeeVee*

corresponding to 1669 CE. Today, the village of Medaraninganahalli mentioned in the inscription lies bisected by the New BEL Road; most of the old village now forms part of the campus of IISc, with the Central Power Research Institute now standing on portions of it. As Narasimhachar says, 'This epigraph is interesting as it informs us that Mallesvaram had the almost identical name of Mallapura about 250 years before the extension was formed with its present name.'[49] Evidently, the old name was lost sometime in the intervening years. The record also makes it clear that the Kadu Mallikarjuna temple already existed in 1669.

X. Dhobi Ghats

Double back down 2nd Temple Street, turn left at the next intersection and then take the first left onto the diagonal 6th Temple Street. A short walk of about 200 metres brings you to two *kattes* in front of the dhobi ghats. You may want to rest under the shade of the generously spreading canopy of the trees at this *katte*. One of the *kattes* here has a single tree while the other, a few metres away, is of the more commonly seen pattern with one peepal and one neem tree, traditionally said to be male and female respectively. Researchers Harini Nagendra, Hita Unnikrishnan and Seema Mundoli have documented and studied *kattes* around the city.[50] Like the ones seen here, *kattes* usually have raised seating around the trees, and there are one or two idols or *nagakals*, snake stones, placed on them. Nagendra documents how *kattes* were once used for diverse activities including as spaces for community gatherings and where the village headman traditionally dispensed justice. These functions are now almost forgotten. Most *kattes* now serve only for rest and religion.

One of the oldest, and certainly one of the most interesting, examples in Bengaluru of adaptive reuse—the repurposing of an old structure—is that of the conversion of Malleswaram's old swimming pool into dhobi ghats! Survey of India maps of the area dating from the late 19th and early 20th centuries show that a water body existed in this area; this *kere* was downstream of Sankey Tank and received water from its overflow. In the mid-1930s, bathing ghats were made along the banks of the *kere* and a swimming pool was added next to it. In the 1970s, the pool was converted into dhobi ghats. You can still see vestiges of the old pool just below the stone's edge, along the northern end of the ghats. Old-timers here recall that at one time, there was also a dhobi ghat on the banks of Sankey Tank.[51] Later, when that ghat was closed, all the washermen were given facilities here: Bengaluru's largest dhobi ghat, spread over about 6 acres. Water for the ghats is still supplied from Sankey Tank. About 75,000 to 200,000 clothes from homes, hotels and other institutions are washed here every day, by nearly 300 washermen.[52]

The Dhobi Ghats in Malleswaram, one of the largest in Bengaluru. © *Aravind C*

In about 2010, the establishment was modernised, with the installation of several automatic washing machines and dryers. However, the old-fashioned method of washing clothes by hand still continues alongside, especially for some clothes that the washermen deem delicate.[53]

Despite the huge numbers of clothes, men, and machines at work here, not to mention a few donkeys too, Malleswaram's dhobi ghats are essentially tranquil. The grand old peepal trees filter out the harsh sun and the dappled lighting lends a soothing atmosphere to the whole scene. One can spend hours here, walking along the ghats or watching from the sidelines or chatting with the men and women as they work, most of whom are quite happy to share their stories with visitors who wander in.

Other Must-see Places in Malleswaram

Two other places that anyone interested in Malleswaram must see may be a little too far to include in a walk on one day.

St Peters' Pontifical Institute

St Peter's seminary, as it is popularly known, was established towards the northern end of 8th Main Road, in 1934. But its history goes back much further, all the way back to 1778 when the Société des Missions Etrangères de Paris (the Society of Foreign Missions of Paris), or the MEP as it is known, set

The 1934-built St Peter's Pontifical Institute. © *PeeVee*

At the St Peter's Pontifical Institute. © *PeeVee*

up the St Peter's Seminary near Puducherry. As the seminary began to expand, it was decided to move it to a place with a more temperate climate and so naturally, Bengaluru was chosen. In 1962, the seminary was affiliated to the Pontifical Urban University of Rome.[54] Several Roman Catholic priests have received their training in theology here.

The seminary was established here thanks partly to Sir Mirza Ismail. In August 1934, when he visited the seminary, the priests who received him gushed their thankfulness that their seminary 'occupies such a beautiful site at the doors of Bangalore', that they enjoyed the 'pure and invigorating air, and feasted [their] eyes on the grand scenery that surrounds us.'[55] Much of that remains in this seminary that stands at one end of Malleswaram.

The seminary building is a majestic, three-storeyed structure built in stone. The central part of the building projects out with a porch on the ground floor level and rooms above. The plan of the building has arched colonnades at all levels; interestingly, the arches are different at each level. The linearity of the building is further accentuated by projecting stone bands at all levels.

Jewell Filters

In 1896, a momentous event took place in Bengaluru: for the first time, modern technology was applied to quench the city's perennial thirst.[56] This was when the Hessarghatta water supply project began supplying water to the city. The project involved expanding a 15th century reservoir on the Arkavathy river. An aqueduct carried water from this newly expanded Hessarghatta reservoir to a pumping station, from where it was pumped about 10 km up to Chimney Hills; from there, gravity carried it to filtering and distribution stations in the city, including one at the northern end of Malleswaram. With this, for the first time, the city went beyond its tanks and wells in search of water, thus sounding the death knell for these centuries-old traditional sources. Water from Hessarghatta first flowed to the city in June 1896.

The first so-called Jewell Filter (named after the inventor Omar Hestrian Jewell) to be erected in India was installed in 1903 in Kolar Gold Fields by the Mysore government.[57] These were procured from the New York-based Jewell Filtration Company. When this system was seen to work successfully in Kolar, the old sand-bed filters in Bengaluru, which had been quite unsatisfactory in filtering the water from Hessarghatta, were also replaced with the Combined Jewell Filters in 1905. The system initially comprised two settling tanks and six filters, constructed of concrete. The tank for clean water was constructed below these filters.

An old tank in the BWSSB premises housing the Combined Jewell Filters. © *Aravind C*

In the early days, this plant in Malleswaram supplied 3 million gallons of filtered water a day to both the city and the C&M Station. Later, additional tanks were constructed. In the 1930s, when the water works at Thippagondanahalli were installed, these, too, pumped water to these Combined Jewell Filters.

You can still see this old installation in Malleswaram. The Jewell Filters are no longer functional, nor is the tank built on a tower that once supplied wash water for the filters; however, many of the other storage tanks are still in use.

● ● ● ● ●

The peaceful grounds around the Jewell Filters, where you can hear the leaves rustle in the wind and watch lizards skitter in the grass, is a pleasant place with which to end your Malleswaram experience. But we are sure you will come back for more, perhaps to experience the area's cultural dimensions by attending a concert or two in one of the various institutions here, or to buy some lip-smacking traditional delicacies from some of the many mom-and-pop establishments here. Or you may do as many Bengalureans do and buy your next saris or *panches* (dhotis) in one of the shops here. Like the rest of Bengaluru, Malleswaram is not immune to change. As elsewhere, old-timers here rue the razing of many of their familiar haunts and buildings. But a city is more than its buildings. And so, even as the winds of change gust through here, like elsewhere, Malleswaram retains its quintessence as a leafy, genteel, cultural hub of Bengaluru.

Notes

1. See the 1885 map. Also see later in the chapter for the village of Mallapura.
2. In the early official correspondence, the extension is spelled variously by officials and residents as Malleswaram, Mallesvarum, Mallesvarum, Malleswara, Mallesvaram and Malleshwaram. This book uses the first spelling which is most commonly used; it is also what the post office uses.
3. Anon 1920, 92.
4. File Sani 27 of 1900, Sl 1–9, KSA.
5. File ML 80 of 09, Sl 1, 3–4, KSA.
6. File Sani 26 of 00, Sl 1–8, KSA.
7. File Sani 27 of 1900, Sl 1–9, KSA.
8. File Sani 144 of 1900, Sl 1–4, KSA.
9. File GF 146 of 1901–02, KSA.
10. File ML 238 of 1912, Sl 1, 6, 8, KSA.
11. Anon 1931, 72.
12. Report on the administration of Mysore for the year 1941–42.
13. http://www.mlafgcw.org/history.html, accessed September 2018.
14. http://www.mesinstitutions.org.in, accessed September 2018.

15. Interviews with 70-year-old Sundar Prasad, great-grandson of HV Nanjundayya, and Udhav Patankar, great-grandson of Dewan VP Madhav Rao, August 2018. Both are residents of Malleswaram.
16. Anon 1927.
17. Subba Rao 1933.
18. Visvesvaraya 1917, 37.
19. Lee 1874.
20. Francis 1988.
21. File Sani 1 of 1891, Sl 1–2, KSA.
22. DeSouza 1970.
23. Report on Public Instruction in Mysore, for the Year 1877–78.
24. As per documents shared by Krishnama Raju, Raman Research Institute Trust.
25. Parameswaran 2011.
26. Raman had planted a huge number of roses in his house in the Raman Research Institute and he tended to them every day, very carefully. Personal communication, Dominique Radhakrishnan, daughter-in-law of Sir CV Raman, 31 October 2018.
27. Raman was a voracious reader. His eclectic reading included several classics. Kaushalya Ramaseshan, his nephew's wife, recalls how Raman, who often sleep-talked, once rattled off some lines from one of Thomas Hardy's novels in his sleep! Personal communication, 31 October 2018.
28. Ramaseshan 1978.
29. Ramaseshan 1988, 163.
30. Raman 1930.
31. Parameswaran 2011, 134.
32. Baweja 2015.
33. Lee 2012.
34. Dutt 1955.
35. Gundappa 2018.
36. The house was possibly sold to BN Gopala Rao. Interview with Indira Ramakant and Seetha Ravindra, both great-granddaughters of HV Nanjundayya, 9 September 2018. Gopala Rao later became notorious for having defrauded thousands of people of their money, including the redoubtable Sir CV Raman who 'invested' his Nobel winnings with the scamster. The house was probably later bought by the government from Gopala Rao.
37. Gundappa, quoted in Chandrasekharayya 1966, 1.
38. Interview with Indira Ramakant and Seetha Ravindra, 9 September 2018.
39. Interview with Surendra Reddy, Jayaram Reddy and Vinatha Reddy, grandson and great-grandchildren of T Baiyanna, 8 April 2019; Iengar 1985.
40. Interviews with Udhav Patankar and Sunder Prasad, residents of Malleswaram, September 2018.
41. Interview with Vatsala Rao, great-granddaughter of PN Krishnamurti, November 2017.
42. File Muz 36 of 1896, Sl 1–4, Section VI, KSA.
43. File Muz 36 of 1896, Sl 1–7, Section I, KSA.
44. Mathur 2001; Karunakaran 2014.
45. Sundara Rao 2015.
46. Radhakrishna 1997.

47. Issar 2002, 134.
48. File Muz 23 of 1903, Sl 1–10, Section III, KSA.
49. Annual Report for the year ending 30th June 1909, Archaeological Survey of Mysore, 25.
50. Nagendra 2016.
51. Interview with Muniraju, a washerman at the dhobi ghat, August 2018.
52. 'Dhobi Ghat gets a washover', The Times of India, 23 December 2009.
53. Interview with washerman Muniraju, August 2018.
54. https://stpeters.org.in/seminary/, accessed 31 October 2018.
55. Ismail 1936, 334.
56. Many thanks, for discussions, to S Vishwanath of Rainwater Club, who has written and lectured on this subject extensively.
57. Iyengar 1913.

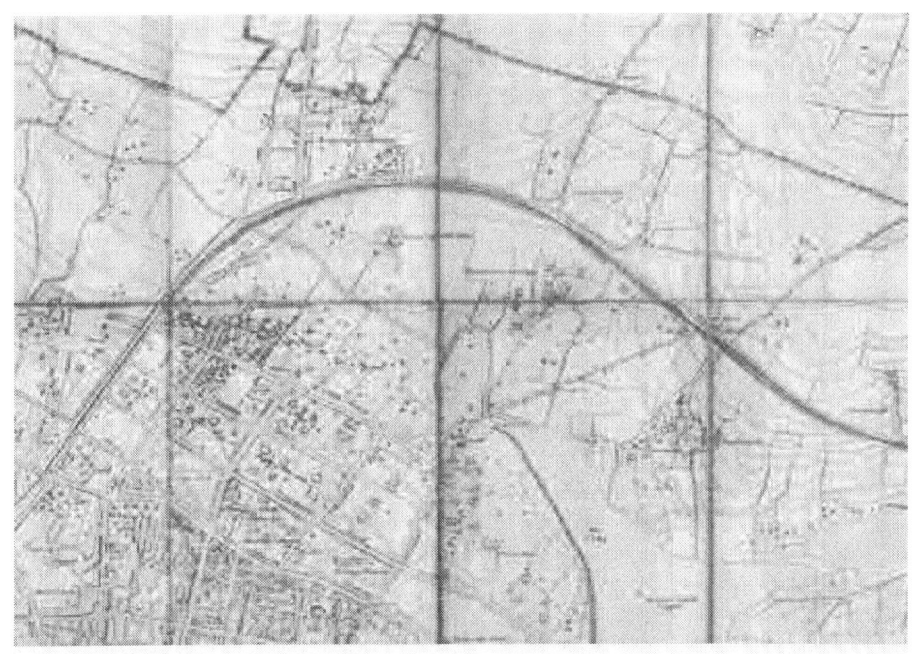

The Fraser Town area in 1884-85. From, Survey of India. *Cantonment and City of Bangalore and Environs, Season 1884-85. Courtesy of Mythic Society, Bengaluru.*

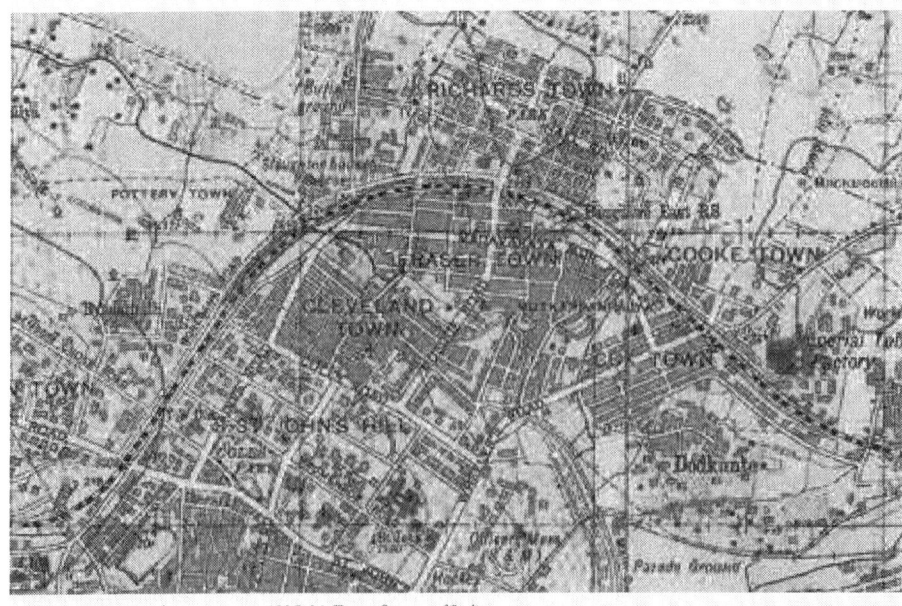

Fraser Town and its vicinity in 1935-36. From, Survey of India. *Bangalore Guide Map. Surveyed 1935-36. Courtesy of Naresh Narasimhan.*

CHAPTER 6

Towns of the City: Fraser Town, Richards Town, Cooke Town

Extensions of British Bangalore

The plague that led to the expansion of the city on the south and north also had its effects on the other side of the administrative divide, in the Civil and Military Station. Newspaper articles from the late 1890s onwards began carrying alarming reports: 'Plague spreads in Bangalore', 'Plague active in Bangalore', '371 cases since 28 September', disturbances, plague riots, and so on.[1] And frankly, it is not really surprising, given the unhygienic conditions that prevailed. The Swiss doctor Alexandre Yersin had established beyond doubt the connection between rats, plague and humans in the 1890s. In the mid-1900s, by which time this connection was more generally (but still not wholly) accepted, the C&M Station embarked on a programme of 'destruction of these vermin'. Between 1906 and 1908, over half a million rats and mice were killed. In other words, the population of vermin in the C&M Station was several times that of people, which at that time was 90,000.[2]

Inoculation drives were undertaken but, at least at first, these did not meet with great success. The authorities sought to encourage further inoculations by making the whole event rather like a mela, complete with music, drums and dance!³ Despite all this, the war against plague was only partly effective, for the disease continued to strike throughout the first two decades of the 20th century. And while the City Municipality had already begun work on establishing the two new extensions of Malleswaram and Basavanagudi within a month of the plague first making its appearance in Bengaluru, opening up new residential areas was implemented at a much tardier pace in the C&M Station.

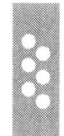

The problems were bureaucracy and money, in that order. Proposals for relieving congestion had been discussed since at least 1899, but the financing of such schemes was caught in bureaucratic tangles. The crux of the issue: could the authorities give loans under the Land Improvement Loans Act of 1883 or should a new law be formulated? Seven years of discussing and letter-writing later, a special law called the Bangalore Sanitary Improvements Loans Law was enacted in 1906, under which the C&M Station Municipality could give loans on favourable terms to those whose houses were demolished, to enable them to build in the new extensions.[4]

Meanwhile, even as the bureaucratic wrangles were going on, in 1902, Col Robertson, the then Resident of Mysore State, submitted to the Government of India a proposal to relieve congestion in the Station; the estimated budget was almost Rs 18 lakhs! The government blanched at the cost and politely dismissed the proposal. Finally, in 1905, it agreed to sanction a loan for a pilot project: show us your scheme works and we shall see, they said.[5] Some more missives and even a few telegrams later, in early 1906, the Government of India finally advanced a paltry sum of about Rs 20,000 to begin laying out a new extension to the C&M Station.

Fraser Town

Land was acquired in Papareddipalya which fell within Doddigunta village and work began in February 1906. The extension was bounded on its north-western, northern and north-eastern perimeters by the curving railway line that linked the Bangalore Cantonment station to Chennai. On its southern end

Newspaper reports from 1907-1909 on the Northern Extension. *Courtesy of KSA, Mysore.*

was Promenade Road, to the south of which was the older suburb of Cleveland Town. On its east ran Wheeler Road.

To begin with, about 50 acres of land were acquired at a cost of about Rs 18,860 and divided into 476 plots. In the meantime, some houses in the most crowded areas of Blackpully (now Shivajinagar) were demolished and those lands acquired. Those whose houses were dismantled were given some compensation and also a site in the new extension. The acquired land was divided into plots; those who were given sites were told to build houses on them within a certain period. And so began the Blackpully Extension Scheme as it was then called. The extension itself was at first referred to as the Northern Extension (because it was north of the C&M Station; not to be confused with the Northern Extension of the city which later became Seshadripuram) and later named Fraser Town after the then British Resident Stuart M Fraser, who had supported and pushed for it. In 1988, Fraser Town was renamed Pulikeshi Nagar after Pulakesin II, the seventh-century ruler of the Chalukya kingdom. However, most Bengalureans still know it as Fraser Town.

A plague-proof town

The primary aim of all this demolition of houses and relocation of people being to prevent plague, particular care was given to planning to keep plague away. JH Stephens, the Municipal Engineer in charge of laying out the new extension, implemented several ideas to keep Fraser Town plague-proof. First, the area was broken up into 1-acre blocks by intersecting streets and roads. The main roads were 99 feet wide, while the other streets were 66 feet and 33 feet wide.[6] Each of the 1-acre blocks was divided into 20 plots measuring 66 by 33 feet. Those who wanted to build larger houses could buy a maximum of two plots. Importantly, only one-third of the site could be built upon; the remaining was compulsorily to be left open and unbuilt. This meant that houses could only be a maximum of 726 square feet on a single plot, or 1452 square feet in case of a larger plot, and would be surrounded by large open spaces. These dimensions, Stephens says, were arrived at after measuring the houses where people lived in Blackpully.[7] Incidentally, by law, no large trees were to be planted around the house.[8]

Like many of his time, Stephens makes much of houses being 'free from damp' if they were to be free from plague. This was a period when, though the connection between plague, rats and fleas had been established, it was still thought that dampness and lack of ventilation abetted, if not caused the disease. Stephens for example, declares, 'Fermentation caused by damp on the soil of Bangalore is the cause of plague at that place.'[9] The idea then was to keep houses rat-free but also well ventilated. Accordingly, Fraser Town's drains were dug 1.5 feet below ground level, so that water would drain quickly out of the building sites. Additionally, to keep rats from burrowing into them, all houses had to have basements that were 1.5 feet high and made of granite rubble mixed with stone. For the same reason, floors were to be made of stone slabs or tiles, and not mud, and were certainly not to be covered with cow dung.[10] Finally, the roofs were to be made of Mangalore tiles, not country tiles or thatch. Stephens waxes eloquent about how the Mangalore tiles allowed air circulation but kept water out. Additionally, he believed '[t]hese tiles also afford no lodgement to mice or rats'.[11]

Later, British Resident Stuart Fraser noted that since the houses were built on modern sanitary lines, plague did not visit Fraser Town; the conditions had 'designedly been made averse to the rat establishing himself there on terms of domestic familiarity with the inhabitants'.[12]

The improved sanitation that thus resulted led to a marked drop in cases of plague and Fraser Town indeed lived up to its reputation of being 'the only plague-proof town in all India'. The Government of India must have been impressed, for it did eventually part with more funds to keep this 'scheme to relieve congestion' going.

Within two years of work beginning on the extension, more than 400 sites had been sold, about 175 houses had been constructed, and a few hundred people had already moved to Fraser Town, including from Blackpully. And, as planned, the density of population was low—about 50 per acre, as against about 300 per acre in Blackpully. But perhaps it was too low: the extension was not growing quite as quickly as had been hoped. The problem was that people were a little chary of moving so far—why, it was almost 2.5 km away from Blackpully!

It took a few good men to throw their weight and their money behind Fraser Town to help it succeed. Prominent among them were Annasawmy Mudaliar, merchant, contractor and philanthropist, and Hajee Sir Ismail Sait, merchant, banker and philanthropist. Their investments and involvement helped the extension grow and become popular. Both realised that people needed facilities to make the move to a new place. In addition to their other charitable activities, both these gentlemen also built small houses in Fraser Town for people to rent at nominal rates of Re 1–Rs 2 per month.

An early view of cottages and houses in Fraser Town. From Stephens, JH. 1914. *Plague-Proof Planning in South India.* Madras: Methodist Publishing House.

Two Merchant Philanthropists

Grain merchant, contractor, philanthropist. **Rao Bahadur Bangalore Perumal Annasawmy Mudaliar** was all this and more. Born in 1849 and educated at Mission High School in Bengaluru, he is said to have become a contractor for the Railways while still in school.

Mudaliar was also a contractor for the Public Works Department and it was in this capacity that he built the so-called Government Offices, also called the Public Offices. Until 1881, the offices of the British administration were housed in the Attara Kacheri (also called the Public Offices) located in Cubbon Park. With the Rendition in 1881, the Attara Kacheri was taken over by the Mysore Maharaja's government, leaving the C&M Station's administration suddenly homeless. After several years of being housed in rented buildings scattered around the Station, and after previous plans for a new building were turned down, the administration finally agreed that a new building was indeed required. The new offices for the C&M administration came up next to Mayo Hall, and was built in an architectural style similar to it. It was opened in July 1904. Annasawmy Mudaliar was lauded for his work on this building and received the Kaiser-i-Hind, 2nd class, in recognition of this work.[16]

Rao Bahadur BP Annasawmy Mudaliar. *Courtesy of B Anantharam, great grandson of Annasawmy Mudaliar.*

Annasawmy Mudaliar served as Municipal Commissioner in the Station Municipality. He was also Director of the Bangalore Bank.[17]

Apart from his business and building deals, Annasawmy Mudaliar was well respected for his many charitable works. In 1900, he, along with Hajee Sir Ismail Sait and four other citizens of Bengaluru, funded and established the Lady Curzon Hospital in Shivajinagar, a hospital especially for women. In the early days of Fraser Town, Annasawmy Mudaliar realised people needed certain basic amenities before they could move in. Accordingly, he built a dispensary and a market, and handed them over to the Municipality. He also built a school for children of all castes and creeds.

Annasawmy Mudaliar's spirit is revealed in this story about an inoculation drive held in October 1907 at a market in the C&M Station. The administration was out in full force, from the Resident, his First Assistant and the Municipality President to health officers and doctors. But the crowd was suspicious of the whole enterprise. Until up stepped BP Annasawmy Mudaliar, the prominent and well-respected citizen of the Station. He first spoke to the gathering about the benefits of inoculation and then, to show his confidence in the method, bared his arm and was inoculated even as the crowd cheered![18]

Three roads in Fraser Town are named after his three sons: Madhavaraya, Cheluvaraya and Achyutaraya. Annasawmy Mudaliar himself has a road named after him in Ulsoor, where he lived almost all his life.

Hajee Sir Ismail Sait was born on 7 March 1859 in Mysuru. In 1870, his family moved to Bengaluru. Four years later, when his father passed away, 15-year-old Sait plunged into the business of buying and selling goods. It was something he obviously had a flair for. His first commercial venture seems to have been an extremely successful shop called the English Warehouse, strategically located on St Mark's Road, close to where his (mainly English) customers were. The shop sold all manner of goods imported from England, from milk powder to machinery. Soon, there were branches of English Warehouse in Chennai and Secunderabad too.

Hajee Sir Ismail Sait. *Courtesy of Zaffar Sait, great grandson of Ismail Sait.*

Very quickly, Ismail Sait built on this success to diversify into an astonishing variety of businesses. At 22, he became a Director in the newly established Carnatic Mills (which later merged with another mill to become the well-known Binny Mills). He owned and operated mines in Kolar Gold Fields and Shivamogga; supplied provisions to the British Army establishment in Bengaluru, including horsegram; traded in timber; and ran a distillery and a carbonic acid manufacturing unit in Kolkata. He also served as Director in the Mysore Sandalwood Oil company, the Mysore Sugar company and the Bhadravathi Iron Works.[19]

But success in business was not the reason for honours being heaped upon Ismail Sait. Throughout his life, he donated generously to many causes. His most well-known act of charity was a donation of Rs 1.5 lakhs towards the construction of the Gosha Hospital in Bengaluru, set up in 1925 so that women who observed purdah could avail of modern medical care. Sait also made generous contributions to the Bowring, St Martha's and Victoria hospitals in Bengaluru, the KR Hospital in Mysuru, and hospitals in Chennai and Shimla; to the Aligarh Muslim University and Mysore University; to orphanages, schools, reading rooms and colleges in various parts of the country; and to several other organisations. He also provided invaluable help in relief works during the many plague and cholera outbreaks that Bengaluru suffered in those days. As an active member of the business community, when the Chamber of Commerce was established in Bengaluru in 1916 (a year after Sir M Visvesvaraya had suggested it), Ismail Sait donated money for the construction of new buildings for it.

In Fraser Town, Hajee Sir Ismail Sait donated land and money to build the mosque which is named after him; the road on which it stands was named the Hajee Sir Ismail Sait Mosque Road. He also built the Urdu school opposite the mosque and a *musafirkhana* or travellers' rest house, which no longer exists. His estate still provides scholarships to deserving Cutchi Memon students, and also maintains a school that he built. It was for all his public service that, in 1919, the Mysore Maharaja conferred on Hajee Ismail Sait the title 'Fakhr-ut-Tujjar' (The Pride of Merchants). He was knighted by King George V in Buckingham Palace in 1923.

As a prominent member of Bengaluru society, Hajee Sir Ismail Sait was given the honour of formally opening Russell Market in 1927. He was also a popular fixture in the city's racing circuit, as a racehorse owner and member of the Bengaluru and Mysuru race clubs. He died on 24 April 1934.

Richards Town

Meanwhile, the Station Municipality felt another extension north of Fraser Town was needed. This extension, meant for Europeans, Eurasians and wealthy Indians, aimed to spur trade and livelihoods for people in Fraser Town. In 1911, the C&M Station Municipality acquired about 47 acres of land north of the railway line for the grand sum of Rs 13,075. The land was divided into 112 plots, each measuring a quarter acre; the price of a plot: Rs 300–Rs 600.[20]

The road bridge over the railway line near the Hajee Sir Ismail Sait Mosque was constructed in 1912. Roads were laid out, drains built, culverts made, and in no time, people began to buy, build and move into Richards Town, named after FJ Richards, the then President of the Station Municipality.

One of the ideas for boosting the accessibility of Richards Town and Fraser Town was to set up an electric tramway up to Richards Park. FJ Richards himself had his heart set on it, arguing that Richards Town's success depended upon the tramway. However, the Mysore government seems not to have approved of the idea. But Richards Town proved to be a success even without the tramway. Other incentives were proffered. The C&M Station Municipality encouraged the Peninsular Tobacco Company to establish their factory nearby as a potential employer. The factory opened in 1913. It was later known as the Imperial Tobacco Company and, in 1974, renamed the Indian Tobacco Company (ITC). Incidentally, many older residents of the area associated the smell of roasting tobacco with home!

© Paul Fernandes. First appeared in In and Around, the newsletter of the Richards Town Residents Association.

Cooke Town

Though Fraser Town had been planned primarily to accommodate people from Shivajinagar whose houses had been demolished, within a few years, it attracted many others: retirees from various government departments, retired defence personnel and so on. The area was particularly popular with Anglo-Indians, Mangalore Christians, Kodavas and Mudaliars. As demand grew, so did the extensions.

Cooke Town was laid out in the early 1930s, again on a grid pattern. Plot sizes here were intermediate between Richards Town and Fraser Town. This extension was peopled largely by Anglo-Indians. Beyond Cooke Town lay guava orchards and vineyards growing the famous Bangalore Blue grapes.

In the 1950s and 1960s, as the Anglo-Indians who lived here emigrated elsewhere, people from other communities began moving in. Among those who moved here were pensioners, many who served (or had served) in the army, and employees of Hindustan Aeronautics Ltd (HAL). Some of those who left donated their houses to the Church, which explains the large number of convents that dot this area. Some of these churches ran orphanages, schools, hostels and other institutions. One of Bengaluru's premier institutions, St John's Medical College, was established in one such Christian institution in Cooke Town in 1963.

A Confluence of Communities

The earliest settlers of the new extension of Fraser Town were mostly Muslims and Hindus, and a few Christians, many of whom moved in here from Shivajinagar. Very soon, people from different communities—Anglo-Indians, Mangalore Christians, Tamil-speaking communities and so on—began to call this area home.

What distinguished these Towns from the rest of Bengaluru was their very cosmopolitan nature. Growing up here meant your neighbour on this side would be a Christian, on the other side a Hindu, and one house away, a Muslim. As Peter Colaco says in his book *Bangalore*, 'Temples, mosques and churches were the familiar landscapes of our childhood ... We took for granted the existence of different people around us, their different beliefs, their different languages.'[21]

This pluralism meant a bonanza of foods and festivities for children (and adults). For Christmas, all children, including Hindus and Muslims, went carol singing, and everyone got rose cookies, *kulkuls* (a crisp, deep-fried snack made with flour, sugar and coconut milk), cake and other goodies from their Christian friends and neighbours. At Ramzan, you would get biryani and *sheer kurma*

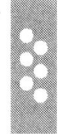

(a dessert made with milk, vermicelli and dry fruits) from your friends. Ugadi meant *holige* (a flat bread with a sweetened stuffing) from the aunty next door. And for Deepavali, everyone would turn out to burst crackers and, of course, to eat![22]

The People Behind the Names

Fraser Town is named after **Stuart Mitford Fraser** who, in 1905, became British Resident of Mysore State, a post in which he enjoyed great popularity. Appointed to the Indian Civil Service (ICS) in 1884 as Assistant Collector in Bombay, he was later tutor to the Maharaja of Bhavnagar and then to the young Maharaja of Mysore, Krishnaraja Wodeyar IV. Afterwards, Sir SM Fraser was Resident in Kashmir and Hyderabad.

In Bengaluru, Fraser facilitated and pushed for the formation of Fraser Town, which is why the extension was named after him. Incidentally, this was also the period when the famed Bishop Cotton School was floundering and on the verge of being closed down. Fraser was instrumental and actively assisted in the process of the takeover of the school by a new management, which helped the hoary institution rise, phoenix-like, from imminent collapse.

George Henry Cooke was the longest-serving President of the Municipal Commission of the C&M Station, serving from 1928 to 1934. Born in Dungarvan in Ireland in 1895, Cooke did not pursue his father's business of jewellery and watchmaking: having excelled in school, particularly in mathematics, football and cricket, he went on to study in Trinity College in Dublin. He then joined the ICS in 1920 and was first posted to Madras. Later, he moved to Bengaluru where he served as Assistant Collector and Magistrate, Sub-Collector and Joint Magistrate. Other posts he held under Mysore State included Inspector of Schools, Additional Joint Registrar of the Cooperative Societies, and Secretary to the Education and Public Health Departments.[23]

Richards Town was formed thanks to the efforts of **Frederick John Richards**. Born on 26 June 1875, he studied at Oxford's Exeter College. After obtaining his Masters degree in Arts, he joined the ICS in 1898 and was first appointed Assistant Collector in Madras.[24] He was President of the Municipal Commission of the C&M Station from 1908 to 1912, and was also Collector and District Magistrate.

Richards was a keen antiquarian; most of the stone tools and ceramic objects from Karnataka in the University of Oxford's renowned Pitt Rivers Museum were donated by him. He was later appointed Honorary Lecturer in Indian archaeology at University College, London.[25] He was also a founder of the Mythic Society in Bengaluru. He authored several articles on south Indian gods, goddesses and rituals. In fact, Richards's detailed article about Bengaluru's Karaga festival in the society's journal is one of the first documentations of this festival.

FJ Richards, who was instrumental in the establishment of Richards Town. *Courtesy of Mythic Society.*

Bungalows of the Towns

— by Anjali Cheriyath and Sonali Dhanpal

There are several gracious old bungalows remaining in Fraser Town, Cooke Town and Richards Town—about 215 as of April 2017.[26]

A typical layout

Set within large, tree-filled compounds, bungalows usually (but not always) have symmetrical layouts. The typical bungalow in this area has a verandah, a large central hall flanked by two bedrooms on either side, and a separate dining room. Often there was a large pantry behind the dining hall or adjoining it. The kitchen and the servants' quarters were in a separate 'outhouse'. Some old houses, particularly in Richards Town, also had stables set against the compound wall. Most bungalows had grand or elaborate gates, marked by decorative gate posts.

You may have noticed how colonial bungalows often have multiple roofs and terraces. The central hall of the bungalows of the area usually has a high ceiling with a sloping roof and Mangalore tiles, while the rooms on either side have lower, flat Madras terrace roofs. Sometimes, two of the side rooms may have pitched roofs while others have flat roofs. These height differences may have been governed by the need for ventilation, or perhaps it was an architect's whim!

A bungalow in Richards Town. © *PeeVee*

Most bungalows used brick as the building material, plastered with lime plaster. Stone was used but rarely, sometimes as quoins at the edge of the buildings.

Monkey tops and more

You can see a distinct difference between the older Cantonment bungalows and the bungalows of the early 1900s that are found in the three Towns. The linear, low bungalow gave way to bungalows with vertical aspirations: pitched roofs, peaked gables, turrets, a profusion of ornamentation, and of course the famous monkey tops, the pointed hoods over windows that project from the wall. Monkey tops are usually made of a close trelliswork of slats, suspended from the eaves of the window hood or the gable of the porch. The bottom edge of the trellis is shaped with fanciful curves. The trellis is often painted green.

Other period details you see here are cast iron sunshades and ornamental parapets. Several houses have coats of arms emblazoned on their pediments. A few houses, especially in Richards Town, have classical semi-octagonal bays with castellated turrets and little pointed windows. In Cooke Town, the youngest of the three Towns, you can also see Art Deco motifs and decorations in some of the bungalows that were built in 1940s, '50s and '60s.

Monkey tops! © *PeeVee*

Walk 1: Through Promenade Road, Fraser Town

In which you visit several churches and their educational institutions

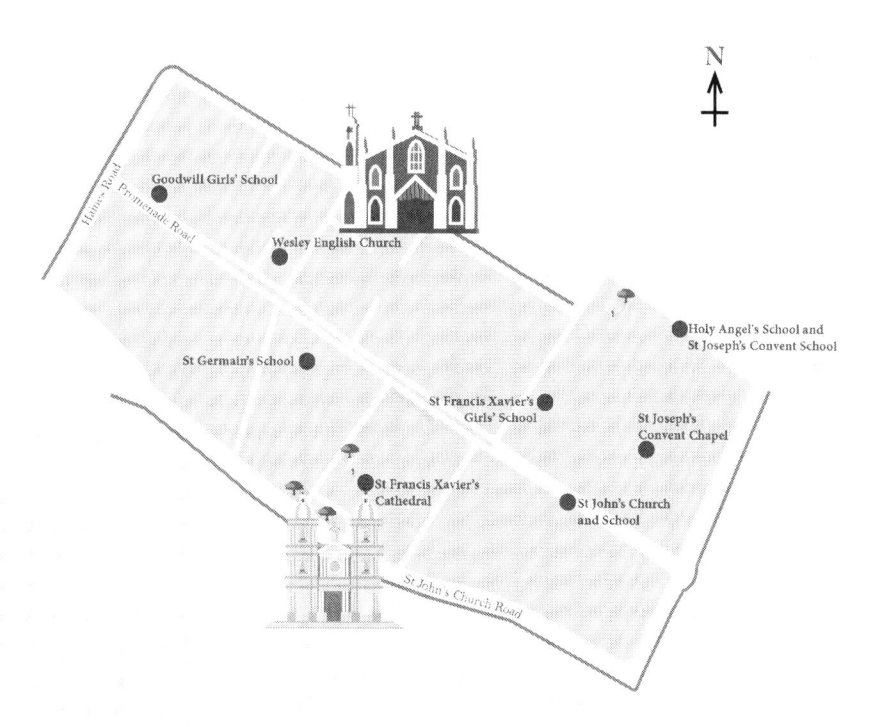

Walk 1: Through Promenade Road, Fraser Town. © *INTACH Bengaluru Chapter*

Walk 1: Through Promenade Road

– by Krupa Rajangam

Promenade Road teems with churches and institutions that have helped make Bengaluru an educational hub. Promenade down this road, beginning from the Thom's Bakery end, and unravel the sometimes confusing, often intertwined, history of these churches and schools. (However, do keep in mind that most schools and their grounds are typically not open to casual visitors.)

Incidentally, Promenade Road was carved out of lands north of 'Mootoocherry', the 'native' settlement beyond Cantonment Bazaar (Shivajinagar's markets). It defined one edge of Cleveland Town, a suburb which predates Fraser Town by several decades. Today, however, these areas are considered a part of Fraser Town.

1. St John's Church and School

This striking red church is just past Thom's Bakery. This church is built in the Neo-Gothic style, with pointed arches, spires and crenellations on its parapet. It looks pretty much as it did when it was completed in 1858 (though bits and pieces were added later).

The story behind its founding is interesting because it gives us a glimpse into the regimented and segregated life of the 19th century Cantonment. The church was conceived as a pensioners' chapel to serve the elderly residents of Cleveland Town. It owes its foundation to Rev Posnett, Assistant Chaplain at St Mark's Cathedral. Rev Posnett had observed that Eurasians, pensioned soldiers and their children were not really welcome in St Mark's Cathedral or the Cantonment schools, and so conceived the idea of a separate parish (and thus schoolroom and church) for them. With the Bishop's support he petitioned the Directors of the East India Company (which ran the Empire at that time) for permission to set it up. Permission was needed because the Company had a 'one station, one church' rule at the time.

St John's Church, with its distinctive red spire. © *PeeVee*

By 1853 a foundation to build the 'Mootoocherry' church was laid near an existing pensioners' chapel, along with two schoolrooms. These were completed in 1854 to serve as a school for 'boys, girls, and infants'. Additional funds were then sought for the church building based on a guarantee by the Cantonment priests and the Bishop that the structure would be 'plain and simple with no adornment as befitting its location'.[28] While work was underway, the priests decided to add a tower. There was some opposition to this from Cantonment residents, as their church, St Mark's, didn't have a tower—so why should a pensioners'/Eurasians' church have one? However, the priests managed to raise funds privately and the church with tower was consecrated in 1858, when it was renamed St John's Church; the area became known as St John's Hill. Further construction followed (chancels and stained glass panels were added), and finally, with the installation of the organ in 1898 the church began to look like it does today. St John's Church is affiliated with the (Protestant) Church of South India (CSI).

The spire of this church, visible amidst trees, with cottages dotting the slopes, made for an attractive view from the Cantonment and reminded residents of their countryside parishes back in England. Over the years the two schoolrooms grew to become today's St John's High School.

II. St Joseph's Convent Chapel

Across the street from St John's Church is St Joseph's Convent Chapel, used by the Sisters of St Joseph of Tarbes, a congregation founded in France in 1843, for their private worship. It is a Neo-Romanesque stone structure with semi-circular arches and a central lanterned dome. Indeed, it resembles the French Romanesque style of cathedral architecture likely because of its French origin—much like St John's Church is modelled after the English Gothic architectural style because of its English origin.

Its foundation was laid in 1898 by Monseigneur Kleiner, who belonged to the Missions Étrangères de Paris (MEP) or the Paris Foreign Mission, a group of French Jesuits already active in Bengaluru at that time.[29] The Jesuits, both Portuguese and French, had been in India for about 400 years by then. The Tarbes Sisters were invited to Bengaluru by Msgr Coadou, then Bishop of the French Jesuit Mysuru Diocese (of which Bengaluru was part). They initially assisted at the then newly opened Bowring Hospital in Shivajinagar. An

Monseigneur Eugène-Louis Kleiner. From, *Les Missions Catholiques*, Vol 31, 1899, p544.

212 | Discovering Bengaluru

St Joseph's Convent Chapel, as seen from the bell tower of St John's Church, early1900s. The new extension of Fraser Town is in the distance. *Courtesy of Jane Smith, granddaughter of Fred Goodwill, from the collections of Fred Goodwill.*

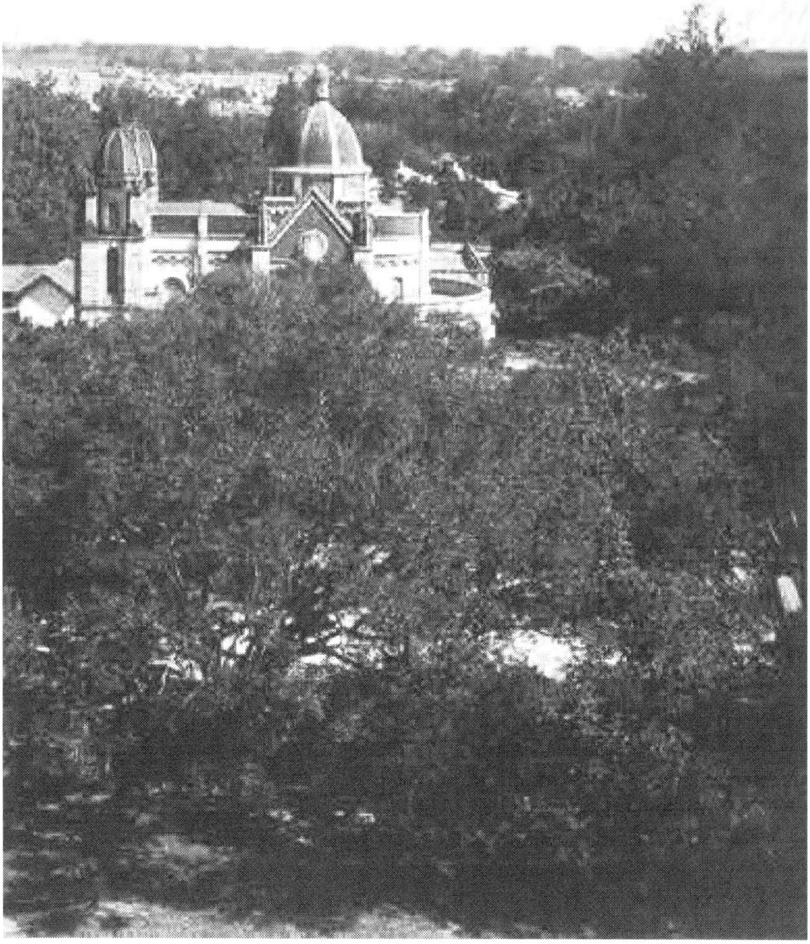

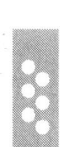

interesting incident that affected the history of the Tarbes Sisters in Bengaluru is that before their arrival here, another France-based congregation, the Sisters of the Good Shepherd, had been invited to Bengaluru in 1854. Clashes with the Good Shepherd Sisters over division of hospital work at Bowring and teaching led to the Tarbes Sisters being given charge of the day school attached to the parish school of St Francis Xavier's Cathedral (*see below*), and they moved their convent house to Promenade Road. After the laying of the foundation stone in 1898, the chapel was finally consecrated in 1907 with the MEP donating Rs 40,000 towards its construction.

Incidentally, Jyoti Nivas College in Koramangala, which most Bengalureans will have heard of, was started by the Tarbes Sisters in this very compound on Promenade Road in 1966. It moved to its current location in 1976. A record of that time wishes the Sisters well in the new venture and notes their spirit in setting up a college at a location amidst grasslands well outside the city.

III. Holy Angels Higher Primary School and St Joseph's Convent Girls' High School

Adjacent to St Joseph's chapel is St Joseph's Convent Girls' High School and the RTC School. Rajamma Thumboo Chetty, wife of Raja Dharma Pravina Thumboo Chetty, the then Chief Justice of Mysore, wished to start a school for Indian girls. She donated a house on Narayan Pillai Street for the cause and the Sisters of Tarbes opened the Rajamma Thumboo Chetty School (RTC School) here in 1899. The school moved to larger premises near St Francis Xavier's School (see below) in 1915. It was bifurcated into three schools in 1944: Holy Angels Higher Primary School, St Joseph's Convent Girls' High School, while the RTC School continued to exist as RTC Girls Middle School.

Rajamma Thumboo Chetty. From, *Les Missions Catholiques*, Vol 31, 1899, p544

IV. St Francis Xavier's Cathedral

One of the grandest edifices on Promenade Road, on the same side of the road and occupying the block next to St John's Church, is St Francis Xavier's Cathedral.

This Catholic church was built in 1851 thanks to the efforts of Father Chevalier (later Bishop Chevalier of Mysuru) of the MEP. He bought land for the church from the widow of an English commander for Rs1000. By the time Father Servanton took over as parish priest in 1898, the congregation had grown considerably and need for a new church was felt as the old church could only accommodate 350 to 400 people. Finally, when the cross fell from the tower of the old church in 1905, it was interpreted as a sign that a new building was required. The foundation stone was laid in 1911. After 21 years of persistent fundraising by Father Servanton, the new church finally opened in 1932.

This is the Neo-Romanesque stone structure we see today, similar in style to St Joseph's Convent Chapel but conceived on a far grander scale—one befitting a grand church or cathedral. The domes on top of the entry towers are, however, a recent addition. In keeping with the architectural style of European cathedrals this structure is oriented east–west with a grand entry to the west (St John's Road side). This entry is defined by a large central entrance doorway, a rose window above (circular window above the doors with a radiating pattern, typical of European cathedrals), and towers on either side. This entrance leads straight to the slightly curved altar end (apsidal shape), also a typical feature

St Francis Xavier's Cathedral, 1980s. © *INTACH*

The domes over the entry tower were added in 2009. © *PeeVee*

of European cathedrals. The east–west orientation is so that light can fall on the stained glass panels that are installed both at the grand western facade and eastern altar end to create a spectacular lighting effect within.

The cathedral also has stained glass panels but these were added gradually with the support of patrons, mainly the Thumboo Chetty family. Currently the grand western entry is closed and a smaller doorway to the north provides access.

In the same compound is St Anthony's Boys' School; Father Servanton is credited with founding this school as well, in 1913. When St Francis Xavier's School (*see below*), then in the same compound, was set up as an independent institution, its old building was transformed into St Aloysius Primary School, possibly in 1898 and later made a high school. A more recent addition within this compound is St Rock's Girls' High School, established in 1997, though a higher primary school of the same name has been in existence since 1957.

When Bengaluru was declared an independent Catholic diocese (splitting from Mysuru) in 1940, St Francis Xavier's was designated as the diocesan cathedral. In 1942, Rev Thomas Pothacamury became the first Indian Bishop of the Bengaluru Diocese and the church structure was formally consecrated as St Francis Xavier's Cathedral on 24 January 1948.

The mortal remains of Father Servanton, Rev Pothacamury and patrons from the Thumboo Chetty family were all laid to rest inside the cathedral as a mark of honour. The intersection of St John's Church Road and Seppings Road was renamed Father Servanton Circle in honour of his dedicated service.

V. St Francis Xavier's Girls' School

Diagonally across the street from the cathedral is St Francis Xavier's Girls' School, part of the same compound as St Joseph's Convent Chapel. The parish school associated with St Francis Xavier's Cathedral was run by the Sisters of St Joseph of Tarbes. It began in a small house somewhere in the area in 1889 and then moved within the cathedral compound. Land for the current premises was bought two years later, and a new building constructed by 1894 and formalised as St Francis Xavier's Girls' School. By 1898 the school was running in a full-fledged manner in its current premises with a total of 139 pupils.

The original 1894 school building still stands; a simple rectangular stone structure with sloping roof topped by Mangalore tiles and used occasionally for school events.

VI. St Germain's School

Head back onto Promenade Road, walk towards Coles Park, and cross over to St John's Church Road to see this building, which was originally part of the SFX compound. It has an interesting past, going from school to exalted residence and then back to school once again. The structure is neoclassical in style, with a columnar entrance corridor, semi-circular arches and pediment roof, but has been added to and altered over the years as the school grew.

The well-known St Joseph's Boys' School was first started in these premises by the MEP in 1858. It moved to its current location near Residency Road in 1898 and the vacated school building began to function as the (Catholic) Bishop's house. When Bengaluru became a separate diocese in 1940, a new house was constructed for the Bishop, and this building fell vacant again. In 1944, Rev Pothacamury started St Germain's School here. The school was named in memory of Father St Germain, a much-loved French priest who had taught at St Joseph's Boys School.

St Germain High School. © *PeeVee*

VII. Wesley English Church

Walk 100 metres and cross over to the other side of Promenade Road to see this church at the junction of Promenade and Saunders roads. It was established as a Wesleyan church,[30] and briefly called St John's Hill Church, and finally renamed Wesley English Church in 1953. It was originally located in Haines Road within 'Mootoocherry' (now part of Shivajinagar), currently where the Wesley Tamil Church stands. Over time, the Wesleyan missionaries felt the need for separate English and Tamil churches; so the church was split in 1888, and the English church moved to its current location.

The structure was built in the Neo-Gothic style, similar to that of St John's. Parts of it have been altered over time. The bell tower at the entry, built in the same style, is a recent addition. There is a missionary school room within the same compound dating to the colonial period. It was built in a similar style but has since been restored and altered.

The neo-Gothic styled Wesley English Church, built in 1888. © *PeeVee*

VIII. Goodwill Girls' School

About 50 metres further down Promenade Road on the same side as the Wesley Church is Goodwill Girls' High School and Composite Junior College, an institution that began life as the Wesleyan Tamil School in 1855.

Established by Mrs Little, wife of a Wesleyan missionary, it moved to its present site in 1888. An 1855 Mission Report notes: 'Mrs. Little's native girls school numbers thirty-five and the Tamil branch of the native educational establishment continues to do well.' A Mission Report dated four years later notes that the aim of the school was 'to impart useful knowledge to the girls in their own language and thus prepare them for the sphere in which they were likely to move'.

The school was renamed Goodwill Girls' School in honour of Rev Fred Goodwill who was Superintendent of the Bangalore Wesleyan Mission and took over as Manager of the school in 1904. He appears to have re-energised the school. He believed in education for women and was dedicated to the cause of 'native' languages with particular interest in Tamil (he was a Tamil scholar), making sure the schoolgirls were taught and examined in Tamil. Rev Goodwill lived in Bengaluru for 26 years before moving back to England. His granddaughter Jane Smith notes: 'He kept up, by reading, his knowledge of the Indian languages and often used to sing hymns in Tamil or Canarese and when the first Indian migrants came in the 1950s he loved stopping Indians in the street and talking to them.'[31]

Fred Goodwill in 1900. *Courtesy of Jane Smith, granddaughter of Fred Goodwill, from the collections of Fred Goodwill.*

The school building is a simple structure of partly stone and partly brick masonry with a sloping Mangalore tile roof. It has gradually been added to over time.

The Goodwill Girls School. © *PeeVee*

Walk 2: Through Parts of Fraser Town and Richards Town

In which you encounter a charming medley of bungalows, cows, stations, parks and more schools

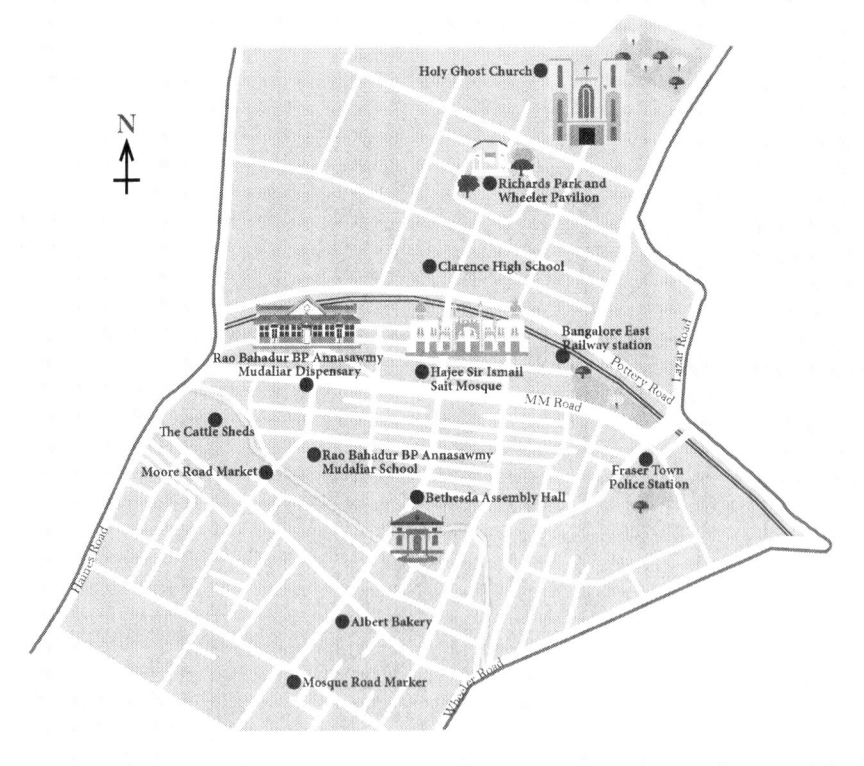

Walk 2: Through Parts of Fraser Town and Richards Town. © *INTACH Bengaluru Chapter*

I. Mosque Road Marker

At the corner of Coles Road and Mosque Road is a stone marker recording the (re-)christening of the extension, née Northern Extension, as Fraser Town, after Stuart M Fraser. The extension was so renamed in response to a petition from some Municipal Commissioners and several houseowners of the area.[32] This was formally done in August 1910, by Mrs FJ Richards, wife of the then President of the Station Municipality.

Mosque Road today is a hive of activity, buzzing with shops and brisk with business. But even in the 1980s, it was a quiet street, with very few commercial establishments. One resident, Rajshekhar Ramachandran, recalls sitting with his aunt some evenings, just waiting for someone to pass by! Another remembers how the only traffic on the road were the pushcarts he and his friends played in; one boy would sit in the little cart and another would give a big push, sending cart and boy hurtling down the road all the way to the Bethesda Assembly. Others recall how they were forbidden from walking down the street after 6 pm because it was deserted![33]

The Mosque Road marker.
© PeeVee

II. Albert Bakery

A walk of about 120 metres down from the marker brings you to this iconic institution on Mosque Road, which is easy to overlook in the daytime if you aren't looking for it. Come 4 o'clock, it is usually hard to miss because of the crowds that throng it for its famous brain puffs, mutton samosas, khoya naan and other such freshly baked goodies. The bakery has been operating since 1902, and at its present location since 1921. Mohammad Sabir Faizan, son of the owner Nawab Jan, says the bakery was started by his great grandfather, Mohammad Yacoob in a lane off Kamaraj Road. Why Albert? So that Europeans could relate to it, say the current owners!

However, others have a different origin story for the bakery. Some old-timers assert that Albert Bakery was started by and named after its founder Albert White. Carolyn Pais née White, who now lives in Australia, is a great-granddaughter of Albert White who, she says, used to live on Richmond Road. 'For years, the family used to get free bread,' she remarks.[34]

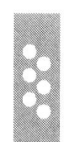

III. The Cattle Sheds

— by Jahnavi Pai

As you walk down Mosque Road, take the first left onto Robertson Road and walk half a kilometre to reach a part of Fraser Town that has remained practically unchanged from a hundred years ago. For here is a unique community facility that still retains its original granite blocks, wooden pillars, Mangalore tile roofs and the unhurried pace typical of a cattle shed.

The C&M Station Municipality constructed the shed in 1915 to house 144 cows, as part of its sanitation drive and to provide services for the new extension. (Incidentally, a second community facility that the C&M authorities constructed was the slaughterhouse on Tannery Road, which came up around 1909. This was both to provide meat for the residents of Fraser Town and to encourage butchers to move out of Shivajinagar.[35]) The cattle sheds now have about 150 cows, owned by 30 milkmen. Milk is sent to dairies, picked up from here by some customers, and door-delivered to others. The milkmen rent the stalls from BBMP, as did their fathers before them. Vittal Rao, one of the oldest milkmen here, supplies 100 litres of milk to 50 customers. Earlier he used to live nearby but has now moved 6 km away. He comes here by 5am, cleans the shed, washes the cows and then milks them. He leaves for home at 11am and returns by 4 pm to repeat the exercise.[36]

This unique structure requires some maintenance and upgrading. The milkmen have sought assistance from the BBMP for a biogas plant. The request has not yet been granted.

The cattle sheds in Fraser Town. © PeeVee

IV. Moore Road Market

A short walk from the cattle sheds back onto Moore Road, towards MM Road, brings you to this no-frills market which was probably built by Annasawmy Mudaliar, as part of his efforts to provide amenities for residents of Fraser Town. A typical market structure of the early 1900s, it has two rows of shops opening out onto a large central open space.

Moore Road is named after PL Moore, an ICS officer and administrator of the C&M Station who served as District Magistrate, Collector and President of the Station Municipality. He helped galvanise the scheme to lay out Fraser Town and was also responsible for clearing some of the congested areas in Shivajinagar.[37] Interesting factoid: PL Moore's daughter Joan Mary Moore, who was born in Bengaluru in 1905, is the grandmother of Hollywood actor Ralph Fiennes!

Just behind the market is a *nala* or drain. You can also spot the same drain along Mosque Road, just past Ahmed Sait Road. Though it has now been barricaded from view there, you can detect its presence a few hundred feet away thanks to its stench. But can you imagine it as a little stream running through your neighbourhood, in which you could sail paper boats, fish and, yes, even swim? As children, residents of the area have done all this and more in this very *nala*. Residents recall how the *nala* had sloping grassy banks and clean water even until the 1970s![38] No sewage, no garbage, no smell. This *nala* is a storm water drain that carried rainwater from upstream and channelled it to Ulsoor *kere*. Today, it receives sewage and garbage, and we can only say in dismay, 'What have we done to our city?'

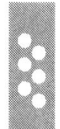

V. Rao Bahadur BP Annasawmy Mudaliar School

A little further down Moore Road to your right is the school built by Rao Bahadur BP Annasawmy Mudaliar for children of all castes and creeds. This is significant at a time when there were very few other schools within C&M Station limits that Indian children could attend (RBANM's School in Ulsoor being the only other), and hardly any that catered to children of lower castes. The school still functions, and is managed by the Rao Bahadur BP Annasawmy Mudaliar Trust.

The school building is almost a textbook example of construction that strictly followed the anti-plague rules written down by JH Stephens: the basement is about a metre high; the floors are of close-fitting Cuddapah tiles; and the roof is of Mangalore tiles. The Trust has maintained the building almost entirely in its original condition except for a minor alteration towards the rear.

The Rao Bahadur BP Annasawmy Mudaliar School. © *Aravind C*

Up until the 1980s, the vast ground that is now part of the school had been leased out to some families who farmed the land. Old-time residents recall with wonder how one could watch the entire workings of a farm right on Mosque Road. The land was later recovered by the Trust and is now a part of the school grounds.

Take a closer look, if you can, at the foundation stone. It was formally laid on 13 March 1907 by Mrs Fraser, wife of Sir Stuart M Fraser after whom the Town is named.

VI. Rao Bahadur BP Annasawmy Mudaliar Dispensary

A walk of about 200 metres up Moore Road brings you to MM Road; at the junction to your right is this charming old building. The name of the building is emblazoned on the pediment: Rao Bahadur BP Annasawmy Moodrs Dispensary 1909. Inside, the foundation stone informs us that it was laid on 11 March 1907 by Mrs PL Moore, wife of the then President of the Station Municipality, Pierce L Moore.

Annasawmy Mudaliar built this dispensary and handed it over to the Station Municipality. In the early 1900s, even minor surgeries were performed here. This dispensary, the school and the market were all inaugurated on 8 January 1909, by SM Fraser. Speaking at the event, Sir Fraser said: 'The three ceremonies which Mr Moore and myself have performed today, at the request of Mr Annasawmy Mudaliar, in the opening of a school, a market and a dispensary, may be regarded as marking the final stage of completion of this offshoot of the Civil and Military Station...'⁴⁰

The dispensary is built like a typical bungalow of its times, with a combination of a central room with a high, pitched roof, side rooms with flat Madras terrace roofs (some have since been replaced by RCC slabs during a recent renovation), tall arched windows with granite sills, finials on the roof (though many have been lost), and so on. Like other period buildings, it is built of brick and lime plaster, though much of the latter has been recently been replaced with cement.

Just opposite the dispensary on MM Road, you can see a row of small houses, identically built with sloping roofs. These were among the houses BP Annasawmy Mudaliar built to accommodate poorer people on low rents. Though they appear quite small from the road, the houses actually also incorporate a well and a small backyard. Until the 1980s, both sides of MM Road were lined with these houses.

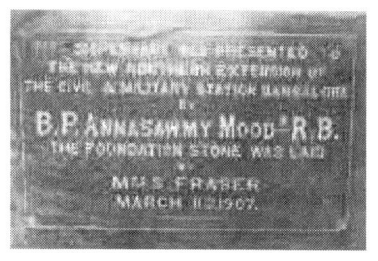

Foundation stone of the Annasawmy Mudaliar dispensary. © *Aravind C*

The Rao Bahadur BP Annasawmy Mudaliar Dispensary, for which the foundation stone was laid by Mrs Fraser. © *Aravind C*

VII. Hajee Sir Ismail Sait Mosque

A short walk down MM Road towards its intersection section with Mosque Road brings you to the mosque that gives one of Fraser Town's main roads its name. It was built thanks to a donation of land and the generous sum of Rs 50,000 from Hajee Sir Ismail Sait. The mosque is named after the donor whose name boldly decorates the entrance arch. Sir Ismail Sait had built it primarily for people from his community of Cutchi Memons. However, Muslims from all communities now gather for prayers at this mosque. When built, it accommodated 300 worshippers. It was expanded in 1990. The capacious courtyard now accommodates about 3000 people.

The Hajee Sir Ismail Sait Mosque. © *PeeVee*

VIII. Bethesda Assembly Hall

You can walk back about half a kilometre down Mosque Road to see this handsome building which opened on 1 December 1918. Church records note that it had its beginnings in a small house somewhere on Moore Road in Fraser Town, and opened for worship with seven members. Bethesda Assembly is part of the Brethren Church, a community of Christians separate from Protestants and Catholics.

The church was founded by Alfred Redwood, who also established Clarence High School (*see below*) with his brother Walter. Incidentally, Walter Redwood is fairly well known in Indian law quizzes for an unusual reason. In 1929, he was authorised by the British Resident of Mysore State to solemnise marriages in the C&M Station between Christians. Unfortunately, Redwood did not realise

The Bethesda Assembly Hall on Mosque Road. © *PeeVee*

there was a rider to this: he could solemnise marriages provided neither party was a British citizen. And so he merrily solemnised several marriages, little knowing these unions would not be legally recognised. When it was discovered that marriages he had solemnised that involved a British citizen were invalid, the Government of India had to rectify the matter by passing the Bangalore Marriages Validating Act of 1936 expressly for this purpose.[41]

Bethesda Assembly Hall is sited in the centre of a large open site. This brick and lime mortar structure is built on a stone foundation. The windows and doors have semi-circular fanlights and arched mouldings. The pedimented front has a circular window in the centre. An entrance porch, seemingly added later, is supported on four pillars.

IX. Bangalore East Railway Station

Head back towards the mosque and continue past it. Take the lane to the right of the flyover and turn right towards the railway station.

The station has undergone some renovations with longer sheltered platforms and extended booking counters. However, much of the station still retains its original look and feel, with its stone building, Mangalore tile roofs, segmental-arched windows and its long, low architectural profile.

Even as Fraser Town was being planned, C&M authorities convinced the Madras and Southern Mahratta Railway Company to establish a station here. Accordingly, the Bangalore East station opened around 1908–09 as a 'flag station': this meant trains could be flagged down or would stop only if required. Many residents of these Towns marked the passage of time by the passages of trains. Some recognise the particular trains by their whistles. As children, they sometimes ran ahead to ask the engine driver to wait even as their fathers or mothers followed, huffing and puffing as fast as they could![42]

X. Fraser Town Police Station

Continue on MM Road for about 150 metres to reach the police station. As the building itself proudly proclaims, this police station was built in 1917. Interestingly, though the building was ready in 1917, it was not inaugurated and formally occupied until 1921 thanks to a shortage of staff. So severe was the shortfall in numbers that 'undersized or overage' policemen were employed just to keep the force going! Until then, the building served as an 'outpost'.[43]

This building was renovated in 2004 thanks to funding from a former resident of Fraser Town and currently houses the traffic police. The new building behind it was also built in 2004–05.

As you exit the police station, take a look at the urn sitting a little lopsidedly in the small fenced-off garden on your left. This urn stood at the intersection of Mosque and MM roads until it was removed sometime in the 1990s. An enterprising policeman with a sense of history saved it from destruction and moved it here.

XI. Clarence High School

From the police station, you can either walk back on MM road about half a kilometre, turn right on Mosque Road and then take the railway overbridge. Or you can take the underpass near the police station towards Pottery Road, turn left and walk up 550 metres towards Clarence High School, which is at the intersection of Pottery and Clarke roads.

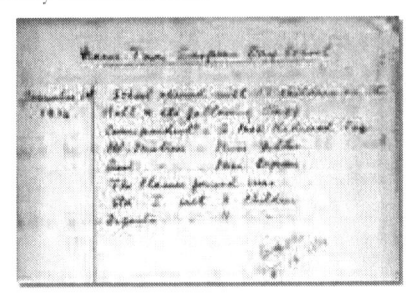

Clarence School opened in 1914 as the Fraser Town European Day School. *Courtesy of Clarence High School.*

The site where Clarence School now stands, in 1922. *Courtesy of Clarence High School.*

The school did not always stand here. Clarence School, which began on 1 December 1914 and was initially named Fraser Town European Day School, opened in a small house somewhere in Fraser Town, with six children, eleven infants, two ladies and a gentleman. From this first location, it soon moved to where the Fraser Town Post Office now stands on MM Road, then to a bungalow in No 2, Hall Road. The land for its current premises was bought in 1921 and the school finally moved here in September 1922.[44]

As the school expanded, several new buildings were added to the campus. The Wilcox Block, which houses the offices of the principal and the administration, were built by modifying and extending the original building. You can still the windows and doors which have been retained from the 1920s building.

Like the Bethesda Assembly, this school also owes its existence to the Redwood brothers. They named it Clarence after their own school (which no longer exists) in Weston-super-Mare in Somerset, England. Hundreds who have been through the portals of this Clarence School have a fierce fondness for their alma mater for the lifelong values and discipline it instilled in them.

The Redwood brothers Walter and Alfred, who helped establish Bethesda Assembly Church and Clarence High School. *Courtesy of Clarence High School.*

XII. Richards Park and Wheeler Pavilion

Richards Park is about 180 metres up Clarke Road. Residents of Richards Town are inordinately proud of this park, the green heart of this Town. The bandstand in the park is called the Wheeler Pavilion. This unusual, multipurpose structure was built in 1925. (See if you can spot the name and year inscribed on it. Warning: you do need eagle eyes to see this!) The top was a water tank while the space below was used as a bandstand where police and military bands used to play. Today, the water tank is no longer needed since water is piped to the Town from elsewhere. The music concerts are also a thing of the past.

You can see the urn that once graced the intersection near Clarence High School—the twin to the one in the Fraser Town Police Station—in the park.

A meander along Richards Town's broad footpaths is highly recommended, especially to see some of the beautiful old bungalows that still stand here. You can also see another relic of the past: the conservancy lanes between the bungalows. However, in some instances, these have been filled with grass and plants, converting the lanes into vibrant strips of green.

The Wheeler Pavilion in Richards Park. © *PeeVee*

XIII. Holy Ghost Church

At the end of Clarke Road is the Holy Ghost Church, a part of the Catholic Church in the Archdiocese of Bengaluru, consecrated in 1953.

The Holy Ghost Church. © PeeVee

The church building came about thanks to the efforts of Matthew Hickey, an Irish Redemptorist. Redemptorists are Roman Catholics who belong to the Congregation of the Most Holy Redeemer. In the 1940s, the Redemptorists bought a dilapidated old bungalow (it came with a tomb in the middle!) on John Armstrong Road, completely renovated it, and used it for worship. When this proved too small, Hickey bought the land where the church now stands, with the idea of building both a church and seminary.

The design of the church, by architect Stanley Fernando, is remarkably original. The building is designed to resemble a dove, with the church forming the body of the dove. The two wings house a seminary and accommodation for faculty and priests.

In the 1960s, '70s and '80s, the Holy Ghost Church was also the cultural hub of the area. The church used to organise talent shows and summer camps for young people. These were events that residents of Richards Town, Fraser Town and Cooke Town, including non-Christians, looked forward to and participated in with enthusiasm.

We end our stroll through these little Towns at this church. Bengaluru is one of the few Indian cities to have such enclaves that are strong reminders of our colonial legacy, in name, character and layout. Layouts like the three Towns we have just visited, or Richmond Town, Langford Town, Austin Town, Cox Town and so on, are today still distinct entities, adding to the character of the city as one that has multiple centres and several strands in its history, a salad bowl of several identities where the flavours remain distinct yet enhance each other.

Notes

1. See, for example, 'Indian telegrams', *The Singapore Free Press and Mercantile Advertiser*, 18 October 1898.
2. 'Spreaders of plague', *The Straits Times*, 3 April 1909.
3. Jenks 1919.
4. File Resy 479 of 1905, Sl 1,3,4,7, KSA.
5. File Resy 286 of 1899, Sl 95--117, KSA.
6. Stephens 1922. Incidentally, these unusual lengths were based on the old imperial units called rods and chains which were used by surveyors. A rod was 5.5 yards (5 metres). Four rods made a chain, which equalled 66 feet (20 metres). So a road that was 6 rods would be 99 feet (30 metres) wide.
7. Stephens 1914.
8. File Resy 286 of 1899, Sl 139–163, KSA.
9. Stephens 1922, 35.
10. File Resy 286 of 1899, Sl 95–117, KSA.
11. Stephens 1914, 19.
12. 'Improving Bangalore: New district opened', *The Times of India*, 11 January 1909.
13. Stephens 1922, 238.
14. Amritaraj 1912.
15. 'The Northern Extension', *The Daily Post*, 18 January 1909.
16. 'New Government Offices, Civil and Military Station, Bangalore', in Doyle 1905, 144.
17. Anon 1909, 396.
18. 'Plague inoculation', *Eastern Daily Mail and Straits Morning Advertiser*, 4 November 1907.
19. 'Patron of racing: Death of Hajee Sir Ismail Sait', The Straits Times, 10 May 1934.
20. File Resy 45 of 1912, Sl 1–8, KSA.
21. Colaco 2003, 76.
22. See *Towns of our City: Fraser Town, Richards Town, Cooke Town*, a film by INTACH Bangalore, 2018, https://www.youtube.com/watch?v=b9YNDdiJkCg&feature=youtu.be.
23. 'Obituary: Mr George Henry Cooke MC', *The Irish Times*, 25 June 1940.
24. Anon 1923, 203.
25. Hicks, Petraglia and Boivin 2013.
26. Cheriyath 2016.

27. Various church histories and annual missionary reports were consulted for this section, particularly that of the Wesleyan Mission and *The History of the Sisters of St. Joseph of Tarbes in India (1882–2006)* by Sister Victorine Lobo, *The History of the Arch-Diocese of Bangalore*, compiled by Rev Father Anthony Simo, and *Wesley English Church, Bangalore. 123 Years of Life. 1888–2011*, by Professor Hemalatha John and Rev Florence Deenadayalan.
28. Penny 1922, 209.
29. Jesuits and consequently St Joseph's Convent Chapel were part of the Catholic congregation unlike St John's Church, which was initially under the Church of England (before Indian Independence) and later moved to CSI (which was established after Independence). Both are distinct forms of Christianity with well-established doctrines.
30. The Wesleyan movement was started within the Church of England by John and Charles Wesley in 18th century England based on their interpretation of the Bible. Its missionaries travelled across the globe including India. This church is now part of CSI for administrative purposes along with former Church of England churches, all under the broad umbrella of Protestantism.
31. Personal communication, 2015.
32. File Resy 131 of 1901, KSA.
33. Personal interview with long-time residents of the area, Rajshekhar Ramachandran, Parveen Nayeem and Sampath Mudaliar, January 2017. Also see the film *Towns of Our City: Fraser Town, Richards Town, Cooke Town*, INTACH Bangalore, 2018.
34. Personal communication, 2018.
35. File Resy 286 of 99; Sl 139–163, KSA.
36. Interview by Jahnavi Pai with Vittal Rao, February 2017.
37. 'A successful administrator', *The Daily Post*, 25 February 1905.
38. Personal interviews with long-time residents Rajshekhar Ramachandran, Deepak Pinto and Pradeep Sinnas, February 2017. Also see the film *Towns of Our City: Fraser Town, Richards Town, Cooke Town*, INTACH Bangalore, 2018.
39. Interview with Deepak Pinto, January 2017. Also see the film, *Towns of Our City: Fraser Town, Richards Town, Cooke Town*, INTACH Bangalore, 2018.
40. 'Improving Bangalore: New district opened', *The Times of India*, 11 January 1909; Anon 1909.
41. https://indiankanoon.org/doc/1479956/, accessed 16 August 2018.
42. *Towns of Our City: Fraser Town, Richards Town, Cooke Town* (film), INTACH Bangalore, 2018.
43. Cobb 1918, 5; Barton 1923, 5.
44. *Clarence High School Centenary Celebrations Book*, 2014.

The Whitefield area in the 1820s. Wurtoor is Varthur, Curgoory is Kadugodi. From, Walker, John, *Atlas of India, 1786-1873*. India Office, Great Britain. *Courtesy of Library of Congress, Geography and Map Division, Washington.*

Whitefield in 2015. The Inner and Outer Circles are near the right end. The hatched area in the top left is the International Technology Park Limited (ITPL). In the centre is the Nallurahalli kere. From *Comprehensive Development Plan 2015. Bengaluru Development Authority.*

CHAPTER 7

The Eurasian and Anglo-Indian Pensioners' Paradise: Whitefield

- by Krupa Rajangam

Whitefield is named after David Emmanuel Starkenburgh White, a retired Anglo-Indian civil servant who conceptualised the Eurasian and Anglo-Indian settlement in the 19th century.[1] It was meant to be a 'self-sufficient' farming community with the aim of making the Eurasian community, 'especially its poorer members', independent and 'thus raise their social status'.[2] For this purpose, in 1882, he sought and obtained 3900 acres of land on easy terms from the Maharaja of Mysore.[3] This was through the Anglo-Indian Association of Mysore and Coorg, which he founded along with a few other active members of the community such as Sausmond and Duckworth. Subsequently, two other settlements were planned nearby, named after Sausmond and Duckworth, but Whitefield appears to have been more successful.

Portrait of DS White, the founder of Whitefield
Courtesy of The Whitefield Club

In *Narratives of Travels in India*, which records the travels of JD Rees through British India along with Lord Connemara (they visited Whitefield in 1890), Rees introduces Whitefield and Sausmond as settlements where 'somebody had tried to accomplish the supposed impossibility' of making the Eurasian a farmer.[4]

He extensively quotes from DS White's *A Guide to the Eurasian and Anglo-Indian Villages (1879)*, where White states that the aim of these settlements was to lead 'them [Eurasians] into agricultural and industrial pursuits, and to remove forever the feeling of anxiety as regards their own future and that of their children'. White's view was that in laying the foundation of the first settlement, the Association was but 'laying the foundation of thousands of others'.[5]

Though British administrative circles of that time shared Rees's scepticism about the feasibility of such an experiment, the settlement became popular among pensioners due to its proximity to Kolar Gold Fields where many Anglo-Indians and Eurasians worked. It saw fairly steady growth with a number of people taking up plots and constructing houses, though not for the original purpose of setting up as agriculturalists; rather, the houses served as weekend getaways for shooting parties due to the open countryside for miles around.

Access to the settlement was by means of a pass between two hills, Kaolin Hill (to the north of Our Lady of Lourdes Church—*see below*), and Hamilton Hill, the hill across the road (to the east). Kaolin Hill was so named because of the presence of china clay on its surface.[6] There were proposals to commercially extract this and set up a pottery unit but the venture does not appear to have been successful. These are JD Rees' first impressions of the settlement as he and Lord Connemara rode towards it from the railway station, 2 miles (approximately 3.2 km) to the north:

> *From the top of the Kaolin hill a good view is obtained of Whitefield. You see the village school, the church, and a dozen cottages more or less, well laid out upon a plan somewhat too ambitious for the actual circumstances of the case. It was intended that from a central circus, different avenues should radiate, these avenues being connected by parallel lines of streets made up of houses, each standing in its own walled garden. A small church is almost completed, and the largest building is the now unused storehouse constructed by Messrs. Arbuthnot and Co. for the abandoned business of working the kaolin clay. An undulating country stretches all around the settlement. In the trifling depressions the soil is good; on the higher ground it is rocky, and more than indifferent. Here and there are groves of casuarinas and orchards of fruit trees. There were no crops on the ground, and abundant evidence was forthcoming that crops are sparsely raised. The settlement had not a very flourishing appearance. Some of the cottages were moderately neat, but in no case apparently had any settler the time or inclination to sacrifice to the Graces ... The houses do not look like homes, and many of the settlers in fact live in Bangalore.*[7]

The original village consisted of 20 plots (each 3/4th of an acre), with five plots in each quadrant, and additional triangular wedges to the eastern and western ends; there were also 20 farm plots, each of 20 acres. The eastern wedge was marked for the church and the western one was meant to be the 'Whitehouse'—the house DES White meant to build for the family but which never came to fruition. The layout as originally planned was an ambitious one of five concentric circles, each with an array of plots, served by the circular 'First Street' and 'Second Street', intercepted by avenues (to be named Jack Avenue, Mango Avenue, Gulmohar Avenue and so on) radiating from the central village green. The green had a pond at one end (to the west) and it is believed that soil excavated to create the pond was used to build the first few houses in the village. Eventually only two of the five circles were executed.

By 1895, 'permanent residents numbered 115 with 12 cottages built on the village site and 14 houses on the farm holdings, a Protestant Church, holding both Church of England and Dissenting services with the parsonage under construction and a school with 31 pupils'. There is further mention that as all land holdings in Whitefield had been taken up, more land was leased from the *jodidar* (zamindar) of Pattandur, adjoining Whitefield to the north, and this portion 'contained the Roman Catholic chapel, parsonage and 8 houses'.[8]

Today very little remains of the original village except for a few isolated bungalows and the circular layout of the Inner and Outer Circle roads of Whitefield along with the central circular open area that was the village green. The 20 farm plots have evolved to become Jimmy Giddens Layout, Prashanth Nagar Extension, Chaitanya Armadale (once Armadale Farms), Prestige White Meadows, Silver Oak, Dodsworth Layout and so on.

The Village

The style of houses in the settlement (both village and farm plots) appears to have been fairly uniform: a central porch supported on two pillars; ornamented gable ends perpendicular to the porch with a circular skylight at each end; and a central pitched roof taller than the lean-to attached to it on either side. In other words, the typical 'colonial bungalow' style. However, their appearance is different from the more well-known bungalows of the Cantonment—which are larger in size and more richly ornamented, with decorative monkey tops and carved finials, and barge and eaves boards.

White's pamphlet on Whitefield encloses sketches of the typical style of cottages or 'model cottages' that could be built at the settlement. The pamphlet also mentions a number of suitable trades and occupations for residents: apart from agriculture, pisciculture, viticulture and sericulture, White says residents could keep pigs, goats and sheep; breed horses, ponies and mules; and cultivate tobacco, vanilla and arrowroot.[9]

'Perfect Peace,' a typical bungalow in Whitefield. It was originally called 'Hill Side' and was visible from the two hills nearby. *Courtesy of Paul D'Souza.*

The two main churches in Whitefield, Memorial Church and Our Lady of Lourdes Church (*see below*), both date to the time of the Anglo-Indian settlement. The former was a non-denominational Anglican or Church of England church and is now administered under the Church of South India (CSI). The latter is a Catholic church. The cemetery came up in 1893 across the main road from the settlement. Local records document that the need for a cemetery was not felt till much after the settlement was established; it was set up following a petition to the Mysore government. The plot was subdivided into four: the first to be used for burials of all denominations, the second set aside for Dissenters, the third for Church of England and the fourth for

Roman Catholics, which appears to have been a unique arrangement. Till the retrocession of the settlement in 1935 by the Mysore government the plot was used only for European and Anglo-Indian burials.

The Social Whirl

The excerpt below—from a letter written in 1950 by three visitors ('Pam, Betty and Cynthia') to Whitefield during the Christmas vacation—gives us an idea of the social life at that time.[10]

NOT THE 'SLEEPY HOLLOW' THE HAMLET IS BELIEVED TO BE

As the time of our Christmas vacation was approaching, we three lady teachers from Colleges in Madras were at a loss as to where we should spend our holiday. Various places were suggested but the objections seemed insuperable, and so the youngest, Betty, who had some contacts at Whitefield, proposed we go there. Cynthia, who had been there a decade ago, raised stormy protests and, as I had heard the place described as Sleepy Hollow was inclined to agree with her. But Betty was insistent, for reasons we now understand.

A warm and kindly welcome was extended to us from many quarters and willing escorts took us over the town. It was my first acquaintance with a place laid out in this unique fashion, two circles intersected by avenues of fruit and other trees, with five houses in each cluster. The church and Institute are conveniently situated in the Inner Circle near the main road.

A few [who] have passed the ninetieth mile stone reminisce on the chequered history of their little town or village. They proudly state this is the best English village on Indian soil, and we feel this is a point none will dispute.

That evening we were invited to the Institute; that this little hamlet still under a Panchayat, should have a cosy well furnished Club (we understand it was extended a year ago) and have a regular attendance of 50 or more members to whist drives and other functions, held four times a week, was a matter of great surprise to us.

We were given a programme of the Christmas activities, extending from Dec 21st to Jan 2nd and a hearty invitation was extended to us.

The one function that pleased us immensely was the Children's Fancy Dress Carnival. There were no less than 30 costumes, many were strikingly original and others entirely pretty. The concert which followed was thoroughly enjoyable. It gladdened one's heart to see tiny tots of three to teenagers go on the stage and entertain us with recitations. Piano solos, Hula dances and romantic songs sung with sentiment and expression. For the Adults were Bumper and Pagal [?] Whist drives, Socials and the New year dance, and all proved evenings of fun and merriment,

```
and were run by those who know 'how to make things go'.
Several Pianists, Violinists and Vocalists and the comic
element is not lacking, suitable entertainment was provided
without much difficulty. We witnessed a very amusing sketch
written and produced by the members, and were delighted
to once again meet a Cabaret Artiste whom we had known in
far away Mussorie.

We can but say that Whitefield is extremely fortunate in
having a very capable, efficient and experienced Committee
who not only possess the necessary talent but work
indefatigably to produce such gratifying results.

Well, dear friends, we were truly sorry our stay had come
to an end, and here's a warm 'thank you' to all, for
taking us into your happy circle and giving us a memorable
and happy holiday.
```

The 'Crisis' of Independence

Besides ongoing challenges in terms of lack of water supply dating from when it was founded, the failure to make the Anglo-Indian a farmer,[11] or conflicts between the settlers and the Association over control, a major crisis for the Anglo-Indian community at Whitefield was Indian Independence. Residents were confused over whether to sell up and go back to Britain or remain in India. India was home to many of whom were born and brought up here and had never seen the UK, but on the other hand they felt insecure about staying back as they were 'half-white' and not 'all brown'. Many reluctantly chose the offer of free passage to Britain (provided they could prove their 'white' ancestry) while a few moved to much larger Anglo-Indian settlements elsewhere in India. Some returned in the 1960s and '70s from Britain and Australia as those countries proved too alien for them.

Take a walk along the Inner Circle one day, preferably around twilight when the golden rays of sunlight filter through the tamarind trees that were planted in White's days. You might just end up walking back in time to the original pensioners' paradise of Bengaluru.

A Walk through Whitefield
In which you see the surviving traces of an experiment in planned living

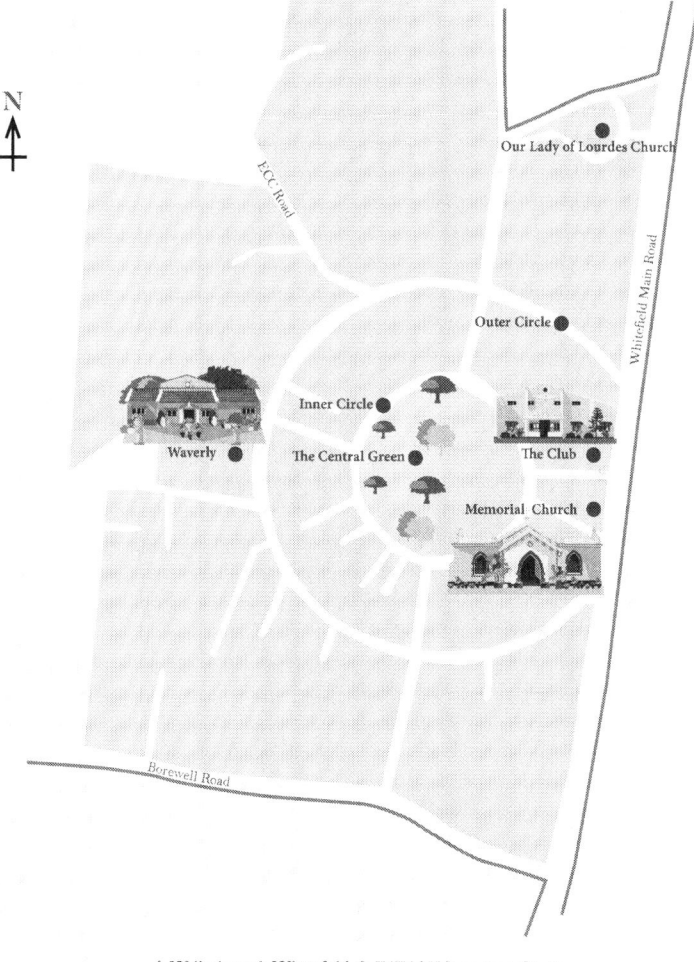

A Walk through Whitefield © *INTACH Bengaluru Chapter*

Weekends are good days to walk through the village as the churches are generally open through the day except for a few hours in the afternoon. (Do note that only the churches and cemetery are open to visitors; all other properties including Waverley and the club are privately owned. We urge you not to disturb the residents.)

1. Memorial Church

Begin at the Memorial Church on the Inner Circle. A well-maintained property, the church was constructed in 1886 on three-fourth of an acre of land donated by the Anglo Indian Association. It was uniquely planned as a non-denominational church and managed by a committee whose members were chosen from across all denominations. Catholic services were discontinued when their own church was built to the north, but other sects/denominations continue to share the church.

As the church was well beyond city limits it was served by a visiting priest from the Cantonment. He would stay overnight at the Church Institute next door before departing for the long journey back to the city.

The rectangular church was built in the Neo-Gothic style. The vestries on either side of the entrance and the front porch were added in 1940 in a similar

The Memorial Church, in 2007.© *Krupa Rajangam*

style, through the Hardinge Fund (bequeathed by one Mrs Hardinge). The masonry construction is roofed in Mangalore tiles supported on timber trusses while the vestries are roofed in the Madras terrace style.[12] The story goes that the altar was originally planned to the west where the current entrance is. When the church was to be consecrated the officiating priest noticed the error. So the ceremony was hurriedly put off, and the altar and doorway positions switched. The two small square rooms to the rear of the church housed the dispensary (a doctor used to visit weekly) and kitchen.

There is a small brass plaque on the reredos (ornamental screen covering the wall behind an altar) which notes that it was set up in memoriam of lives lost in 'the Great War' (First World War). There are other commemorative plaques on the walls including that to the church organist who was with the church 'for the longest time'. There was a time when the organ went missing and, after a frantic search, was located in the middle of the village pond. It was cleaned, restored and reinstated. Though still in working condition it is no longer used and has been set aside in the vestry to the left as you enter the church.

II. Inner and Outer Circles and the Central Green

As you walk south along the circular road from the Memorial Church, to your right is the central village green and on your left the bungalow plots, each of which have since been subdivided into six or eight plots, or for the most part rebuilt as apartments/villas and sometimes contemporary bungalows. The southern half of the Circle has almost completely transformed, but as you complete a semi-circle and reach the western end right across from Memorial Church, you can catch glimpses of Whitefield as it might have been. There are mature trees, whose canopies shade the road, and the occasional bungalow or cottage that is set back from the road.

What used to be the village green at the centre, with a pond at one end (now filled in), is now the Krishnaraja Wodeyar Playground and Park. Close to where the HOPCOMS outlet stands was the old village school building (it collapsed due to neglect and deterioration).

III. Waverley

As you continue walking along Inner Circle, a short walk on the road leading west to Outer Circle gets you to 'Waverley', one of Whitefield's more famous bungalows. This property was originally an inn with a general store attached to it, the only one in Whitefield at the time. While the year of construction is unknown, it is popularly supposed to have been owned or at least run by

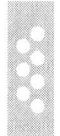

Waverley in 2009, the only unaltered plot from the
original settlement of Whitefield. © *Krupa Rajangam*

a Mr Hamilton; a 1936 map notes Mr Mahoney as the owner but mentions Mr Hamilton's name beneath. It is also widely believed that Winston Churchill, no less, visited or stayed here as he was courting Ms Hamilton, the innkeeper's daughter. Local legend has it that one of the large boulders behind Our Lady of Lourdes Church had an engraving of a heart with the initials WC and RH, which old-timers believe stood for Winston Churchill and Rose Hamilton. (A popular pastime among local children in the 1960s was to slide down these boulders on large leaves. The boulders were dynamited a few years ago to make room for a housing project.)

The structure is a masonry construction with timber trusses supporting a tiled roof similar to the other bungalows; the plan layout, however, is different, given its original function as an inn. This is the only unaltered plot and structure of the original settlement, and hence of significance in the historical narrative of the place. During the Second World War it was supposedly used as an army canteen.

IV. Our Lady of Lourdes Church

Walk along the Outer Circle, past the ECC Road intersection; the lane going north takes you to Our Lady of Lourdes Church.

This church was constructed in 1889 due to the efforts of Rose White, wife of DES White, the founder of the settlement. Mrs White (who was Catholic while her husband was Protestant) was buried inside the church to the left of the altar; her husband's grave is in Chennai. The Whites supposedly stayed in the parish priest's residence located within the church grounds before moving to their own house north of the village.

Attached to this church is the Mission of the Sisters of St Joseph of Tarbes, who run the St Joseph's Convent School nearby. The mission history documents that the Whitefield Sisters were supplied with water by the Home Mission in Fraser Town. Once a week bullock carts would trundle to the Whitefield convent due to acute water shortage in the area; the arterial road Borewell Road is so called as it had the only borewell that supplied water to the whole of Whitefield.

Both the Whitefield churches show the influence of the Neo-Gothic style of architecture popular in the Cantonment with their pointed arches and crenellated parapets. The Memorial Church structure largely remains intact though it has additions, but the Catholic church retains only its altar end. The nave portion has been reconstructed; and the whole is roofed in GI sheets. Currently the structure's future is a question mark as a new church has been built and consecrated on the premises.

Kaolin Hill, to the north of the church building, houses the Stations of the Cross.

V. Whitefield Club

You can retrace your steps back to Inner Circle to the Memorial Church; across the road from the church is Whitefield Club. En route, you get to walk past one of the few largely intact houses (though the plot has been subdivided), with a well-maintained garden, originally called Hill View Cottage (it had a view of Kaolin and Hamilton hills). The club building used to be the Church Institute. In keeping with the spirit of its original function, a clause stating that one room should be made available to visiting clergy remains part of the club charter. It was remodelled around 2007–08, but before that it looked pretty much like the other Whitefield houses of the colonial period.

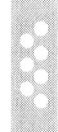

Our short walk in this once quaint outpost of Bengaluru ends here. Today, of course, most people know Whitefield only for its IT industry. In the 1980s the area was known for the Sathya Sai Baba Ashram nearby while in the 1960s and '70s, it was known as an industrial region with its four factories: the Brooke Bond factory (earlier Moody's Tea which morphed into Hindustan Uni Lever, that is, the Brooke Bond label), Joy ice cream factory on Hamilton Hill, Rao Insulating and Usha Martin. All the factories have shut down now. Few remember or know why Hope Farm junction (on buses the stop is often rechristened 'O Form') is so called (a farm of that name existed at that junction) or why Varthur Kodi is so named (*kodi* means overflow weir; the term refers to the Varthur end of Whitefield). Today, Varthur *kere*—where residents of Immidihalli, the village to the east, and Whitefield would swim, fish and source their drinking water from about 20 years ago—is infamous for the foam that rises on the surface of the lake. Nor do many people remember the pass between the Kaolin and Hamilton hills; the pass no longer looks like one as Hamilton Hill and the factory have since been demolished to make way for real estate development.

Besides the handful of scattered structures, what endures, at least amongst some of Whitefield's long-term residents, are countless stories and anecdotes: of the 'shooting spinster' of Whitefield, who was known to first shoot at any noise or disturbance and ask questions later; of Kenneth and Donald Anderson (father–son wild game hunters and later conservators, who lived here) taking their pet

The Whitefield Club before it was remodelled in 2007-08. © *Krupa Rajangam*

The kodi or overflow weir of Varthur kere, 1970s. The house seen behind the cart is now a petrol pump. *Courtesy of Christa Moss.*

iguana for walks or letting their hyena escape; of a Panchayat chairman who was said to refuse government development grants because he wanted Whitefield to remain a village; of an elderly couple who slept with their coffins ready, under their beds, to make it easy for their neighbours to bury them when their time came; or the dog that liked to climb trees.

Notes

1. Detailed history, analysis and architectural documentation of the settlement and structures are available in the peer-reviewed article Rajangam 2011.
2. 'All about Whitefield', from the collections of Rev Peck, past Whitefield resident.
3. Rice 1897b, 93.
4. Rees 1891, 298.
5. Rees 1891, 299.
6. 'All about Whitefield', from the collections of Rev Peck.
7. Rees 1891, 305–306.
8. Rice 1897b, 93.
9. White, quoted in Rees 1891, 299.
10. Letter source: V D'Souza, Whitefield resident. It appears to have been published in the 'Bangalore Gazette', perhaps a newsletter for the community, on 30 March 1950.
11. Rees 1891.
12. Anon 1977.

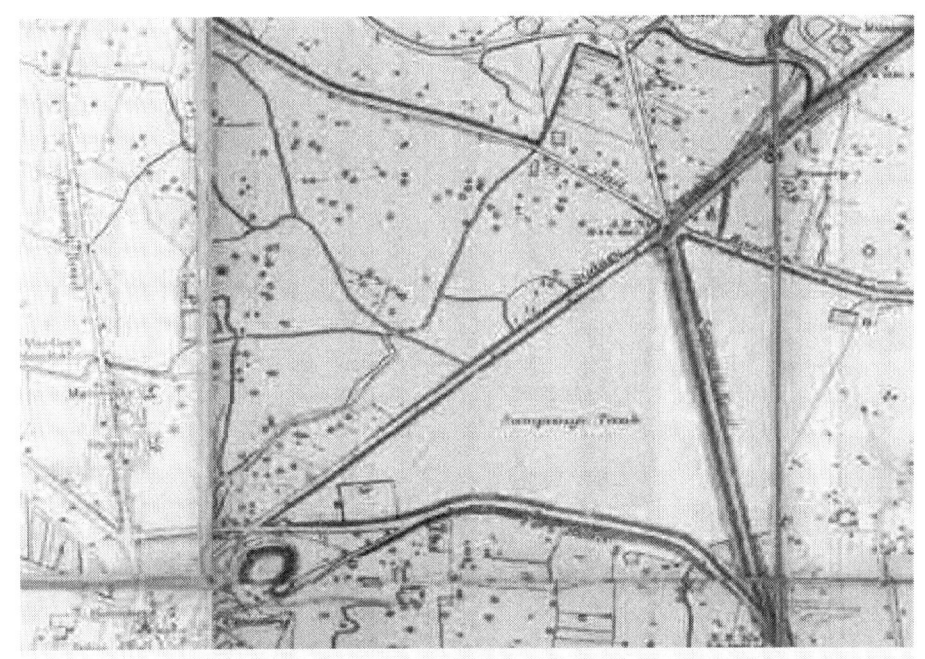

Sampangi kere and its vicinity in 1884-85. From, Survey of India. *Cantonment and City of Bangalore and Environs, Season 1884-85. Courtesy of Mythic Society, Bengaluru.*

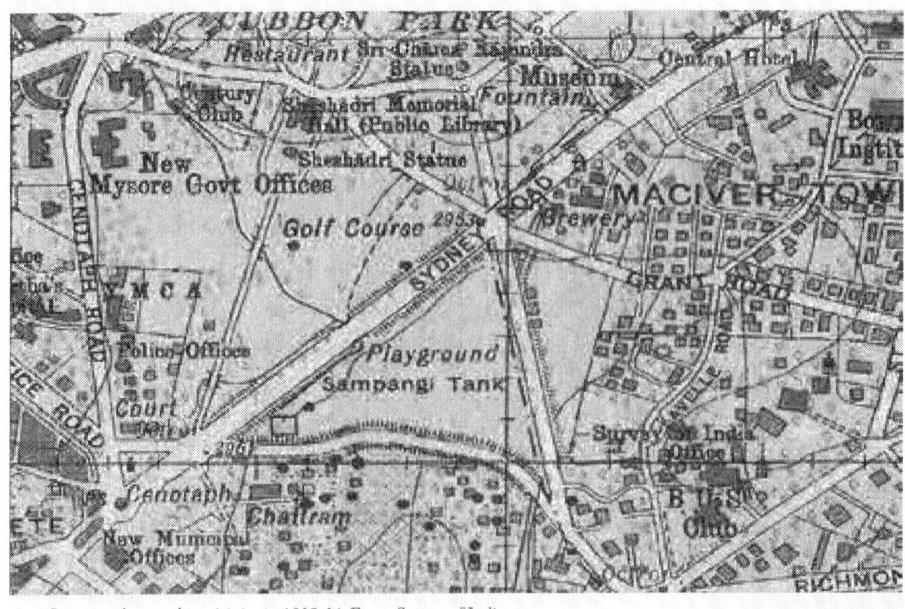

Sampangi kere and its vicinity in 1935-36. From, Survey of India. *Bangalore Guide Map. Surveyed 1935-36. Courtesy of Naresh Narasimhan.*

CHAPTER 8

The Watery Past of a Modern Stadium: Sampangi Kere

- by Hita Unnikrishnan,
B Manjunatha and Harini Nagendra

Lake District: A Background to Bengaluru's Lakes

Known as the 'Garden City', and now the world over as the 'IT City' of India, Bengaluru has been an important settlement for successive dynasties since the mid-15th century because of its strategic location on the Deccan Plateau. It also formed an important military outpost for colonial India. In fact, the area has been occupied by settlements long before that, as evidenced by pottery shards, bones, inscription stones and other artefacts that have been excavated.[1] Such a long history of settlement is rather unusual for a city that lies within a rain shadow and lacks a major water source.

Early occupants of this city recognised this geographical shortfall and created a system of networked reservoirs (*keres*—tanks, or lakes as they are known today) that provided water to the entire city. The earliest recorded tanks date back to the ninth century CE; inscriptional evidence suggests that this network was strengthened and expanded over the centuries. It reached its prime in the middle of the 19th century, when British colonialists observed that there was no further space for the construction of new reservoirs within the city.[2] They were the only source of water for the area till about 1895–96, when the city started looking to other distant sources to meet its increasing water demands.

This system of tanks was rather special in several ways. They were built along the natural gradient of the city, making good use of its undulating terrain, and were connected by means of channels (known as *rajakaluves*). Built to harness rainwater and support a primarily agrarian landscape, this networked system ensured that water overflowing from one reservoir would travel downstream through the channels into the next one in the network, thereby creating a system of flow in an otherwise static infrastructure.[3] As these reservoirs were seasonal (depending heavily on the monsoons), they operated in tandem with open wells associated with them.[4] These open wells drew water from shallow aquifers that were recharged by the tanks associated with them and were made use of especially in drier seasons. Such a system also meant that the city had a fairly reliable source of water through the year.

Each tank was associated with one or more villages bordering them and it was usually the responsibility of these villages to ensure its maintenance. The tanks were not just important for provisioning of water for agriculture and domestic needs, but also served as communal spaces for a variety of village requirements. They were associated with adjoining communal pasturelands (known locally as *gomalas*) and village forests (which served as both shelter for nomadic communities and a source of fuel wood and fruits mostly for large gatherings in the village). Water being considered sacred by many communities, tanks were also associated with temples. Ritualistic offerings were made to related deities, seeking divine protection from floods or disease or to ensure good harvests. Water was let out by means of sluice gates (known locally as *thoobu*) by specific community members known as *neergantis* (or the village watermen) into the fields as required.[5] These sluice gates were often ornate structures and, by way of their architectural styles, offer clues to the history of the tanks.

Post 1799, these water bodies passed into state ownership and management; thereafter communities had reduced stakes in the resource. That, coupled with the arrival of piped water supply into the city in 1896 (from a distant northern reservoir, at Hessarghatta), began to spell doom for the city's water bodies. Tanks began to be neglected, had sewage diverted into the channels, or simply became polluted by increasing amounts of domestic, industrial and agricultural run-off. Several of them were drained for sanitary purposes, and yet others went dry and were built over as a result of their channels being cut off by the expanding city infrastructure. Today, very few tanks remain; the few that exist are in varying states of degradation, prompting a renewed call in recent decades (following spells of water shortage in the city) for their rejuvenation and restoration.[6]

A Lost Lake

Sri Kanteerava Stadium is a prominent landmark of Bengaluru. Boasting of a state-of-the-art indoor stadium as well as extensive outdoor space, this stadium in the heart of the city, with its distinctive domed facade, is immediately recognisable to most Bengalureans. It is a popular retreat for people who wish to indulge in a spot of rock (well, wall) climbing, archery or team sports such as cricket and football. But what many people of present-day Bengaluru don't know is that the roughly triangular patch of land upon which this stadium stands was once a lake whose origin dates back to about the mid-16th century—about the time the city was founded by a medieval war chieftain called Hiriya Kempegowda. Today, nothing gives away the former watery identity of this place as much as torrential rain, when the entire stadium floods.[7] It is then that Bengaluru collectively laments the loss of its once beautiful landscape dotted with networked, interconnected lakes that provided water to the masses.

For all the city's preoccupation (selective as it may be) with its lost lakes, not much is known either about the circumstances causing their decline or even whether some traces of their existence have been left behind. Some such forgotten relics from the past are indeed hidden in plain sight in the heart of the city. Around the area presently occupied by Sri Kanteerava Stadium, for instance, there are remnants of its earlier watery identity—Sampangi lake—scattered amidst malls, educational institutions and shops selling exquisite silk items.

Believed to have been built in the mid-16th century by Immadi Kempegowda,[8] the son of the city's founder, Sampangi lake is associated with at least two tales related to its name. One story holds that the lake was named Sampangi after one of Immadi Kempegowda's daughters-in-law. The other ascribes the name to a large Sampige (*Michelia champaka*) tree that used to grace this landscape.[10] This tree is also believed to be the inspiration for the name of the village that thrived on the banks of the lake: Sampigehalli. Today we know Sampigehalli as Sampangiramnagara.

Sampangi lake was an impressive water body, indispensable to communities living around it. Up until the establishment of colonial rule in Bengaluru (around 1799), this lake provided water to meet the needs of the prominently agricultural community living in Sampigehalli.[10] This community includes some of the oldest migrants to the city, the Tigalars or the Vannhikula Kshatriyas—horticulturists par excellence who moved from Tamil Nadu in the 16th century and were responsible for much of the city's earlier gardening achievements.[11] Their festival—the Karaga—is one of the oldest celebrated festivals in the city, and it revolves around lakes and water bodies; the festival provides reflections of the former waterscape of Bengaluru.[12]

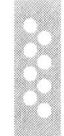

In the colonial era (specifically around the year 1865), Bengaluru consisted of two distinct zones: the anglicised Cantonment governed by the British, and the native city or the *pete* governed by the Wodeyars of Mysore who had become subsidiaries of the British. The Cantonment was a reflection of the British ethos of life, complete with gardens, bungalows, boulevards, fountains and parks, while the *pete* was the industrial and agricultural hub of the city. The Cantonment, with the excellent land it occupied, was also a continuing expression of military presence in the region—a character it retains to the present day. Every effort was made to separate the colonial and native populations, even going so far as to set up a separate brewery with British sensibilities! Yet, this sharp line of separation blurred and thinned out when it came to Sampangi lake.

This lake, by virtue of its presence right on the borders of the Cantonment and the *pete*, defied all attempts to keep the native and colonial populations separate. It was needed as much as a water source to the Cantonment (until piped water arrived from the Hesarghatta lake further north in 1865), as it was to nurture the lush horticultural fields in the *pete*. As much as the waters

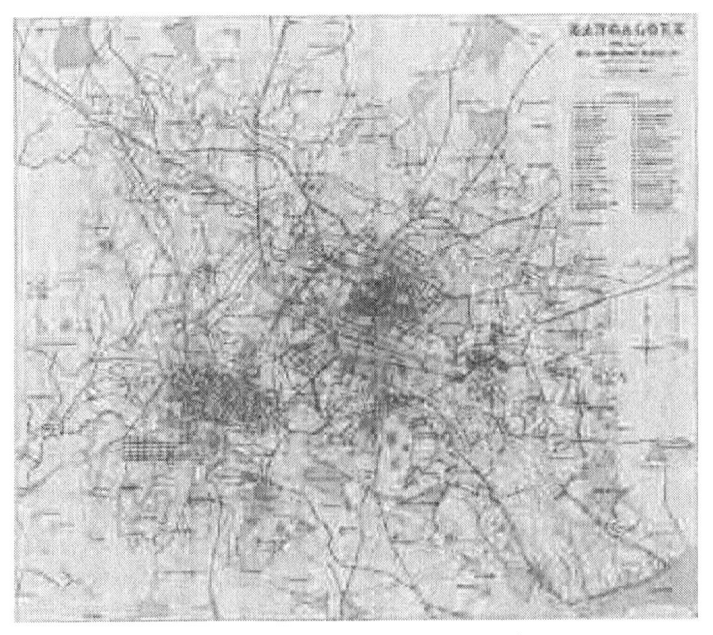

Lake District: Bengaluru at the turn of century, showing its vast network of connected lakes. *Courtesy of British Library; Bangalore (1935).*

provided a picturesque backdrop to the bungalows of the British, it also helped the villagers wash themselves, their animals, clothes and vessels, while allowing local youngsters to swim about or fish in its depths. While paddy, millets, vegetables, flowers, and green leafy vegetables were cultivated on one side of the lake, the other saw the establishment of hospitals, public institutions, schools, bungalows and the aforementioned brewery. And while the native population valued the water body for the water and the resources it provided, the colonial population valued it more for the real estate opportunities it afforded. Naturally, with such differing viewpoints, both among the users of the lake and its managers, conflicts were bound to arise.

Between the years 1900 and 1945, the lake was the site of fierce debate about whom it served best. Was it really necessary to deepen the channels of the lake to provide more water for the farmers? Would that not endanger the public buildings, bungalows and brewery on the opposite banks if the lake were to be breached any time? By this time, Bengaluru was not dependent upon its lakes for water, choosing instead to pump in water from reservoirs and rivers further and further away from the city to meet the demands of its expanding populations. The lakebed and its wetlands began to be slowly drained to make way for Jesuit educational institutions, hospitals and other public buildings. Reclaimed land was given away as compensation to people who lost their lands during times of war. Imperial regiments used the lakebed as a polo ground (often to the dismay of the Wodeyars), and later on, it was used as a playground by local youth.

The lake transformed in people's imagination from being a nurturer and provider into a social hazard, a vector for mosquitoes and therefore dangerous diseases, and a place suitable for use as a public toilet. By the early 1940s, the lake had dried up completely, save for a small square of water that remains even today. There were official discussions exploring the possibility of converting this empty space into a sports stadium following similar models of development in the neighbouring city of Mysuru. The sports stadium was officially inaugurated in 1945, giving a new identity to a much-used and often-maligned water body.

Maps 1–4 document this transition of the lake and its surroundings between the years 1885 and 2014.

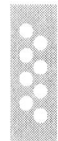

254 | Discovering Bengaluru

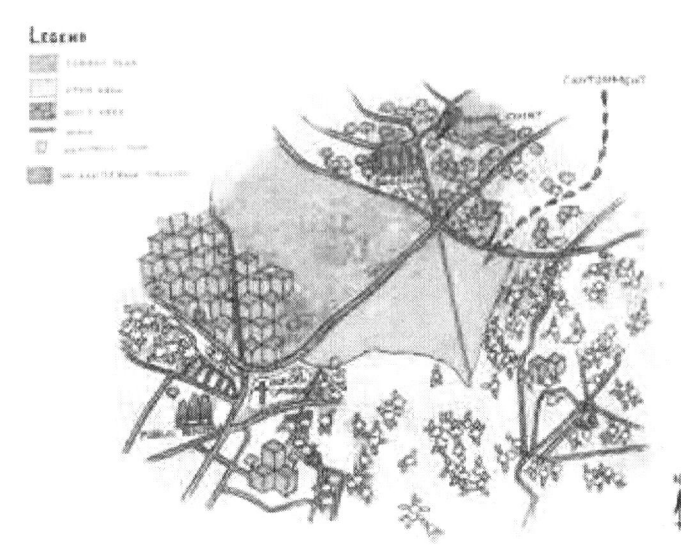

Illustration of the landscape in and around Sampangi lake in the year 1885.
Based on a map created by Hita Unnikrishnan, and illustrated by Shubhika Malara

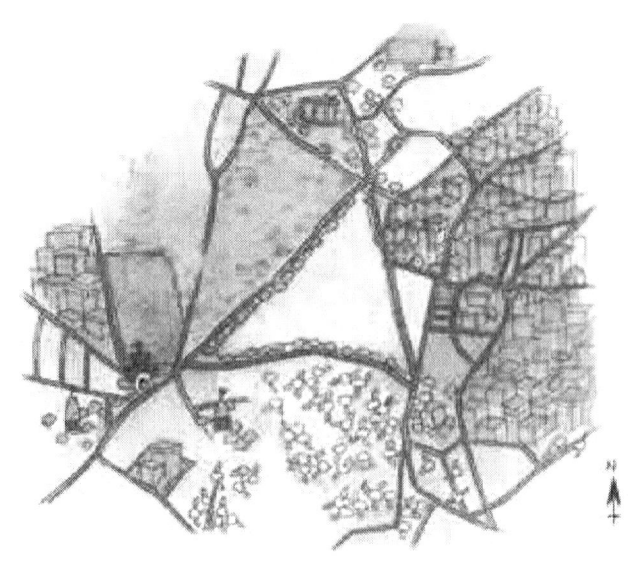

Illustration of the landscape in and around Sampangi lake in the year 1935.
Based on a map created by Hita Unnikrishnan, and illustrated by Shubhika Malara

Illustration of the landscape in and around Sampangi lake in the year 1973.
Based on a map created by Hita Unnikrishnan, and illustrated by Shubhika Malara

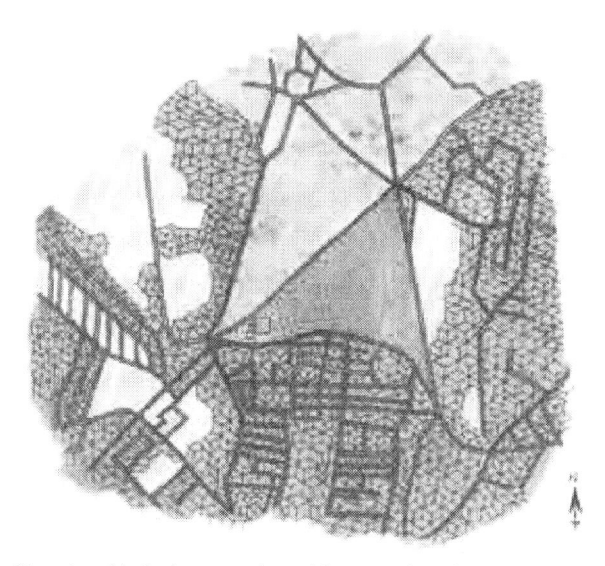

Illustration of the landscape in and around Sampangi lake in the year 2014.
Based on a map created by Hita Unnikrishnan, and illustrated by Shubhika Malara

A Walk through Sampangiramnagara

In which we meet ghosts of a past lake and a culture still present

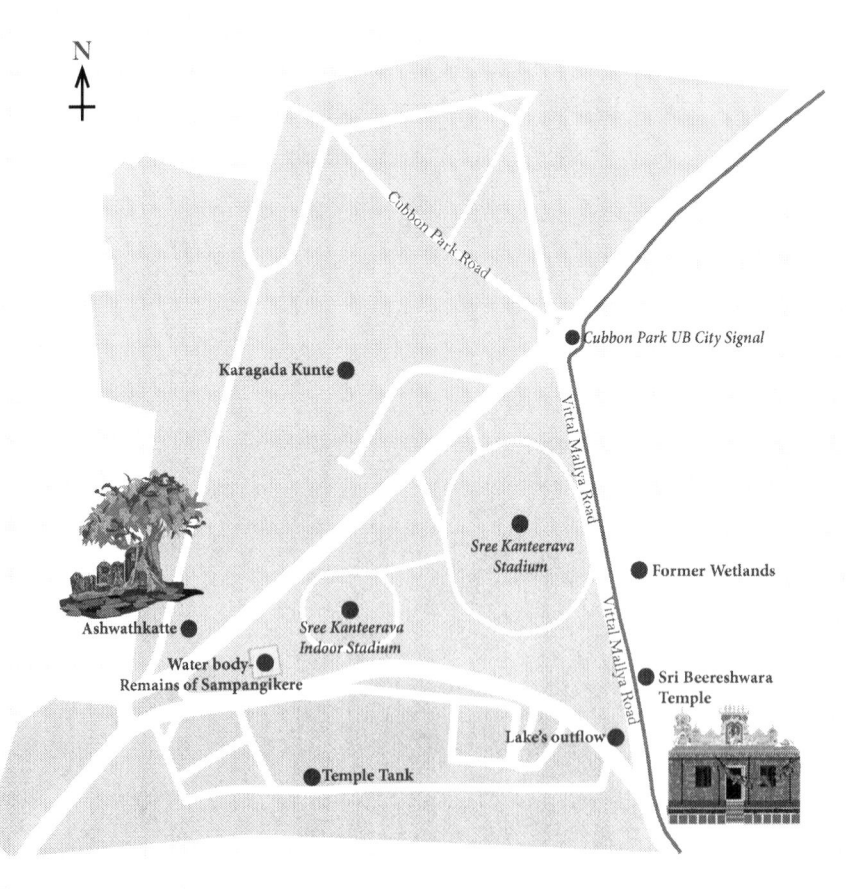

- Karagada Kunte
- Cubbon Park UB City Signal
- Ashwathkatte
- Sree Kanteerava Stadium
- Former Wetlands
- Sree Kanteerava Indoor Stadium
- Water body- Remains of Sampangikere
- Sri Beereshwara Temple
- Lake's outflow
- Temple Tank

A Walk through Sampangiramnagara © *INTACH Bengaluru Chapter*

I. Storm Water Channel

Today, save for the obviously low-lying ground occupied by the stadium, very few traces of Sampangi lake are to be found in this triangular patch of land. A former storm water channel—now carrying sewage and floodwater—still flows next to the stadium grounds on Vittal Mallya Road; it may be glimpsed by walking on the footpath right next to the stadium. Following the trail of this channel, at the end of the road next to the junction is the site of the lake's outflow. Here one can see the remains of the pipes carrying water away from the lake, though obscured by tall shrubs. They stand as testimony to the numerous fields irrigated and the many households served by this once important water body.

II. The Former Wetlands

Vittal Mallya Road, with the concrete UB City Mall and the Mallya Hospital (named after Vittal Mallya, the father of a rather beleaguered beer baron), offers some more glimpses into the past of the area surrounding Sampangi lake, as we shall see. On this road stands St Joseph's Educational Institutions—established in the year 1898 to provide quality education to children—occupying what were once the sprawling wetlands irrigated by this lake.[13] Indeed, as the institution's website proudly states, 'It did take a lot of time and energy to see that the tank bed was drained out to prepare the sprawling playgrounds for the students.'

The remains of Sampangi lake's overflow visible today. © *Hita Unnikrishnan*

III. Sri Beereshwara Temple

Next to the Mallya Hospital, on the same road, is a rather quaint temple: the Sri Beereshwarana Devastana, sacred to the Kuruba (shepherd) communities of the state.

The passing visitor might be forgiven for not paying attention to the small nondescript arched entrance to this temple, flanked as it is by the Mallya Hospital on one side and the opulent ITC Gardenia on the other. Prepare to be astonished at your first glimpse of the veritable oasis hidden behind that arch: lush sprawling grounds dotted with large rain trees and copperpods, upon which bonnet macaques practise their gymnastics, and squirrels scamper for their food. It is one of the few undisturbed green spaces in the heart of the city.

Within this compound to the right is a youth hostel run for the youth of the Kuruba community. Sri Beereshwarana Devasthana dominates the rest of the property. It is a rather ordinary looking temple till one notices the rows of elaborately chiselled stones that make up its base. Undated to the present day, these stones tell tales of valour and sacrifice of men and women who lived long ago and were a part of this landscape. While the Kuruba community itself possesses no written record of when these stones were placed here, relying instead on oral traditions passed down through generations, historians have put forth a number of propositions regarding this site.

One of the theories is that this place was a site where special acts of bravery (such as victories in cattle raids) were recorded and immortalised in stone.[14]

The Beereshwara Temple on Mallya Road. © *Hita Unnikrishnan*

The chiselled stones that make up the base of the Beereshwara Temple. © *Hita Unnikrishnan*

Yet another view is that these stones represent sites where the practice of sati had occurred.[15] This hypothesis is lent some credence by the presence of specific motifs (such as depiction of a woman with her right hand raised, bestowing a benediction) chiselled on the stones that are common to hero stones in other places that have commemorated sati. The oral tradition of the Kuruba community holds that these stones have been placed to commemorate special acts of worship that community members from far-off places have performed. None of these viewpoints are mutually exclusive, and it may very well be that this site represents a combination of all of these events.

IV. A Kalyani

Vittal Mallya Road connects to Raja Ram Mohan Roy Road, with the left of the road leading into the settlement today known as Sampangiramnagar. This area too formed part of the irrigated wetlands downstream of Sampangi lake, which used to be cultivated with paddy. Indeed, local residents can even today point to the stretches irrigated by the overflow of the lake, and where the water used to be channelled into fields through strategically placed sluice gates. Scattered throughout this area are places that evoke the watery history of this landscape. Thus, there is the *Kalyani* slum, purportedly built over one of the many temple tanks or kalyanis that once dotted the landscape[16]; a dried up step well is the only trace left of the *kalyani*.

Temple tanks, as the name suggests, refer to step wells or ponds associated with temples. Constructed to serve as a source of sacred water for rituals performed in the temple, they also doubled as a secondary source of water. Old maps of the region show numerous step wells dotting the area. Most of these have since disappeared. The one located within Sampangiramnagar is drained of its water, yet highly evocative of a time long gone by.

The *kalyani* or temple tank filled up and used for the *Karthika Deepotsava* in Sampangiramnagar. © *Hita Unnikrishnan*

Situated next to the Government High School in Sampangiramnagar, this structure is hard to miss with its rectangular structure and steps leading down to what used to be the water body. Massive stone pillars grace the four sides of the rectangle, and the entrance is sculpted with motifs of people and various mythical creatures. The water body has been filled up and the space is used for various activities by the residents of the area. It functions as a playground for the government school next door; it is also used as a space to teach and learn various art forms such as Taekwondo and dance. The space is lit with numerous lamps during the Hindu festival of Karthika Deepotsava, and the entire community gathers here for an evening of music, dance, theatre and feasting. In a sense, this space represents the repurposing of an urban commons for new uses that foster different forms of community building and forge new identities for a historical landscape.

Sampangiramnagar, where this tank is situated, is also a reflection of a space where discrete cultural tapestries come together and weave conspicuous identities of their own. Walking along these roads, one comes across several spaces for specific community groups or sanghas—those of the Vannhikula Kshatriyas (horticultural cultural community belonging to the warrior caste), the Devangas (weavers) and the Vaishyas (merchants). Oral histories of these communities that we recorded indicate that these buildings came about because of intense communal conflicts which took place in this region around the late 1920s. Historical records too indicate that this was a period of intense communal clashes all across the city, particularly between the Hindus and the Muslims who lived in the area.[17]

V. A Water Body and a Shrine

At the junction of Raja Ram Mohan Roy and Kasturba roads, and directly across from Cubbon Park, one encounters the small, square water body that is all that remains of the former Sampangi lake. It lies within a space called the Sampangi Tank Park, as proclaimed by a rusty green board visible only from the side of the property that faces Kasturba Road. Adjacent to this water body and linked to it is a small plot of land upon which stands a small shrine surrounded by decorative lawn grass. On most days, this shrine and water body are quite deserted except for the caretakers who live within the premises along with their numerous cats and dogs. Maintained by the community of Tigalars (or Vannhikula Ksahtriyas) for whom Sampangi lake holds great cultural significance, the water body is also populated with fish that are periodically caught and used mostly for subsistence by one family belonging to the same community. In a quaint tradition, the fisherman feeds a portion of the catch to a group of Brahminy kites circling overhead.

This water body, however, comes to life in the collective consciousness of the urban population exactly once a year during the festival of Karaga. Celebrated by the Tigalars, this tradition involves worship and rituals conducted around several lakes in the city. Sampangi lake represents the second water body in this cycle of rituals that honour Draupadi, who is believed to be the mother of the Tigalars.[18]

Sampangi tank with the Sri Kanteerava Stadium in the background. © *Hita Unnikrishnan*

VI. A Katte

The ashwathkatte with its trunk partially obscuring some of the snake deities. © Hita Unnikrishnan

The first water body to be worshipped during Karaga also lies in this general vicinity within the premises of Cubbon Park, on the side that faces Kasturba Road. While approaching this, one comes across a temple and an old *ashwathkatte*[19] — a raised stone platform flanked by two large peepul trees and decorated with images of the snake gods venerated in Hindu tradition.[20] Oral traditions hold that these trees marked one of the waterfronts of Sampangi lake in its heyday and were worshipped as such. The age of this katte is obvious even to the casual observer as one of the peepal trees has grown around and obscured a part of the snake motifs. This *katte* is also the site of a quaint annual tradition when Kamadeva, the Hindu equivalent of Cupid, is worshipped on a full moon night in summer and offerings are laid out for him in the form of food, flowers and fruits.

The idols of Kamadeva and his consort worshipped beneath the katte. © Hita Unnikrishnan

VII. Karagada Kunte

A little ahead of this *katte* is the Karagada *kunte:* the first water body that is visited as part of the Karaga festivities. Its approach is marked by a metal grill shaped into a dome-like structure upon which letters are formed to spell the Kannada term *'Shakti peetha'*—literally translating to the 'seat of power'. The Tigalas regard this water as sacred and integral to their belief of divine manifestation during the Karaga rituals. Maps dating to 1885 show this space as a significant water body next to Sampangi lake but separate from it. Over the years however, the water disappeared, leaving behind a depression that is artificially filled once a year to, ironically enough, mark the celebration of a festival that involves the city's waterscape.

The landscape around Sampangi lake is not unique in having relics that testify to its former watery identity. Among the plethora of sights and experiences the bustling metropolis of Bengaluru offers the casual traveller—fancy shopping malls, multiplexes and eateries dotting the streets, the swanky silver and pink Metro rail system, old, narrow streets lined with large flower markets that open in the wee hours of the morning and sell a variety of blooms, traffic build-ups that stretch across kilometres—it becomes quite easy to

The *Karagada Kunte*. © *Hita Unnikrishnan*

overlook other features that contribute to the unique identity of this city. Such as structures that symbolise ancient bonds forged with nature that lie scattered through the landscape, and yet are subtle enough to escape attention. For, as unusual as it may seem, nature is and has always been a strong force shaping the city's past, present and, very likely, its future.[21]

The terrain around many lost lakes of Bengaluru (and there are many) is dotted with reminders of the past if only one looks carefully for these signs. Magnificent old wells with stone steps spiralling down to their depths scattered across the city in dilapidated states today were once most likely associated with water bodies or huge irrigated fields.[22] The remains of the sluice gate that once served Dharmambudhi tank (today, the city's central bus terminal) may still be found very close to the bus station. An old stone venerated as the *grama devathe*[23] (village deity) near the Alliance Française on Millers Tank Bund Road indicates the location of the former series of 'Miller's tanks' (another set of lakes connected to the Sampangi lake by means of channels) that were drained to prevent water-borne epidemics.[24]

These spaces bear testimony to the city's engagement with its natural resources—an engagement that has slowly dwindled as it expanded and became

Remnants of a lost lake: flooding at the Sri Kanteerava Stadium. *Courtesy of Deccan Herald Archives.*

more urban, and less dependent upon them for meeting its basic requirements of food and water. They are reflective of a growing city's obsession with development that prioritised aesthetics and recreation; this became manifest in the relations it held with its water bodies such as Sampangi lake, which was eventually drained to become an entity that mirrored these notions. The formerly utilitarian aspects of water bodies (relating to the farmer, fisherman or pastoralist, and even recharge of the water table) have become forgotten aspects of the city's past, as they slowly get subsumed by layers of urbanisation and development.

The few remaining urban lakes of the city today are vulnerable to threats such as encroachment, pollution and reclamation. Despite their critical importance for various aspects of the city's ecology (microclimate regulation, recharge and preserving biodiversity, to name a few), many of them continue to be neglected and a shadow of their former selves. Indeed, newspapers in recent years have been abuzz with reports of one of the city's largest lakes catching fire. It is indeed paradoxical that a water body should be associated with the one element that water douses: fire! In other lakes that have been rejuvenated or where attempts to rejuvenate them are ongoing, the focus is primarily on notions of aesthetics and recreation. This is reflected in the engagement with real estate, parks, boulevards, water sports, playgrounds, jogging tracks and eateries that are encouraged around such spaces, which are usually also enclosed and inaccessible for a large part of the day, thus cutting them off from more marginalised user groups.[25] Thus, conspicuously absent from these spaces are people such as the humble farmer, shepherd or the washerman, for whom a lake represents more than just a space for relaxation. Most of the lakes have lost their former cultural and utilitarian connection with communities.[26]

Such relics of the past serve to remind us that our situation is precarious. We live in an era that is characterised and beset by water shortages, dry spells of scorching heat, and continued disputes over inter-state sharing of water. With such bleak prospects, it is time to look inward to the city to enhance its ability to nurture and provide for the millions dependent upon it. Even if we cannot restore the waterscape of Bengaluru to its former glory, we can at least hope to protect and nurture our existing water bodies in a just, equitable and sustainable manner. It is time we go back to the stories of our long forgotten engagement with our resources, read the histories of the landscape that have silently stood witness to drastic changes, and look to incorporating lessons from the past to secure a resilient future for the city.

Notes

1. Annaswamy 2003.
2. Nagendra 2016.
3. Sudhira, Ramachandra and Subrahmanya 2007.
4. Rice 1897a; Unnikrishnan, Sen and Nagendra 2017.
5. Unnikrishnan, Mundoli and Nagendra 2017.
6. Nagendra 2016.
7. For example, see 'Constables turn heroes in rain', *Bangalore Mirror*, 27 September 2014; 'Bengalureans caught unaware as rain cripples city', The Hindu, 16 May 2015; 'Skies open up, Bengaluru on its knees', *Deccan Chronicle*, 7 May 2016.
8. Rice 1897a; Annaswamy 2003; Nair 2005.
9. Oral history interviews conducted by the authors around Sampangi lake between 2014 and 2015.
10. Srinivas 2004; Unnikrishnan, Manjunatha and Nagendra 2016.
11. Mirza 1949.
12. Srinivas 2004.
13. http://sjihs.org/history.html, accessed February 2016.
14. Oral history interviews conducted by the authors around Beereshwara temple between 2014 and 2015.
15. Aruni 2013.
16. Oral history interviews conducted by the authors between 2014 and 2015 in and around Sampangiramnagar.
17. Anon 1928.
18. This community believes that it has descended directly from Draupadi, a character central to the Mahabharata. As the story goes, at the end of the Mahabharata, when Draupadi and her five husbands begin their journey to heaven accompanied by a dog, each of them falls down and fails in their quest due to their various worldly attachments. Draupadi is the first to fall down (explained in the epic as a consequence of her excessive love for one of her husbands over the others). The oral traditions of the Tigalars pick up at this point when they relate that as she fell down, Draupadi (still a beautiful woman) attracted the lustful eyes of a demon. She created the first Tigalars out of her blood and sweat to defend herself at this moment. The warriors thus born fulfilled their role in defending their mother and found themselves aimlessly wandering. At this point in time Draupadi inspired them to lead normal lives with the assurance that she would manifest herself among them once every year. The seven-day festival of the Karaga is believed to be this manifestation of the goddess among them.
19. *Ashwathkattes* have traditionally been spaces where village disputes were solved and justice meted out in the precolonial era. Today, such raised platforms, usually flanked by one or more peepal or neem trees, are used for rituals centred around marriage and finding prospective grooms. These shaded spots are also used by people to relax and gossip on a sunny day.

20. Nagendra, Unnikrishnan and Sen 2013.
21. Nagendra 2016.
22. Unnikrishnan 2017.
23. Village or lake deities are often associated with many lakes across the city. Offerings are made to these deities for a range of reasons including protection from disease, a bountiful harvest, protection against floods and rituals celebrating the various stages of life. See Unnikrishnan, Mundoli, Manjunatha and Nagendra 2016.
24. Nagendra 2016.
25. Field visits to over 21 lakes of the city made by the authors over two seasons between 2014 and 2015.
26. Unnikrishnan, Manjunatha and Nagendra 2017.

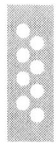

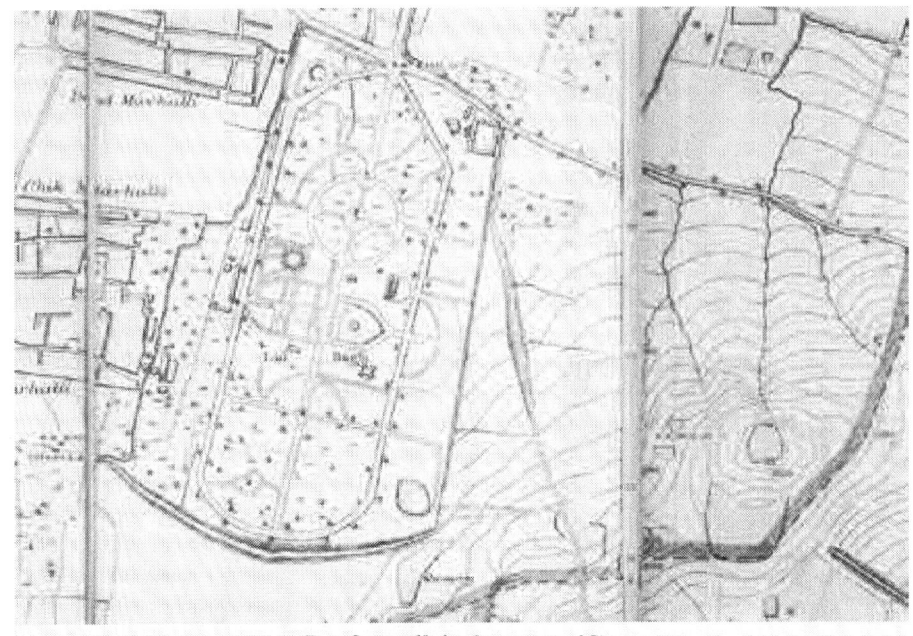

Lalbagh and tis vicinity in 1884-85. From, Survey of India. *Cantonment and City of Bangalore and Environs, Season 1884-85.* Courtesy of Mythic Society, Bengaluru.

Lalbagh and its vicinity in 1935-36. From, Survey of India. *Bangalore Guide Map. Surveyed 1935-36.* Courtesy of Naresh Narasimhan.

CHAPTER 9

From Royal Gardens to Urban Green Lung: Lalbagh

A Short Account of Bengaluru's Green Spaces

Garden City. Until a few decades ago, this was the moniker applied to Bengaluru. The name derived from the large compounds of all the larger bungalows—compounds that were filled with fruit trees and flowering plants, with butterflies and birds. And then there were the parks and gardens that dotted the city, and its thousands of grand old street trees, all of which contributed to the city's well-deserved image as a beautiful garden city, a gardener's paradise.[1]

The image of Bengaluru as a city full of trees and gardens has a hoary past. In fact, the city's very name may well derive from a tree: one of the theories for the origin of the name is that it derives from the *benga* tree (*Pterocarpus marsupium*).[2] Thanks to its elevation and the resulting balmy climate, Bengaluru has long been a horticultural paradise. In her wonderfully interesting analysis of inscriptions found in Bengaluru (beginning with the earliest dating from 517 CE which mentions Begur), Harini Nagendra outlines how the earliest settlements came up in fertile valleys, and later, in the 1200s or so, in the slopes of the hills around the area. Apart from tracing the settling of this region, these inscriptions also provide valuable information on the landscape of the area. As Nagendra shows, the southern and western areas of the city were dominated by dense scrub and jungle, with several inscriptions alluding to attacks by wild boars and tigers. The inscriptions paint a picture of cultivated lands irrigated by *keres* in the north and east. However, even these agricultural settlements were surrounded by trees.[3]

The earliest literary description we have of the city, written in the 1600s by Kavindra Parmanand *(see chapter 1)*, shows that despite being a dense settlement, it was still known for the 'trees thick with flowers and shade [that] lined each home garden'.[4] About a hundred years after Parmanand wrote this, Hyder Ali and, later, his son Tipu Sultan ruled this area; both were known for their fondness for gardens and trees.[5] However, the late 1700s were also a time of numerous battles and one of their casualties was the trees. In keeping with military requirements, the areas around forts, including the Bengaluru forts, were often kept intentionally free of trees to preclude enemies from using them for cover. Paintings of the period show a rather bare landscape, devoid of trees, around the stone fort. However, maps dating from the same period, drawn by Europeans after their battles against Tipu, do show a number of gardens around the city. Echoing earlier inscriptions, there are trees above the bunds of several of the lakes, there are well-defined gardens here and there, and there are trees lining many of the city's main roads.

When the British set up the Cantonment, they brought with them their ideas of gardens and urban parks, which were subsequently also adopted by the City Municipality administered by the Mysore Maharaja. Apart from Cubbon Park, the city boasted several neighbourhood parks like Coles Park, Richards Park, MN Krishna Rao Park and so on. And so was perpetuated the idea of Bengaluru as a city of gardens and trees, where bustling commercial areas are shaded by canopies of century-old rain trees, and where modern IT parks lie cheek by jowl with *kattes* harbouring venerable peepal and neem trees.

Lalbagh, Bengaluru's oldest garden, has an especially interesting history that is intertwined with the history of the city and the Cantonment. It reflects the importance of botany in the Empire and continues to hold a special place in the heart of every Bengalurean.

From Mango Orchard to Botanic Garden

A mango orchard, a royal garden, a botanic garden, a zoo, even a battleground—Bengaluru's Lalbagh has been through various incarnations over the years. What has remained unchanged for two and a half centuries has been the care lavished upon it by successive administrators and rulers. Lalbagh has also been at the centre of the development of horticulture not just in Karnataka but also in India, thanks to the connections of its administrators with the principal botanical gardens around the world, especially so with Kew in England. The garden today covers almost 240 acres, and has 673 genera and 1854 species of plants, according to the official website.

The earliest evidence of human activity here dates from thousands of years ago. In the early 1900s, remains of numerous prehistoric burials were discovered east of what is popularly called the Lalbagh Rock. These relics, including potsherds and large urns, were characteristic of the Early Iron Age period, approximately 1800 to 3000 years ago. Sadly, no traces remain of our prehistoric ancestors in Lalbagh.

However, evidence suggests that Lalbagh went from being a burial ground to a battleground. Near the northern base of the rock is a hero stone depicting a warrior accompanied by a woman. Close to the bandstand, nestled amidst some rocks and trees, stands a second, very interesting two-tiered memorial stone. The upper layer depicts Nandi and a linga while the lower layer shows a resplendent royal couple flanked by two attendants. Based on their distinctive styles of dress, hairdos and weapons, these memorials have been placed in the Vijayanagar period. With no inscriptions to guide us, we can only wonder about the kinds of battles Lalbagh was witness to hundreds of years ago.

Fast-forward about a hundred years and we come to the time of the Kempegowda family, when Kempegowda II built one of his iconic towers atop the rock. Legend claims there was already a mango grove in the vicinity when he built the tower but we cannot be sure. What we are sure of is that another two centuries later, Hyder Ali picked this very spot to set up a series of gardens growing, among other things, mangoes. And so in 1760 begins the official history of Lalbagh.

A medieval period hero stone in Lalbagh. © *Meera Iyer*

The Lalbagh Rock

The Lalbagh Rock, a National Geological Monument. © PeeVee

The botanical garden teems with artefacts made by our ancestors. But Lalbagh is also home to a monument that is far, far older. About three billion years old, to be a little more precise. Just to put that in context, the Earth itself is about 4.5 billion years. (We modern humans have been around for a paltry 250,000 years.) This means the Lalbagh Rock comes from a time when the Earth was still undergoing major volcanic activity and witnessing the beginning of tectonic upheavals. This is pretty exciting because though, as laypeople, we tend to think of rocks as permanent, the reality is that the Earth's rocks have been consumed and refashioned by tectonic activity and erosion over the aeons; so it is rare to find remnants from the Earth's infancy, so to speak. This makes the Lalbagh Rock of immense interest to geologists.

The rock is peninsular gneiss, a term coined in 1916 by the then Director of the Mysore Geological Department, William F Smeeth.[7] In 1975, it was declared a National Geological Monument by the Government of India. According to the Geological Survey of India, 'gneisses and related granitoids constitute one of the most abundant rocktypes exposed on earth'. The Lalbagh Rock 'is composed of dark biotite gneiss of granitic to granodioritic composition containing streaks of biotite. Vestiges of older rocks are seen in the form of enclaves within the gneiss. Peninsular Gneiss of the region is dated 2500 to 3400 million years that accreted in three major episodes, i.e. 3.4 Ga, 3.3-3.2 Ga and 3.0-2.9 Ga. The quarries of Lalbagh are of great importance for researches on earth sciences towards evolution of the terrain.'[8]

Royal Gardens

Hyder Ali set up several garden plots in this area. His son Tipu Sultan expanded the gardens his father had created. These gardens were formal, with cypress-lined walkways separating the plots.[9]

There are various theories for the origin of the name Lalbagh. The garden always had a profusion of roses. The story goes that when Tipu the child was brought to the garden, he saw the roses and exclaimed 'Lalbagh! Lalbagh!' (red garden). And so the name Lalbagh was given to all of Hyder's gardens including the one in Srirangapatna.[10]

Right from those early days of the 1700s, Lalbagh became a repository of exotic, unusual and useful plants from around the world. Hyder brought in plants from Delhi, Multan and Lahore, Tipu from even further afield, including Mauritius, Turkey, Persia and parts of Africa. How he procured these plants is interesting. In 1785, for example, he wrote several times to Meer Kazim, his commercial agent in Muscat, asking him to send young date palm, almond and pistachio saplings, and saffron seeds.[11] The many battles he was mired in did little to curb his enthusiasm for plants and trees. In December 1797, less than two years before his final defeat, Tipu sent two ambassadors to Mauritius. They returned in April the following year, bringing with them 20 cases of plants and seeds. Camels and horses were sent all the way from Srirangapatna to bring this precious cargo.[12]

Several economically valuable trees were introduced, including spices such as clove, nutmeg and cinnamon, as well as other kinds of trees such as the annatto, said to have been very common in the garden.[13] Tipu also stocked his gardens with fruit trees including pomegranate, jackfruit, rose apple, fig, orange and mango. One of these trees fell a few years ago but a seed from that was planted and a healthy mango sapling now takes forward that particular tree's legacy. Close to the famous sapling are a few more mango trees which are also from Tipu's period.

During this period, the garden was looked after by a head gardener who was given the title 'daroga'. Like the rulers, a father–son pair of darogas named Mohammad Ali and Abdul Khader, looked after the garden in Hyder's and Tipu's times respectively.[14]

Did you know that Lalbagh even played a bit part in defending Bengaluru during this period? During the 1791 siege of Bengaluru, Tipu stationed some

East View of Bangalore, by Robert Hyde Colebrooke, 1792. Note how the Kempegowda Tower looks, and the different plots of garden that are visible. *Courtesy of British Library Shelfmark WD4461*

of his troops in these very gardens. Equipped with 10-12 guns, they fired on British troops attacking the fort, but their efforts proved futile, for the fort fell *(see chapter 1)*.

European soldiers found the gardens utterly charming and in 1791–92, several of them produced paintings of the gardens which they called variously the Mango Tope, the Cypress Garden and Sultan's Gardens.[15] The earliest contemporary description of the Lalbagh of yore is by Francis Buchanan. Soon after the British had managed to finally overcome their most implacable enemy Tipu Sultan, Governor General Richard Wellesley appointed Buchanan to survey and report on the territories that until recently had been with Tipu. Buchanan was a Scottish surgeon, and also a botanist, zoologist and geographer.[16]

Buchanan visited Lalbagh on 11 May 1800, a year and a week after Tipu had been killed in Srirangapatna. Here is an extract from his report:

> I visited the gardens made by the late Mussulman princes, Hyder and Tippoo. They are extensive, and divided into square plots separated by walks, the sides of which are ornamented with fine cypress trees. The plots are filled with fruit trees, and pot-herbs. The Mussulman fashion is to have a separate piece of ground allotted for each kind of plant. Thus one plot is entirely filled with rose trees, another with pomegranates, and so forth. The walks are not gravelled, and the cultivation of the whole is rather slovenly; but the people say, that formerly the gardens were well kept. Want of water is the principal defect of these gardens; for in, this arid country every thing, during the dry season, must be artificially watered. The garden of Tippoo is supplied from three wells, the water of which is raised by the capily, or leather-bag, fastened to a cord passing over a pulley, and wrought by a pair of bullocks, which descend an inclined plane. This, the workmen say, is a much more effectual machine than the yatam. Hyder's garden is watered from a reservoir, without the assistance of machinery. The taste of Hyder accorded more with the English, than that of his son. His walks are wider, his cypress trees are not so much crowded; and in the means for watering the plots there is not so much masonry, or bricklayer's work, employed. There is, indeed, so much of these in the parts of Tippoo's garden which he probably considered the finest, as almost to cover the ground, and to leave nothing but holes, as it were, through which the trees grow.
>
> In this climate the cypress and vine grow luxuriantly, and the apple and peach both produce fruit; the former much better, and the latter much worse than at Calcutta. Some pine and oak plants, lately introduced from the Cape of Good Hope, seem to be thriving. I think there can be little doubt, but that in this country all the valuable plants of the Levant would succeed.[17]

It is not altogether surprising that Buchanan commented on the 'want of water', given that he visited in the month of May. It is, however, very interesting that even when describing gardens, Britons lost no opportunity to deride Tipu, though they displayed no such animosity towards Hyder!

Tracing the Original Lalbagh

It is generally believed that the garden Hyder Ali set up in 1760 was located north of and adjacent to the Lalbagh tank. Maps published by the Department of Horticulture, for example, depict the garden covering a roughly rectangular patch of about 40 acres adjacent to the tank during 1760–1856.

Using a combination of historical maps, old paintings and recent remotely sensed images, Iyer, Nagendra and Rajani attempted to determine the boundaries of the garden during Tipu Sultan's time.[18] We used two maps, one of which showed the fortress and the other the fort as well as surroundings up to a radius of about 8 km. These maps were first registered (geo-referenced or geo-coded). They show that in 1791, the gardens of Hyder Ali and Tipu Sultan comprised not one contiguous area but a series of five rectangular plots of varying sizes. The plan of these plots corresponds well with historical information that the Hyder–Tipu Sultan gardens, including those elsewhere such as at Sira and Srirangapatna, were laid out in the Persian *char bagh* style, with four plots separated by walks. From Francis Buchanan's report, too, we know that these gardens were divided into plots which were separated by walks. Buchanan describes the gardens as separate entities, which agrees with the map showing separate plots rather than one contiguous garden.

We used the historical paintings as a second line of evidence to locate the original gardens. A 3D simulation of the old landscape was generated on ERDAS software virtual GIS module using Digital Elevation Model (DEM) and overlaying registered maps. That the garden in Tipu Sultan's time consisted of a series of plots and not of one contiguous plot is evident from these paintings of Lalbagh. In 1791–92, shortly after the capture of Bengaluru by the British, a number of British army draughtsmen, surveyors and artists, both official and amateur, painted scenes showing the 'Cypress Garden'. *East View of the Cypress Garden* by an official army artist Robert Home, *East View of Bangalore* by army surveyor Robert Hyde Colebrooke, and *Southerly View of Bangalore*, painted by Col Claude Martin of the Grand Army, all clearly show distinct garden plots, though it is difficult to discern the exact number of plots.

The total area of the plots adds up to 17–18 ha (depending on which map we refer to), which matches with the figure of approximately 17 ha recorded

Benches, tree canopies and solitude at Lalbagh. © *PeeVee*

for Lalbagh in 1800.[7] Of the five gardens clearly demarcated on the maps, four are completely outside the modern Lalbagh. Today they form part of the crematorium to the north of Lalbagh, Muslim burial grounds and the Al-Ameen educational institutes. It is the southernmost rectangular plot, or at least most of it, that falls within the current Lalbagh. The views of the gardens and the fort as shown in the paintings, and the information gleaned from the maps, indicate that the only portion of the Hyder–Tipu gardens encompassed within the modern botanical garden is not adjacent to the Lalbagh Tank (as is generally accepted) but north of it.

Interestingly, as per our analysis, the famous mango tree said to have been planted during Tipu Sultan's time, and hence known as Tipu's mango tree, is indeed within the southernmost rectangular plot, just at the corner; it is located a few metres within the southern boundary and few metres on the west side of the cypress avenue. Another tree that is sometimes pointed out as having been planted during Tipu's times is the large silk cotton tree near the old Aquarium (*see below*). This may have been planted during his time but falls outside the original garden laid out by Tipu.

It is likely that the garden was consolidated into one plot when it was taken over by Gilbert Waugh, in about 1814 (*see below*).

The Company Garden

When the British finally defeated Tipu Sultan in Srirangapatna, practically the entire peninsula was open to them. In 1800, Governor General Richard Wellesley commanded that the 'Sultan's garden in Bangalore was to be appropriated' to establish a botanical garden. He also decreed that the Scottish botanist Benjamin Heyne be put in charge of the garden, which would become a 'depository for useful plants sent from different parts of the country'. The stress was on useful flora rather than 'those which are recommended merely by their rarity or their beauty'.[19]

In March that year, Heyne came to Bengaluru, bringing with him one European painter of plants, two Indian painters, two experienced Indian plant collectors, and a whole bunch of plants (including oaks, pines, nutmeg and cinnamon) and hundreds of seeds. And so the tradition of introducing different species into Lalbagh continued.

Other plants that Heyne introduced to the early Lalbagh when it was under his care were coffee (though other enterprising chaps had already started growing this in their own gardens in Bengaluru), durian, clove, rambutan, mangosteen and, not to forget, potatoes—for, like many Britons, Heyne seems to have been obsessed with potatoes.[20] Under Heyne's husbanding of the garden, parts of the 41-acre or so garden were given over to cultivating mulberry, about 3 acres were under potatoes, and a further 2 acres under grape vines with the aim of making wine, of course![21] He also grew peaches, apples, loquats and other fruit. A part of the garden also turned pastureland for he bought several sheep so that they could provide manure for his precious potatoes and turnips.[22]

Heyne also prepared several botanical drawings which he sent to England. He employed gardeners to work on the garden while he himself flitted in and out of Bengaluru, haring off to study copper mines near Ongole (while his boss, the surveyor Colin Mackenzie, sent him innumerable, peremptory summons, most of which he ignored!) or to carry out his own investigations elsewhere. Meanwhile, he also contracted hepatitis and was moved to Cuddapah. What with all this, Heyne's involvement with the garden came to an end in the second half of 1806. He proposed that it be turned over to the Mysore government, but that attempt appears not to have worked out. Regardless, by 1807, the East India Company had decided 'to incur no further expense on account of the Garden at Bangalore'.[23] In his own report written in 1812, Benjamin Heyne refers to the garden being given over to 'a negro'—presumably an Indian!—who he says sold all the trees and brought the land under rice and ragi.[24]

When next we hear of it, the garden has become the private property of an East India Company soldier named Gilbert Waugh. From being the Sultan's Gardens, they were now referred to as Waugh's Garden. As it happens, Waugh, too, put a lot of serious and patient effort into growing sugarcane, coffee and several kinds of fruits in Lalbagh. He brought in mangosteen (again) from Malaysia and crossed them with varieties from Kerala; he also grew and grafted plums on to existing pear trees in a successful effort to acclimatise them.

Major Gilbert Waugh who 'owned' Lalbagh for a few years. *Courtesy of National Army Museum, UK. Accession no. NAM. 1953-03-22-1.*

The Garden and the Mountain

Gilbert Waugh was born in Scotland and joined the Madras Army as an Ensign in 1798, when he was 15 years old. It was during his stint as a Barrack Master in Bengaluru that Lt Waugh seems to have come into possession of the garden. He was promoted to Major in 1818, and became a Paymaster in Bengaluru. He died in 1844 in Malaysia, at the age of 61, by which time he was Maj Gen Waugh.

Incidentally, there is a connection, tenuous as it may be, between Lalbagh and Mount Everest: Gilbert Waugh's elder son Andrew Waugh was an army officer and a surveyor who was part of the Great Trigonometric Survey. He succeeded George Everest as Surveyor General of India and is credited with having named the peak after his predecessor.[27]

Gifted, Accepted, Declined

A curious episode took place in the garden's history in 1819. In January that year, the recently promoted Major Waugh generously offered to gift 'his' garden to the East India Company's government, then under Governor General Hastings. The offer was made through Arthur H Cole, the then British Resident of Mysore State, who wrote that over the last 15 years, Major Waugh had 'devoted time, attention and fortune to the liberal and useful pursuit of enriching this country with the most valuable productions of Europe and China', and that this work had 'been brought to perfection through a happy combination of industry and the congenial climate and soil of Bangalore'. Cole added that the garden was flourishing thanks to the care Waugh lavished on it, but that it would decay without him.[28]

In April that year, the Marquess of Hastings enthusiastically accepted the gift and suggested it could become a branch of the botanical garden in

Calcutta, which was headed by the renowned surgeon and botanist Nathaniel Wallich. Wallich himself opined that the garden would be 'of great advantage' in introducing in India trees and fruits of Europe and China.[29] However, inexplicably, in August that year, just four months after it first accepted the gift, the Company retracted its acceptance, saying that the value of the garden was too great for them to accept it.

Accordingly, the garden reverted to Waugh, who presumably retained it for a while longer. At some point, the garden was probably returned to the Mysore Maharaja's government. Either way, the exact ownership and trajectory of the garden is a little murky during this period. What is clear is that in 1831, when the British took over the administration of Mysore State from the Maharaja, the garden—though still belonging to the Maharaja's government—came under the care of the Chief Commissioner of Mysore State, General Mark Cubbon

In early 1836, the Agricultural and Horticultural Society of Bangalore was established by some Europeans in Bengaluru, with some lofty aims, including: 'to improve the method of cultivating indigenous plants, to introduce exotic ones to excite competition among the natives [*sic*], and to lay open to the scientific world at large the botany of Southern India, at present but partially and imperfectly known'.[30]

The organisation requested that the erstwhile Waugh's Garden, which was then with the Maharaja, be made over to them. Agreeing to their proposal, Cubbon said, 'Great public benefit may be expected to arise from this institution, not only in regard to objects merely horticultural and the extension of botanical knowledge, but in the promotion of the agricultural interests of the country, by introductions suited to the climate.'[31] Accordingly, in June 1836, the Society reported: 'His Highness the Rajah of Mysore has been pleased most liberally to place at the disposal of the Society for the purpose of a botanical garden a valuable piece of ground commonly known as the Lalbagh.'[32]

The government supported the organisation in various ways, including by providing convict labour. The Society was quite active, growing sugarcane, mulberry, oats, wheat and barley; constructing a house for a Superintendent; conducting exhibitions; and so on. However, perhaps because a number of the members were soldiers and officers who kept getting transferred out of Bengaluru, the members were not constant. The constant churn took a toll; the Society was disbanded in 1842 and the garden reverted to Cubbon's care.[33] The next few years saw a lull in activity here; apart from keeping the walks clean, nothing was done in Lalbagh.

However, the idea of a botanical garden that could be useful had taken firm hold. In 1855, Hugh Cleghorn, the Conservator of Forests in the Madras

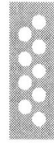

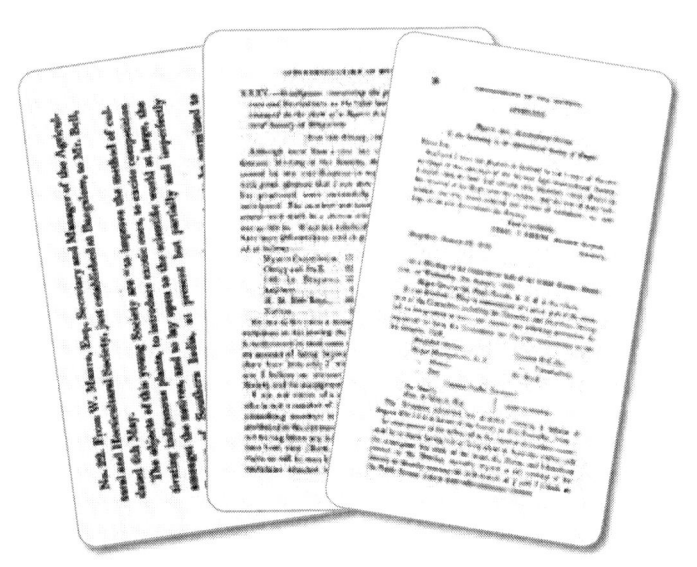

Members of the Agri-Horticultural Society experimented with growing coffee, apples, mulberry and more in Lalbagh. From, Journal of the Agricultural and Horticultural Society of India, various volumes.

Presidency, in his report on the Government Gardens at Udhagamandalam (or Ooty as the British called it), outlined the need for a garden at an intermediate climate between the plains and the Nilgiris. 'The difference of temperature between the Nilgiri Hills and the Carnatic plains is so great that I fear many valuable plants acclimatised in the former would not succeed if at once transplanted to the latter,' he noted.[34] Naturally, Bengaluru with its salubrious climate was the prime candidate for such a garden. By 1856 it was found that the area where Hyder and Tipu had established their gardens 'was, on the whole, the most eligible spot for the purpose': the soil was good, the water abundant and the tank nearby could be enlarged if required.

The proposal immediately found favour. In October that year, the Government of India in Calcutta approved the scheme for the establishment of a 'Horticultural Garden in Bangalore', and sanctioned a sum of Rs 4000 for the construction of a house for a new Superintendent for the garden and for laying out the grounds. The government also provided a monthly grant of Rs 300 for the expenses incurred and a further sum of Rs 200 per month as a salary for the Superintendent of the garden.[35]

And so it was that the Mango Tope and Cypress Garden of yore became the Government Botanical Gardens in 1856.

A Plant Research Laboratory

Lalbagh's association with the Royal Botanic Gardens at Kew in London, the world's pre-eminent centre for botanical research, began almost immediately after it officially became a government botanic garden. Cleghorn called upon the noted botanist Sir William Hooker, then the Director at Kew, to assist in finding someone suitable for the garden in Bengaluru. The First War of Independence then engulfed the country and the candidate who was to join declined to come to India. In the interim period, Cleghorn appointed a gardener named Heera Lal to look after the garden. A committee was set up to administer the garden. They got ready a house for the Superintendent built at a cost of Rs 2000.[36] You can still see this house which (now considerably expanded) houses the Mari Gowda Library.[37] The first official Superintendent of the garden was William New (*see below*).

The original purpose of the garden being to acclimatise (mainly economically beneficial) plants that could profitably be introduced to the colonies, a furious exchange of seeds and plants began that continued till well into the 1930s. Initially, this exchange was predominantly with the mother garden at Kew, but very soon, plants began arriving in Lalbagh from all around the world. The 1905 report on the garden, for example, lists seeds and plants that were received from various places in India and also Cape Town and Cuba. The next year, plants and seeds were received at Lalbagh from Sri Lanka, Trinidad, Philippines and Italy. Lalbagh maintained an exchange of information and plant material with more than a hundred botanical, agricultural and horticultural institutions around the world in the early 1900s.[38] Meanwhile, experimental plantings were always underway in some parts of the garden on various species that could be introduced, including several fruits and vegetables, as well as crops such as coffee and cotton.

But Lalbagh was not only a centre of research; it was also a place of recreation, and a captivating one. From its very early days, the garden has been the delight of Bengalureans and a must-see for all visitors. Horticultural shows have been held here twice every year since the late 1800s, earlier known as the Summer and Winter shows and held in August and February, now held around Republic Day and Independence Day. The who's who of the world have visited the garden and been charmed, including world leaders like Nikita Krushchev, royalty from Britain and other countries, rulers of former Indian principalities, and many, many others. Author Edward Lear, famous for his nonsense verse, visited Lalbagh in August 1874 and called it the Kew of India. He writes in his diary, 'Never saw a more beautiful place, terraces, trellises etc.' He wandered over the rocks and then walked over to the tank where he drew for a while. 'There is something very rural quiet about this green place,' he says,[39] a sentiment we can all identify with even today.[40]

Men Who Made Lalbagh

The pioneer

The first Superintendent of Lalbagh who was trained as a botanist was William New, who was recommended by William Hooker of Kew. New had previously worked at the Belfast Botanic Garden and also at Kew. He reached Bengaluru in April 1858, bringing with him cases of plants from Hooker, which included species from Australia, North Africa, Madeira and Tenerife.

New spent the next couple of years energetically setting up the paraphernalia required in a botanical garden. Several wells were dug, paths laid, pavilions built. He brought in plants from the botanic gardens at Ooty and elsewhere. Nurseries and greenhouses were established which still exist today. He also made the walkway on top of the bund, a walk that is still one of the favourite spots for visitors to the gardens. Some of the eucalyptus trees (from Australia) below the bund of the tank date from William New's period. At Cleghorn's request, New also undertook the first ever census of plants in Lalbagh in 1861. The census enumerates approximately 620 genera and 1033 species.[41]

Interestingly, New began reshaping the garden into a typical formal English garden, with all the usual elements associated with such gardens including urns, circular and sweeping carriageways, terraces and a 'rustic octagon' for creepers.

New left in 1863 but was brought back after the short stint of his replacement Allan Adamson Black (who incidentally has a genus named after him, *Allanblackia*); he continued till his death in August 1873.

Apart from plants, New also introduced elements typical of formal English gardens into Lalbagh, such as urns and terraces. © *Aravind C*

The father of horticulture in Karnataka

John Cameron took over as the Superintendent of Lalbagh in March 1874. Like his predecessor, Cameron had a background in botany and had trained at the Royal Botanic Gardens in Kew. Whatever little we can glean from stray records and his correspondence reveals a man full of ideas, action and passion for plants and horticulture.

In the first six years after he took charge of Lalbagh, Cameron managed to introduce an average of 160 new plants every year, so that Lalbagh's second plant census in 1880 records 2020 species![42] And 11 years later, the garden had an astonishing 3222 species though, of course, by this time the garden had also increased in size.[43] It's no wonder that the 33 years that Cameron was in charge of Lalbagh are regarded by horticulturists as the golden era of plant introductions.

Cameron cast his net far and wide, using his contacts around the world to bring new plants to the garden: clematis from Greece, oil palms from West Africa, silk rubber from Indonesia, khat or qat from Yemen, fish poison tree from Sri Lanka, blackthorn from Australia, and many more. He also tried to introduce several commercial crops, including varieties of coffee, apples, rubber and grapes.[44]

In fact, many of the vegetables we think of as an integral part of our diet were introduced during Cameron's period. The next time you chew your chayote squash (*seeme badnekayi*, or the 'foreign brinjal'), ponder how this may not have been possible but for Cameron. Sometime in 1890, Cameron received three chayote fruits from Sri Lanka. After trying them out in Lalbagh, he realised the vegetable could be useful. But convincing the farmers was no simple task. To persuade them to try out this new crop, Cameron personally toured the surrounding countryside on horseback, talking to farmers and distributing the seeds. A few months later, he revisited them to find out if they had tried the vegetable and how their crop was doing. It is said that the indefatigable Cameron even stood at the toll gate on Hosur Road to distribute these fruits to farmers.[45] Perhaps this is why people of neighbouring states still refer to this vegetable as the 'Bangalore brinjal'.

From January 1887, Cameron was also given charge of the Mysore Government Museum in Bengaluru. But the additional responsibility does not seem to have made a dent in his commitment to horticulture. Cameron kept up a steady stream of scientific publications, some based on botanical tours that he undertook to various parts of the erstwhile Mysore State. He gave advice to plantation owners on coffee cultivation. There were also always experiments underway at Lalbagh to learn the potential value of new plants. Students and volunteers were encouraged to come and watch these for free so that they may learn. Outstanding volunteers were also given certificates of merit. Cameron began a class for gardeners in Lalbagh to train 'native' gardeners, with six scholarships available for deserving candidates.[46] He even edited a 115-page book in Kannada on kitchen gardening, titled *Mysore Seemeyalli Kaithotagala Vyasaya*, which was all about the cultivation and care of exotic and native vegetables.[47]

Cameron's second mission was to enlarge the area under his care. He was helped in this by the change in administration in Mysore State that occurred during his tenure: the Rendition in 1881 whereby the administration of Mysore State reverted to the Durbar. Since Lalbagh was within the Bangalore City Municipality and not in the British-administered C&M Station, it came under the Maharaja's administration. The Maharaja supported Cameron's quest to enlarge the garden. When Cameron assumed office, Lalbagh had an area of about 45 acres. In 1889, 30 acres were added to the eastern side, followed by 13 more in 1891, including the rock atop which stands the Kempegowda Tower. Three years later, Cameron managed to add a whopping 94 acres to Lalbagh, just east of and below the Lalbagh Rock.[48]

Another pet project of Cameron's seems to have been the zoo. Lalbagh had a zoo since at least 1866, and Cameron appears to have collected animals for it with quite as much enthusiasm as he collected plants for the garden. Among other things, he procured a tiger cub (for an exorbitant Rs 50!), orangutans, bears, hoolock gibbons and rhinos, besides innumerable birds (including from Australia and Singapore) and small animals such as rabbits.[49]

He also continued the work begun by his predecessor of giving the garden a decidedly English character. The ornamental flight of stone steps leading up to the tank bund is one of his additions. In 1891, he had an elegant new main

The Glass House, initially used as a conservatory, was built thanks to John Cameron's efforts. *Courtesy of Harish Padmanabha.*

The ornamental steps up to the tank bund were Cameron's idea. © *Aravind C*

gate built. The grand wrought iron railings of the Cameron Gate, as the Main Gate was called for many years, were designed so that people outside could have a view of the garden inside. He was also the man behind the Glass House (see below). Cameron retired in 1908, returning to England.

Horticulturist, botanist, garden designer, town planner, architect

Gustav Hermann Krumbiegel was a German horticulturist, architect, town planner, Rotarian and more. Born in Lohmen near Dresden, he moved to London in 1881 after his initial training and early work in horticulture in Germany. He worked at Hyde Park so that he could improve his English before attending a course in the Royal Botanic Gardens in Kew and later joining the staff there.[50] His first appointment in India was with the princely state of Baroda, where he was the Superintendent of State Gardens there. His fame as horticulturist and garden designer spread to other states and soon, he was helping the royal families of Kapurthala and Cooch Behar with their gardens as well. When Cameron retired, the Maharaja of Mysore immediately sought out Krumbiegel to replace him.[51]

Krumbiegel served as the Superintendent of the Government Gardens (including both Lalbagh and Cubbon Park, besides other parks and gardens around the state) during 1908–1928. Like Cameron before him, he also served as the Director of the Government Museum in Bengaluru. During 1928–1932, he was appointed the first Director of Horticulture in Mysore State.

GH Krumbiegel. *Courtesy of Alyia Phelps-Gardiner Krumbiegel.*

In Lalbagh, Krumbiegel was responsible for introducing several species into the garden from Java, Indonesia, Singapore, Italy, England, Australia and elsewhere. He emphasised the economic benefits of horticulture by introducing plants that yielded fibre, resins, and so on. As outreach, he prepared and disseminated literature for the public on the plants that had economic potential. Trials of new and improved varieties of fruits and vegetables were also introduced. Improving upon Cameron's classes, Krumbiegel established a formal Horticultural Training School, then the only one of its kind in India. The library and herbarium that he improved in Lalbagh were useful resources for this school.[52] A major task he undertook was the replacement of the old system of water supply (which relied on tanks and cisterns) with pipes that fed all parts of the garden. He was also the first to provide labels for all the trees.[53] The vision that guided Krumbiegel was articulated thus by him: 'The work of the department does not begin and end in sweeping lawns and roads, and planting a few flower beds, but ... the development of its economic, scientific and educational work is its ultimate and legitimate aim.'[54]

Krumbiegel helped design and remodel several gardens in the city, including the Silver Jubilee Park, the Victoria Hospital Gardens, Bengaluru Palace gardens, the grounds of the Indian Institute of Science, and the garden in NIMHANS, to name just a few. He also designed parks elsewhere in India, including in the steel city of Jamshedpur, where he designed the town's popular Jubilee Park, the Raj Ghat in New Delhi, and the Brindavan Gardens at the Krishnaraja Sagar dam.[55] As the *Journal of the Kew Guild* put it, 'Whatever he touched, he adorned.'[56]

One of Krumbiegel's most visible and beautiful interventions in Bengaluru, for which we must forever be grateful, is the concept of serial blossoming: tree species planted along Bengaluru's streets were chosen so that they flowered sequentially. This means there is never a time when flowers do not add their colours to the streetscape: at any time of the year, there are always some species in bloom in the city.

After 1932 and till his death in 1956, Krumbiegel served as Consulting Architect for Mysore State. It was in this last capacity that he designed several buildings and gardens around Mysuru, Mandya and of course Bengaluru. Some of the projects he worked on included the layout of the extension at Bhadravati, layout of the Intermediate College at Shivamogga, some extensions in Mandya, Madhugiri and Kunigal, and improvements to parks and markets at Tumakuru and Shivamogga. In Bengaluru, you can see his hand in the layout of some areas near Jakkasandra and behind NIMHANS, and of sites in Wilson Garden.[57] Another example of Krumbiegel's architectural oeuvre in the city is the Asiatic

Building, also known as the Janatha Bazaar building, on Kempegowda Road. (In September 2018, INTACH Bengaluru Chapter filed a PIL against a government plan to demolish this building; in March 2019, the High Court granted an interim stay against demolition.)

Within Lalbagh, Krumbiegel designed the rather majestic office of the Director of Horticulture and also a small cottage-like building that was to serve as a museum. In addition, there was a lecture hall where he used to conduct classes on horticulture, subsequently named Krumbiegel Hall after him. Sadly, this building was lost to the city in October 2017 (*see below*). In his honour, the Karnataka government named one of the roads adjacent to Lalbagh after him.

Interestingly, during both the First and Second World Wars, being a German national, Krumbiegel was interned in a so-called parole settlement by the Government of India as an 'enemy foreigner'. Both times, at the request of the Maharaja's government, he was allowed to continue working much as usual while he was interned in Kodaikanal.[58]

The man who groomed Lalbagh

Hirehally Chennaiah Javaraya was born in 1889, the year the Glass House was inaugurated in Lalbagh. He trained in agriculture in the Agricultural College in Coimbatore that was then in its second year of existence, and eventually joined as Assistant Superintendent of Government Gardens in Bengaluru. The tumultuous effects of the First World War were felt in Lalbagh too. When the (Imperial) Government of India interned Krumbiegel in Kodaikanal for four years, it fell to Javaraya, 30 years old at the time, to manage Lalbagh in his absence, a duty he discharged admirably well.[59] When Krumbiegel returned to his post, Javaraya asked the government if he could go for further training at Kew Gardens. Permission was readily granted and Javaraya spent a year at Kew. In 1932, on Krumbiegel's retirement, Javaraya took over and became the first Indian to hold the post of Superintendent of Government Gardens. Later, he was also made the Director of Horticulture for Mysore State.

HC Javaraya. *Courtesy of Harish Padmanabha.*

Like his predecessors, Javaraya continued the popularisation of plants of economic value. To him goes the credit of popularising Rome Beauty, a variety

In 1935, Javaraya had the Glass House enlarged to make it the symmetrical structure of today. Seen here, along with Mirza Ismail and others, at the foundation-laying ceremony of the extension. *Courtesy of Harish Padmanabha.*

of apple first introduced here by Cameron. In fact, one of Javaraya's articles on apples is regularly cited in horticultural papers on apple cultivation even today.[60]

Javaraya's time saw several additions to Lalbagh, which we today tend to see as an inherent part of the garden. It was he who added the fourth wing of the Glass House to make it the symmetrical structure we know today. To him also we owe the distinctive lantern-shaped guardhouse at the West Gate to Javaraya (*more on both these below*). Another of his additions was the so-called Javaraya Cascade, an artificial waterfall that he got constructed, connecting the Lalbagh Tank to the small lotus pond nearby. It is said that the sound of the waterfall was a great attraction; even the ladies of the royal family used to come to Lalbagh to see this waterfall.[61]

Javaraya was also the one who pushed for setting up an experimental station for fruit research, which was finally established in Hessarghatta with financial aid from both the Government of Mysore and the Government of India. In 1940, he was given the title 'Rao Bahadur' by the Viceroy of India, the Marquis of Linlithgow, for his contributions to the nation.

After his retirement in 1944, Javaraya served as a horticultural advisor in the princely state of Bhopal.[62] At the time of his death in 1946, he was the Vice-President of the Horticultural Society of India.

Bengaluru's Lost Apples

Bengaluru had for long been known for its wonderful, crunchy apples. In 1897, many varieties that had been under cultivation were destroyed by the American blight disease. Apple cultivation was revived in 1914 with important new varieties and disease resistant stock around 1914.[63] By the 1920s and 1930s, the lands in and around Bengaluru were filled with fruit orchards, many of them apple orchards.

Writing in 1934, Javaraya said about apples: 'This is one of the important fruits grown commercially in Bangalore and there is great scope for its extension. Rome Beauty, Cox's Orange Poppin, Jonathan and Cleopatra have been found to do well here. There is hardly any crop which is as profitable as the Rome Beauty apple.'[64] He goes on to list no less than 54 varieties of apples that had been introduced by Lalbagh. A far cry from today when the only apples we see in the markets are imported varieties.

A continuing legacy

MH Mari Gowda, who did his MSc in botany from Lucknow, joined Lalbagh in 1942 as an Assistant Superintendent under HC Javaraya. In 1947, he was sent to Kew Gardens for additional training in horticulture. Post his training at Kew, Mari Gowda hopped across the pond and joined Harvard University where he received a doctoral degree in botany in 1951, and also published several papers in scientific journals.[65] Mari Gowda returned to India that same year and became Deputy Superintendent in August 1951, and six months later, Superintendent.[66] In 1963, he also became Director of Horticulture.[67]

A bust of MH Mari Gowda in Lalbagh. © *Aravind C.*

The Flora of Lalbagh

One of the many interesting things about Lalbagh is that you can still see traces of its past history and management in its current layout of trees and plants.[68]

Remnants of its earliest management history are seen in the mango trees popularly attributed to Tipu Sultan. A sapling marks the spot where one of the mango trees supposedly planted by Tipu stood; the tree itself fell a few years ago, as mentioned earlier. It is almost certain that the other mango trees that you see along the same road also date from that period, meaning they are almost 250 years old! Little of Tipu's hand is otherwise seen in the garden.

Of Waugh's time in the garden we can discern nothing. But it was during New's times that planting occurred based on the geographical regions of the plants' origins. Thus we have a section between the statue and the bandstand where several species from Australia are planted together. This is also when the garden began to take on the characteristics of a formal English garden: terraces, wide, circular carriageways, urns, parapets and so on.

In 1859, just a year after New took over as Superintendent of the garden, in England, a clergyman with a fondness for natural history and science published a book titled *On the Origin of Species*. Charles Darwin's concept of evolution is the foundation of all plant science today and it did not take too long for its effects to be felt even here. The original stated purpose of the Lalbagh gardens was to acclimatise plants that could be of economic benefit to the Empire. Though this broad mandate remained, alongside there was equal importance given to science and the scientific classification of plants. Perhaps this is why entire sections of the garden were given over to particular botanical families (as opposed to a region): the magnolia garden and the coniferous garden, for example. Can you discern other signs of the past in the present?

Trees—standing tall

— Karthikeyan Srinivasan

Watching a Mahogany seed detach itself from the woody seed case and come down twirling in the gentle breeze can delight the young and old alike![69] Many of us may have witnessed this phenomenon umpteen number of times. Some trees use means other than wind, like birds and animals to move their seeds farther away, ensuring better survival possibilities. Just put yourself in the shoes of a tree (or should we say get into the roots of a tree?!). It will then be easier to appreciate the capabilities and strategies required to transport seeds away from the parent tree. Apart from movement, trees exhibit a variety of other behaviours as well—all this while being rooted to one place!

We must remember that trees have been on Earth for much longer than humans. Consequently, they have evolved strategies over several millennia and in response to a variety of situations and stimuli that they have experienced from time to time over that period. They have also evolved closely with a multitude of organisms that have been part of their environment as they were evolving. We just have to think differently to gain a deeper understanding of trees and the ecosystem they are a part of.

A large component of the Lalbagh Botanical Garden is trees—trees that are both native and exotic. Here are some that draw the attention of even the casual disinterested visitor by the sheer show they put on!

The Gulmohur is native to Madagascar. Owing to its stunning show of scarlet during the summer months it is grown for ornamental purposes across India. This species is often planted on roadsides because of its flat, spreading canopy and feathery leaves that look beautiful, particularly when young. The tree has conspicuous buttresses that at times spread extensively. Children use parts of the bud to 'grow' long, red-coloured nails instantaneously! Small Green Barbets often find the bare branches of this tree ideal for nesting.

Similarly, the Copper Pods, African Tulip trees and the like are valuable real estate for barbets and often used by them to make their nests. These fruit-eating birds are capable of excavating a neat hole to nest in. This then becomes the subject of quarrels with other birds such as mynas vying to occupy the nest; at times mynas even go to the extent of evicting the nest builders without waiting for them to finish raising their brood. Parakeets, Magpie Robins, Cinereous Tits are all birds that need holes in branches for nesting. In Lalbagh, these birds are almost entirely dependent on the barbets to excavate holes in branches.

Dry branches of trees are often lopped for the fear of them falling on people or damaging property. Little do people realise that even these dry branches have a very important role to play. Those that are spared or go unnoticed by humans are always in great demand amongst other denizens.

Apart from providing homes to many feathered bipeds, the Copper Pods and the African Tulip trees also add colour to Lalbagh. The Copper Pod starts flowering around the time the Gulmohur does but continues to be in bloom

Gulmohur (*Delonix regia*) flowers. © *Karthikeyan S.*

A Copper Pod (*Peltophorum pterocarpum*) in bloom. © *Karthikeyan S.*

The Queen's flower, or Pride of India (*Lagerstoemia flos-reginae*). © *Karthikeyan S.*

for much longer. Their yellow blossoms placed amidst green leaves is a welcome relief to weary eyes. The yellow carpet under the tree is a beautiful sight as well. The African Tulip tree comes into flower when the Copper Pods are tired of flowering. The bright orange tulip-shaped flowers are quite enchanting. Mynas, in particular, are attracted to the nectar of this tree, as are the bees.

Lalbagh also has one of my all-time favourites, which calls the river banks in the Western Ghats its home: the Queen's Flower. It is popularly known by the name 'Pride of India', and rightly so. The tree seems to wear a floral crown when in bloom. The foot-long inflorescence of pink flowers pointing outward are a spectacle to behold! The tree can be easily identified even after the flowering season by the smooth bark (it peels as in a Guava tree) and the woody seed capsules which remain on the tree for a long time—sometimes even up to the next flowering season.

A red carpet welcome is what people wish for in life. However, at Lalbagh, the Jacaranda trees can treat you to a picturesque mauve-coloured one. The experience can be one of bliss! The Jacaranda is a very beautiful tree, especially when in flower. Sunbirds come by to steal the nectar from the flowers. The tree has a canopy of fine, feathery leaves, which render it of ornamental value. Its leaves are lost during winter and bunches of flowers grow on the leafless tree. The seeds are enclosed in a round, woody capsule that hangs from the tree for a long time before dropping off.

A large umbrella-like canopy carrying out its daily exercise of opening its leaves in the morning and closing them in the evening can be fascinating. I am referring of course to the Rain Tree. The flowers are white and pink, resembling an open brush, which contrasts against the green crown. An ideal species for planting along broad roads, it also provides for roosting and nesting of many birds.

Trees are not just about a visual experience. Stand under a Mahogany and your olfactory organs will go into overdrive, especially on a summer morning or evening! The flowers themselves are tiny and can easily go unnoticed. You might recollect that this article started with a reference to the winged seeds of this tree. Each seed is long, brown and flat. The arrangement of these seeds is in itself a lesson in design and efficient packaging!

Plants and trees have accompanied man since he started travelling. The Cannonball Tree is no exception. Though a native of tropical South America, interestingly, it is considered sacred in India (the structure of the flower is likened to snake hoods sheltering a Shiva linga). The big, impressive flowers have a strong albeit pleasant smell. The tree produces brown, spherical woody fruits almost the size of a human head!

Butterflies, when it comes to laying eggs, are very host specific. The female locates the right plant by merely touching the leaf to ensure that the larvae emerging from her eggs will be well provided for. Butterflies like Emigrants and Grassyellows seek the Indian Laburnum besides other related species to lay eggs on. The tree has somewhat sparse foliage. This moderately sized tree is truly spectacular when in bloom. People seek this tree out for the beautiful inflorescence of golden yellow flowers borne on green stalks and resembling a chandelier. All this makes it an excellent choice for ornamental purposes.

For seed dispersal, trees use several strategies. Depending on the type of fruit, using animals could be an option. The very familiar Mango tree, in more

The Cannonball Tree (*Couroupita guianensis*).
© *Karthikeyan S.*

recent times, has perhaps used humans to ensure that it is cultivated on vast tracts of land! The larva of the Baron butterfly, which is known for its excellent camouflage, seeks its leaves to feed on.

Banyan and Peepal are perhaps the more familiar species among figs though Lalbagh has several others as well. Figs are unique in more ways than one. Before some recent research, their flowering and pollination had been but an enigma. An attempt at understanding their natural history can be very educative in itself. For good reason, they are called 'keystone species'. During their fruiting season and otherwise, they support a plethora of organisms. Each tree can be a complete ecosystem in itself. Besides, figs have also greatly influenced traditions and cultures.

Trees and other life forms

Birds are among the better-known group of organisms supported by trees in the city. They use trees for roosting, foraging and nesting, besides other things. They also disperse using the cover of these trees.

Macaques and squirrels, among mammals, are the better-known inhabitants of trees in an urban setting. They find food on the trees and they and spend considerable time on them. In Lalbagh, many birds such as cormorants and pelicans along with Brahminy Kites and Common Kites roost on trees. Tree branches also serve as vantage points for a variety of birds to hunt from. Some birds also play an important role in dispersing the seeds of certain trees.

Mammals that are very important to the ecosystem and often ignored are bats. Some of the large trees in the city are used by the Indian Flying Fox as communal roosting sites. They fly out at dusk in search of fruiting trees. After feeding, they are also responsible for dispersing seeds along their flight path. Similarly, Short-nosed Fruit Bats can be seen roosting in ones and twos amid the foliage of trees and, like the Indian Flying Fox, also help in dispersal of seeds whereby they plant their own little garden! Many insectivorous bats like the Pipistrelles roost in crevices of trees, particularly the older ones—for example, old fig trees that create ample opportunities to hide.

A Short-nosed Fruit Bat. © *Karthikeyan S.*

Trees provide a shoulder to lean on for climbers that reach the canopy in search of sunlight. For their part, these climbers support a variety of other organisms. Trees are also home for a whole variety of other organisms ranging from geckos, praying mantids, spiders, bugs and other plants as well.

Many creatures camouflage themselves beautifully on the trunks of trees. A close examination of a tree trunk can reveal a lot to a discerning eye. The denizens of a tree trunk could range from that Bark Gecko peeping out of a crevice to a Two-tailed Spider lying flat against the bark waiting for an unsuspecting insect to come within reach of its long legs. Bugs and bark mantids also happily share the space.

Can you spot the Two-tailed Spider camouflaged against the bark? © *Karthikeyan S.*

Many little creatures call the leafy canopy their home. An excellent example is the larva of the Common Jay butterfly whose caterpillar blends in very well with the leaves of the Mast Tree. Any mature old tree could possibly be home to four to five different species of ants even in Lalbagh. This includes the very obvious Weaver Ant that builds large leaf nests and is typically seen on Mango and Jamun trees, though is not exclusive to them.

Not just animals; there are also many plants that eke out a living in the canopy. This is best represented by the mistletoe that grows on the branches of various trees. How it gets to the branches of the trees is a story very interesting in itself. A tiny bird called the flowerpecker disperses the seeds of the mistletoe as it tries to dislodge its sticky seed. The mistletoe is a partial parasite and uses the raw material from the host tree for its own survival. In turn, the mistletoe plays host to the very beautiful Common Jezebel butterfly which requires this plant to lay eggs on. So, by carefully choosing trees and other plants, we encourage and support a whole community of butterflies that liven up our environment and our lives. Lalbagh, by virtue of housing so many species of plants, harbours a good diversity of butterflies.

Trees as ecosystems

While generically trees have various important functions in the environment, each tree has a unique place in our ecosystem. Trees, as we have seen, are crucial habitats for several forms of life. The older trees tend to support a greater diversity of wildlife. The composition of organisms depends on the assemblage of plants in any given place. Large parks and gardens connected by tree-lined avenues help in creating a mosaic of habitats for a variety of species to thrive. Several species use this vegetation cover to disperse to newer areas conducive for their survival while others use the vegetation in a variety of ways, such as shelter or food, at various stages of growth.

A majority of our society today perceives trees only as things that provide shade and wood. However, trees have this unique ability to draw and support an abundance of life. They create a microclimate wherever they stand. Many species have even gained cultural and religious importance through history. Once we start looking at trees as living entities we might be able to shift away from the general mindset and attribute to them abilities that are typically regarded as the domain of the animal world. Let us enjoy and appreciate trees for what they bring to our environment, be it in a botanical garden like Lalbagh or, for that matter, wherever they are!

Buildings and Other Structures in Lalbagh

Apart from the botanical wealth of the garden, Lalbagh has over the years accumulated a collection of very interesting buildings and other structures that are well worth more than a look.

In its early days, the garden boasted a building aptly named Darwinia which was popular as a dancing saloon in the 1800s,[70] and was also used as a venue for flower shows.[71] In December 1915, it was converted to a restaurant, or rather into two separate restaurants, one serving Indian food and the other European.[72] Old-timers recall with great fondness the dosas that used to be served here. This building was demolished in the 1960s and was replaced by a Mughal garden.[73] Most of the other buildings added to the garden over the years still stand.

A Walk through Lalbagh

In which you see some of the handsome human-made structures in the greens

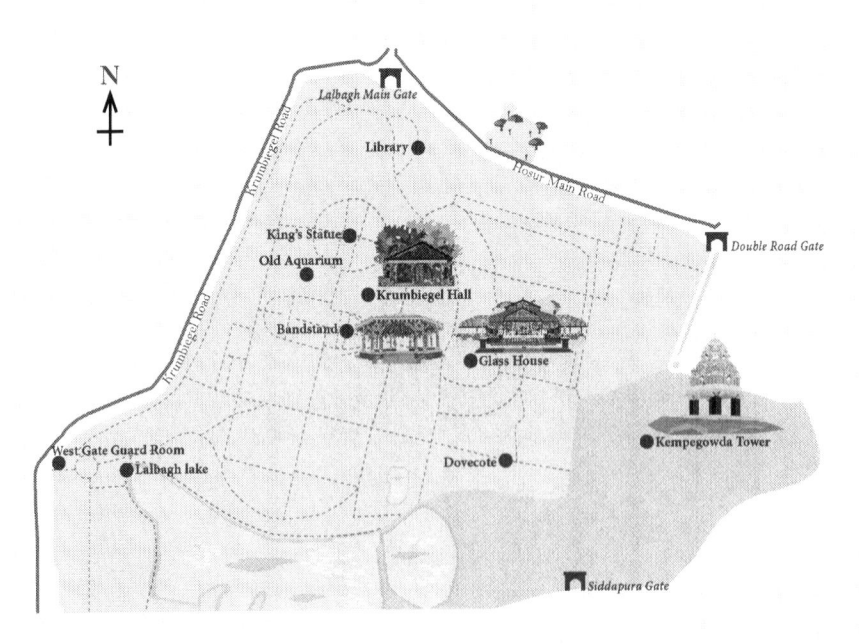

A walk through Lalbagh. © *INTACH Bengaluru Chapter*

The main attractions of Lalbagh are its trees, its gardens areas and the many trails that wind through them. For this reason, we have mostly given general directions from one stop to another. We encourage you to explore the garden languorously!

1. The West Gate Guardroom

We recommend you begin your ramble at the West Gate. Before you step in, take a look at the lantern-shaped guardroom that forms a part of this entrance into the gardens. There is a heart-warming story behind this little granite structure that says much about the concern for aesthetics and heritage some administrators of that time had, unlike today.

This guardroom stood at the entrance to 'Poorna Prasad', a house built by Dewan PN Krishnamurti, grandson of Dewan Purnaiah of Tipu's times who later also worked with the British. In the 1940s, when a part of Krishnamurti's bungalow was acquired by the government, there was a move to raze the compound wall and this guardroom. It so happened that Dewan Mirza Ismail and HC Javaraya visited the site to see the progress of this work. When he saw the guardroom, it struck Javaraya that the structure could be saved. He requested the Dewan to be allowed to carry out the dismantling work himself. The stones were all numbered, dismantled and reassembled in the centre of the West Gate. It took two months and about Rs 5250. When it was all done, Javaraya invited Sir Mirza to see the end result; the Dewan was very pleased with Javaraya's idea, work and his commitment to saving the structure.[74]

The West Gate itself was made in 1907–08 thanks to the urging of VP Madhava Rao, who suggested that an entrance here would be useful for the newly established suburb of Basavanagudi.[75]

The West Gate Guardroom. © *Meera Iyer*

II. The Lake and Its Bund

A short walk brings you to Lalbagh lake, or tank (*kere*) to be more precise, which probably predates the garden itself. As we mentioned earlier, the original garden was probably not adjacent to the tank, as is popularly believed. However, from at least the time of the Agricultural and Horticultural Society's management of the garden, the lake has been an important part of the garden.

The brick-lined channels that you see leading out from the tank were added by William New in the late 1850s, as was the walkway.[76] The eucalyptus trees growing near the bund were brought from Australia and are also from that time.

Like the other *keres* in Bengaluru, Lalbagh's lake is an excellent place in which to see birds and is a popular spot for birdwatching. It is also a particular favourite of morning walkers, photographers who love to capture the mist hanging over the lake in the early mornings, and lovers of nature.

III. Dovecote

Walking along the bund till the very end and then heading roughly east will bring you to the little round building that was built in 1893 during the time of Cameron. Its purpose was to house pigeons.[77] It is said to have accommodated about a hundred pairs of pigeons. However, it stopped being used for this purpose from the first decade of the 1900s.

The Dovecote, built in 1893. © *Aravind C*

IV. Kempegowda Tower

This is one of the four so-called Kempegowda towers which, as we have seen, were probably built as lookout towers. This particular tower has undergone some interesting transformations. Paintings of the garden made by British army officers (see Colebrooke's) in the 18th century show a two-storeyed structure topped with a dome. Postcards from the early 1900s show the same structure, often labelled Tippoo's observatory! Sometime in the early 1950s, the tower was modified to its present form.[78]

V. Glass House

A few hundred metres northwest of the dovecote, you will come upon the Glass House, often called the Jewel of Lalbagh.

On 30 November 1889, the who's who of Mysore State (along with about 5000 others) gathered at Lalbagh Botanical Garden. The occasion was a reception party hosted by His Highness Chamaraja Wodeyar for Prince Albert Victor, heir to the Prince of Wales, then on tour in India. During this function, the dapper young prince laid the foundation stone for a building that was initially called the Horticultural Exhibition Building (or simply the Exhibition Building), then the Albert Victor Conservatory, and is now known as the Glass House.

The Foundation Stone of the Glass House, laid by Prince Albert Victor. © *Aravind C*

At the gala that afternoon, the Prince was handed a silver trowel inscribed with the words 'Presented by His Highness the Maharajah of Mysore to Prince Albert Victor Christian Edward, KG, KP, for the purpose of laying the foundation-stone of the Exhibition building at the Lal Baugh, Bangalore, 30th November, 1889'.[79]

It was Cameron who mooted the idea of a building for horticultural shows and as a conservatory. The building was designed and executed by MacFarlane and Company, Glasgow,[80] at a cost of Rs 75,000.[81] Built of glass and cast iron, the building is modelled after the famed Crystal Palace built in 1851 in London. The Crystal Palace was designed by a gardener named Joseph Paxton, who was inspired by the water lily *Victoria regia*: 'Nature has provided the leaf with longitudinal and transverse girders and supports that I, borrowing from it, have adapted in this building.' Paxton's revolutionary design did not need any bricks or stone. Covering 19 acres, the building was built almost entirely with glass and iron. The Crystal Palace inspired other similar structures elsewhere, including Madrid's Palacio de Cristal and the Palm House in the horticultural gardens in Gothenburg, Sweden.[82] The original Crystal Palace was moved to Sydenham in 1852; it was destroyed in a fire in 1936.

But our Glass House still happily stands and was, in fact, expanded. In 1934, HC Javaraya proposed adding a fourth wing to it. Dewan Mirza Ismail and the Maharaja agreed to the proposal. The cast iron for this fourth, eastern wing was procured from Bhadravathy Iron and Steel Company.[83]

The building also used to have a trellis similar in pattern to the porch of the Mari Gowda Library. This was removed sometime after the 1960s.

The Glass House, the Jewel of Lalbagh. © *PeeVee*

This 'Jewel of Lalbagh' has been the cynosure of all visits to the garden by dignitaries and officials. Apart from the two flower shows held every year, it has also been the venue for several tea parties and banquets in honour of important visitors, and has hosted several historic events including a public meeting with Mahatma Gandhi on his visit here in 1927.[84] In 1956, Prime Minister Jawaharlal Nehru famously addressed an All India Congress Committee session held in the Glass House. (Incidentally, nine years later, Lal Bahadur Shastri did the same.[85]) Nehru then also planted a sapling of *Tecoma argentea* in front of the Glass House which is now thriving. Later that year, Dag Hammerskjoeld, then the Secretary General of the United Nations, also planted a *Tecoma argentea*. In February 1961, Queen Elizabeth visited and planted a sampling of *Araucaria*

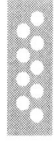

cookii, or Cook's pine. A few years later, Khan Abdul Ghaffar Khan, better known as Frontier Gandhi, also planted an *Araucaria cookii*.[86]

At present, you can usually admire the Glass House only from outside. You have to wait for the two flower shows held in Lalbagh to enter this elegant, gossamer-like structure that, like the water plant that inspired its parent, seems to float in the air.

VI. Bandstand

An ornamental fountain punctuates the grand path that leads from the Glass House to the bandstand, which is Bengaluru's first. It was established sometime prior to 1870, possibly in 1863 according to a retired horticulture official.[87] Like the bandstand in Cubbon Park, this too played host to military bands. James Furneaux, subeditor at the then British-owned *Times of India* newspaper, wrote how 'on certain occasions when the moon is at the full, the many military bands of Bangalore perform to the enjoyment of thousands of the public. There are few spots in Bangalore so charming in all seasons as the Lal Bagh.'[88]

Before the Glass House was built, flower shows were conducted in this bandstand. It was extensively repaired some ten years ago, at which time much of the older material was replaced.

The bandstand in the early 1900s. *Courtesy of Harish Padmanabha.*

VII. Old Aquarium

About 150 metres northwest of the bandstand is a circular building that once contained an aquarium and, earlier, an aviary. Some reports suggest that the building also housed animals at some point.

The old Aquarium has a very unusual, circular floor plan.
© *INTACH Bengaluru Chapter*

There has been a zoo in Lalbagh with animals and birds since possibly the late 1860s (as per a memo written by Cameron in 1900, though New's report of 1860–61 mentions no animals).[89] Various annual reports over the years have recorded that the zoo in Lalbagh had tigers, Indian and African lions, panthers, hyenas, monkeys, wild boar, lynx, bears, guinea pigs, bears and orangutans, to name just a few. The menagerie was initially located in some sheds on the western side of the garden. Later, cages were built near the southeastern end of the tank bund. And as mentioned above, the old Aquarium may have also housed animals. There was also a deer paddock with deer and nilgai. The zoo was finally closed in the 1930s and the animals moved to Mysore Zoo.

Among the birds in the aviary as listed by Cameron are cockatoos, peafowl, pigeons, Himalayan partridges, water birds and more. Cameron also mentions that a circular building was constructed before his time to house an aviary. This would suggest that the old Aquarium is about 150 years old. In 1910–12, the original structure was extensively rebuilt.

At some point, the aviary was abandoned and the building was converted to an aquarium. However, that too was closed several years ago, and the building has not been used or maintained since. Rainwater channels on the roof lie blocked with leaves and other debris, as a result of which parts of the roof have been severely damaged. Portions of the building are on the verge of collapse.

It would be a pity if this building too were to be demolished, because it is not only a bit of history, but also unusual architecturally. The structure has a circular plan. A large central open space is enclosed by a circular wall with one set of colonnades facing inside, towards the open space, and another opening outwards. The circle is divided into four quadrants with intermediate openings or rooms. A wide entrance between two quadrants leads into the large central space. The structure has a flat roof and an ornamental parapet wall.

VIII. King's Statue

A stone's throw from the old Aquarium is the King's Statue, the central ornament of Lalbagh's statue circle. This equestrian statue of Chamaraja Wodeyar, who reigned from 1881 to 1894, was originally in Curzon Park in Mysuru; it was moved here in 1908, during Krumbiegel's time, when that park got another statue of the Maharaja.

This bronze statue was sculpted in about 1899 by Edward Onslow Ford, a celebrated English sculptor whose works can still be seen all over the UK.[90] This particular statue cost Rs 70,000 and was shipped to India from the artist's studio in England.[91] Take a closer look at the highly decorative details on the caparisoned horse and on the King's clothing: Ford was known for both his ornamentation and the realism in his subjects.[92]

The statue stands on a marble pedestal about 3 metres high. On the eastern and western faces of the pedestal are two female figures. On one side is Justice, helmeted, blindfolded and bearing scales. On the other is a lady symbolising Knowledge who appears to be considering a long scroll draped over her knees. Photographs of the statue when it was still in Curzon Park show that the four small pedestals at each corner once bore winged angels balancing themselves on one foot on little orbs. These angels are long gone, thought to have been stolen. Today, the pedestals sometimes bear flowerpots but are mostly left bare.

This statue of Chamaraja Wodeyar was made by Edward Ford. © *PecVee*

Requiem for Krumbiegel Hall

Not far from the statue of Chamaraja Wodeyar there stood a little red building. A simple, striking, symmetric structure, it had a front porch with a colonnade of slender Ionic columns supporting a pedimented wooden gable roof. Emblazoned on the pediment was a prominent, beautifully made *gandrabherunda*, the symbol of the Wodeyar dynasty of Mysore. The pillars, both inside and outside, were made of granite. Unusually, the ones on the porch were thickly plastered with lime mortar, with rope wound around it for additional strength. The prominent *gandabherunda* suggests that the building was likely built in the late 1880s, after the Rendition, when the Maharaja's government was in charge of Lalbagh.[93]

Initially called simply the Lecture Hall, it was renamed Krumbiegel Hall sometime later. Lectures on horticulture were given here as part of the diploma in horticulture that was offered in the early 1900s. When the diploma course was scrapped, lectures on horticulture continued here on Sundays.[94] When new buildings and classrooms were built elsewhere in Lalbagh, the hall gradually fell into disuse. In 2010, when we visited the building, Krumbiegel Hall was being used as a dumping ground for old files, papers, tickets and other kinds of unwanted paperwork.

The years of neglect told on the building. Plaster began to peel and fall, the building began to decay. In response, the Horticulture Department put up a sign saying the building was dangerous. In 2010, INTACH submitted a proposal to the Department to restore the building for less than Rs 20 lakhs. An MoU was signed to restore the Krumbiegel Hall, the old menagerie and the library. However, the Department then rescinded the MoU. In October 2017, a portion of the building finally fell. Even as INTACH members and other heritage activists were preparing to meet the Department to see how best the remaining portion of the building could be salvaged, in November 2017, the authorities brought in a JCB and demolished the remaining portions of the building. Krumbiegel Hall was no more. Today, not even a trace remains of the building that carried the name of one of the garden's most beloved superintendents who was also one of the city's illustrious residents.

IX. Library Building

This is one of the garden's oldest buildings. The building dates from 1858; in his early reports on the garden, Hugh Cleghorn mentions that 'an elegant cottage' was built for the Superintendent at a cost of Rs 2000.[95] Over the years, it has served as the residence of several illustrious superintendents of Lalbagh, including Cameron, Krumbiegel and Javaraya.

The library, one of the oldest buildings in Lalbagh. © *Aravind C*

The building has undergone several additions and alterations since it was first built. Yet it still remains a charming, colonial bungalow, with its typical trellis work in the front porch, arched doorways, semi-circular arched windows, Mangalore tile roofs (the old pot tiles were replaced in 1910[96]), and patterned floor tiles in some of its rooms.

A porch with a beautiful tiled and sloping roof leads to a verandah that runs on three sides of the central hall. The sloping roof of the porch continues over the hall and the verandah. The hall has large openings on the sides which open into the verandah. These areas have patterned heritage tiles. Rooms at the rear lead to a space that opens into another large hall.

In 1988, this building was converted into a horticultural library named after Dr Mari Gowda.[97] For anyone with a love of history or books, a visit to the library is a treat. There are about 7000 books in its collection, including many fascinating treatises and reports from the 1800s. It is also home to a treasure in the form of over a thousand superb botanical drawings. There are 700 water colours, 300 pencil drawings and 12 ink drawings of local flora.[78] Many of these illustrations were commissioned by Cameron who first appointed the artist K Cheluviah Raju to make these drawings. Most of the drawings are by Raju, who worked at Lalbagh from 1884 to 1923. Raju's illustrations are not just botanical drawings; they transcend into the realm of art. Other artists include Vishnudas Ramdas and Vasan; several artists who worked on these drawings remain unknown. These rare and precious drawings are currently not available for public viewing.

In 2010, INTACH had proposed to restore this building for approximately Rs 40 lakhs. The building was renovated by the State Department of Archaeology in early 2018 for Rs 95 lakhs.

Heading out of the Main Gate nearby will take you to one of Bengaluru's iconic eateries, Mavalli Tiffin Rooms, better known as MTR; a feast there is a good way to celebrate the completion of the walk!

Notes

1. For a comprehensive review of the green history of Bengaluru, see Nagendra 2016.
2. Kamath 2008.
3. Nagendra 2016.
4. Translated and quoted in Nagendra 2016, vii.
5. For example, see Schwartz 1826.
6. Personal communication, Dr SK Aruni, Indian Council for Historical Research, Bengaluru, August 2010.
7. Smeeth 1916.
8. https://www.gsi.gov.in/webcenter/portal/OCBIS/page17/pageGEOTOURISM/page1945?_afrLoop=1998455017854658&_adf.ctrl-state=19syv2rj9g_1#!%40%40%3F_afrLoop%3D1998455017854658%26_adf.ctrl-state%3D19syv2rj9g_5, accessed 23 June 2018.
9. Buchanan 1807, 46.
10. Mari Gowda 1967.
11. For example, Letter CCLXXII to Meer Kazim, in Kirkpatrick 1811, 300.
12. Mari Gowda 1967.
13. Heyne 1814, 412.
14. Cameron 1891.
15. Incidentally, apart from the usual suspects—Robert Home, Robert H Colebrooke, James Hunter, all British army officers who drew and painted scenes near the fort and the palace—we also have a painting of the garden by Claude Martin, a man of many parts. Martin came to India as a soldier in the French army but then switched to the British side. He eventually retired as a Major General after serving all over India, in various capacities. He left a part of his fortune to three schools that he started in Calcutta, Lucknow and Lyon in France. All the schools bear the name La Martiniere.

16. Prain 1905.
17. Buchanan 1807, 46.
18. Iyer, Nagendra and Rajani 2012.
19. Phillimore 1950, 113.
20. Heyne 1814, 411.
21. IOR/P/242/73, 21 January 1805, 684–688, British Library.
22. IOR/F/4/275, British Library.
23. IOR/F/4/275, British Library.
24. Heyne 1814, 412.
25. Anon 1828.
26. Anon 1836a.
27. Anon 1878.
28. F/4/751/20526, British Library.
29. Quoted in Mari Gowda 1967, 86.
30. Anon 1836a, 273.
31. Venkatasubba Sastri 1932, 205.
32. Anon 1836b, 523.
33. Kamath 1991.
34. Cleghorn, quoted in Anon 1856.
35. File GM 1 of 1856, Sl 1–2, KSA.
36. Cleghorn 1861.
37. Kamath 1991.
38. Annual Report of Government Gardens and Parks in Mysore for the official years 1905–1906 and 1906–07.
39. Murphy 1953, 176–177.
40. In the Report on the Working of the Government Gardens and Parks in Mysore, 1908–1909, Gustav Krumbiegel writes, 'Of visitors in general, it must be said that 90 per cent form a most desirable and appreciative clientele. There are, on the other hand, the remaining 10 per cent who seem to be entirely untouched by the refining influences of nature's beauty and whose sole object of a visit seems to be annoying fellow-visitors, wanton destruction, and even deliberate theft. One cannot but pity these unfortunates and it is to be hoped that sympathetic efforts of the higher society and a broad-minded educational policy of Government may help to speedily raise their morals.' Another sentiment that some can identify with today!
41. Cleghorn 1861.
42. Cameron 1880.
43. Cameron 1891.
44. Hittalmani 1991.
45. Hittalmani 1991.
46. GM File 33 of 91, KSA.
47. Hittalmani 1991.
48. Kamath 1991.
49. Report on the Government Botanical Gardens and Parks for the year 1891–92.
50. Eppert 2015; Anon 1937.
51. Bowe 2012.
52. Jayaram 2010.
53. Annual Report of Government Gardens and Parks in Mysore for the official year 1908–1909.

54. Eppert 2015, 592.
55. Bowe 2012.
56. Anon 1937, 674. This is also the title of the book on Krumbiegel by artist Suresh Jayaram. See note 52.
57. File Home/Political/E/1941/F 30–31, NAI.
58. File Home/Political/E/1941/F 30–31, NAI.
59. Anon 1996.
60. Javaraya 1943.
61. Anon 1996.
62. Bowe 2012.
63. Report on the Progress of Agriculture in Mysore, 1939, 167.
64. File Agriculture 1934 F 241/34A, NAI.
65. For example, Mari Gowda 1951.
66. Hanumaiah 1967.
67. Anon 1991.
68. Many thanks to Krishna MB for discussions on this subject.
69. As per the request of the author of this section, the common names of trees (as also of animal and bird species) have been capitalised in this section since that is the tradition followed in the community of naturalists in India.
70. Furneaux 1895, 419.
71. Anon 1875, 278.
72. Annual Report of the Government Botanical Gardens and Parks for the years 1915–1916.
73. Anon 1967, 139.
74. Narayana Swamy 1991.
75. Annual Report of Government Gardens and Parks in Mysore for the official year 1907–1908.
76. New 1861.
77. Narayana Swamy 1991, 31.
78. Narayana Swamy 1991, 30.
79. 'Prince Victor's tour in India', *The Times of India*, 4 December 1889.
80. Narayana Swamy 1991, 28.
81. Furneaux 1895, 419.
82. http://www.crystalpalacefoundation.org.uk/history/the-complete-guide-to-crystal-palaces, accessed 30 August 2018.
83. Anon 1996, 11.
84. Annual Report of the Government Botanical Gardens and Parks for the Years 1908/9–1931/32.
85. Mari Gowda 1967.
86. Hanumaiah 1991.
87. Iyer 2013.
88. Furneaux 1895, 419.
89. File GM 132 of 1900, Sl 1–16, KSA.
90. Mapping Sculpture (online database), 2011; for more on this sculptor, see Dixon 1898.
91. Report on the Administration of Mysore, 1900, ii.
92. Nevill 2016.

93. A popular belief is that the building was built in the 1860s, the proof cited being the date 1860 on the tiles on the building. This is a misconception: a tile from a prominent tile factory was often inscribed with the year that the factory was set up, not the year the tile itself was made.
94. Narayana Swamy 1991.
95. Cleghorn 1861.
96. Annual Report of the Government Botanical Gardens and Parks for the years 1910–1911.
97. Narayana Swamy 1991.
98. White 1999.

Epilogue

In 1974, CJ Padmanabha, son of the horticulturist HC Javaraya, wrote a note titled 'The Future of Bangalore'. Padmanabha had served in the government in various capacities including as Commissioner of the Bangalore City Corporation in the late 1960s and as Chairman of the City Improvement Trust Board (CITB) between 1971 and 1974. The locality of Padmanabhanagar in south Bengaluru is named after him. Here, we reproduce extracts from his previously unpublished note (shared with us by his son Harish Padmanabha) which provide a synopsis of its more recent history of growth, especially from an administrator's point of view, and also prescribe some solutions to the problems facing the city.

Padmanabha was one of the first advocates of ring towns around Bangalore to decongest the city; both Kengeri Satellite Town and Yelahanka New Town were developed to serve as satellite/ring towns. While some of the issues he talks about (such as people rearing cows and buffaloes in their compounds) are a thing of the past, many others—air pollution, waste disposal, and the loss of trees and tanks—have only been exacerbated since the 1970s. Some of his predictions, such as the shortage of water, have indeed come to pass in the almost half a century since Padmanabha wrote this note.

The Future of Bangalore

Bangalore was well known as 'The Garden City', with its salubrious climate, being situated on a small hillock of 3,002 ft height. It was popularly known as 'Poor Man's Ooty', 'Pensioner's Paradise', and as a health resort. It was considered a well-laid out, clean city. Well-planned extensions were being formed from time to time.

Bangalore was considered a Garden City not because there was a Cubbon Park or Lalbagh, or a few gardens of the Corporation here and there, but because every house had a garden of its own charm. Bangalore was called the Pensioner's Paradise because it had all the amenities, such as electricity, water supply, sewerage, plenty of fruits and vegetables, and well-supplies food grain markets at low cost.

Some thirty years ago, the population of Bangalore was one-and-half lakhs in the City, and one lakh in the then Civil & Military Station, the two being administered separately by two Municipalities. Between the two portions, a green belt ran from the Sanatorium [the SDS TRC and Rajiv Gandhi Institute of Chest Diseases], the Wilson Garden Burial Ground, the then

Sunkal Farm [now the BMTC bus depot in Shantinagar], and nurseries on either side of Lalbagh Road, the Monkey Thope of Shantinagar [an area in Shantinagar; Kengal Hanumanthaiah Road, or Double Road as it is popularly called, was known as Monkey Thope Road until 1953], Cubbon Park, Residency Race Course and on to Palace Orchards, dividing the two population areas of Bangalore City and the Civil & Military Station. In 1949, Bangalore Corporation was formed, merging the two Municipalities. The then Administrators, His Highness the Maharaja of Mysore, Late Shri Krishnaraja Wadeyar [sic] Bahadur, and the then Dewan of Mysore, later Sir Mirza Ismail, had taken a keen interest in the orderly development and cleanliness of Bangalore. Their one aim was to make Bangalore a beautiful, international city. However, with rapid industrialisation, starting with the Hindustan Aeronatuics Ltd, then the Hindustan Machine Tools Ltd, the Bharat Electronics Ltd Indian Telephone Industries and a number of ancillary industries, Bangalore, which was just a capital city, became an industrial and commercial city. The influx of population due to employment potentialities increased tremendously. ... Bangalore today is a cosmopolitan city, having grown up to 17 lakhs of permanent population as per the 1971 census, and about 3 lakhs of floating population, together coming to nearly 20 lakhs. The city which had a population of 2.5 lakhs and planned then for 5 lakhs expected in the next 25 years, suddenly finds itself outgrowing this plan. The result has been a shortage of housing, water supply and sewerage, and deterioration of roads, cleanliness, law and order, etc. The cost of living has tremendously gone up.

With the demand for housing, big and vast extents of agricultural lands are being acquired all round by the City Improvement Trust Board, and layouts are being formed on modern town planning principles and sites are being allotted to deserving persons. As a result of this, the cost of land has gone up. The green belts around the city, consisting of casuarina plantations, mango gardens (*thopes*), honge trees [Indian beech], are all sold out, due to the high price of firewood. Today, firewood has to come from nearly 50-60 miles, incurring heavy transport charges. Green belts are all destroyed. Air and water pollution are increasing. The City Improvement Trust Board (CITB) hitherto [was] planning for individual sites and houses. It is now better to plan for collective living in multistoreyed buildings, by having big plots in addition to having plots for individual housing in the proportion of 50:50 in the lands that have now been acquired and layouts that are being planned.

Bangalore was cool for three reasons: One, that it is at a height of 3,002 ft above sea level; secondly, it had a series of tanks like Miller Tank,

Sampangi Tank, Mavalli Tank, Koramangala Tank, over which the wind blew and cooled the atmosphere. The other series of tanks are Sankey Tank, Malleswaram Tank, Dharmambudhi Tank, Jakkarayanakere, Kempambudhi Tank, etc. Most of these tanks are breached, expect for Sankey Tank, Kempambudhi Tank and Ulsoor Tank. The third reason is that the increase in [the] number of houses, with [a] greater number of hearths, factories, generating heat, and the automobiles running about, has made the atmosphere warmer and polluted. The cement concrete houses, the metal surface of vehicles and cement and asphalted roads, also reflect heat and make the city sultry during the day-time.

The other tanks, like Marenahalli Tank, Yediyur Tank, Channamanakere, are still there, and are being polluted with sullage and sewage waters [of these, Marenahalli and Channamanakere no longer exist]. It is necessary now that these tanks should be preserved, by preventing sullage from getting into them, and maintaining them as fresh water tanks. There must be tanks in Bangalore for the growth of trees and plants and to keep the water table high, so that water would be well supplied in the wells. Otherwise, the wells will go dry. It is generally argued that tanks are responsible for the mosquito nuisance, but it is not so. When it is a fresh water tank, fish live in it and devour the mosquito larvae. It is only when citizens let sullage water into tanks and pollute them, that the fish die, mosquito larvae thrive and the mosquito nuisance is increased. Therefore, one should see that no sullage water is allowed from any house into storm water drains and into these fresh water tanks. Virtually, the storm water drains have to be dry in most parts of the year.

As stated above, due to the increase of population and acute shortage of houses, acquisition by the CITB, private layout owners and industrialists, land prices went up. Secondly, due to the increased taxation policy, particularly on vacant land, by the Corporation, wealth tax, estate duty, etc., people [with] big compounds started bifurcating their plots into small plots. As a result, houses are coming up too close to each other—sometimes with the window chajjas almost touching—without observing the correct set-backs for each plot, or each site. No doubt, the municipal bye-laws have prescribed the open spaces to be kept in the front, rear and sides of each building site, and that the built area ratio to open spaces should be 55-45% respectively. This is not being observed strictly. When there are no set-backs, naturally there are no gardens. One could observe the change-over, from what was a Garden City, gradually becoming concrete slums in some parts. It is necessary to change the building bye-laws to suit the present-day needs of multistoreyed buildings, owned flats and zoning regulations.

It is time that one should ponder over and decide to what extent Bangalore should grow and where it should be halted. Bangalore should not go beyond the metropolitan boundaries now drawn and the population should not be allowed to exceed 30 lakhs. It should be the endeavour of all to see that the population is checked and a limit be put on the establishment of industries and housing in Bangalore, if it should be really a Garden City, with all comforts and facilities to live in. There should be a green belt around the metropolitan boundary. People should be encouraged to grow fast-growing and useful trees, like casuarina and eucalyptus, in the green belt, and under no circumstances should the land be permitted to be converted from agricultural to non-agricultural purposes, either for having a dairy, poultry, industry or housing, etc., but kept on for agriculture. If this green belt is to be seriously implemented, the only course would be either that the Forest Corporation should develop forests, or the Horticultural Department or societies should develop fruit gardens, as it used to be once. This green belt should be worked out also from the point of commercial purpose, so that the green belt could be perpetually maintained as such by the Forest Department or Forest Corporation itself by afforestation, and later deforestation for realising the firewood value or timber value.

There is also a tendency for the people to have cows, buffaloes, poultry, piggery, horses, etc., in their compounds. It is very necessary that these should be shifted outside Bangalore into ring towns. ...

Bangalore will again face water supply difficulty. Today the city is being supplied with 30 mg [million gallons] from Hesarghatta and Thippagondanahalli Water Works. It is working out at 10 gallon per head. As this was not sufficient, the Cauvery Scheme is being implemented. The first stage is costing about Rs 35 crores and will be bringing in 30 mg. The second stage would supply 30 mg. This will also be at about Rs 35 crores, or even more. This would only increase the per capita consumption from 10 gallons to 30 gallons while the standard is 40 gallons per head per day. However, as the city grows, the supply may again come down to 20 to 15 gallons per head. The price of water could go up to Rs 3.50 or Rs 4 against the present Rs 1.30. This cannot be afforded by people. Therefore, water problem would also be more if Bangalore is allowed to grow indiscriminately.

However, to meet the requirements of the growing population, it would be worthwhile to develop ring towns in places like Yelahanka, Nelamangala, Gollahalli, Doddaballapur, Hoskote, Whitefield, Kengeri, Ramanagaram, Magadi, Anekal, etc. around Bangalore. In the first phase, preference should be given [to] developing these towns with industrial complexes only in places where facilities for movement, such as railways and road transport, are available at present. In the second phase, ring towns could be developed where only road transport facilities exist. Kengeri ring town is a success and there is a demand for houses. A separate municipality is formed for a ring town. The citizens of Kengeri could take more interest in developing Kengeri than being merged in the unwieldy Bangalore and getting lost. [Yelahanka New Town was also developed as a ring town/satellite town.]

Though a large number of residential sites are distributed by CITB and residential houses built, the allottees are violating the conditions and are leasing out for commercial and industrial purposes. This is resulting in a housing shortage and also violation of zoning prescribed by the planning authority. This conversion from residential to commercial should be prevented and use for residential purposes only strictly enforced; for instance, in Kengal Hanumanthiah Road, Jayanagar Main Road, Rajmahal, etc., residential houses are being leased as offices and for commercial purposes.

The Housing Board could go in a big way for constructing houses in the proposed ring towns and reducing their activities in Bangalore. Industrial Estates also should be built in these ring towns. Heavy industries could arrange to have small ancillary industries started in these ring towns. This, in the long run, would help each ring town to grow by itself with its own Municipality, water supply, sewerage, which would in turn be administered better, without becoming unwieldy. If timely action is not taken from now on, Bangalore may also become [an] uncontrollable city, and unmaintainable from the point of law and order, transport, water supply, sewerage, good roads, etc. when people and goods will have to move long distances at very heavy costs. Even removing the dirt, garbage and debris to outside the city would become difficult and costly. Hence, advance planning is necessary in the development of Bangalore and its ring towns. From now on, a cry for halting the growth of Bangalore should be made and ring towns developed, if Bangalore should be preserved as a 'Beautiful City'. The people of Bangalore should decide the type of city they want and work together to build a beautiful city of their choice and live happily.

CJ Padmanabha
5 March 1974

Glossary

Ashtadikpalas	guardians of the eight directions
Choultry	wedding hall
Damru	small drum that Shiva holds in one of his hands
Gandabherunda	double-headed eagle, the symbol of the Wodeyar dynasty
Garadi Mane	traditional gym
Garbagriha	sanctum sanctorum
Gavaksha	horseshoe-shaped arch used as a decorative motif
Gomala	pastureland
Grama Devathe	village deity
Gruhapravesham	house-warming ceremony
Hobli	cluster of villages
Holige	flat bread with a sweet stuffing
Jagali	ledges lining the front walls of a house or the entrance itself
Jodidar	zamindar
Kalyani	small stepped tank
Katte	open space
Kere	lake or tank
Killedar	commandant of a fort
Kodi	overflow weir
Kulkuls	deep-fried snack made with flour, sugar and coconut milk
Kunte	pond or small water body
Makara	sea creature
Mantapa	pillared hall
Manya	sacred offering
Maths/Matha/Matt	religious institutions
Mukhamantapa	central hall of a temple
Murti	idol
Musafirkhana	travellers' rest house
Nagakal	snake stones
Nathasampradaya	Natha cult
Naubat Khana	performance space for musicians in Mughal courts
Nava Nathas	the nine Shaiva saints
Neerganti	village waterman
Pete	town or area
Pradakshinapatha	circumambulation path
Rajakaluve	water channel
Sangha	a group of people of a specific community or profession
Saptarishis	the seven great sages revered in Hinduism
Sheer Kurma	dessert made with milk, vermicelli and dry fruits
Silsila	here, order of Sufi saints
Swayambhu	self-manifested
Thoobu	sluice gate
Trishul	trident that Shiva holds in one of his hands
Utsava	festival
Yali	a mythical horse–beast amalgamation

Bibliography

Archival Sources

IOR - India Office Records, British Library
KSA - Karnataka State Archives
NAI - National Archives of India
WP - Wellington Papers

Other Sources

Aitchison. CU. 1909. *A Collection of Treaties, Engagements, and Sanads Relating to India and Neighbouring Countries*, Vol 9. Calcutta: Superintendent Government Printing.

Amritaraj, S. 1912. 'Relief of Congestion in the C and M Station, Bangalore and Results'. In *Proceedings of the Second All India Sanitary Conference, Madras*, 1–15. Simla: Government Central Branch Press.

Annaswamy, TV. 2003. *Bengaluru to Bangalore: Urban History of Bangalore from the Pre-Historic Period to the End of the 18th Century*. Bangalore: Vengadam Press.

Annesley, James and Thomas Joseph Pettigrew. 1855. *Researches into the Causes, Nature and Treatment of the More Prevalent Diseases of India and of Warm Climates Generally*. London: Longman, Brown, Green and Longman.

Annual Record of Queen's Victoria's Own Madras Sappers and Miners for 1923–24. Bangalore: Sappers Press.

Annual Report for the Year ending 30th June 1909, Archaeological Survey of Mysore. Bangalore: Government Press.

Annual Report of Government Gardens and Parks in Mysore, various years. Bangalore: Government Press.

Annual Report of the Government Botanical Gardens and Parks, various years. Bangalore: Government Press.

Anon. 1791. 'Extract of a letter from the President and Council at Fort St George, in their Political Department, to the court of Directors, dated April 14, 1791'. *The European Magazine and London Review* 20: 233–236.

Anon. 1828. 'On the Cultivation of Coffee in Bangalore'. *Oriental Herald* 18: 360–362.

Anon. 1836a. 'Agricultural and Horticultural Society of India'. *The Calcutta Monthly Journal* (July): 270–273.

Anon. 1836b. 'Abstract of letters which have been received by the Secretary since the last General Meeting on the 7th November 1835'. *The Calcutta Monthly Journal* (November): 522–524.

Anon. 1852. 'Opening of a New Chapel at Bangalore'. *The Missionary Magazine and Chronicle* 188 (January): 62–63.

Anon. 1854. 'Bangalore and the Monkey Tope'. *The Home Friend* 4 (Society for Promoting Christian Knowledge): 181–184.

Anon. 1856. 'Proposed Establishment (or Restoration) of an Agricultural and Horticultural Garden at Bangalore in the Madras Presidency'. In *Hooker's Journal of Botany and Kew Garden Miscellany* 9: 24–27.

Anon. 1865. 'Native Girls School and Preaching-room, Alasoor, Bangalore'. *The Wesleyan Juvenile Offering* 22: 185–187.

Anon. 1875. Notice in *The Gardener's Chronicle* (27 February 1875): 278.

Anon. 1878. 'Sir Andrew Scott Waugh'. *The Geographical Magazine* 5 (March): 68–69.

Anon. 1880. 'Cholera in India'. *The British Medical Journal* 1 (15 May): 750–751.

Anon. 1891. Notice in *Electrical Engineer* 7(1): 530.

Anon. 1905. 'New Government Offices, Civil and Military Station, Bangalore'. *Indian Engineering* 36: 144.

Anon. 1909. *The Cyclopedia of India*, Vol 3. Calcutta: Cyclopedia Publishing.

Anon. 1913a. 'India'. *British Medical Journal* 1(2725): 633–634.

Anon. 1913b. 'The Minto Ophthalmic Hospital'. *Indian Review* 14(1): 169.

Anon. 1913c. *Tour of His Excellency the Viceroy to Mysore State November 1913*. Bangalore: Government Press.

Anon. 1917. 'Dedication and Opening of the Rice Memorial Church, Bangalore'. *The Harvest Field* 37(2) (February): 75–77.

Anon. 1920. *Campbell's Bangalore and Mysore Directory*. Madras: Campbell and Sons.

Anon. 1923. *Merchant Taylors' School Register, 1851–1920*. London: Merchant Taylors' Company.

Anon. 1927. *Indian Statesmen: Dewans and Prime Ministers of Native States*. Madras: GA Natesan and Co.

Anon. 1928. *Disturbances in Bangalore City July 1928: Evidence given before the committee of enquiry appointed by the Government of His Highness, The Maharaja of Mysore*. Bangalore: Government Press.

Anon. 1931. *City of Bangalore: Municipal Handbook*. Bangalore: City Municipal Council.

Anon. 1937. 'Kew Garden Personalities: GH Krumbiegel'. *Journal of the Kew Guild* 1(1): 673-677.

Anon. 1945. *Agricultural Marketing in India: Report on the Marketing of Bananas in India*. New Delhi: Government of India.

Anon. 1963. 'Venue of the Eighteenth General Conference of the CMAI'. *Journal of the Christian Medical Association of India* 37: 576–608.

Anon. 1967. *Horticulture in Mysore State*. Bangalore: Department of Horticulture.

Anon. 1977. *The Story of a Church* (pamphlet). Bangalore: Perpetual Help Press.

Anon. 1991. *Glass House: The Jewel of Lalbagh*. Bangalore: Mysore Horticultural Society.

Anon. 1996. *Rao Bahadur HC Javaraya: A Centennial Memoir*. Bangalore: Mysore Horticultural Society.

Anon. 2008. *Marked to Witness*. Bangalore: St Mark's Cathedral.

Anon. 2014. *Dhanyosmi BK Mariappa Dharmasamsthe Smarana Sancheke (Dhanyosmi BK Mariappa Charities Commemoration Volume)*. Bangalore.

Archer, Mildred. 1980. *Early Views of India: The Picturesque Journeys of Thomas and William Daniell, 1786–1794*. London: Thames and Hudson.

Aruni, SK. 2007. *Yelahanka Nada Prabhugala Vastushilpa-Shilpakale* (Architecture and Sculptural Art of the Yelahanka Nada Prabhus). Edited by M Jamuna. Bangalore: Prasaranga and Bangalore University.

Bibliography

Aruni, SK. 2013. 'What do 106 memorial stones reveal?' *The Hindu*. 29 October 2013.

Barton, WP. 1923. Report of the Administration of the Civil and Military Station of Bangalore for the year 1922–23. Bangalore: Mysore Residency Press.

Baweja, Vandana. 2008. 'A Pre-history of Green Architecture: Otto Koenigsberger and Tropical Architecture, from Princely Mysore to Post-colonial London'. PhD thesis, University of Michigan. https://deepblue.lib.umich.edu/handle/2027.42/60709. Accessed 8 August 2018.

Baweja, Vandana. 2015. 'Messy Modernisms: Otto Koenigsberger's Early work in Princely Mysore, 1939–1941'. *South Asian Studies* 31(1): 1–26.

Bell, George. 1867. *Rough Notes by an Old Soldier during Fifty Years' Service*. London: Day and Son.

Bentinck, Lord William Cavendish. 1809. *Memorial Addressed to the Honourable Court of Directors Containing an Account of the Mutiny at Vellore*. London: John Booth.

Blakiston, J. 1829. *Twelve Years' Military Adventure in Three Quarters of the Globe*, Vol 1. London: Henry Colburn.

Bowe, Patrick. 2012. 'Lal Bagh: The Botanical Garden of Bangalore and its Kew-trained Gardeners'. *Garden History* 40(2): 228–238.

Bowring, LB. 1871. *Eastern Experiences*. London: Henry S King and Co.

Bowring, LB. 1893. *Haidar Ali and Tipu Sultan and the Struggle with the Musalman Powers of the South*. Oxford: Clarendon Press.

Bremer-David, C. 1997. *French Tapestries and Textiles in the J Paul Getty Museum*. Los Angeles: J Paul Getty Museum.

Buchanan, F. 1807. *A Journey from Madras through the Countries of Mysore, Canara and Malabar*, Vol 1. London: T Cadell and W Davies.

Butler, T. 1983. *Plague and Other Yersinia Infections*. New York: Plenum Press.

Cameron, J. 1880. *Catalogue of Plants in the Botanical Garden, Bangalore*. Bangalore: Mysore Government Central Press.

Cameron, J. 1891. *Catalogue of Plants in the Botanical Garden, Bangalore*. 2nd edition. Bangalore: Mysore Government Central Press.

Campbell, Walter. 1864. *My Indian Journal*. Edinburgh: Edmonston and Douglas.

Chandrasekharayya, HV. 1966. *Biography of Rajamanthra Pravina Sri HV Nanjundayya*. Bangalore: Sri Power Press.

Cheriyath, Anjali. 2016. *Listing of Fraser Town, Cooke Town and Richards Town*. Unpublished. INTACH Bengaluru Chapter.

Clark, James. 1885. *Historical Record and Regimental Memoir of the Royal Scots Fusiliers*. Edinburgh: Banks and Co.

Cleghorn, Hugh. 1861. 'Bangalore Garden'. In *The Forests and Gardens of South India*, 330–343. London: WH Allen.

Cobb, HV. 1918. Report of the Administration of the Civil and Military Station of Bangalore for the year 1917–18. Bangalore: Mysore Residency Press.

Colaco, Peter. 2003. *Bangalore*. Bangalore: Via Media Books.

Compton, Herbert. 1897. *A King's Hussar: Being the Military Memoirs of a Troop-Sergeant-Major of the 14th (King's) Hussars*. London: Cassell and Company.

Curzon, Lord. 1902. *Speeches of Lord Curzon of Keddleston*, Vol 2. Calcutta: Office of the Superintendent of Government Printing.

DeSouza, F. 1970. *The House of Binny*. Madras: Associated Printers.

Dhanraj, AK, R Isaac and Mercy. 2010. *Fortified Revival*. Bangalore: St Luke's Church.

Dixon, Marion Hepworth. 1898. 'Onslow Ford R.A.'. *The Art Journal* 157: 294–296.

Dobbs, Richard Stewart. 1882. *Reminiscences of Life in Mysore, South Africa, and Burmah*. Dublin: George Herbert.

Doveton, Captain. 1844. 'The Bangalore Conspiracy'. *The Asiatic Journal and Monthly Miscellany* 2, Third Series (November–April): 620–624.

Doyle, Patrick. Ed. 1905. *Indian Engineering*, Vol 36. Calcutta: CJA Pritchard.

Dutt, K Guru. 1955. *Chitrapur Saraswat Retrospect*. Bangalore: BBD Press.

EC *(Epigraphia Carnatica)*, various volumes.

Echenberg, Myron. 2007. Plague Ports: *The Global Urban Impact of Bubonic Plague, 1894–1901*. New York: New York University Press.

Eppert, Anja. 2015. 'The Maharajah's Gardener: The Revised Story of Kewite Gustav Hermann Krumbiegel'. *Journal of the Kew Guild* 16(1): 590–593.

Fisher, George Park. 1890. *History of the Christian Church*. London: Hodder and Stoughton.

Francis, W. 1988. *The Gazetteer of South India*, Vol 2. Reprint. New Delhi: Mittal Publications.

Furneaux, JH. 1895. *Glimpses of India*. Bombay: CB Burrows.

Glass House: *The Jewel of Lalbagh*, Mysore Horticultural Society: Bangalore

Govind, Ranjani. 2017. 'Kempe Gowda era "mantapa" emerges from Hosakerehalli lake'. *The Hindu*, 25 January 2017. https://www.thehindu.com/news/cities/bangalore/Kempe-Gowda-era-%E2%80%98mantapa%E2%80%99-emerges-from-Hosakerehalli-lake/article17090134.ece. Accessed June 2018.

Gowda, M. 1951. 'The Genus *Pittosporum* in the Sino-Indian Region'. *Journal of the Arnold Arboretum* 32(4): 303–343.

Gundappa, DV. 2016. 'Prof. Bellave Venkatanaranappa: Founder of Basavanagudi Club, Exemplary Citizen'. https://www.prekshaa.in/prof-bellave-venkatanaranappa-founder-basavanagudi-club-exemplary-citizen. Accessed 7 August 2018.

Gundappa, DV. 2018. *Jnapaka Chitrashale, Vol 1: Sahiti Sajjana Sarvajanikaru*. Reprint. Hubbali: Sahitya Prakashana.

Hall, Basil. 1833. *Fragments of Voyages and Travels*, Vol 1. Philadelphia: Edward C Mielke.

Hanumaiah, L. 1967. 'The Set-up and the Development of the Department of Horticulture: The Past, the Present and the Future'. In *Horticulture in Mysore State*, 1–14. Bangalore: Department of Horticulture.

Hanumaiah, L. 1991. 'The Glory of Lalbagh and Glass House'. In *Glass House: The Jewel of Lalbagh*, 19–27. Bangalore: Mysore Horticultural Society.

Hasan, Fazlul. 1970. *Bangalore through the Centuries*. Bangalore: Historical Publications.

Hasan, Mohibbul. 1971. *History of Tipu Sultan*. 2nd edition. Delhi: Aakar.

Henry, JR. 1962. 'A History of Tamil Churches in Mysore Diocese'. Unpublished thesis, United Theological College, Bangalore.

Herbert, Trevor. 2000. 'Nineteenth-century Bands: Making a Movement'. In *The British Brass Band: A Musical and Social History*, edited by Trevor Herbert, 10–67. Oxford: Oxford University Press.

Hervey, Albert. 1850. *Ten Years in India; or the Life of a Young Officer*, Vol 2. London: William Shoberl.

Heyne, B. 1814. *Tracts, Historical and Statistical, on India*. London: Robert Baldwin, Paternoster-Row.

Hicks, Dan, Michael Petraglia and Nicole Boivin. 2013. 'India and Sri Lanka'. In *World Archaeology at the Pitt Rivers Museum*, edited by Dan Hicks and Alice Stevenson, 482–503. Oxford: Archaeopress.

Hittalmani, SV. 1991. 'Lalbagh: The Garden Paradise'. In *Glass House: The Jewel of Lalbagh*, Mysore Horticultural Society: Bangalore.

Hobble, AC. 1906. 'Largest Hydroelectric Installation in Southern Asia, Mysore Province, India'. *The Far Eastern Review* 3(1) (June): 20–22.

Home, R. 1808. *Select Views in Mysore, the Country of Tippo Sultan, from Drawings Taken on the Spot*. London: Mr Bowyer.

Hourihane, C. Ed. 2012. *The Grove Encyclopaedia of Medieval Art and Architecture*, Vol 1. New York: Oxford University Press.

Hudson, J. 1893. 'Native Christians and the Public Wells'. *The Harvest Field* 5 (August): 41–51.

Iengar, KN. 1985. 'List of the Buildings of Bangalore Surveyed for the Bangalore Urban Arts Commission'. Unpublished. INTACH Bengaluru Chapter.

Ismail, Sir Mirza. 1930. *Speeches by Amin-ul-Mulk Sir Mirza Ismail*, Vol 1. Bangalore: Government Press.

Ismail, Sir Mirza. 1936. *Speeches by Amin-ul-Mulk Sir Mirza Ismail*, Vol 2. Bangalore: Government Press.

Ismail, Sir Mirza. 1949. *Speeches by Amin-ul-Mulk Sir Mirza Ismail*, Vol 3. Bangalore: Government Press.

Issar, TP. 2002. *The City Beautiful*. 2nd edition. Bangalore: TP Issar.

Iyengar, K. 1914. 'Extension of Bangalore City'. In *Proceedings of the Third All-India Sanitary Conference*, Vol IV, 206–215. Calcutta: Thacker, Spink and Co.

Iyengar, V Rangaswamy. 1913. 'Mechanical Filters for Town Water Supply'. In *Proceedings of the Second All-India Sanitary Conference held at Madras in November 1912*, Vol 2, 199–215. Simla: Government Central Branch Press.

Iyer, M, H Nagendra and MB Rajani. 2012. 'Using Satellite Imagery and Historical Maps to Study the Original Contours of Lalbagh Botanical Garden'. *Current Science* 102(3): 507–509.

Iyer, Meera. 2010. 'Bangalore's rock-solid lung space'. *Deccan Herald*, 7 June 2010.

Iyer, Meera. 2013. 'Where the music played'. *Deccan Herald*, 18 March 2013.

Iyer, Meera. 2015. 'Treasure trove of history'. *Deccan Herald*, 13 October 2015.

Iyer, Meera. 2017. 'When the electric age dawned on Bangalore 112 years ago'. *The Hindu*, 30 July 2017.

Iyer, K Seshadri. 1914. 'Address of the Dewan of Mysore to the Dasara Representative Assembly at Mysore, on Tuesday 17th October 1899'. In *Addresses of the Dewans of Mysore to the Dasara Representative Assembly from 1881–1899*, Vol 1, 255–268. Bangalore: Government Press.

Jain, Sanjeev, Pratima Murthy and SK Shankar. 2001. 'Neuropsychiatric Perspectives from Nineteenth Century India: The Diaries of Dr Charles I Smith'. *History of Psychiatry* 12: 459–466.

James, Lawrence. 1998. *Raj: The Making and Unmaking of British India*. New York: St Martin's Press.

Javaraya, HC. 1943. 'Biannual Cropping of Apple in Bangalore'. *Indian Journal of Horticulture* 1(1): 31–34.

Jayaram, Suresh. 2010. *Whatever He touched, He Adorned*. New Delhi: Khoj International Artists Association.

Jenks, HN. 1919. 'Public Health Work in India'. *American Journal of Public Health* 9(12): 943–951.

John, Hemalatha and Rev Florence Deenadayalan. Nd. *Wesley English Church, Bangalore. 123 Years of Life, 1888–2011*. Bangalore: Wesley English Church.

Kamath, SU. 1991. 'The Early Long History of Lalbagh'. In *Glass House: The Jewel of Lalbagh*, 4–11. Bangalore: Mysore Horticultural Society.

Kamath, SU. 1996. *A Handbook of Karnataka*. Bangalore: Karnataka Gazetteer Department.

Kamath, SU. 2008. 'A City Yet Unborn'. In *Multiple City: Writings on Bangalore*, edited by Aditi De, 6–9. New Delhi: Penguin Books.

Karnataka State Gazetteer, various years. Bangalore: Government Press.

Karthik, S. 2015. 'Shasanagalali kanda Bengaluru'. Talk at Gokhale Institute of Public Affairs. Archived at https://soundcloud.com/udaya-kumar-p-l/karthik-gokhale-institute?fbclid=IwAR3pzghkkiRn1JRFcdvY3cJNFXeRgczkZ0ukkvNQT8_XaV-YvDu-5AAy1d4. Accessed February 2019.

Karthik, S. 2016. *Bengaluru sthalanama nishpatti likitha aakaragala hinnaleyalli* (The etymology of the name Bengaluru based on written sources). In *Nudijaagara: A Special Commemorative Volume on Bengaluru City*, edited by KL Rajashekar, 122–136. Bengaluru: Bengaluru Nagarajilla Kannada Sahitya Parishattu.

Karunakaran, K. 2014. 'Rediscovering a lost spring'. *Deccan Herald*, 21 May 2014. https://www.deccanherald.com/content/408096/rediscovering-lost-spring.html. Accessed January 2018.

Kirkpatrick, William. 1811. *Select Letters of Tippoo Sultan*. London: Black, Parry and Kingsbury.

Krishnamurthy, PV. 2011. 'Yelahankarajya prabhugalada Bengaluru Kempegowdaru shasanegalu hinneleyalli ondu sookshma adhyana' (The Kempegowda family rulers of Bengaluru as reflected in contemporary inscriptions). *Itihasa Darpana 2* (October–December): 40–49.

Lang, Jon T, Madhavi Desai and Miki Desai. 1997. *Architecture and Independence: The Search for Identity—India 1880 to 1980*. New Delhi: Oxford University Press.

Lee, Rachel. 2012. 'Constructing a Shared Vision: Otto Koenigsberger and Tata & Sons', *ABE Journal Architecture beyond Europe* 2: 1–26.

Lee, Standish. 1874. *The Sewerage of Madras, a Report Submitted to the Municipal Commissioners of that City*. Vepery: Foster Press.

Lee, Standish. Ed. 1882. *Guide to the Eurasian and Anglo-Indian Villages, Proposed to be Established in the Province of Mysore, and Hand Book of Industries and Pursuits*. Madras: Eurasian and Anglo-Indian Association.

Lewis, B. 2012. 'British Assessments of Tipu Sultan's Hill Forts in Northern Mysore, South India, 1802'. *International Journal of Historical Archaeology* 16: 164–198.

Lobo, Sister Victorine. Nd. *The History of the Sisters of St. Joseph of Tarbes in India (1882–2006)*. Bangalore.

Mackenzie, R. 1793. *A Sketch of the War with Tippoo Sultaun*, Vols 1 and 2. Calcutta.

Manjunatha, MG. 2010. 'Historical Memoir of Bangalore'. In *Tipu Sultan: The Tiger of Mysore*, edited by R Gopal, 393–396. Mysore: Directorate of Archaeology and Museums.

Mapping Sculpture. 2011. 'Maharajah of Mysore'. Mapping the Practice and Profession of Sculpture in Britain and Ireland 1851–1951. University of Glasgow History of Art and HATII, online database. http://sculpture.gla.ac.uk/view/object.php?id=msib7_1207134896. Accessed 19 July 2018.

Mari Gowda, MH. 1951. 'The Genus *Pittosporum* in the Sino-Indian Region'. *Journal of the Arnold Arboretum* 32(4): 303–343.

Mari Gowda, MH. 1967. 'History of Lalbagh'. In *Horticulture in Mysore State*, 79–97. Bangalore: Department of Horticulture.

Marryat, Florence. 1868. *'Gup': Sketches of Anglo-Indian Life and Character*. London: Richard Bentley.

Martin, M. 2014. 'Tipu Sultan's Ambassadors at Saint-Cloud: Indomania and Anglophobia in Pre-Revolutionary Paris'. *West 86th* 21(1): 37–68.

Mathur, Meghana. 2001. '7000-year-old temple in Malleswaram'. *The Times of India*, 15 October 2001. https://timesofindia.indiatimes.com/bangalore-times/7000-year-old-temple-in-Malleswaram/articleshow/129602326.cms. Accessed January 2018.

Matthew, John Morgan. 1793. *Nine Letters from a Very Young Officer Serving in India under the Marquis Cornwallis*. London: GGJ and J Robinson.

Moona, Suresh. 2011. *Dharmaprakasha SV Sreenivasa Setty: A Source of Inspiration for Generations to Come*. Bangalore: CVMS Hostel.

Morrison, Kathleen. 2015. 'Archaeologies of Flow: Water and the Landscapes of Southern India Past, Present, and Future'. *Journal of Field Archaeology* 40(5): 560–580.

Muddachari, B. 1965. 'Mysore-Maratha Relations in the 17th Century'. PhD thesis, University of Mysore.

Muddachari, B. 1966. 'Maratha Court in the Karnatak'. *Proceedings of the Indian History Congress* 28: 177–179.

Munivenkatappa, B. 1936. 'Buildings, Bridges and Road Construction in Mysore State'. *Asiatic Review* 32(3): 780–784.

Murphy, Ray. Ed. 1953. *Edward Lear's Indian Journal*. London: Jarrods.

Nagendra, H, H Unnikrishnan and S Sen. 2013. 'Villages in the City: Spatial and Temporal Heterogeneity in Rurality and Urbanity in Bangalore, India'. *Land* 3(1): 1–18.

Nagendra, H. 2016. *Nature in the City: Bengaluru in the Past, Present and Future*. New Delhi: Oxford University Press.

Nair, J. 2005. *The Promise of the Metropolis: Bangalore's Twentieth Century*. New Delhi: Oxford University Press.

Narasimha, R. 1985. 'Rockets in Mysore and Britain, 1750–1850 A.D.'. https://www.researchgate.net/profile/Roddam_Narasimha/publication/37179995_Rockets_in_Mysore_and_Britain_1750-1850_AD/links/564d75e708aefe619b0df11c/Rockets-in-Mysore-and-Britain-1750-1850-AD.pdf. Accessed 10 August 2018.

Narayana Swamy, S. 1991. 'Artistic Structures in Lalbagh'. In *Glass House: The Jewel of Lalbagh*, 28–34. Bangalore: Mysore Horticultural Society.

Nevill, Alexandra. 2016. 'The Career Choices of the Victorian Sculptor: Establishing an Economic Model for the Careers of Edward Onslow Ford and Henry Hope Pinker through Their Works'. Masters thesis, University of Leiden. https://openaccess.leidenuniv.nl/bitstream/handle/1887/44837/Masters%20Thesis%20-%2021.12.16.pdf?sequence=3. Accessed 19 July 2018.

New, William. 1861. 'Summary of Operations at the Lal-Bagh during 1858–59'. In *The Forests and Gardens of South India*, Vol 9, by Hugh Cleghorn, 336–338. London: WH Allen.

Nicholson, Edward. 1873. *Medico-topographical Account of the Station of Bangalore: Army Medical Department Report for the Year 1873*, Vol 25. London: Harrison and Sons.

O'Callaghan, RW. 1832. 'Court Martial: The Bangalore Conspirators'. *The Asiatic Journal and Monthly Register for British and Foreign India, China and Australasia* 11 (May–August): 84.

Parameswaran, Uma. 2011. *CV Raman: A Biography*. Gurgaon: Penguin.

Penny, Frank. 1922. *The Church in Madras: Being the History of the Ecclesiastical and Missionary Action of the East India Company in the Presidency of Madras From 1835 to 1861*, Vol 3. London: John Murray.

Phillimore, RH. 1950. *Historical Records of the Survey of India*, Vol 2. Dehra Dun: Survey of India.

Prain, D. 1905. 'A Sketch of the Life of Francis Hamilton (once Buchanan)'. *Annals of the Royal Botanic Garden, Calcutta* 10: I–lxxv.

Proceedings of the Government of Mysore, various years, KSA.

Puttaiya, B. 1923. 'The Kempe Gowda Chiefs'. *Quarterly Journal of the Mythic Society* 13(4): 723–741.

Radhakrishna, BP. 1997. 'Yele Mallappa Settaru: Forgotten Benefactor of Bangalore'. *Journal of the Geological Society of India* 49: 119–122.

Rajangam, K. 2011. 'Whitefield: An Important but Forgotten Chapter of India's Colonial Heritage'. *South Asian Studies* 27(1): 89–110.

Rajangam, K. 2013. 'Mootoocherry and St Mark's: these are districts the English built'. *Citizen Matters*, 27 June 2013.

Rajani, MB. 2007. 'Bangalore from Above: An Archaeological Overview'. *Current Science* 93: 1352–1353.

Ram, Theja. 2017. 'From a thriving bazaar to a garbage-strewn dump: Tracing the history of Bengaluru's KR Market'. *The News Minute*, 29 July 2017. https://www.thenewsminute.com/article/thriving-bazaar-garbage-strewn-dump-tracing-history-bengalurus-kr-market-65970. Accessed 10 August 2018.

Raman, Sir Chandrasekhara Venkata. 1930. Nobel Lecture. https://www.nobelprize.org/prizes/physics/1930/raman/lecture. Accessed 5 November 2018.

Ramaseshan, S. 1978. 'CV Raman: A Life Sketch'. *Science Today* 13(5): 50–52. http://dspace.rri.res.in/handle/2289/6450. Accessed August 2018.

Ramaseshan, S. 1988. 'Research with Style: The Story of Raman's Study of Light Scattering'. *Current Science* 57(4): 163–171.

Rao, CH. Ed. 1929. *Mysore Gazetteer*, Vol 4. Bangalore: Government of Karnataka Publication.

Rao, CH. Ed. 1930a. *Mysore Gazetteer*, Vol 2. Bangalore: Government of Karnataka Publication.

Rao, CH. Ed. 1930b. *Mysore Gazetteer*, Vol 5. Bangalore: Government of Karnataka Publication.

Reed, Stanley. 1906. *The Royal Tour in India*. Bombay: Bennett, Coleman and Co.

Rees, JD. 1891. *Narratives of Tours in India*. Madras: Government Press.

Report on Public Instruction in Mysore, for the Year 1877–78. Bangalore: Government Press.

Report on the Administration of Mysore, various years. Bangalore: Government Press.

Report on the Medical Topography and Statistics of the Mysore Division of the Madras Army. In *Report on the Medical Topography and Statistics, of the Provinces of Malabar*, 1844. Vepery: RW Thorpe.

Report on the Progress of Agriculture in Mysore, 1939. Bangalore: Government Press.

Report on the Working of Archaeological Researches in Mysore during 1914–15. Bangalore: Government Press.

Report on the Working of the Government Gardens and Parks in Mysore, 1908–1909. Bangalore: Mysore Government Press.

Review of the Progress of Education in the Mysore State for the decennium 1922–23 to 1931–32. 1935. Bangalore: Government Press.

Rice, BL. 1889. *Archaeological Department: Report for the year ending 31st March 1889*. Bangalore: Mysore Government Central Press.

Rice, BL. 1897a. *Mysore: A Gazetteer Compiled for Government*, Vol 1: Mysore in General. Revised edition. Westminster, UK: Archibald, Constable and Co.

Rice, BL. 1897b. *Mysore: A Gazetteer Compiled for Government*, Vol 2: Mysore by Districts. Revised edition. Westminster, UK: Archibald, Constable and Co.

Rice, BL. 1905. *Epigraphia Carnatica*, Vol 9: Inscriptions in the Bangalore District. Bangalore: Mysore Government Central Press.

Rice, Edward P. Nd. *Benjamin Rice: Or, Fifty Years in the Master's Service*. London: Religious Tract Society.

Roberts, Emma. 1837. *Scenes and Characteristics of Hindostan: With Sketches of Anglo-Indian Society*. London: WH Allen and Co.

Romilly, FJ. 1880. 'Report on the Ulsoor Water-works'. In *Professional Papers on Indian Engineering*, Vol 9, edited by AM Brandreth, 311–349. Roorkee: Thomason College Press.

Sankey, Richard H. 1853. 'On the Geology of Some Parts of Central India'. *Quarterly Journal of the Geological Society of London* 10: 55–56.

Sankey, Richard H. 1873. 'Offices of the Mysore Government at Bangalore'. In *Professional Papers in Indian Engineering*, Vol 2, edited by Major M Lang, 1–7. Roorkee: Thomason College Press.

Schwartz, CF. 1826. *Remains of the Rev CF Schwartz, Missionary in India*. 2nd edition. London: Jaques and Wright.

Sewell, J. 1858. 'Bangalore Mission of the London Missionary Society'. In *Proceedings of the South India Missionary Conference, 1858*, 97–102. Madras: Society for Promoting Christian Knowledge.

Shama Rao, M. 1936. *Modern Mysore: From the Beginning to 1868*. Bangalore: Higginbothams.

Sharma, RS. 2010. *Cratons and Fold Belts of India*. Berlin: Springer-Verlag.

Sharma, Y. 2016. *Bangalore: The Early City*. New Delhi: Partridge India.

Shivakumar, AR. 2012. 'No more dry spells at dhobi ghat'. *Deccan Herald*, 9 January 2012. http://www.kscst.iisc.ernet.in/rwh_files/rwh_dh_publications/22%20No%20more%20 dry%20spells%20at%20dhobi%20ghat%2009.01.12.pdf. Accessed 19 October 2018.

Shyam Prasad, S. 2018. 'Advocate aims to tell Sir Cubbon: On your Mark, get set, go!' *Bangalore Mirror*, 18 August 2018. https://bangaloremirror.indiatimes.com/bangalore/cover-story/ advocate-aims-to-tell-sir-cubbon-on-your-mark-get-set-go/articleshow/65445378.cms. Accessed 25 August 2018.

Simo, Rev Father Anthony. Ed. 1997. *The History of the Arch-Diocese of Bangalore*. Bangalore: St Paul's.

Smartt, J. Ed. 1994. *The Groundnut Crop: A Scientific Basis for Improvement*. Dodrecht: Springer Science+Business.

Smeeth, WF. 1916. 'Outline of the Geological History of Mysore'. *Bulletin of the Department of Mines and Geology, Mysore State* 6: 1–21.

Srinivas, S. 2004. *Landscapes of Urban Memory: The Sacred and the Civic in India's High Tech City*. Hyderabad: Orient Longman.

Srivatsa, Sharath. 2014. 'Prehistoric sites lost to rapid urbanisation'. *The Hindu*, 3 May 2014.

State Government Archives, 1936, Revenue Department Proceedings of the Government of His Highness the Maharaja of Mysore.

Steggles, Mary Ann. 2000. *Statues of the Raj*. London: BACSA.

Stephens, JH. 1914. *Plague-Proof Planning in South India*. Madras: Methodist Publishing House.

Stephens, JH. 1922. 'Fraser Town: A Plague-Proof Town in India'. *The American City* 26: 235–238.

Stocker, Mark. 2014. 'Review of Thomas Brock: Forgotten Sculptor of the Victoria Memorial'. *The Sculpture Journal* 23(2) (1 December): 257–265.

Stronge, S. 2009. *Tipu's Tigers*. New Delhi: Lustre Press.

Stubbs, FW. 1877. *History of the Bengal Artillery*. London: Henry King and Co.

Subba Rao, KA. 1933. *Revived Memories*. Madras: Ganesh and Co.

Subba Rao, TK. 1926. *Tourists' Guide to Mysore*. Nd.

Sudhira, HS, TV Ramachandra and MHB Subrahmanya. 2007. 'Bangalore'. *Cities* 24(5): 379–390.

Suganya, Kuili. 2011. INTACH Gavipuram listing. Unpublished. INTACH Bengaluru Chapter.

Sundara Rao, BN. 2015. *Bengalurina Itihaasa* (Bangalore's History). 3rd edition. Bengaluru: Ankita Pustaka.

Sundara, A. 1989. 'Benjamin Lewis Rice: A Biographical Sketch'. In *Archaeological Survey of Mysore, Annual Reports: 1885–1905*, edited by A Sundara, vi–ix. Mysore: Directorate of Archaeology and Museums.

Towns of Our City: *Fraser Town, Richards Town, Cooke Town*. 2018. A film by INTACH Bangalore. https://www.youtube.com/watch?v=b9YNDdiJkCg&feature=youtu.be.

Troup, Jack. 1997. *The life that Jack Led: Experiences of a Norfolk Soldier and Policeman, 1918–1974*. London: Larks Press.

Unnikrishnan, H, B Manjunatha and H Nagendra. 2016. 'Contested Urban Commons: Mapping the Transition of a Lake to a Sports Stadium in Bangalore'. *International Journal of the Commons* 10(1): 265–293.

Unnikrishnan, H, B Manjunatha and H Nagendra. 2017. 'Urban Commons in a Globalizing City'. *Seminar India* 690: 63–67.

Unnikrishnan, H, S Mundoli and H Nagendra. 2017. 'Making Water Flow in Bengaluru: Planning for the Resilience of Water Supply in a Semi-arid City'. *Journal of Sustainable Urbanization, Planning and Progress* 2(1): 68–78.

Unnikrishnan, H, S Mundoli, B Manjunatha and H Nagendra. 2016. 'Down the Drain: Tragedy of the Disappearing Urban Commons of Bengaluru'. *South Asian Water Studies* 5(3): 7–11.

Unnikrishnan, H, S Sen and H Nagendra. 2017. 'Traditional Water Bodies and Urban Resilience: A Historical Perspective from Bengaluru, India'. *Water History* 9(4): 453–477.

Unnikrishnan, H. 2017. 'The Changing Nature of Social and Ecological Vulnerabilities of an Urban Lake Social-ecological System in Bangalore'. Thesis submitted to Manipal University.

Urs, Anil. 2016. 'State Bank of Mysore: Into the sunset after 104 years'. *Business Line*, 1 April 2016.

Urs, Sir M Kantharaj. 1953. *Speeches of Sirdar Sir M. Kantharaj Urs, Dewan of Mysore, 1919–1922*, Vol 1. Bangalore: Government Press.

Venkatasubba Sastri, KN. 1932. *The Administration of Mysore under Sir Mark Cubbon*. London: George Allen and Unwin.

Verghese, Anila. 2001. 'A Rare Depiction of Nine Yogis in the Somesvara Temple, Ulsoor'. *Journal of the Asiatic Society of Bombay* 75: 179–187.

Vibart, HM. 1883. *Military History of the Madras Engineers and Pioneers from 1743 up to the Present Time*, Vol 1. London: WH Allen and Co.

Visvesvaraya, Sir M. 1917. *Speeches by Sir M Visvesvaraya, Dewan of Mysore*. Bangalore: Government Press.

Vyasanakere, PJ, K Sudeesh and BS Shylaja. 2008. 'Astronomical Significance of the Gavi Gangadhareshwara Temple in Bangalore'. *Current Science* 95(11): 1632–1636.

Wadia, BP. 1947. 'The Indian Institute of Culture'. *The Aryan Path* 18: 231–233.

Wadiyar, KR. 1921. *Speeches by His Highness Sri Krishnaraja Wadiyar Bahadur, 1902–1920*. Bangalore: Government Press.

Waltraud, Ernst, Biswamoy Pati and TV Sekher. 2017. *Health and Medicine in the Indian Princely States: 1850–1950*. Routledge: New York.

Wellesley, Arthur. 1851. 'Memorandum upon Seringapatam'. In *Selections from the Dispatches and General Orders of Field Marshal the Duke of Wellington*, edited by Lt Col John Gurwood, 26–33. London: John Murray.

White, DS. 1879. *Guide to Eurasian and Anglo-Indian Villages* (pamphlet).

White, James J. 1999. 'Lalbagh Botanical Garden Artworks on the Web'. *Bulletin of the Hunt Institute for Botanical Documentation* 11(1): 2.

Wigington, Robin. 1992. *The Firearms of Tipu Sultan*. Hatfield, UK: John Taylor Book Ventures.

Wilks, Mark. 1817. *Historical Sketches of the South of India, in an Attempt trace the History of Mysoor*, Vol 3. London: Longman, Hurst, Rees.

Williams, Rev Arthur. 1840. *Mission to the Mysore, with Scenes and Facts*. London: Partridge and Oakey.

Contributors

ANJALI CHERIYATH is a conservation architect and an assistant professor in the Wadiyar Centre Architecture in Mysore.

SONALI DHANPAL is an architect, built heritage conservationist and the current recipient of the Forshaw PhD Scholarship at Newcastle School of Architecture, Planning, and Landscape, United Kingdom. Her doctoral research explores residential extensions, bungalow culture and the production of everyday spaces in the Princely state of Mysore by focusing on its mutually constitutive capitals, Mysore and Bangalore during high colonialism (1881 to 1920).

B MANJUNATHA is with the Azim Premji University, Bengaluru, and is also a freelance researcher with considerable knowledge about urbanisation in Bengaluru. He shares a strong concern for the protection of urban commons.

PANKAJ MODI is a conservation architect and Coordinator of Projects at INTACH, Bengaluru Chapter. He has more than a decade of dedicated experience in the field with specialisation in Wood Architecture from Norway. He has been involved in several restoration projects around the country with both government and private agencies. He has co-authored a book Domes and Vaults in South India. He is visiting faculty in several architecture schools in Bengaluru.

HARINI NAGENDRA is professor of sustainability at Azim Premji University, Bengaluru. She has conducted research on the interaction between people and nature in forests and cities for over twenty-five years. Her books include Nature in the City: Bengaluru in the Past, Present, and Future, and Cities and Canopies: Trees in Indian Cities.

JAHNAVI PAI is an ecologist based in Bengaluru. Her has studied the state-owned grazing pastures known as Amruthmahal Kaval, co-authored and coordinated the production of a bilingual nature guide, worked on the mapping of avenue trees in Malleswaram, and studied Giant Squirrels, among other things. She is currently with the Karnataka State Biodiversity Board.

KRUPA RAJANGAM is a Bangalore based conservation architect with over 15 years field based experience in various aspects of heritage conservation. She is Founder-Director of the collaborative heritage practice 'Saythu…linking people and heritage'. She is committed to democratizing the heritage idea through past and current initiatives like Bangalore City Project, Nakshay and Neighbourhood Diaries.

SWATHI REDDY is a qualified Chartered Financial Analyst and financial journalist with a longstanding passion for the crafts and heritage of India. She channels this interest into her work as a corporate social responsibility (CSR) consultant, focusing on fundraising and corporate gifting programmes for handcraft entrepreneurs and artisans. Prior to this, she was actively involved with the Bengaluru chapter of INTACH as its co-convenor.

KARTHIKEYAN SRINIVASAN has nurtured a deep love for wildlife for over 30 years. He is a birdwatcher, an amateur photographer with a keen interest in insects like butterflies & ants and spiders. He has authored Discover Avenue Trees and various articles published in leading dailies and magazines. He was conferred the Carl Zeiss Wildlife Conservation Award in March 2013.

HITA UNNIKRISHNAN is a Newton International Fellow (British Academy) at the Urban Institute, The University of Sheffield. She is also a visiting faculty at the Azim Premji University in Bengaluru. Her work examines the historically changing vulnerabilities of urban ecological commons in India using multiple perspectives drawing on both the social and the natural sciences. She was the recipient of the Professor Elinor Ostrom International Fellowship for Practice and Policy on the Commons in 2013.

Acknowledgements

We gratefully acknowledge the support of the Karnataka State Archives, Bengaluru, and the Mythic Society, Bengaluru, in providing us archival material used for this research.

This chapter draws partially on two papers published in 2014 and 2016 by the Nehru Memorial Museum and Library (NMML) and the International Journal of the Commons, respectively. We thank Dr Meera Iyer and Seema Mundoli for their invaluable help with archival material that enriched our understanding of the landscape surrounding the lake.

We also thank Shubhika Malara, whose creativity has beautifully brought to life the maps created for this project.

Funding for this study was provided from the Centre for Urban Sustainability in India, Azim Premji University, a USAID peer grant to Harini Nagendra at the Ashoka Trust for Research in Ecology and the Environment (ATREE), Bengaluru, and a Newton International Fellowship from the British Academy awarded to Hita Unnikrishnan.

Hita Unnikrishnan, B Manjunath
and Harini Nagendra

I would first to thank the Bengaluru Chapter of the Indian National Trust for Art and Cultural Heritage with whom I have been associated for several years now. It is thanks to the friendship and steadfast support of colleagues at INTACH that this book has finally taken shape: first and foremost Aravind C, who has unfailingly helped and encouraged me to get on with the writing – this book would have taken a few more years if not for him! Swathi Reddy, whose friendship I have always greatly valued; and Pankaj Modi, who always freely shared his time and architectural expertise – a lot of the architectural descriptions in the book are thanks to him. Thank you, all three of you.

Thank you very much, Sujaya Shashikiran and Shashikiran Mullur of HiCal, long-time friends of INTACH, for your financial support for this book.

I would like to thank Dr SK Aruni, Director, Indian Council of Historical Research, for always being generous with his time and knowledge; the staff at the Karnataka State Archives and the Madras Sappers Museum and Archives, Madras Engineer Group for permission to access and use their archives; Krishnam Raju of Raman Research Institute and the RRI Archives for the use of their photographs; and the Mythic Society and the ICHR for the use of their excellent libraries.

Thank you, Harish Padmanabha for sharing photos and old postcards and the note by CJ Padmanabha. I also thank Clarence High School; Rohit Hangal; Jane Smith; Ranganath; Alyia Krumbiegel; Zaffar Sait; B Anantharam; Surendra Reddy, Jayaram Reddy and Vinatha Reddy; TV Annaswamy and Sanjeev Narrrain; the MG Rangaiah family; Paul Fernandes; Krishna and Aruna Chidambi; and Malini White; for being so generous with postcards, sketches, photographs and information.

Several people have gladly spared time and shared inputs: K Jairaj, Krishnarao Jaisim, M Narendra, Udhav Patankar, Indira Ramakanth, Surendra Prasad, Deepak Pinto, Anaheeta Pinto, Megha Shyam, Krishna MB, Zaffar Sait, B Anantharam, Seetha Ravindra, Surendra Reddy, Rajshekhar Ramachandran, Ajay Kadam, Ravikumar Kashi, Ananthanarayana K. and Sanjeev Narrain among others.

Thank you, Rimli Borooah. I am so glad you worked on the editing of this book. Thank you Jaya Jha and Abhaya Agarwal for being the first to believe in the book. Thank you muchly Sneha Prasad for coming in along with Samanvita and Varsha to work on the lovely illustrated maps. And PeeVee, you rock!

And a big, big thank you to my family: To my parents and sisters for blowing my trumpet for me! To S for not interfering. And to my children, for putting up with my frequent absences from home and my crabbiness and dottiness while writing—you two make everything worthwhile.

Meera Iyer

Index

A

Agrahara 164
Agricultural and Horticultural Society 279, 280, 300, 319
Ahmed Buildings 33
Albert Bakery 221
Albert Victor, Prince 301
Anglican Church 146
Anglo-Indian vii, 235, 238, 239, 240, 324, 325, 327, 329
Anjaneya temple 22, 28
Ankamma Choultry 121, 122
Apples 277, 280, 283, 289, 290
Aquarium 276, 305, 306
Armoury 56
Arsenal 40, 42, 43, 71
Aruni, SK 320, 321
Assigned Tract 43, 87, 107, 108
Attara Kacheri 43, 87, 107, 108
Avenue Road 43, 87, 107, 108
Ayre, Lt 18

B

Bahadur Shah 37, 38
Baiyanna, T 182, 194
Balfour, Edward Green 101
Bamboo Roofs 9, 89, 98, 115
Bandstand - Cubbon Park 84, 89, 95, 96, 98, 101, 103
Bandstand - Lalbagh 271, 291, 304, 305
Bangalore City Municipality 132, 284
Bangalore Sanitary Improvements Loans Law 198
Bank of Mysore 19, 20, 21, 132, 328
Banyan 295
Basavanagudi Union 149, 150
Bats 154, 295
Batteries 28, 41
Battle for Bengaluru 35, 40, 41, 112
Battle for the 'Pettah' 18
Beagles Basketball Club 174
Beatson, Capt Alexander 41
Begur 1, 6, 7, 103, 269
Bell, George 70, 91, 115, 127, 212, 218
Bengaluru fort 38-47
Bengaluru Inscription 7
Benga Tree 269

Benjamin Lewis Rice 26, 328
Benjamin Rice 23, 25, 26, 74, 327
Bethesda Assembly Hall 226, 227
Bhaktavatsala, M 98, 99, 109
Bharat Sports Union 174
Bhojagade, Venkatarao 157
Binnys 171
Bishop Cotton School 206
BK Mariappa Charities Hostel 154, 155
Black, Allan Adamson 282
Blackpully 79, 199, 200
Blakiston, Lt John 78, 79, 81, 107, 108, 321
Botanical drawings 277, 309
Bowring Institute 95, 96
Bowring, Lewin Bentham 26, 48, 51, 73, 89, 95, 96, 103, 107, 108, 203, 211, 214, 321
British Resident 51, 62, 81, 127, 146, 172, 199, 200, 206, 226, 278
Brock, Thomas 94, 328
BRV Theatre 107
Buchanan, Francis 67, 75, 274, 275, 309, 310, 321, 326
Bugle Rock 154
Bull Temple 13, 137, 141, 151, 152, 153, 154, 157, 159
Bungalows 1, 2, 55, 79, 80, 82, 86, 87, 114, 121, 133, 137, 151, 165, 176, 207, 208, 220, 230, 237, 243, 244, 252, 253, 269
Byramma 159

C

Cameron, John 95, 283, 284, 285, 286, 287, 289, 300, 301, 305, 308, 309, 310, 321
Campbell, Walter 321
Canara Union 173, 174, 179, 180
Cantonment vii, 10, 12, 40, 42, 43, 51, 62, 76, 77, 78, 79, 80, 81, 82, 83, 84, 85, 86, 87, 88, 89, 91, 92, 93, 99, 100, 101, 107, 110, 112, 113, 114, 126, 127, 130, 131, 135, 168, 171, 183, 196, 198, 208, 210, 211, 237, 242, 245, 248, 252, 268, 270
Car Street 121, 122, 125
Caste 133, 155, 260
Cauvery Falls Power Scheme 50
Central High School 23

Chamarajpete 20, 58, 59, 133, 134, 137, 138, 139, 141, 154, 155, 156, 165
Chickpete 6, 9, 22, 32, 34, 68
Chief Architect 35, 53, 145, 174, 178
Chikkadevaraja 9, 34, 35, 45, 60
Chinese Bell 115
Chitrapur Math 179
Cholera 131, 203
Churchill, Winston S 244
City Improvement Committee 35, 44, 132, 134
City Market 36
Civil and Military Station 10, 43, 197, 225, 232, 320, 321
Clarence High School 226, 228, 229, 230, 233, 333
Cleghorn, Hugh 279, 281, 282, 308, 310, 312, 321, 325
Cleveland Town 82, 199, 210
Colaco, Peter 205, 232, 321
Communities 8, 15, 113, 128, 137, 139, 142, 169, 170, 205, 226, 250, 251, 258, 260, 265
Conservancy lanes 133, 138, 140, 171, 230
Cooke, GH 206
Cooke Town vii, 197, 205, 207, 208, 231, 233, 321, 328
Cornwallis, Charles 17, 19, 37, 41, 325
Courtyards 45, 46, 114, 164
Crystal Palace 301, 302
Cubbon, Mark 42, 62, 89, 98, 279
Curzon, Lord 49, 321
Cypress 272, 274, 276

D

Daniell, William and Thomas 2, 3, 159, 320
Darwinia 297
Delhi Gate 41, 44, 45, 47, 51
De Lotbinier, Major ACJ 51
Department of Public Instruction 22, 23
Dhobi Ghats 126, 165, 188, 189, 190
Dovecote 301

E

Early Iron Age 6, 103, 271
East India Company 10, 19, 42, 77, 78, 81, 87, 126, 210, 277, 278, 326
East West School 148, 149
Ekoji (Venkoji) 9, 187
Electricity 50, 51, 182

Epigraphia Carnatica 26, 322, 327
Eurasian vii, 235, 324, 329

F

Fernandes, Paul 204, 333
First War of Independence 62, 86, 96, 281
Floyd, Col John 19
Fort High School 45, 58, 59
Fountain 63, 64, 65, 69, 304
Fraser, Stuart M 146, 199, 200, 206, 221, 224
Fraser Town vii, 82, 107, 196, 197, 198, 199, 200, 201, 202, 203, 204, 205, 206, 207, 209, 210, 212, 220, 221, 222, 223, 226, 227, 228, 229, 230, 231, 232, 233, 245, 321, 328
French influence
 - on motifs 66
 - on the Fort 47
Friends Union Cricket Club 174

G

Gandabherunda 33, 47, 69, 103, 118, 155, 307
Gandhi Bazaar 150, 151, 152, 166
Gandhiji 22, 151
Gandhi, Mahatma 151, 156, 303
Garden City 1, 249, 269, 313, 315, 316
Gavigangadhareshwara temple 13, 161, 163, 164
Gibbs, Harry Parker 51
Girija Kalyana (marriage of Shiva and Parvathi) 118
Glass House 285, 286, 288, 289, 301, 302, 303, 304, 320, 322, 323, 324, 325
Gokhale Institute of Public Affairs 154, 324
Goodwill, Fred 219
Goodwill Girls' School 218, 219
Government Museum 6, 99, 101, 283, 286
Grand Army 19, 37, 41, 47, 275
Grand Magazine 56
Gulmohur 292
Gundappa, DV 22, 148, 149, 154, 166, 181, 194, 322
Gupta, SVS 29, 30, 73

H

Hanumanthaiah, Kengal 58, 98, 105, 314
Harihara Gudda 161, 164, 165
Hasan, Fazlul 11, 81, 322
Hero Stone 7, 102, 271
Hessarghatta 192, 250, 289

Heyne, Benjamin 277, 309, 310, 323
High Court 62, 87, 96, 97, 98, 99, 100, 102, 105, 288
Holy Ghost Church 231
Home, Robert 17, 18, 41, 64, 275, 309
Home School 146, 147
Hostel 29, 30, 53, 154, 155, 157, 167, 325
Hyder Ali 9, 19, 34, 45, 56, 57, 61, 77, 270, 271, 272, 275

I

Ibrahim Shah 35
Indian Institute of Science 107, 173, 176, 177, 287
Indian Institute of World Culture 148
Indian Tobacco Company (Imperial Tobacco Company) 204
Inner Circle 239, 240, 242, 243, 245
Inscription
  - Begur 1, 6, 7
  - Bull Temple 153
  - Malleswaram 186, 187, 188
  - Ranganathaswamy Temple 26, 28
  - Tipu's Palace 61, 62
INTACH Heritage Award 31, 104, 147, 156
Ismail, Mirza 144, 191, 195
Iyengar, Masti Venkatesh 149, 150, 165
Iyer, Parvatiamma Chandrashekar 156
Iyer, Seshadri 26, 49, 50, 96, 103, 104, 132

J

Jackfruit 111, 273
Jagali 122
Jakkarayana Kere 169, 171, 186
Janatha Bazaar 288
Javaraya, HC 288, 289, 290, 299, 302, 308, 311, 313, 320, 323
Jewell Filters 192

K

Kadlekayi (Kadlekai) Parishe 153
Kadu Mallikarjuna Temple 186, 188
Kalyani 120, 121, 185, 186, 187, 259, 260
Kanteerava Stadium 251, 261, 264
Karaga 38, 206, 251, 261, 262, 263, 266
Karagada Kunte 263
Karanji Kere 137, 138, 183
Kattes 15, 28, 188, 189, 270
Kempambudhi Kere 13, 159, 160, 161
Kempegowda 5, 8, 11, 13, 15, 16, 17, 23, 28, 34, 35, 45, 73, 111, 112, 113, 115, 117, 118, 120, 126, 129, 154, 158, 159, 160, 161, 162, 170, 251, 271, 273, 285, 288, 301, 324
Kempegowda Towers 161
Khan, Ranadullah 162
Kites 295
Kleiner, Monseigneur 211
Koenigsberger, Otto 145, 174, 178, 321, 324
Kote Venkataramanaswamy Temple 60
Krishnamurthi, PN 51
Krishna Rajendra Market (KR Market) 35, 36, 52, 326
Krishna Rao, MN 74, 141, 142, 144, 145, 146, 147, 270
Krishna Rao Pavilion 145
Krumbiegel, GH 95, 286, 287, 288, 306, 307, 308, 310, 311, 320, 322, 333
Krumbiegel Hall 288, 307

L

Lake, Kempambudhi 13, 159, 160, 161, 315
Lake, Lalbagh 300
Lake, Sampangi 251, 252, 254, 255, 257, 259, 261, 262, 263, 264, 265, 266
Lake, Ulsoor (also Halasuru) 81, 111, 112, 126
Lakshmidevamma 29, 30, 53
Lakshminarasappa, SH 35, 53, 74
Lalbagh Rock 271, 272, 285
Lear, Edward 112, 281, 325
Lee, Standish 133, 136, 139, 169, 171, 324
Leonard, TT 133, 134, 136
London Missionary Society 24, 25, 327
London Mission High School 23

M

Macintire, Lt Col 44, 132
Mackenzie, Lt Roderick 37, 41, 42, 65, 73, 75, 277, 324
Madhava Rao, VP 22, 137, 140, 146, 169, 172, 174, 299
Madras Terrace 23, 24, 31, 33, 59, 98, 157, 180, 207, 225, 243
Mahila Seva Samaj 156
Mahogany 291, 294
Makara Sankranti 163
Malaria 77, 138
Mallapura 187, 188, 193
Malleswaram Girls' High School 180
Malleswaram Market 174, 184
Mango Tope 274, 280
Mango Tree 276

Manik Mastan 34, 35
Mariappa, BK 154, 155, 167, 320
Mari Gowda 281, 290, 302, 308, 309, 310, 311, 324, 325
Mari Gowda, MH 281, 290, 302, 308, 309, 310, 311, 324, 325
Market 1, 35, 36, 52, 184, 203, 223, 326
Marochetti, Carlo 98
Martyrs' Memorial 21
Mayo Hall 85, 93, 97, 99, 202
Meade, Richard 89
Medaraninganahalli 187, 188
MEG 81, 106, 107, 115, 132
Megaliths 6
Memorial Church 24, 25, 73, 105, 238, 242, 243, 245, 320
Military Architecture 45
Mineral Enterprises Limited 59
Minto Ophthalmic Hospital 68, 69, 320
Missions Étrangères de Paris 211
MN Krishna Rao Park 144, 145, 270
Mohan Buildings 32, 33, 34
Monkey Tops 59, 182, 208, 237
Moorhouse, Lt 18
Mootoocherry 82, 210, 211, 218, 326
Mosque Road 203, 221, 222, 223, 224, 226, 227, 228
Mudaliar, Annasawmy 6, 94, 200, 202, 223, 224, 225
Mudaliar, Arcot Narrainsawmy 100
Municipal Commission 133, 135, 136, 206
Munivenkatappa, B 53, 74, 325
Music 58, 62, 144, 148, 173, 177, 197, 230, 260, 323
Mutiny of Bangalore 85, 86
Mysore Bank 17, 19, 20, 21, 22
Mysore Bank Circle 17, 21
Mysore Gate 17, 44, 45
Mysore Maharaja Hall 100
Mysore Public Offices 62

N

Nagendra, Harini v, 8, 11, 73, 188, 249, 269, 332
Nanjundayya, HV 51, 180, 181, 183, 194, 321
Narasimhachar, R 26, 187, 188
National Geological Monument 272
National High School 155, 156
Nava Nathas 118, 119, 318
Networked Reservoirs 249
New, William 325

NIMHANS 20, 53, 287
Northern Extension 133, 198, 199, 221, 232

O

Old Taluk Cutcherry 32
Our Lady of Lourdes Church 236, 244, 245
Outer Circle 237, 243, 245

P

Pagodas (Currency) 78
Paint 269
Paintings 65, 66, 102, 103, 164, 274, 275, 276
Panchalingeshwara Temple 6, 7
Panchavati 176, 179
Papareddipalya 198
Parade Ground 62, 63, 78, 82, 87, 88
Parmanand, Kavindra 14, 270
Peepal 15, 28, 188, 190, 262, 266, 270
Peninsular Gneiss 272
Pettigrew, Rev 92, 107, 319
Plague 15, 58, 120, 121, 131, 135, 136, 140, 141, 142, 146, 166, 169, 172, 197, 199, 200, 203, 223, 232
Plague Camps 141
Plague-defined architecture 141
Poddar, Basant 59
Poo Pallaki 124
Posnett, Rev 92, 210
Pothacamury, Rev Thomas 216, 217
Prakash Padukone 174, 179
Prince of Wales 93, 301
Promenade Road 199, 209, 210, 214, 215, 217, 218
Pterocarpus Marsupium 269
Public Interest Litigation (PIL) 98
Public Offices 62, 97, 100, 202
Puttana Chetty, KP 132, 133

Q

Queen's Flower 293
Queen Victoria 49, 93, 94, 96, 106, 107, 109
Queen Victoria Memorial Fund 93
Quit India 22

R

Railway Station 227
Rajani, MB 74, 275, 310, 323, 326
Raju, K Cheluviah 309

Ramakrishna Math 152
Raman, CV 3, 173, 176, 177, 178, 194, 326, 333
Raman Research Institute 173, 176, 177, 178, 194, 333
Ranganathaswamy Temple 27
RBANMs Educational Charities 101, 109, 223
Reddy, Subbaiah 121
Red-Oxide 31, 115, 147, 182
Redwood, Alfred and Walter 226, 229
Rendition 10, 42, 43, 48, 87, 97, 202, 284, 307
Rice Memorial Church 24, 25, 73, 320
Richards, FJ 204, 206, 221
Richards Park 204, 230, 270
Ring Towns 313, 316, 317
Roberts, Emma 83, 327
Rome Beauty 288, 290
Rotten Row 78, 83, 84, 85
Royal Botanic Gardens (Kew) 281, 283, 286

S

Sait, Hajee Sir Ismail 200, 202, 203, 204, 226, 232
Sajjan Rao 1, 53, 55, 156, 157, 162
Sajjan Rao Choultry 156, 157
Sampangi Tank (also Sampangi lake) 261, 315
Sampige Road 170, 184
Sankey, Lt Col RH 89, 97, 99, 102, 327
Sankey Tank 99, 172, 186, 189, 315
Sanskrit College 71
Sati 259
Seeme Badnekayi 283
Serial Blossoming 287
Servanton, Father 215, 216
Seshadri Iyer Memorial Hall 96, 103, 104
Seshadripuram 103, 133, 199
Setty, Chinthalapalli Venkatamuniah 29
Setty, Srinivasa SV 29
Setty, Yele Mallappa 186, 326
Shahaji 8, 9
Shivabharath 14
Shivaji 8, 9, 14, 32, 187
Silver Jubilee 37, 38, 53, 96, 181, 287
Sisters of St Joseph of Tarbes 211, 216, 245
Sluice Gates 160, 167, 183, 250, 259
Smyth, Lt Col John 68
Someshwara Temple 6, 111, 119, 120, 124
Sport 84, 85, 174
Sri Beereshwara Temple 258

Sri Dakshinamukha Nandi Tirtha Kalyani Kshetra (Nandishwara Temple) 185, 186
Srirampura 171
Srirangapatna 9, 40, 57, 65, 67, 77, 78, 131, 272, 273, 274, 275, 277
Statue
 - Chamarajendra 103
 - Mark Cubbon 98
 - Queen Victoria 93
Stephens, JH 199, 201, 223, 328
St Francis Xavier's Cathedral 214, 215, 216
St Germain's School 217
St John's Church 210, 211, 212, 215, 216, 217, 233
St John's School 92
St Joseph's Convent Chapel 211, 212, 215, 216, 233
St Luke's Church 52, 70, 322
St Mark's Church (also Cathedral) 79, 81, 82, 84, 91, 92
Storm Water Channel (also, storm water drain) 223, 257, 315
St Peters' Pontifical Institute 190
Swami Vivekananda 126, 152
Swimming Pool Extension 172
Syed Tipu 86

T

Tanks 13, 99, 120, 126, 159, 192, 193, 249, 250, 259, 264, 287, 313, 314, 315
Tank system (system of tanks) 99
Tawakkal Mastan 34
Tharagupete 6, 15, 132
Theosophist 148
Thumboo Chetty 214, 216
Tigalas 263
Tipu Sultan 9, 19, 40, 45, 47, 52, 56, 57, 60, 61, 62, 67, 77, 112, 270, 272, 274, 275, 276, 277, 290, 321, 322, 324, 325, 329
Tipu Sultan's Palace 61-67
Tramway 170, 204
Trinity Church 81, 126, 127

U

Ulsoor Lake (Halasuru Lake) 81, 111, 112, 126

V

Vani Vilas Hospital 30, 52, 53, 54, 70, 71, 157

Vani Vilas Institute 54, 56
Vannhikula Kshatriyas 251, 260
Vema Lodge 182, 183
Venkatanaranappa, Bellave 149, 322
Venkataramayya, D 171
Venkatarangiengar, S 171
Venugopalaswamy Temple 183, 184
Venugopal, KC 59
Vernacular architecture 23, 55, 59, 121, 122, 123, 146, 147, 164
Victory plaque 47
Vidhana Soudha 2, 97, 98, 105, 106
Vijayanagar style 27, 117
Village Green 237, 243
Villa Pottipati 182
Visvesvaraya, M 2, 19, 69, 142, 154, 171, 181, 194, 203, 329

W

Wadia, BP 148, 166, 329
Washermen 189, 190
Waugh, Gilbert 276, 278, 279, 291, 320
Waverly 92
Wesleyan Church 218
Wesley English Church 218, 233, 324
Western Extension 133
West Gate Guardroom 299
Wetlands 253, 257, 259
Wheeler Pavilion 230
White, DS 235, 329
Whitefield vii, 234, 235, 236, 237, 238, 239, 240, 241, 243, 244, 245, 246, 247, 316, 326
Whitefield Club 235, 245, 246
Wodeyar, Chamaraja 48, 63, 87, 101, 103, 133, 301, 306, 307
Wodeyar, Krishnaraja 19, 38, 40, 52, 68, 81, 94, 96, 100, 183, 206, 243

Y

Yediyur Nagasandra 137
Yelahanka Gate 17, 18, 19
Young Men's Mandyam Association 174
Young Pioneers Sports Club 174

Z

Zoo 270, 285, 305

Printed in Great Britain
by Amazon